Indian Wars Everywhere

AMERICAN CROSSROADS

Edited by Earl Lewis, George Lipsitz, George Sánchez, Dana Takagi,
Laura Briggs, and Nikhil Pal Singh

Indian Wars Everywhere

*Colonial Violence and the Shadow
Doctrines of Empire*

Stefan Aune

UNIVERSITY OF CALIFORNIA PRESS

The publisher and the University of California Press Foundation gratefully acknowledge the generous support of the Peter Booth Wiley Endowment Fund in History.

University of California Press
Oakland, California

© 2023 by Stefan Aune

Library of Congress Cataloging-in-Publication Data

Names: Aune, Stefan, 1988– author.
Title: Indian Wars everywhere : colonial violence and the shadow
    doctrines of empire / Stefan Aune.
Other titles: American crossroads ; 71.
Description: Oakland, California : University of California Press,
    [2023] | Series: American crossroads ; 71 | Includes bibliographical
    references and index.
Identifiers: LCCN 2023013089 (print) | LCCN 2023013090 (ebook) |
    ISBN 9780520395398 (cloth) | ISBN 9780520395404 (paperback) |
    ISBN 9780520395411 (epub)
Subjects: LCSH: Indians of North America—Wars—Influence. |
    America—Colonization. | United States—History, Military.
Classification: LCC E81 .A87 2023 (print) | LCC E81 (ebook) |
    DDC 973—dc23/eng/20230407
LC record available at https://lccn.loc.gov/2023013089
LC ebook record available at https://lccn.loc.gov/2023013090

Manufactured in the United States of America

32 31 30 29 28 27 26 25 24 23
10 9 8 7 6 5 4 3 2 1

For my parents, Mark and Janis Aune

Contents

Contents

Illustrations

Acknowledgments

I owe innumerable people a debt of gratitude for helping me transform a set of nebulous ideas into *Indian Wars Everywhere*. Much of this book was written and revised during the COVID-19 lockdowns. Those challenging circumstances led to an even greater appreciation for the intellectual communities that helped me develop this project under conditions that were sometimes less than ideal. I will attempt to thank some of you, but I could never thank all of you.

The Program in American Culture at the University of Michigan was the perfect environment for beginning this project. Philip Deloria's influence on *Indian Wars Everywhere* cannot be overstated; your mentorship is a model I will do my best to replicate. Penny Von Eschen, Gregory Dowd, and Kristin Hass guided my research from start to finish with unwavering intellectual generosity. The Settler Colonialism Reading Group and the Native American and Indigenous Studies Interest Group at Michigan were an invaluable source of insight and friendship—thanks to Scott Lyons, Michael Witgen, Tiya Miles, Joseph Gaudet, Emily Macgillivray, Kathleen Whiteley, Mallory Whiteduck, Kris Klein Hernández, Sophie Hunt, Frank Kelderman, and so many others. Additional thanks to Anthony Mora, Susan Najita, Maria Cotera, Magdalena Zaborowska, Matthew Lassiter, Joo Young Lee, Iván Chaar-López, Stephen Molldrem, Sophie Cooper, Rachel Miller, Kyera Singleton, Katherine Lennard, Meryem Kamil, Maryam Aziz, Peggy Lee, Michael Pascual, and others for their friendship and collaboration.

I was fortunate to spend three years as a faculty fellow in the History Department at New York University. The support of NYU and the Elihu Rose Fellowship in Modern Military History was crucial in the development of this project. I found a home in the Native Studies Forum at NYU—thanks to Dean Saranillio, Rebecca Goetz, Sam Iti Prendergast, Ried Gustafson, Madison Bastress, Tony Brave, Cliff Whetung, and the rest of that community. Elizabeth Ellis organized an invaluable manuscript workshop during my time at NYU that guided the final revisions to this project. Thanks to Jodi Kim, David Fitzgerald, Andrew Lee, Andrew Needham, and Sinclair Thomson for their comments. I have been fortunate to receive a warm welcome from my new colleagues at Williams College. Thanks to Jan Padios, Dorothy Wang, Kelly Chung, Cassandra Cleghorn, Mark Reinhardt, Phi Su, Lisa Conathan, and the rest of the Williams community. I also need to thank the faculty at Macalester College for setting me on this intellectual path, particularly Andrea Cremer, Karin Aguilar-San Juan, Lynn Hudson, Peter Rachleff, Kiarina Kordela, and Duchess Harris.

I am grateful for the many archivists, librarians, and researchers that helped me with this book, particularly the staff at the Library of Congress; the National Archives in Washington, DC; the Newberry Library; the United States Military Academy Archives and Special Collections; the Carroll University Archives; the Chester Fritz Library at the University of North Dakota; the Special Collections Research Center at the University of Michigan; the Howard Gotlieb Archival Research Center at Boston University; and the library staff at the University of Michigan, Cornell University, New York University, and Williams College.

Thanks to Niels Hooper, my editor, for believing in this project and guiding me toward the finish line. I am grateful to Naja Pulliam Collins and the rest of the staff at the University of California Press for their unending assistance. Jeffrey Ostler and Alex Lubin carefully read the manuscript and provided essential feedback that helped me refine the argument, structure, and archive; I am grateful for their assistance as well as the other anonymous readers that took the time to comment at various stages of this project.

This book is dedicated to my parents, Mark and Janis Aune, for their unconditional love, support, and encouragement. You nurtured an intellectual curiosity in me without which none of this would have been possible. Thanks to my sister Ingrid, and the rest of the Aune and Blomgren families, particularly my grandparents: Harry, Elaine, Eldon, and Helen.

Finally, to Leigh York: you are my best friend, the person who has taught me the most in life, and the person with whom I have shared this academic journey. I could not have done this without the family we have built together.

Abbreviations

CGSC	United States Army Command and General Staff College
CIA	Central Intelligence Agency
GPO	Government Printing Office
JMSI	*Journal of the Military Service Institution of the United States*
LOC	Library of Congress, Washington, DC
NARA	National Archives Building, Washington, DC
NLF	National Liberation Front
TTU	The Vietnam Center and Archive, Texas Tech University, Lubbock, TX
USACAC	United States Army Combined Arms Center
USAWC	The United States Army War College

Introduction

On May 2, 2011, President Barack Obama, Vice President Joe Biden, and other members of the United States national security team sat in the White House situation room (Figure 1). In tense silence they listened as CIA Director Leon Panetta narrated the unfolding of Operation Neptune Spear, a mission targeted at Al-Qaeda leader Osama bin Laden.[1] When the Special Forces operatives reached the target Panetta reported, "We have a visual on Geronimo," and after a few minutes he proclaimed, "Geronimo EKIA." Geronimo, the name given to Chiricahua Apache leader Goyahkla by his Mexican enemies, was code for bin Laden, and the coded message that reported a successful mission was "Geronimo—EKIA," or "enemy killed in action," a comparison that Fort Sill Apache Tribe chairman Jeff Houser would later call "painful and offensive."[2] The ensuing debate over the code name controversy, which was taken up in newspapers, blogs, and the Senate Committee on Indian Affairs, pointed to the enduring legacy of the so-called "Indian Wars," those conflicts fought during the period of US continental expansion.[3] Geronimo has been held up as one of the most intractable resisters of American colonialism, the last Native leader to surrender. He has been represented as incurably savage, impossibly elusive, and unwaveringly cruel. In short, Goyahkla the person has been overshadowed by a representation, "Geronimo," which has been appropriated to serve a variety of interests.[4]

1

FIGURE 1. President Barack Obama and members of the national security team monitor the mission targeted at Osama bin Laden. National Archives photo no. 118817935 by Pete Souza.

So why Geronimo, and why bin Laden? Regardless of the code name's intentionality, the comparison is embedded with historical weight. The terror attacks of September 11, 2001, led to the War on Terror, a global military campaign so broad that definitions of the "terrorist" became increasingly fluid, applied to revolutionaries, militias, religious fundamentalists, and a host of enemies in a range of countries. The war was everywhere, the war was endless, and the enemy was invisible.[5] At the same time, the War on Terror made apparent that the conflicts of the United States are still understood, in part, in racial terms, as a variety of ethnic and religious groups were coded as "terrorist" and subjected, at home and abroad, to a range of disciplinary practices justified through wartime necessity.[6] After 9/11, terrorism was often understood as "Islamic," boiling complex political histories down to cultural and racial essences. Even as terrorist networks remained hidden, "we" knew who "they" were, and the vagueness with which terrorism was defined drove an expansion of the national security apparatus while enabling domestic surveillance, repression, and other forms of state power.[7]

The War on Terror, like almost every war the United States has engaged in, also saw numerous references to conflicts with Indians. These representations still relied on race to make sense of the United States' enemies but did so through comparisons to the era of US continental expansion.[8] Policy makers argued that "if the government of Iraq collapses . . . you've got Fort Apache in the middle of Indian country, but the Indians have mortars now." Journalists reported that "welcome to 'Injun Country' was the refrain . . . heard from troops from Colombia to the Philippines, including Afghanistan and Iraq. . . . The War on Terrorism was really about taming the frontier." A Marine Corps veteran noted that "the common thread between Vietnam, Afghanistan, or Iraq to the Indian Wars is counterinsurgency."[9] More than one hundred years had passed since Goyahkla surrendered to the US Army, but it seemed as if the United States was still fighting the Indian Wars.

INDIAN/FIGHTING PAST AND PRESENT

These connections between the Indian Wars and the War on Terror did not come out of nowhere, and it is precisely this history that *Indian Wars Everywhere* interrogates. The violence of US continental expansion continually circulates throughout the history of US militarism, influencing everything from helicopter names to military violence.[10] For much of the twentieth century it was commonplace for Americans to refer to enemy territory as "Indian country." They did so in the Philippines, during the World Wars, the Vietnam War, and the Gulf War, and they continue to do it today.[11] References to "Indian country" could be interpreted as casual comparisons born of the proliferation of "cowboys and Indians"–style violence in American popular culture.[12] On some level these connections are unsurprising coming from people raised on Old West novels, John Wayne films, and the *Red Dead Redemption* videogames. Even so, a number of scholars have helped paint a more complicated picture, charting the ways in which the United States' colonial *history* is also its perpetual colonial *present*.[13] Foremost among these studies are the works of Richard Slotkin and Richard Drinnon, which demonstrated how the "frontier" and similar concepts acted as organizing metaphors for American violence.[14] Other works, notably Jodi Byrd's *The Transit of Empire*, show how the history of US empire begins with the colonization of Indigenous peoples in North America. US empire emerges from, and is built on, the conquest of Indian country. Further, Indian country is not solely a *place*, but also a category, "Indian," that can be applied to those upon whom US imperial power descends to justify the imposition of that authority.[15]

Indian Wars Everywhere will fill in the blanks where other scholars made assumptions about *whether* and *how* the Indian Wars continue to resonate into the present.[16] It is partly motivated by how often US military violence is compared to the Indian Wars without fully excavating that history. Previous studies have paid less attention to US military doctrine, strategy, and tactics, or assumed a consistent transfer of Indian warfare across time and space. Excellent critical work on the history of counterinsurgency and other forms of irregular warfare sometimes makes assumptions about the coherence of "Indian fighting" doctrine and how it influenced later conflicts.[17] A careful examination of whether and how the Indian Wars persist has proved more elusive. To be sure, ideologies such as "manifest destiny," "the frontier," and the "savage" have shaped how later generations of Americans view the world. But there is more to this story, particularly the ways in which colonial violence has (and has not) been institutionalized in the US military, or in the broader American culture. Telling this story will help historicize the violent continuities embedded in US history.

This book is an attempt to more fully understand why the Indian Wars seem to be *everywhere*. It moves from the violence of US continental expansion all the way through the War on Terror, examining why Indian/fighting has remained such a consistent aspect of US imperial power. The slash (/) in Indian/fighting is intentional and will be used throughout this book to denote the competing discourses that have rendered US military violence as both "fighting against Indians" and "fighting *like* Indians."[18] The chapters that follow explore the persistence of the Indian Wars not just as an imaginative structure that shapes how people view conflict, but also as a "shadow doctrine" that informs the practice of US military violence. I use the term *shadow doctrines* to describe those military practices that emerge from the traces of colonialism embedded in American culture, as opposed to the military's official doctrine as compiled in manuals, training, and education. Where doctrine for the US Army constitutes the "principles the Army uses to guide its actions in support of national objectives," shadow doctrines are the resonances of ongoing US colonialism that intrude on those principles.[19] Shadow doctrines should not be taken to imply a sharp divide between the US military and the broader culture in which it is embedded. Military institutions exist within national cultures, shaping (and being shaped by) that broader culture.[20] There is not an explicit continuity of Indian/fighting doctrine in US history, but there is a *shadow* of one.

The concept of shadow doctrines is particularly useful when exploring moments in US history where violence intersects with race and colonialism, as these conflicts are often viewed as "savage" or outside the mainstream of military action. There is a persistent tension between "savage" and "civilized" warfare throughout US history, and that tension has often been negotiated through references to the Indian Wars. The ongoing colonialism that results in "savage wars" is perpetually at odds with the desire for a *finished* colonialism, a *civilized* war, and the friction between these two poles forms an important part of the history of American violence. Stated plainly, ideas about race have always been present in the contours of US militarism, and Indian/fighting has been a mechanism for transmitting some of those ideas across time and space.

Indian Wars Everywhere concludes with the War on Terror because the shadow doctrines of US empire have been increasingly visible since the attacks on 9/11. Those waging the War on Terror did more than reference the frontier when drawing connections between the Indian Wars and the War on Terror. They articulated the United States' history of colonial violence as a template, tutor, and validator of twenty-first-century warfare. The clearest examples are found in the institutions of US military training, education, and strategy, which published materials that analyzed the Indian Wars as a blueprint for contemporary conflicts. Returning to the comparisons of Geronimo and bin Laden, we can find a similar example from 2003 written by an officer at the United States Army War College (USAWC):

> Both the Apaches and the Islamists possess a charismatic group of leaders. The Apaches were led by Cochise, Natchez, Victorio, Geronimo and others, names that still echo throughout the world. Today the leaders include Osama bin Laden, Mullah Omar and dozens of others unknown to most American citizens but important in their regions stretching throughout the Middle East, Asia, Europe and pockets of the United States. All these historical and current leaders preach a fantasy ideology that seek[s] to have the US depart from "their" territories and for "the people" to return to an imagined life that is forever gone.[21]

This officer at the USAWC constructs Indigenous sovereignty as the original "fantasy ideology" in a long line of attempts to resist the power of the United States. In doing so, the writer conflates Indigenous resistance to settler colonialism with the atrocities carried out by Al-Qaeda, stating explicitly the implicit logic behind the bin Laden/Geronimo code name controversy. This is one example of the many connections traced throughout this book that collectively constitute the shadow doctrine of Indian/fighting. The United States' formative acts of colonial violence persist in the actions, imaginations, and stories that have facilitated the spread of American empire.[22]

SHADOW DOCTRINES AND THE CULTURAL HISTORY OF VIOLENCE

References to Geronimo or Indian country draw on a long history of representations of Native people found in literature, media, and art. These images act as a fog, obscuring the concerns of Indigenous peoples who continuously assert their sovereignty amid the pressures of ongoing colonialism.[23] At the same time, the US military has a long history of using words and images referring to Indians to represent itself, from Apache helicopters to the paratroopers that shout "Geronimo" as they jump from airplanes.[24] Native people have also served in the US armed forces in large numbers, particularly since World War I.[25] Indianness is deeply coded into the imagination of American culture, and that includes the military. Goyahkla's resonance as the ultimate elusive enemy made him a likely candidate for symbolic deployment in the most significant mission of the War on Terror. However, the use of *Geronimo* as a code word was also a reminder that some of the earliest experiences of the US military with what is now referred to as *irregular warfare* (which includes unconventional warfare, counterinsurgency, stability operations, counterterrorism, and more) were in conflicts with Native people resisting the imposition of US sovereignty (see Figure 2).[26] The image of the Indian casts a long shadow that solidifies whenever the words *savage*, *guerilla* or *insurgent* are deployed in the service of empire.

But what does it mean for an image or idea to *solidify*? What are these things we call "culture" and "discourse," and how do they relate to the fingers on the triggers of guns, the hands that grasp the controls of airplanes? Cultural history, as a field of inquiry that focuses on language, representation, and the production of meaning, has much to offer the analysis of violence.[27] Culture functions in a myriad of ways: as the symbolic structures within a given society, as the glue that ties members of a group together, as the "commonsense" ideologies that shape the beliefs of individuals, and as a *process*, a set of meanings that continually shift over time, giving shape to social relationships and the material world.[28] Culture is both the symbolic terrain on which meaning is made and the expression of cultural ideas in physical actions, objects, and events.[29] When cultural ideas resonate, they do so not only through language, but

FIGURE 2. Crew of the Martin B-26 "Geronimo" of the 552nd Bomb Squadron, 386th Bomb Group, Essex, England, September 1, 1943. National Archives photo no. 204859027.

through bodies, through actions. These cultural ideas often take shape as a discourse, a historically specific set of beliefs, terms, and statements. For example, we might think of "manifest destiny," the belief that the United States' continental expansion was divinely ordained, as a particular kind of colonial discourse.[30] The shadow doctrines examined in this book are another such discourse. *Indian Wars Everywhere* is both a cultural history attentive to the materiality of warfare, and a history of violence attuned to the ways culture shapes that violence.

Shadow doctrines reframe the mythologies of colonial violence into more concrete prescriptions for military action. These resonances of US continental expansion function as powerful discursive structures, making meaning out of violence and conscripting military action into a familiar narrative and form. They draw on the legacy of US colonialism to produce a potent justification for the projection of US empire on a global scale. We must account for interactions like the following, which occurred during the congressional hearings into the My Lai massacre during the Vietnam War:

Captain Robert B. Johnson: Where I was operating I didn't hear anyone personally use that term ["turkey shoots"]. We used the term "Indian Country."

Congressman John Seiberling: What did "Indian Country" refer to?

Johnson: I guess it means different things to different people. It is like there are savages out there, there are gooks out there. In the same way we slaughtered the Indian's buffalo, we would slaughter the water buffalo in Vietnam.[31]

When Captain Johnson says "the same way we slaughtered the Indian's buffalo, we would slaughter the water buffalo in Vietnam," you can hear the unspoken subtext: in the same way we fought Indians, we fight the Vietnamese. Remember, this was in the context of congressional hearings on the most visible, but hardly unique, massacre of the Vietnam War, a massacre that recalled the killing of Native people at Bear River, Sand Creek, and Wounded Knee.[32] Captain Johnson was not only talking about how he imagined the Vietnamese; he was talking about how he *fought* them.

SAVAGE WAR AND IRREGULAR WAR

The United States has nearly always been at war, and for much of the twentieth and twenty-first centuries has seemingly been at war *everywhere*.[33] Despite an understandable preoccupation with large battles and global wars in the narrative of US history, the country has spent just as much time (if not more) engaged in smaller-scale conflicts—interventions, occupations, punitive expeditions, small wars, police actions, peacekeeping operations, and counterinsurgencies. These struggles tend to garner less attention, and are often united in their extension beyond defeating opposing armies on the battlefield.[34] Most are conflicts with complex objectives: influencing local politics, legitimating allied governments, protecting US economic interests, or eliminating nonstate actors deemed to be threats to national security.[35] Rudyard Kipling famously called a version of these struggles the "savage wars of peace" in his 1899 poem "The White Man's Burden," written to encourage the United States' occupation of the Philippines. Kipling's poem emphasized that ideas about race were inextricably linked to the expansion of US power at the turn of the century. This imperial paternalism often argued that the colonized were incapable of self-government, and it was the duty of white men to assume the "civilizing" burden.[36]

Kipling's poem calls our attention back to the opposition to savagery written into the founding documents of the United States. The Declaration of Independence criticized the British for endeavoring "to bring on the inhabitants of our frontiers, the merciless Indian savages whose known rule of warfare, is an undistinguished destruction of all ages, sexes, and conditions."[37] From this moment the United States has both reviled and reveled in "savage war," celebrating frontier mythologies while denigrating racialized deviations from Euro-American norms around warfare. Race, often communicated through the code word *savage*, has shaped American conceptions of violence from the nation's origins. The technical language of "civilized" or "modern" warfare has always existed in relation to its shadow, the "savage war."

The phrase *the savage wars of peace* has since been taken up by others to describe those conflicts that blend military violence with governing, developing, stabilizing, and countering insurgent political formations.[38] The "savage" in these wars has often referred not just to the form of violence, but also to the efforts to make the enemy *no longer savage*, integrated into those political and economic institutions favorable to the United States. Over time the "savage wars of peace" have evolved into what the US military now calls irregular warfare, and we can hear the echoes of the "white man's burden" in the more recent emphasis on stability, development, and security.[39] The wars, interventions, and occupations justified through references to security reframe older binaries of savage/civilized into one of underdeveloped/developed. Populations billed as security threats are then subjected to forms of corrective violence.[40] And while much of the scholarship on US national security dates the emergence of the concept to the mid-twentieth century, American "security" has a longer colonial history.[41] Security discourses originate in the idea of "defensive conquest," in which settlers reframed Indigenous nations as security threats to an already-cohesive United States. Settler invasion became a defensive struggle, exemplified by the image of the surrounded wagon train.[42] The besieged settler finds its more recent iteration in descriptions of a dangerous and undeveloped Global South threatening the neoliberal order, a danger often countered by forms of irregular war.

The US Department of Defense defines irregular warfare as "a struggle among state and non-state actors to influence populations and affect legitimacy," and includes under its rubric unconventional warfare, stabilization, foreign internal defense, counterterrorism, and counterinsurgency.[43] *Irregular war* is a more recent term, but it names patterns of violence that have been around since the creation of the United States; violence that is far more *regular* than irregular. The conquest of Native peoples in North America is central to the history of irregular warfare as a particularly imperial form of warfare. In US military history the predominant narrative about irregular warfare is one of continual forgetting. According to this story the military repeatedly neglected to preserve lessons from over two hundred years of conflict, resulting in the effort to "relearn" counterinsurgency and other forms of irregular warfare in places like Vietnam, Afghanistan, and Iraq.[44] And while the "forgetting" narrative is based in valid readings of US military doctrine, education, and practice, it also fails to acknowledge the ways in which Americans have continually reminded themselves that they are, in fact, good at fighting *Indians*. The discourses of US militarism both celebrate and suppress the archive of colonial violence, and this book attends to this dual absence and presence. The US military did not preserve much of the Indian Wars in its doctrine, but it has continually deployed them as a story that gives meaning (and legitimacy) to violence. This mirrors broader patterns in US historical memory, which masks the ongoing presence of Native peoples even as they remain hyper-visible in film, sport, and advertising.[45]

Indian Wars Everywhere is not solely concerned with irregular warfare, but it is no coincidence that the shadow doctrines of Indian/fighting have been most visible in those kinds of conflicts. The different aspects of irregular war—guerilla tactics, blended civil/military programs, small-scale operations, and more—have often confounded mainstream US military doctrine, and Indian/fighting has helped fill in the blanks during these moments. The most recent examples can be found in those writers who drew on the Indian Wars as a source of insight into the War on Terror. They paid particular attention to counterinsurgency when the United States faced protracted insurgencies in Afghanistan and Iraq. These studies argued that the violence of US continental expansion has much to offer the wars in Afghanistan and Iraq.[46] Their arguments largely highlight examples of success in counterinsurgency warfare, saying, "See, the US has effectively fought these sorts of conflicts before." In essence, such work is concerned with asserting what counterinsurgency *is*, and how it can be more successfully applied to current US military efforts.

In contrast, this book is more concerned with where counterinsurgency and other "irregular" forms of warfare *come from*. In US history, irregular warfare has often been as much about cultural attitudes toward those defined as enemies as it has been an attempt to apply a technical form of warfare. And those attitudes, I argue, have colonial roots. There may not be an unbroken chain of doctrinal continuity that links the nineteenth-century Indian Wars to the contemporary War on Terror. There is no "Indian warfare" manual that was read by soldiers in Germany, Vietnam, Afghanistan, and Iraq. However, there is an ever-lurking set of resonances, discourses, and actions, shadow doctrines that find continual expression via ideas about Indian/fighting. There are undeniable continuities in the history of American violence that help us understand the shifting contours of US empire.[47]

INDIAN WARS EVERYWHERE

At the broadest level this book is interested in how military violence has shaped (and been shaped by) the United States' ongoing colonialism. It brings together disparate literatures that investigate the intersections of culture and violence. In this effort I join a group of scholars who have turned a critical eye to the contours of US state violence, at home and abroad. These include analyses of the pervasive influence of militarism in US history, the processes through which war became a central aspect of culture, media, and national discourse.[48] Much of this work has attended to the cultural histories of US empire, tracking the circulation of ideas about race, gender, sexuality, class, citizenship, and more, both at home and abroad.[49] Advancing this historiography, recent scholarship has interrogated the interrelated histories of the World Wars, the Cold War, mass incarceration, policing, and the War on Terror, focusing increasingly on the material aspects of US imperial violence.[50] Building on this work, *Indian Wars Everywhere* demonstrates the relevance of Native American history to the broader historiography of US empire by exploring the continuities between the violence of continental expansion and the increasingly global imperialism that was inaugurated with the Spanish-American War. These are connections that have remained elusive, frequently invoked but less carefully excavated. In large part, this is a separation between the nineteenth and twentieth centuries, a separation hinged by the year 1898 and the Spanish-American War, although that divide seems to be eroding among historians of empire.[51]

Indian Wars Everywhere has a wide-ranging chronology, and ongoing colonialism is the connective tissue binding the various chapters together. Military practices at the center of US global power emerged from the process of continental expansion that attempted to eliminate Native people from the land. "Elimination" can take different forms, including death, removal, legal erasure, or incorporation into the settler-state. What is consistent across the different forms of "elimination" is the attempted elimination of Native sovereignty. Settler colonialism in the United States attempts to transform Native people from an "Indian problem" to an *internal* problem, domesticating indigeneity through the administration of Native life.[52] This focus on managing life, asserting political sovereignty, and rendering external territories as subjects of US security interests is one of the places in which Native and Indigenous Studies intersects with the scholarship on global US empire, and this book enriches our understanding of that intersection. Indian/fighting is the United States' original security discourse. Narrating US history as a set of continually transcended frontiers fails to capture the way in which territories and populations claimed by the United States are held in a permanent state of management, a colonialism that is never fully *settled*.[53] The external and the internal continually bleed together in US history, and both colonialism and irregular warfare are a crucial part of this messy history.

The chronology of this book covers multiple centuries and spans several continents. This breadth is balanced by a series of deep cuts into moments that highlight the ongoing relationship between colonialism and military violence in US history. Our story begins with the continental expansion of the United States before leaping overseas to the Philippines. We then follow the shadow doctrines that have transmitted ideas about Indian/fighting across time and space throughout the twentieth and twenty-first centuries, examining the World Wars, the Cold War, and finally the War on Terror. Following phrases like *Indian country* and *Indian warfare* across a wide range of sources opened avenues I never anticipated: the practices of Civil War guerillas, the imperialism of children's literature, controversies over rifle ammunition, and that time in 1941 when a group of Native Americans awarded Soviet premier Joseph Stalin a feathered war bonnet and declared him warrior of the year. My hope is that *Indian Wars Everywhere* productively revisits some familiar histories while uncovering some lesser-known (but no less important) moments.

Chapter 1 lays a groundwork for the remainder of the book, examining the legal, military, and cultural frameworks through which colonial violence was understood in the United States during the period of continental expansion. Americans inside and outside the military questioned what was appropriate in so-called "savage war," they debated whether the Indian Wars were even a "war" to begin with, and they grasped for ways to characterize Native resistance to US expansion, at times rendering that violence as "terrorism" in ways that long predate modern discourses of terror. By the end of the nineteenth century many US soldiers were confident they were experienced in waging savage warfare, even as that experience largely failed to enter military doctrine. Nevertheless, American soldiers believed they possessed skills that could translate to the maintenance of the United States' burgeoning global empire. These abilities in Indian/fighting would see their most expansive test in the Philippines.

Some of the first US military experts in what is now called "irregular war" imagined themselves as Indian/fighters. These were soldiers that had served in the wars of US continental expansion before finding themselves in places like Cuba, Puerto Rico, and the Philippines. The war and subsequent occupation of the Philippines at the turn of the century was influenced by continental colonialism in particular ways. US soldiers narrated their time in the islands as an Indian war and imagined themselves as Indian/fighters. The Indian Wars were translated, through the actions, imaginations, and writing of soldiers into a flexible discourse able to travel across space and time. Chapters 2 and 3 analyze the histories of Henry Ware Lawton and Charles King. Both were American soldiers who served in the Philippines, and both were producers and subjects of cultural representations focused on Indian/fighting. Lawton, as the man who captured Geronimo, was assumed before he ever arrived in the Philippines to be uniquely suited to defeating the supposedly "savage" Filipinos. While on the islands, he formed a specialized scouting troop called Young's Scouts, led by an "old frontiersman" named W. H. Young. Lawton used the scouts in ways that directly drew on prior experiences with Native people, and this history helps to render visible the linkages between continental colonialism and global empire. Charles King, himself a celebrated general, was more famous as an author. King, in his novels, narrated the experiences of frontier soldiers and helped to cement the "Indian fighter" as an enduring fixation of American culture. King also found himself in the Philippines, and his later novels drew explicit connections between the Indian Wars and the Philippine-American War. Through Lawton and King we can chart the emergence of Indian/fighting as a mobile discourse that helped Americans make sense of the racialized violence that accompanied the spread of US empire.

Chapter 4 examines how early twentieth-century Americans celebrated their history as "Indian fighters" while simultaneously focusing on future "civilized wars." In this period, US citizens from all walks of life confronted a changing world in which anxieties about race, class, gender, and sexuality challenged established norms. In this climate Indian/fighting emerged as a discourse that served to racialize certain types of warfare—particularly the imperial wars that both the US and the British Empire were engaged in during this period. Some celebrated Indian warriors as "the world's tutor in modern warfare," while others argued that "savagery must cease" as they looked toward a future of tanks, machine guns, and bombers. Over time, Indian/fighting became increasingly abstracted from the experiences of nineteenth-century soldiers, associated with the prior "savage wars" that were to have no place in the future. Indian/fighting increasingly moved into the realm of imagination. Those soldiers who found themselves in foreign "Indian country" during World War I were more likely to invoke the Indian Wars as a metaphor for their experience, rather than a template for military tactics. However, during World War II, and then later during the Cold War, these lines became increasingly blurred, as military officers argued that soldiers had to be trained as "Indian fighters" to meet the threat posed by Germany, Italy, and Japan. The further emergence of a shadow doctrine of Indian/fighting is the focus of chapters 5 and 6, which chart the strange blending of myth and method that characterizes the US military's relationship to the Indian Wars. In the early twentieth century, the US military mostly repressed its history of Indian/fighting, but American soldiers during the second half of the twentieth century continually reminded themselves that this very history might, in fact, serve them in the present.

Chapter 6 concludes in Vietnam, a conflict widely imagined as an "Indian war" by the soldiers who fought it and the journalists who covered it. Despite being, in part, a counterinsurgency, the US military declined once more to substantively preserve the lessons learned in that conflict within military doctrine. This meant that when the United States invaded Afghanistan and Iraq in response to the terror attacks of 9/11 there was not a robust counterinsurgency doctrine in place. As the military scrambled to update its approach, the Indian wars emerged as a key historical precedent. In 2006, the US Army and Marine Corps published Field Manual 3-24, *Counterinsurgency*, with a frank admission that the military had neglected to develop and maintain a clear and effective doctrine for that mode of warfare. As the wars in Afghanistan and Iraq continued, and the War on Terror expanded, the military was desperate for effective strategies and a history on which to draw.

In this climate the Indian Wars emerged as an example of the United States' first successful counterinsurgency, with military theorists returning to the study of the wars with Apache, Cheyenne, Lakota, and others. Chapter 7 shows how the Indian Wars reentered US military doctrine as a usable history and blueprint for contemporary irregular warfare. The mythologies of US continental expansion were translated, during the War on Terror, into the technical vocabulary of strategy and tactics.

Over the course of seven chapters, this book will cover more than two hundred years of history, move from North America to Asia to the Middle East, and examine everything from battlefield reports to children's literature. This breadth of content is necessary to show just how intertwined the histories of colonialism and militarism are in the United States. The Indian Wars have been *everywhere*, and they continue to persist as a shadow doctrine of Indian/fighting. The Indian Wars have even circled back to literal Indian country: the conclusion discusses how paramilitary responses to Native resistance to oil pipelines mobilizes counterinsurgency strategies developed during the War on Terror.

Indian Wars Everywhere is a history of the traces of colonialism that continue to reemerge in American culture. It is also an examination of different forms of violence that have mobilized ideas about race, indigeneity, and security to justify an ever-expanding global US militarism. Foremost, however, this book is a critique of the ways in which the United States cannot stop refighting the Indian Wars, imagined or otherwise. As these histories resonate into the present in the form of code words, tactical studies, and historical lessons, we would do well to remember that calling those conflicts "successful" casts a celebratory light on a series of profound losses for Native people. To reckon with the legacy of colonialism means facing up to the influence those conflicts have had on patterns of US military violence.

CHAPTER I

Colonial Violence and the Indian Wars

"UNTIL THE INDIAN PROBLEM IS FINALLY SETTLED"

On June 14, 1876, William Tecumseh Sherman, commanding general of the US Army, addressed the graduating class at the US Military Academy at West Point. It was the country's centennial celebration, and Sherman's speech was forward looking and hopeful. He charged the cadets to "carry into the next century all that is valuable of the lessons and memories of the last." Those lessons included the American Revolution, the War of 1812, the Mexican-American War, and the Civil War, all of which had left an example for these new officers to follow: "Revere the memories of the past," Sherman said, and "love that flag which now waves over you as the symbol of all past glories and the harbinger of greater yet to come."[1]

It is possible that some cadets rolled their eyes at Sherman's patriotic exhortations, envisioning assignment to frontier outposts where they worried that their careers would languish in a haze of dust, boredom, and vice.[2] And while Sherman's genealogy of US military triumph did not include conflicts with Native peoples, he understood, just as the cadets did, that the Army's primary occupation was the conquest of Native peoples. Those cadets inclined to be cynical about the first part of Sherman's speech may have felt he was speaking directly to them when he turned to the Indian Wars: "The mass of you, however, will pass into the cavalry and infantry, destined to be busily occupied until the Indian problem is finally settled. . . . The probabilities are that you will be dispersed and scattered along the line of frontier, pushed farther and farther as military posts become transformed into cities and towns."

The new officers sitting in front of the general may have contemplated a life of monotony, but Sherman assured them that frontier duty would soon disappear. The Army would hasten that day by offering "protection and encouragement to that industrious mass of our fellow citizens who press forward to carry civilization and the arts of the white man to the remotest parts of the center of this great continent." True, Indians stood in the way, but Sherman charged the cadets to hasten their "inevitable fate" with a "due regard to humanity and mercy." Indians, according to Sherman, were unwilling to labor, unwilling to till the soil, and unwilling to abandon their territories, and the general warned against a sympathetic disposition toward people he believed were doomed to vanish. These were questions that Sherman wanted the cadets to consider, particularly since their education at West Point had provided little preparation for frontier duty: "I have thrown out a few of these thoughts," the general said, "because I know you will soon have to grapple with them, and I believe they are not written down in any of your text books."[3] A few of the more thoughtful cadets may have paused at Sherman's warning, reflecting that their military training had offered almost no instruction in combat against Indians. Native warriors featured prominently in the US cultural imagination, but far less prominently in the educational institutions of the US Army.

As the class of 1876 listened to Sherman's prediction of inevitable conquest, Native warriors were preparing to offer a strong rebuttal to US expansion on the northern plains. In the summer of 1876, the United States invaded the territory of the Lakota and their allies, targeting those bands who refused to submit to the reservation system. Just three days after Sherman's speech at West Point a column under General George Crook was rebuffed on June 17 at the Battle of the Rosebud, and on June 25–26, General George Custer and the Seventh Cavalry suffered hundreds of casualties at the Battle of the Greasy Grass (Little Bighorn).[4] "Custer's Last Stand" shocked a nation celebrating its centennial anniversary. One officer encamped with the remaining soldiers of the Seventh Cavalry in the aftermath described the bleak Fourth of July atmosphere in a letter to his wife, writing that "everything is as still as death."[5] As for the freshly graduated cadets, perhaps the anticipated boredom of a frontier posting was replaced with the fear of following in Custer's footsteps.

Custer's defeat certainly tempered Sherman's prediction of inevitable conquest. In the ensuing decades, Sherman's other predictions failed to pan out; the Indians' "inevitable fate" did not come to pass, and tribes emerged from the Indian Wars resolved to carve out a space of self-determination amid the constrictions of ongoing US colonialism.[6] I open this chapter with Sherman's speech because it addresses key questions considered throughout the book: the institutionalization of colonial violence in American culture, the role of militarism in the expansion of US empire, and the presence of persistent continuities in US history. Perhaps the most intriguing aspect of Sherman's speech is his instruction to "carry into the next century all that is valuable of the lessons and memories of the last." Sherman, who viewed the Indian Wars as a temporary impediment to US expansion, probably did not intend that phrase to include the specifics of Indian warfare as a particular branch of military doctrine, strategy, and tactics. And yet it evokes that very question. Would the cadets "carry forward" their experiences in the Indian Wars? Was there actually a doctrine of Indian/fighting that could be transmitted to future conflicts? Would the United States' persistent colonial structures influence future conflicts? This is our story in the ensuing pages. Just as Native peoples did not disappear, the Indian Wars continued to haunt the US military and the broader American culture.[7] The violence that facilitated the United States' colonial expansion lived on—in physical acts of warfare, in the cultural meanings attached to violence, and in the stories told to legitimate the spread of US empire.

Sherman's cadets had been trained in "civilized war," an evolving discourse on what was acceptable in warfare that emerged from Europe's military tradition (and its encounter with non-European peoples or "savages").[8] And yet his warning to the cadets that many would soon embark to settle the "Indian problem" situated their potential future within "savage war," wars we might more critically characterize as *colonial violence*, or the violence deployed in the conquest of Indigenous people's homelands. Taking Sherman as our jumping-off point, the remainder of this chapter explores three aspects of US colonial violence that have resonated across time and space. The first is what I call the "savage exception," a racialized form of violence positioned outside the established norms of law, culture, and politics. The second aspect is what I call, borrowing a phrase from Sherman, the "state of quasi war," the way in which wars with Native people were perpetually positioned at the borders between war/not war, blurring the boundaries of internal and external enemies in ways that delegitimized Indigenous sovereignties and influenced the history of what the US military now calls "irregular warfare." The third is the violence of myth, story, and narrative, the violence that established Indians as the perpetual enemies of the United States. This chapter pays particular attention to the ways nineteenth-century Native resistance was associated with guerilla warfare and terrorism. Over time, these stories became a vehicle for the transmission of Indian/fighting as a shadow doctrine. Examining the history of US colonial violence across these three registers is an attempt to interrupt the continued reproduction of racialized violence that has been transmitted, from the nineteenth century to the present, through ideas about Indian/fighting.

THE SAVAGE EXCEPTION

The conquest of Indigenous peoples in the Americas and the development of the modern rules of warfare occurred on parallel historical tracks.[9] It is thus difficult to untangle this aspect of international law from the spread of European colonialism. Scholars, soldiers, and politicians who contributed to the legal theories we might group together as the rules of war consistently invoked what I call the "savage exception." The savage exception is the belief that war with racialized Indigenous peoples occurs outside the boundaries of law and/or custom that governed "civilized" European warfare. In these conflicts the ameliorating effect of law/custom is discarded in favor of race war. Race becomes a determining factor on the limits placed on violence, as well as a mechanism for delegitimizing "savage" violence.[10] The history of the savage exception has been elaborated in several legal histories of colonialism. Indeed, much of the scholarship in Native and Indigenous Studies discusses the savage exception without naming it as such.[11] Historians have long understood that Europeans waging war in the "new world" willingly transgressed the limits they would have imposed upon themselves in conflicts with other Europeans.[12] A brief survey of this history will help contextualize the development of the United States' approach to wars with Native peoples.

The savage exception emerged through European colonialism in what they called the "New World." In particular, defining Indigenous peoples as savages served to legitimate settler-colonial claims to land. Emer de Vattel, a key figure in the development of international law, argued in his influential work *The Law of Nations* that Native peoples in North America could not claim the entire continent because they did not adequately utilize the land, writing that "the savages of North

America had no right to appropriate all that vast continent to them-selves; and, since they were unable to inhabit the whole of those regions, other nations might, without injustice, settle in some parts of them."[13] These sorts of justifications invoked *terra nullius*, a legal concept used to justify European colonization. Claims to *terra nullius* focused on two related ideas. First, that land was free of cultivation or development; second, that the inhabitants of land were in a "state of nature," lacking organized government. *Terra nullius* made Indigenous peoples—their presence, cultures, and institutions—invisible. Of course, the interac-tions between European settlers and Native polities often laid bare the illusion at the heart of *terra nullius*, since Native peoples *were* there, and often contested colonization through force or negotiated agreements with settlers.[14]

Regarding war, Vattel offers a clear articulation of the savage excep-tion. Concerning the rights of nations in war, he sets out clear limits on the right to kill enemies and cautions that surrendered enemies should be spared. However, enemies guilty of "some enormous breach" of the laws of war can be punished by withholding quarter, a practice known as the law of retaliation. "Savage nations" seem to fall into this category by default: "When we are at war with a savage nation who observe no rules, and never give quarter, we may punish them in the persons of any of their people whom we take." Vattel argued for the right of civilized nations to "join a confederacy for the purpose of punishing and even exterminating . . . savage nations," a viewpoint Jeffrey Ostler notes is resonant with early US foreign policy toward Native peoples as em-bodied in the 1787 Northwest Ordinance.[15] Vattel was not the only founder of international law to invoke the savage exception. Vattel's antecedents, including Jean Bodin, Hugo Grotius, and Alberico Gentili, all characterized Native peoples as savages existing in a state of nature. Gentili argued that Spanish colonizers could engage in just war with Native peoples due to Indians "abominable lewdness." War with Na-tive peoples was "made as against brutes."[16] Similarly, Grotius justified European wars of conquest in North America through overt references to the savage exception, writing, "The most just war is against savage beasts, the next against men who are like beasts."[17]

By the eighteenth century, the European legal tradition had quite clearly enunciated the savage exception, part of a broader imposition of settler law (and sovereignty) on Indigenous peoples. A harsher form of violence was justified in colonial wars of conquest.[18] Articulated as retali-ation, the savage exception transformed European wars of invasion into reprisals for Native transgressions, a phenomenon sometimes referred to as "defensive conquest."[19] As Lisa Ford documents, Indigenous nations had their own traditions of retaliation, and the interaction of Indigenous norms around violence with those of invading settlers grew "into a set of unwieldy, syncretic rules that bound much settler-indigenous interaction." These competing notions of violence could become quite messy at the local level. Settlers became adept at using legal discourses to legitimize their own acts of violence, and, by the nineteenth century, Native violence was increasingly characterized as criminal. And that criminality worked to delegitimize Native sovereignty.[20]

The early English settlements on the Atlantic coast invoked the savage exception in their wars with Native nations, which often involved indiscriminate forms of violence.[21] After the Powhatan Confederacy attacked the Jamestown colony in 1622, the Virginia Company's account of the fighting claimed a right of retaliation, and, by extension, conquest. The author of the company's official history, lawyer Edward Waterhouse, wrote that the "treacherous violence of the savages" meant that the colony could, "by right of war, and law of nations, invade the country and destroy them."[22] Other English settlers made similar legal arguments based on retaliation when justifying their right to claim Native lands. Preacher Robert Gray claimed that a "Christian king may lawfully make war upon a barbarous and savage people" if the end goal was to claim their land and convert them to Christianity and other European cultural norms. The colonists found this advantageous, as wars of conquest were a quicker method of dispossession that would open more land to settlement. Wars could also be endowed with a finality that elided a continuing Indigenous presence. Once "defeated," the settler-fiction could proceed as if Native peoples were gone.[23]

The Declaration of Independence refigured retaliation against "savages" for the purposes of revolution, claiming that the British had sought to incite against the colonists "the merciless Indian Savages, whose known rule of warfare, is an undistinguished destruction of all ages, sexes and conditions." Opposition to savagery was thus written into the founding documents of the United States.[24] During the Revolutionary War, the savage exception was on full display. In 1780, Virginia governor Thomas Jefferson ordered George Rogers Clark into the Ohio Valley against tribes allied with the British. Clark was told to pursue "their extermination, or their removal beyond the lakes or Illinois river."[25] Jefferson was not the only "founding father" who pursued the destruction of Native nations during the revolution. In a campaign the year before that targeted the four nations of the Haudenosaunee confederacy who sided with the British, George Washington ordered Major General John Sullivan to seek the "total destruction and devastation of their settlements." Washington's orders also directed Sullivan to "ruin their crops in the ground and prevent their planting more."[26] This was a policy intended to terrorize the Haudenosaunee. Washington believed that the new nation's security could be secured through "the terror with which the severity of the chastizement they receive will inspire them."[27] During the campaign Sullivan orchestrated daybreak attacks on Haudenosaunee towns, a tactic that would become normalized in US military strategy later in the nineteenth century. The brutality of Sullivan's campaign, marked by mutilation, murder, and atrocity, clearly distinguishes it from clashes with the British during the American Revolution.[28]

American jurists in the new nation echoed their European predecessors when discussing the violence of those they deemed "savage." James Kent's *Commentaries on American Law* groups the United States within the European traditional of international law but excludes Native peoples. In a section devoted to the legality of war, Kent notes that anyone who studied the "Indian character" would know that "war is the natural instinct and appetite of man in a savage state." In a fascinating foreshadowing of current military terminology, Kent also criticizes the conduct of "irregulars" who violate the laws of war. He references the "vexations and irregular warfare of the Indian tribes," evidence that Indian warfare was defined by its perceived "irregularity" in the early nineteenth century, long before that term acquired its current usage. Native peoples were, for Kent, outside the laws that governed war between Euro-American nations, and he believed they would inevitably disappear.[29] Henry Wheaton, another important jurist in the newly formed United States, reiterated the Euro-American right of conquest in the New World. Wheaton argued that international law was premised on "entirely disregarding" the rights of Native nations, and colonizers had "gradually compelled the savage tenant of the forest to yield to the superior power and skill of his civilized invader."[30]

In the decades after the American Revolution, settler militias and US soldiers continued to pursue wars of conquest justified through the savage exception. Nowhere was this more visible than in the wars with the Seminoles, conflicts that brought the legal status of Indian combatants to the forefront of US military/legal discourse.[31] The First Seminole War was an extension of the War of 1812 and the United States' effort to conquer Native peoples in the Southeast. It grew out of Andrew

Jackson's war on the Muscogee (Creek) people, many of whom had migrated south to Florida, forming autonomous communities that often allied with communities of free Blacks, sometimes known as Black Seminoles. The borders between the US and Native territory were fractured by raids, counter-raids, and an escalating cycle of violence that culminated with Jackson organizing an expedition into Florida in 1818.[32] Rallying the Tennessee militia, Jackson told them that Native peoples had been treated with too much "mildness and humanity," and it was now the time to respond with "impunity" to Native attacks on settlers encroaching on their territories.[33]

In 1818, Jackson charged into Spanish Florida at the head of an army to "chastise a Savage foe."[34] They sacked towns, destroyed food supplies, and killed or captured hundreds of Native people and their allies. Evidence of scalps taken by Seminole raiders served to infuriate Jackson's troops, and the campaign was prosecuted with increasing brutality. Jackson's conduct would thrust debate over the laws of war onto the national stage. In one incident he captured and executed two Seminole leaders, Hillis Hadjo and Homathlemico, by tricking them onto a US warship flying the British flag, a clear violation of European laws of war. Even more infamously, Jackson captured and executed Alexander Arbuthnot and Robert Ambrister, two British traders sympathetic to the Seminoles. Arbuthnot and Ambrister were charged in front of a military tribunal with aiding, supplying, and spying for Indians in the Southeast. The tribunal sentenced both to death, Jackson claiming that "the laws of war did not apply to conflicts with savages." They were executed on the morning of April 30, 1818.[35]

Congress formally condemned Jackson's actions. For all of Jackson's brutality against Native peoples it was his execution of two Europeans that dragged his conduct into the spotlight. Indeed, most Americans in and outside Congress found no legal or ethical violation in Jackson's summary execution of two Native leaders.[36] Near the end of 1818, President James Monroe submitted Jackson's actions in Florida to Congress for review. The House Committee on Military Affairs issued a report condemning the executions of Arbuthnot and Ambrister. Jackson's defenders responded with a dissenting report, and a contentious congressional debate raged for days. House Speaker Henry Clay soundly condemned Jackson's conduct in the war, making the somewhat preposterous claim that the United States had, to that point, always followed the laws of war in conflicts with Native peoples, even as he admitted that he also hated "the tomahawk and scalping knife."

Other congressmen responded to defend Jackson, citing international law, including Vattel, as sanctioning Jackson's execution of Arbuthnot and Ambrister. Richard Mentor Johnson argued that all criticism was a moot point in an Indian War. Johnson explained that the US had "a perpetual declaration of war" against Native peoples and that the president was duty-bound to "use the strong arm of power in putting down the savages."[37]

In the end Jackson's defenders in the house succeeded in voting down the censure resolution. A similar resolution in the Senate quietly disappeared after the US finalized a deal to purchase Florida from Spain in the Transcontinental Treaty of 1819. In reflecting on the invasion into Florida, Secretary of State John Quincy Adams cited Vattel, once more, to justify US conduct. According to Adams, international law sanctioned "no rules" in wars with "a ferocious nation." As such, Jackson's expedition against the Seminoles was justified for its "salutary efficacy, through terror." Only through terrible violence could "the barbarities of Indians . . . be successfully encountered."[38] Adams's line of argument was significant. It elevated the savage exception to something adjacent to official US policy, legitimizing a principle that had existed in Euro-American thought for centuries. The savage exception carried significant legal and political weight. It sanctioned Jackson's conduct in Florida, exonerated him from congressional oversight, and did not impede his ascent to the presidency in 1829.[39] Deborah Rosen calls the First Seminole War one of the most significant assertions of US sovereignty during the nation's early years, and a key part of that assertion was the savage exception, the belief that the US could mobilize legally exceptional forms of violence to conquer Native peoples.[40]

EXCEPTIONAL VIOLENCE AND THE MILITARY ARCHIVE

William Smith and Thomas Hutchins's *Expedition against the Ohio Indians*, a history of Henry Boquet's efforts to lift the siege of Fort Pitt during Pontiac's War published in 1765, worried that "scarce any thing has been published on a subject now become of the highest importance to our colonies," and looked forward to the day when "a compleat system is at length formed for the conduct of this particular species of war," namely Indian warfare.[41] They would have waited a long time. US Army officers wrote a great deal during the nineteenth century, but little ended up in formal doctrine. The Army did not produce a singular manual of frontier warfare during the nineteenth century; there was no proto-counterinsurgency document comparable to the Marine Corps' *Small Wars Manual* that arrived in the twentieth century. Instead, a series of guidebooks, memoirs, articles, and written histories function as an archive of informal military doctrine, revealing how American soldiers conceived of their conflicts with Native people.[42]

Many officers wrote eagerly and often, taking on the role of amateur historians, naturalists, linguists, diplomats, scientists, and cultural theorists.[43] Nineteenth-century soldiers were not monolithic in their viewpoints, and many could be sharply critical of US conduct toward Native nations. Those same soldiers could, at other times, champion incredibly harsh military actions or the outright elimination of Native peoples.[44] Take a speech on the "Indian question" given by former officer Henry Carrington in 1875.[45] Carrington argued that "on the one hand, all passions are stimulated to annihilate the savage as a beast because he tears and tortures in the throes of his death struggle; on the other hand, we yearn for his rescue from that oblivion which buried his earlier ancestors, because we feel that his destinies, like his possessions, are in our hands."[46] In Carrington's imperial imaginary, US continental domination is inevitable, producing a simultaneous desire for elimination and incorporation, a euthanasia politics of colonial violence. This spectrum of sometimes-contradictory viewpoints that often criticized the mechanics of a conquest assumed to be inevitable indicates the complexity of this thing we call the "Indian Wars."[47]

What US soldiers did write about their conflicts with Native peoples tended to emphasize the use of Native scouts, increased mobility, and the targeting of Native population centers directly.[48] This body of writing increasingly institutionalized the potential for indiscriminate violence while cordoning off the Indian Wars from the mainstream of military activity into the savage exception. These texts built on the limited engagement antebellum Army officers had given to Indian/fighting. Cadets at West Point received little to no instruction in the specific forms of combat they could expect to face on the frontier. Most learned on the job.[49] One of the few exceptions was a lecture offered by Dennis Hart Mahan in his US Military Academy course taught between 1836 and 1840. Mahan developed the lecture in response to the "Dade Massacre," a defeat suffered by the Army in 1835 during the Second Seminole War. Drawing on Roman military history, as well as the fighting of the American Revolution and Napoleon's struggle against Spanish guerillas during the Peninsular War, Mahan's lecture predicted much of what would become standard Army practice in wars with Native peoples.[50]

Mahan's lecture began with a racialized depiction of Native fighters. They were subtle and treacherous, and they had an "indomitable spirit of revenge." They were elusive enemies but had "all the vices . . . which are peculiar to the savage state." By the 1830s those characterizations were firmly entrenched, and not just in literary venues. Mahan credits George Washington with developing the template for Indian warfare: fix Native populations in position, cut them off from supplies, and attack. Mahan recommended large numbers of troops, carefully guarded marches, and vigilance against surprise attacks. He encouraged the use of Native scouts, alliance with friendly Native nations, and, ultimately, attacks of such aggressiveness that they resulted in extermination or total surrender.[51] Mahan's lectures are one of the only locations for a formalized antebellum approach to Indian/fighting. And that approach emphasized the devastation of Native populations.

Mahan taught many of the officers that would oversee the wars with Native nations in the second half of the nineteenth century. US troops and settler-militias repeatedly attacked Native noncombatants directly during this period, at places like Bear River (1863), Inyan Ska Paha (1863), and Sand Creek (1864).[52] This strategy, which had accompanied US expansion for nearly a century, was more and more acknowledged in the writing of American soldiers. In 1851, Quartermaster General Thomas Jesup recommended that Army policy on the southern plains should focus on concentrating large numbers of troops in a position where they could menace Native villages: "Let them make excursions into the Indian country, find out the positions where the women and children are left when the warriors make their inroads into our territories. . . . The danger to which the Indian families would thus be exposed would restrain the warriors in their warlike and predatory operations."[53] Jesup's solution to the superior mobility exercised by Native warriors, who ignored the national boundaries of the US-Mexico borderlands, was to focus on noncombatants. This recommendation seems to have been accepted without controversy by the secretary of war. The deadly possibilities of campaigning in winter were also under discussion. In 1860, Secretary of War John B. Floyd suggested a winter campaign against the immobilized Navajo was capable of striking "a few decisive blows for the destruction of life," which would enable the US to confine, subjugate, and prevent the otherwise necessary "extermination" of the tribe.[54] These efforts to wield exterminatory violence *in the name of preventing extermination* are characteristic of a euthanasia politics, which takes as its starting point the inevitable disappearance of Indigenous peoples.[55]

When soldiers sat down and attempted to lay out the mechanics of Indian warfare in writing, they often indulged in the usual writerly pursuits of frontier officers, pondering culture, language, and the natural world. When they turned to the actual violence, they usually cordoned those conflicts off from the mainstream of military activity into the savage exception. In 1859, Captain Randolph Barnes Marcy issued "The Prairie Traveler," which was intended to prepare graduates of the US Military Academy at West Point for frontier service and serve as a guide for settlers traveling overland to the West. Marcy's text aimed to correct what he perceived to be deficiencies in the training of army officers, who were well prepared in the European tradition but unready for the fighting they were likely to face on the frontier. In his introduction, Marcy argues that "the education of our officers at the Military Academy is doubtless well adapted to the art of civilized warfare, but cannot familiarize them with the diversified details of border service." Marcy worried that that exposure to frontier violence would corrupt white soldiers. He writes that the "restless and warlike habits of the nomadic tribes renders the soldier's life almost as unsettled as that of the savages themselves."[56] Here the word *settle* takes on a double meaning, as soldiers' efforts in the service of settlement threaten to *unsettle* their differentiation from Native people.

Marcy's text discusses irregular warfare and the unique problems it presents for expansionist empires. Calling standard training inadequate for Indian warfare, Marcy describes a range of practices, including how to march through enemy territory, how to prevent Indians from stampeding horses, how to avoid ambushes, and the necessity of using Indian scouts against other Native peoples. For Marcy the problem was how to fight an enemy "who is everywhere without being anywhere," a phrase that has become something of a counterinsurgency axiom.[57] Invoking the savage exception in tactical terms, Marcy writes that "with such an enemy the strategic science of civilized nations loses much of its importance, and finds but rarely, and only in peculiar localities, an opportunity to be put in practice."[58] In the end, most of Marcy's advice involves vigilance, careful attention to the movement of troops, and treating all Indians as potentially hostile in order to avoid ambush. His text is one of the most thorough guides to Indian/fighting produced by someone affiliated with the US military, particularly before the Civil War.

In 1866, only a year after the Civil War, Marcy published a follow-up to *The Prairie Traveler*, a memoir titled *Thirty Years of Army Life on the Border*. He dedicated it to "a fast vanishing age," and although it struck a more romantic tone, it repeated many of the warnings found in his more prescriptive writing. As the Army transitioned from the Civil War, Marcy cautioned that "the modern schools of military science are ill suited to carrying on a warfare with the wild tribes of the plains." This was because "savages" acknowledged "none of the ameliorating conventionalities of civilized warfare. Their tactics are such as to render the old system almost wholly impotent." It's hard to imagine the carnage of the Civil War as "ameliorating," but Marcy's language embodies the savage exception. These wars were "uncivilized," hence subject to a different set of rules and a different approach.

Looking to another colonial empire, Marcy found inspiration in the French occupation of Algiers. He studied the writings of French officers and in a moment of inter-imperial racialization argued that the "manner of making war is almost precisely the same" between Arab fighters and Native warriors.[59] Drawing similar conclusions to the French colonial soldiers Marcy recommends surprise attacks as the only way to counter Native mobility. Ideally these surprise attacks would occur at night, with columns of soldiers quietly positioning themselves around a Native encampment and charging on a sudden signal. In somewhat dry tones Marcy describes how enemy Indians would be likely to "lose their presence of mind" in response to a sudden onslaught of gunfire and horses.[60] And that was just what soldiers and settler-militias would do in the decades after the Civil War, at places like Sand Creek, Washita, Marias, and Camp Grant.

In the two decades after Marcy published his first guidebook, the US Army accumulated a great deal of experience in Indian warfare. Much of this experience circulated informally, but a handful of officers took it upon themselves to set down a record of these conflicts, two of which deserve particular focus for what they say about the savage exception. In 1881, Edward S. Farrow, an instructor at West Point and former commander of Indian Scouts, published *Mountain Scouting: A Handbook for Officers and Soldiers on the Frontiers*. Farrow was one of the graduating cadets in the audience during Sherman's commencement speech at West Point in 1876 that opened this chapter.[61] A few years after graduation he was passing on his expertise in Indian/fighting to a new generation of US soldiers. Farrow's book moved closer to being an explicit handbook, and at times reads like proto-counterinsurgency theory. Like his predecessors, Farrow was impressed by the military prowess of Native people but wary of emulating the practices of savage warfare. He offers a range of advice like that found in Marcy's *Prairie Traveler*, focusing on the materials, landscapes, ecology, and survival strategies useful for soldiers in the field.

When Farrow arrives at the section focused on Indian warfare he warns that "strategy loses its advantages against an enemy who accepts few or none of the conventionalities of civilized warfare."[62] Farrow even uses a metaphor that has since become an enduring trope of counter-insurgency theory, writing that the Indian "is like the flea, 'put your finger on him and he is not there.'"[63] Farrow warns soldiers that their training in the conservative European tradition will only take them so far once they headed west to face Native irregulars whose character Farrow found both admirable and disgusting. He characterized the Native approach to warfare as a "fiendish thirst for blood" with "no moral restraint."[64] In reality, different Native nations had sophisticated and long-standing military traditions, training, tactics, and conventions.[65] Native practices of warfare were often distinct from the US Army, but the stubborn refusal to confer an organized military legitimacy to Native warriors grew out of the impulse to position them as insurgent to US authority. Farrow's sentiment was shared by many of his peers. In 1868, while preparing to wage war on the Cheyenne, General Philip Sheridan reported to Sherman that he sent Custer to chase down "the small parties of Indians now operating as guerillas" in present-day Kansas, later noting that "Indian tribes should not be dealt with as independent nations. They are wards of the government."[66] A similar assessment in the *Army Navy Journal* argued that Native warfare on the southern plains was "of the guerilla sort" and had to be countered by "making it impossible for him to exist in the country he operates," ideally through the destruction of the bison.[67] Painting Native warfare as chaotic and barbaric was another way to delegitimize Native sovereignty. It pointed to the shifting contours of colonial warfare, with American soldiers (and civilians) often conceiving of their campaigns as attempts to police disobedient subjects of US authority.[68]

Farrow's book recommends dispensing with attempts to defeat Native warriors in the field and instead focusing on destroying Native villages. He advises against offensive maneuvers that try to chase down Indian warriors, whose horsemanship and maneuverability were usually superior to those of US soldiers. Instead, Farrow recommends attacking when noncombatants are present, writing that "at no time are Indians so helpless to make resistance as while moving their families and camps." Additionally, these attacks should achieve the element of surprise, as "the Indian is least prepared to resist an attack made during that uncertain period between darkness and daylight."[69] Farrow specifically recommends the winter campaign, used to devastating effect by Philip Sheridan on the southern plains in 1868–69. Campaigning in the winter eliminated the main advantage of Native fighters, their mobility, and offered the military a desirable target, immobilized groups of Native families. Farrow writes that a commander that can orchestrate a surprise attack in the midst of "cold winds, rain or snow, is surely a good *Indian fighter*" (emphasis his).[70]

The environment and climate on the Great Plains can be unforgiving, particularly in winter. Violent storms, huge drifts of snow, freezing temperatures, and shortages of food can punish the unprepared. Native peoples living on the plains adapted their yearly subsistence cycles to accommodate these environmental factors, congregating in the summer to hunt buffalo and breaking apart into smaller groups to form winter encampments. For tribes engaged in conflict with the United States the winter months could be a time of safety. The Army often refrained from campaigning in winter due to the toll it took on men and horses.[71] Nevertheless, soldiers understood the potential of a winter campaign. As Sheridan noted in a letter to Sherman in 1868, Indians believed that "the inclemency of the weather would give them ample security."[72] When he took over the Department of the Missouri, Sheridan aimed to change that. As part of his strategic plan, Sheridan received permission to conduct extensive campaigning in the winter of 1868–69: "to disabuse the minds of the savages of this confident security, and to strike them at a period at which they were the most, if not entirely, helpless, became a necessity."[73] Helpless: immobilized, hungry, burdened with household items and food, with no separation between warriors and women, children, and the elderly. Sheridan would not be trying to defeat Native warriors in the field. He would be taking the fight to their villages.[74] These were the sort of campaigns Farrow recommended in *Mountain Scouting*, a text written in the aftermath of several campaigns like the one Sheridan describes.[75]

Perhaps the most comprehensive appraisal of American military strategy written in the nineteenth century was John Bigelow Jr.'s *The Principles of Strategy*. And while Bigelow's focus was primarily the lessons to be learned from the Civil War, he did spend some time on the Indian Wars, perhaps in reaction to the near-absence of these conflicts from the education he had received.[76] It was also the first textbook produced by and for the US Army, an appraisal of US Army history written at the end of the nineteenth century when the Indian Wars were considered to be over.[77] Like Farrow, Bigelow highlights the value of surprise attacks on Indian villages. Noting the superior mobility of Indian fighters, he emphasizes the importance of the nighttime march so that troops can catch Indian encampments unawares. These nighttime marches were intended to set up devastating dawn cavalry charges: "Having reached the hostile camp, they silently surround it; and in the morning, as soon as it is light enough to aim, they summon their wily enemy to surrender."[78] In Bigelow's narrative these nighttime marches culminated in a call to surrender, which cannot be attributed to naiveté or ignorance, as Bigelow was well aware of what typically happened when US soldiers caught a Native encampment unawares. American troops were far more likely to charge the camp without warning, guns blazing.

Custer's report of the attack on Black Kettle's Cheyenne village along the Washita River in 1868 paints a clear picture of what was more likely to happen after one of these nighttime marches. Having reached the camp, Custer split his command into four columns with orders to attack at dawn. He would later report that "there was never a more complete surprise. My men charged the village and reached the lodges before the Indians were aware of our presence."[79] This tactic left hundreds of Cheyenne dead, wounded, or captured, including women, children, and elders. And it achieved this goal by focusing on Native populations as units to be surprised, attacked, captured, and driven onto reservations or left dead on the field to be buried by their escaped relatives. Bigelow was aware of this, elsewhere emphasizing the effectiveness of destructive surprise attacks in an essay about the campaign against Apache leader Victorio.[80] These surprise attacks were often the rule, not an exception, and the same goes for the levels of indiscriminate violence they resulted in.

Part of the reason that conflicts with Native people make up a comparatively smaller portion of his writing is because, like his peers, Bigelow positioned colonial violence at the edges of warfare. Military tactics aimed at eliminating Native independence were thus an attempt to actualize settler claims to land, to *settle* the colonial question, and thus might not deserve a permanent place in military doctrine. In an essay for the *Journal of the Military Service Institution* (*JMSI*), one of the primary late nineteenth-century forums in which soldiers exchanged ideas and shared informal doctrine, Bigelow portrayed the soldiers employed against Native peoples as "an army of occupation," controlling Native people and keeping them restricted to their designated areas. He refers to Native warriors as "trespassers and marauders," stripping them of any legitimate military designation and constructing them as insurgents, lacking a preexisting sovereignty.[81] This attempt to grapple with the *status* of these conflicts was not unique to Bigelow. Oftentimes these discussions concerned whether these conflicts were actually wars themselves.

"A STATE OF QUASI WAR"

In the years after the Civil War, the US military turned its attention westward to territories experiencing increasing pressure from settlers. This process was part of the "greater reconstruction" that remade both the American South and West in the aftermath of the Civil War, settler colonialism fueling the capitalist expansion of the Gilded Age.[82] Frontier violence had long been an occupation of the Army, but the postwar years saw an intensified series of conflicts fought over lands that had previously been lightly settled, if at all. Indeed, the territories fought over after the war laid bare the illusion of imperial geography. As much as the country projected a cohesive, coast-to-coast national boundary in 1866, the reality on the ground was that Native nations still controlled large sections of the continent.[83] The colonial process that attempted to wrest these territories away challenged the fixity of temporal, geographic, and discursive boundaries, leaving Americans to wonder: were the Indian Wars actually a war?

In the 1869 *Annual Report of the Secretary of War*, Commanding General of the United States Army William Tecumseh Sherman argued that "a state of quasi war" existed west of the Mississippi in conditions "amounting to anarchy."[84] Sherman's statement came amid discussion of a reduction in the "peacetime" post–Civil War military.[85] American soldiers in the West were thinly spread across a series of isolated forts, many of which provoked conflict with the Native peoples on whose homelands they were erected. Sherman's anxieties were aggravated by increasing settlement, the expansion of the railroad (and the settlement it enabled), and the proliferation of mining and agricultural interests that were all threatened by "nomadic Indians."[86] Nineteenth-century Americans tended to imagine that US civil society was always already present, and that Native resistance was a disruption of a cohesive state, rather than an attempt to maintain sovereign spaces free from settlement. This produced a sense of precariousness, as soldiers were tasked with protecting settlers who demanded (and imagined) Native-free spaces, depicting themselves as constantly under threat of Indian attack.[87] Indeed, the reports by Sherman and his colleagues in the years after the Civil War often border on crisis.[88] Officers found themselves scrambling to meld a variety of imperial practices into a cohesive Indian policy, not just waging war but trying to impose particular kinds of peace, including President Grant's "Peace Policy," which sought to enforce peace on reservations (with the threat of war everywhere else). In practice, "war" and "peace" often aimed at the same object, the acquisition of land and the confinement of Native peoples to reservations.[89]

Army officers complained bitterly about civilian meddlers that stood in the way of military management of Native peoples. Many resented the transfer of Indian policy away from the War Department to the Interior Department, a move that domesticated frontier violence further into a state of "quasi war."[90] The Interior Department controlled most reservations, while the Army was responsible for Native peoples off the reservation, but these roles were often clouded by the realities on the ground.[91] Amid the tangled federal bureaucracy, the Army was often positioned between East Coast "reformers," corrupt federal appointees, and frontier "Indian haters" in their effort to normalize US expansion, sometimes advocating for Native peoples and sometimes crushing their military resistance. Soldiers were asked to serve as conduits of American biopower, administering foods, medicines, and other necessities for sustaining life, goods made necessary by the very reality of US conquest.[92] Many soldiers were exterminationist in their rhetoric, but they could be highly critical of US policies toward Native nations. Philip Sheridan, who oversaw several brutal campaigns, noted that "we took away their country and their means of support, broke up their mode of living, their habits of life, introduced disease and decay among them, and it was for this and against this they made war. Could any one expect less?"[93]

This prevailing state of "quasi-war" frustrated many who attempted to define it. The period between the Civil War and the Spanish-American War saw a rise in US military publications, books, lectures, and educational venues.[94] However, this increase in professional activity was focused on the "civilized" wars the military might face in the future and largely ignored the "savage" wars of the present, the handful of texts discussed in the previous section being an exception.[95] In fact, there was no consensus on whether the "Indian Wars" were actually a war. Politicians, soldiers, and writers often debated whether Native people were sovereign nations, capable of waging war, or government wards, no more than violent criminals. In the aftermath of his winter campaign on the southern plains, 1868–69, Custer reported that the tribes "have, from the commencement of this campaign, been treated, not as independent nations, but as refractory subjects of a common government." However, in that same report Custer also referred to surrendered tribes as "virtually prisoners of war," and one wonders how they can be both "subjects of a common government" and prisoners of war.[96] And, if they were simply the subjects of a common government, Custer's attack at the Washita that destroyed the village of Cheyenne chief Black Kettle takes on even more unsettling overtones given the slaughter unleashed.

This state of quasi war established historical precedents that continue to circulate, most recently during the War on Terror. Attorney John C. Yoo's "torture memos" that sought to legitimize the Bush administration's use of "enhanced interrogation techniques" cited, as precedent, the execution and detention of Modoc Indians in 1873 following the Modoc War. Specifically, Yoo cited US Attorney General George H. Williams, who wrote a legal opinion arguing that captive Modoc men could be tried (and hung) by a military tribunal, and were not subject to a civil court.[97] Williams began with a confusion familiar to readers of this book, writing, "It is difficult to define exactly the relations of the Indian tribes to the United States," before arguing that the Modoc's crimes—particularly the killing of two US representatives under a flag of truce—subjected them indefinitely to US military authority. The Modocs were outside the jurisdiction of both the US constitution and the protections afforded lawful combatants.[98] The resonance to the United States' practices of indefinite detention at Guantanamo Bay are explicit. Indeed, Jodi Byrd calls Indians the "origin of the stateless terrorist combatants." As this chapter will show, Byrd's use of "terrorist" is not an anachronism. Native resistance was often characterized as "terrorism" in the nineteenth century.[99]

Members of Congress could not agree on whether the Indian Wars were actually a war. In an 1876 congressional debate, Senator John Ingalls criticized his colleague John Logan's refusal to award honorary rankings to soldiers who fought in the Indian Wars, saying, "You do not even dignify it with the title of war; you do not acknowledge it to be a condition of war; you dispatch converging columns into an enemy's country, order them to rendezvous at a certain point; they continue for months in the field. And when they ask the Senate for recognition of their heroic deeds, you refuse them the cheap embellishment of a brevet!"[100] The refusal to award Brevet rank—honorary promotions similar to medals—for service on the frontier, illustrates that even Congress was unsure whether they were at war with Native people. Senator Logan argued that he opposed breveting "on the ground that the law recognizes brevets only in time of war for gallant conduct in the face of the enemy. . . . If the senate will not recognize glory in Indian warfare there will not be any glory in Indian warfare."[101]

The Indian Wars are also difficult to define because they encompassed such a broad range of activities. Philip Sheridan's devastating 1868 campaign on the southern plains was certainly a war, but what about First Lieutenant Royal Whitman's decision to allow a community of Aravaipa Apache people to live in proximity to Camp Grant in Arizona in the 1870s? Both actions resulted in the massacre of Native people, but one was a coordinated military campaign while the other was a conscious effort to enforce President Grant's "peace policy" and *reduce* conflict.[102] Are both examples of the Indian Wars? Should we include the attempts to protect, feed, police, house, and control Native peoples under the umbrella of the Indian Wars? The Army was often at odds with the civilian officials tasked with administering reservations, and generals argued they should have greater control over the management of US settler colonialism beyond just fighting.[103] Sherman complained of the difficulties in fighting tribes when they were "construed as under the guardianship and protection of the general government." He called for military control of Indian affairs, arguing that "the Indians should be controlled by the military authorities, and that the commanding officers of the troops should have not only the surveillance of these Indians, but should supervise and control the disbursement of moneys and distribution of presents to the tribes under past and future treaties."[104] Military publications agreed; the *United States Army and Navy Journal* argued that "savages can only be governed by a military system. Their first step toward civilization must be through military discipline."[105] The desire to govern through a "military system" consistently blurred the boundaries between war and peace, between elimination and incorporation.

Sherman's characterization of the frontier as "a state of quasi war" threatening to dissolve into anarchy betrays the always unstable boundaries of the settler-colonial project. Sherman lamented the accompanying strain on his officers, noting that "many of the officers have been required to perform, at great personal risk, the duties of Indian agents, governors, sheriffs, judges and inspectors of elections, &c, &c, duties foreign to their military training, and they have done this duty without a murmur and with marked intelligence."[106] In a later essay published on "The 'Indian Question'" Sherman would report that, as a result of Grant's peace policy, the shadowy ground between war and peace made the Army's job more difficult. He argued that "the Army has a much more difficult task now than if we were actually at war and could anticipate depredations and follow the perpetrators to their very camps." These complaints were not unique to Sherman. Other officers struggled to find a balance "of force and persuasion, of severity and moderation" as one put it.[107] The Native people under Sherman's supposed control inhabited a gray area where their incorporation into the mechanisms of American government created a state of quasi war.

These "duties foreign to their military training" extended beyond the Army's relationship to Native peoples. They explored, built roads, maintained schools, hospitals, and churches, conducted scientific investigations, enforced the rule of law, and generally served as what Michael Tate calls the "multipurpose army." And while direct warfare was sometimes an infrequent pastime, these broader "duties foreign to their military training" helped facilitate US settler colonialism.[108] Sherman wasn't the only officer to worry about this expansion of his mission. The 1882 graduating class at West Point was cautioned that "a soldier is now expected to exert himself within proper limits to preserve and organize peace. He should labor, in unison with the citizen and philanthropist, to impress and extend our civilization . . . in a few short years, whatever may be your age and rank, you may be obliged to administer affairs wherein considerable knowledge of civil matters may be necessary."[109] In statements like this we can see a precursor to the counterinsurgency field manual published during the Iraq War—military and civil affairs blended together in a sometimes confusing mélange.[110] Adding to the confusion, it wasn't until most officials considered the Indian Wars to be over, in 1890, that Congress retroactively awarded brevets for service in the "Indian Wars." These "wars" only became official once they were widely considered to be over.[111] Given the ongoing colonization of Native homelands, we could just as easily say that these wars never ended. These wars/not wars fought with Native nations form an important part of the United States' history with irregular warfare. Moments of violence positioned at the edges of warfare have been a consistent feature of US foreign policy, as has soldiers' discomfort with the subsequent "duties foreign to their military training" that those sorts of conflicts demand. This discomfort originated in the Indian Wars, and explains, in part, why those conflicts have remained an enduring script for irregular warfare.

GUERILLAS AND TERRORISM

The savage exception and the state of quasi war help us view colonial violence within a complex web of law, government, and warfare. Somewhat paradoxically, these frameworks emphasize just how difficult it is to locate Native people within the juridical, national, and discursive borders of colonialism, something Kevin Bruyneel refers to as "colonial ambivalence."[112] These simultaneous inclusions and exclusions extend to violence—both its materiality and its representation in different cultural discourses. Colonial discourses about violence have been a primary mechanism for the transmission of Indian/fighting across time and space, and they have often focused on guerilla tactics and terroristic threats, extensions of the "state of quasi war" that predict contemporary discussions of insurgency. Native people have been linked to each of these categories in ways that have made the figure of the Indian a recurring motif in the history of American violence.

The earliest British colonists were constantly frustrated by the hit-and-run tactics of their Native enemies, referring to them as wolves that fought in a secretive, skulking fashion.[113] The figure of the violent, elusive Indian that struck from the shadows proliferated in early American culture. By the time of the Civil War this was a common image, a tool to critique the tactics and behavior of enemy soldiers.[114] Abolitionist John Brown, who was executed after a failed slave rebellion in 1859, was compared to "the savage Indian, whose war-whoop is the death-knell of whole families" by Confederate soldiers.[115] Reports from the Union occupation of Missouri stated that Confederate guerillas were "committing atrocities more inhuman than those of Indian savages."[116] Confederate guerilla activity was a consistent problem for Union forces, and the long history of warfare against Native peoples provided a ready template to characterize guerilla violence (and justify harsh Union responses).[117]

Indian/fighting cuts both ways, sometimes reviled, sometimes emulated. There were advocates of guerilla warfare in the Confederacy who applauded such "savagery." Writer William Gilmore Simms encouraged the Confederate army to assign several guerillas "painted and disguised as Indians" to every company to "inspire terror" in Northerners who would assume that "scalps are to be taken by the redmen."[118] Other Confederates evoked a more noble savagery in the figure of Turner Ashby, a cavalry commander under Stonewall Jackson who was described by his peers as "active and agile as an Indian hunter" and "the very impersonation of an Indian warrior."[119] One of Ashby's soldiers described his cavalry as "a tribal band held together by the authority of a single chief."[120] References to savage Indians framed violence in multiple ways, sometimes glamorizing it but most often serving as a critique of one's enemies.

Experience in Indian warfare served to legitimize Union officers tasked with halting Confederate raids. This was the case with George Crook, an Army officer who will reemerge throughout this book. At the outbreak of the Civil War, Colonel George Crook left the Pacific Northwest to take command of a regiment in West Virginia. One soldier wrote that "Colonel Crook is a regular Old Indian fighter," while another predicted that Crook would turn the tables on the rebels, "he having been practising those warlike arts for over ten years among the Indians on our western frontiers." Crook's description of his time in the Pacific Northwest, where he fought in the Rogue River War, anticipates much of his military career, with its blend of contempt for Native peoples and criticism of US policy. He described Native peoples as "filthy, odoriferous, treacherous, ungrateful, pitiless, cruel, and lazy," but could be harshly critical of settlers whose atrocities provoked Indian retaliation.[121] The Confederacy was, according to Crook, full of "bushwhackers," and in his autobiography he wrote that "being fresh from the Indian country where I have more or less experience with that kind of warfare, I set to work organizing for the task."[122] With an experienced Indian fighter for a leader, and with a rising tide of anti-guerilla sentiment, Crook's autobiography reports that his troops began executing captured Confederate guerillas rather than sending them to military prisons. Crook seems to have approved of this take-no-prisoners approach, writing that "in a short time no more of these prisoners were brought in."[123]

Partly in response to Confederate guerillas, the US Army commissioned lawyer Francis Lieber to draft instructions for Union soldiers. The document, known as the Lieber Code, went on to be a foundational text in the development of the modern rules of war.[124] It also served to further entrench the savage exception in American warfare. The Lieber Code offered legal protections to uniformed combatants but endorsed punishments for guerillas, insurgents, and those fighting beyond the constraints of what it called "civilized" warfare. It perpetuated the language of political sovereignty that functioned as a tool to exclude Native nations from the formalized discourses of warfare. Article 20 defined war as "a state of armed hostility between sovereign nations or governments," specifying that these categories applied to those living a "civilized existence."[125]

The code established limits on military conduct while authorizing harsh measures against those who flouted the code's prescripts, and a reader of the code could reasonably assert that Native fighters, members of what Lieber called "barbarous armies," fell outside those prescriptions by default. Indeed, Lieber's repeated use of "barbarous" and "uncivilized" fit the code within the longer history of the savage exception, making it a tool to deploy in conflicts with racialized enemies.[126] Articles 24 and 25 of the code warned that "uncivilized peoples" declined to protect noncombatants, in contrast to the "modern regular wars of the Europeans." Articles 27 and 28 endorsed retaliation against "barbarous outrage," codifying a long-running assumption of wars with Native nations that atrocities against Native peoples were justified as retaliation. But even in the discussion of retaliation, Lieber is careful to differentiate between civilized and savage warfare. Under the code, retaliation was only permissible as "protective retribution." Too much retaliation eroded the mitigating effect of the rules of war, sliding violence toward "the internecine wars of savages."[127]

Using the Lieber Code, Union soldiers could argue that Confederate guerillas were not afforded the rights of prisoners of war, and, through comparison to Indians, render them as savages against whom exceptional violence could be deployed. The report on Missouri guerillas in the 1863 *Annual Report of the Secretary of War* complained that "most of these bands are not authorized belligerents under the laws of war, but simply outlaws from civilized society."[128] The figure of the uncivilized "belligerent" striking from concealment and hiding in the woods would have been familiar to a nineteenth-century writer, as those were the terms in which Native warfare was discussed from the earliest colonial conflicts. In North America the language of guerilla warfare has its origins in characterizations of Native violence.

In the aftermath of the Civil War, the precariousness of US settlement resulted in settlers positioning themselves as victims of hostile Indian aggressions, demanding military protection.[129] By the 1870s, settlers were even going so far as to characterize Native resistance to US expansion as "terrorism." The frequent references to Indian terrorism in the late nineteenth century are perhaps the strongest example of how the discursive contours of US colonialism delegitimized Native sovereignty, and particularly Native resistance.[130] "Terrorism" in these examples is not a coincidental utterance.[131] Emerging from the violence of the French

Revolution, the word *terrorism* increasingly entered the vocabularies of Europeans and Americans in the 1870s to describe revolutionary violence. US Army officers worried that the political terror of European radicals, those "dynamite assassins," would find its way to America.[132] It is significant that US settlers began to deploy the term during this same period as a descriptor for Indigenous threats to US expansion. Increasingly, Native violence was "unthinkable" due to both the assumption of US conquest and the emotional investment in manifest destiny.

Native resistance may have been unthinkable in its horror, but it was simultaneously expected. In an article published on February 17, 1879, the *New York Times* loudly proclaimed "ANARCHY IN ALASKA: The Indians Threatening to Massacre the Whites—Terrorism Throughout the Territory." This dire prediction is just one of many instances in the nineteenth century when US newspapers warned of imminent disaster. The threat of possible Indian outbreaks loomed large in the settler consciousness, often expressed in these sorts of alarmist articles. It was most likely an unwarranted fear, and in that sense the story is unremarkable, as similar scenarios of imagined Indian outbreaks played out over and over in the second half of the nineteenth century.[133] These potential outbreaks represented a fear that the *settled* state of US territorial domination could still fracture, that Native people remained a threat to the colonial order. "Outbreak" seemed to induce a titillating thrill in readers, balancing the expectation of Native violence against the brutal successes of US conquest.

What *is* remarkable about the *Times* article is its invocation of both "anarchy" and "terrorism" to describe the threat posed by Native people. The late nineteenth-century discourse around "Indian terrorism" constitutes an early instance of terrorism signifying the violence of racialized nonstate actors. Most histories of terrorism focus on the violence of the French revolution and the spread of the term via the writings (and activities) of European radicals such as Carlo Pisacane in Italy, the Fenians in Ireland, and the Narodnaya Volya in Russia.[134] Writers in the United States were certainly aware of European "terrorism," but they also deployed the term to describe anti-reconstruction violence in the American South and Native resistance to US continental expansion.[135] This is a history that has been inadequately incorporated into analyses of the United States' relationship with terrorism, which unsurprisingly focuses on more recent events. However, as Indians were increasingly defined as subject peoples, rather than independent nations, they were also increasingly designated as terrorists. This constitutes one of the earliest racializations of the word *terrorism*. Scholars have noted the racialized linkage between Arab/Muslim people and terrorism in the twenty-first century.[136] A similar pattern emerged much earlier, in the nineteenth century, and involved the designation of Native people's violent resistance to US colonialism as "terrorism."

As early as 1860, Native resistance to US continental expansion was being referred to as "terrorism." In an editorial titled "Our Indian Policy" published in December of that year, a writer for the *New York Times* complained about the "half-dozen tribes of savages" maintaining "a condition of terrorism over the broad region it scours, wholly irreconcilable with white civilization." Largely concerned with reducing the military budget, the author argued for the mobilization of overwhelming force and eventual confinement to reservations. As with other instances of this language I will detail, terrorism is linked to Indian people's depiction as lawless nonstate actors. The author critiques treaties and other forms of sovereign recognition conferred on Indian "depredators" and argues that treaties be abolished.[137] Of course, in 1860, the Lakota, Dakota, Cheyenne, Apache, and other tribes detailed in this editorial were still very much *external* enemies, but their subsuming into a discourse of state authority rendered their actions as "terrorism."

References to Indian terrorism would multiply in the final decades of the nineteenth century, most often linked to the threat of Indian outbreaks. Apache people, often dehumanized as wolves or tigers, were also characterized as terrorists. In an 1871 news article, the *Chicago Tribune* reported that Apache violence kept Arizona in a state of "terrorism" and voiced support for the Army's policy of vigorously pursuing Apache people "until they submit to the authority of the government."[138] Two years later, on the heels of George Crook's campaign against the Apache, the same paper proclaimed that "civilization through the sword has at last triumphed over the barbarism and terrorism" of a supposedly now-humbled Apache people. In a moment of premature imperial confidence (think George W. Bush on the aircraft carrier in 2003) the paper also declared the Apache wars over, "mission accomplished."[139] The *Oakland Daily Transcript* concurred, writing in June of 1874 that George Crook, freed from the supervision of meddling philanthropists, had administered a "severe punishment," and "deliverance from Indian terrorism" was not far off.[140] What is clear from these articles is that the characterization of Apache resistance as "terrorism" was not solely driven by specific acts of violence. Apache violence was considered to be particularly vicious, but the above writers emphasized that it was Apache disruption of the *settled* state of things in Arizona that was particularly terroristic. In other words, the ability of Apache people to elude, exceed, and fracture the vision of a coherent US authority, to assert that the region was still Apache homeland, was the true root of terror, as settlers attempted to envision a political present in which Indigenous resistance was no longer a reality.[141]

In the final decade of the nineteenth century, depictions of Native violence began to move toward nostalgia as Indian pacification became the prevailing expectation.[142] Speeches and history books now celebrated the victory of Euro-American civilization over Indian terrorism. For example, in 1887, General Nelson A. Miles accepted an award from the citizens of Arizona for his role in the recent campaign against the Chiricahua Apache that resulted in the final surrender of Goyahkla (Geronimo). In his speech, Miles celebrated those settlers at the "vanguard of civilization" who had suffered the "terrorism" of the "fearful scourge" of Apache people. In the end, Miles looked toward a hopeful future for Arizona, trusting that "her progress now in the peaceful advancement of civilization may be more rapid than that of any other State or Territory before." Ultimately, it was precisely this experience with Apache "terrorism" that, according to Miles, would allow Arizona to better achieve the colonial normalcy long denied "the last section of our country to be rescued from the ravages and control of the Indian race." Having experienced the worst offered by "savagery," the citizens of Arizona would move even more rapidly toward the end goal—statehood.[143]

In the 1890s, concerns over Apache violence were renewed at the prospect of some of the Chiricahua, who had been imprisoned in the aftermath of Goyahkla's surrender, being returned to Arizona. A series of editorials in the *Los Angeles Times* warned that the "continuous atrocities of these red devils" would be renewed upon their return to Arizona. One writer complained that "This state of terrorism has lasted long enough. It would be too humiliating to admit that the United States authorities cannot stop it." Another editorial observed that "Arizona has enjoyed a breathtaking spell during the past four years, and has begun to recover from the disastrous effects of protracted terrorism." The author recommended continued confinement and proximity to so-called "civilized Indians" as a mechanism to maintain peace in Arizona. In other words, a maintenance of the colonial controls that had eliminated Apache independence, and the "terrorism" that came with it. The threat of Apache violence lingered in the form of the so-called "Apache Kid," Haskay-bay-nay-ntayl, an Aravaipa Apache and onetime Army scout who fled San Carlos in 1887 and lived as a fugitive in the mountains.[144] A writer for the *San Francisco Chronicle* wrote in 1893 that "Kid's entire career has been one of terrorism to Arizona and Northern Mexico," and that he looked forward to his eventual capture.[145] More than any other reference to Indian terrorism, the threat of the "Apache Kid" hiding out in the mountains evokes the image of the twenty-first century terrorist.

Writers that sought to memorialize the history of Indian warfare at the turn of the century also referenced Indian terrorism. In an 1894 article celebrating Nelson Miles's appointment as commander of the Military Department of the East, the *New York Times* wrote that "Miles started in the heyday of Indian terrorism, fought through its dying stages, and finally conducted the last campaigns, subjugating to lives of domestic pursuit or imprisonment the surviving warriors." The writer even links Miles's suppression of Indian terrorism to the more visible "terrorism" of the nineteenth century, namely anarchist and labor activism. They note Miles's role in suppressing the "industrial revolutionists" during the Pullman Strike in Chicago, which the paper also refers to as an "outbreak" and "uprising," connecting it to the history of Indian outbreaks.[146] Terrorism was a violent threat to state and capital, and these were the terms in which Native resistance was often understood.

Histories of US continental expansion written in the late nineteenth century often invoked Indian terrorism through the lens of nostalgia and pacification. Multiple histories of the Fifth US Cavalry mention how the regiment "ended Indian terrorism" in the states of Kansas and Nebraska in the winter of 1869 with the Battle of Summit Springs, when they destroyed the Dog Soldier band led by Tall Bull.[147] Elbridge Brooks, one of the more famous children's authors of the turn of the century, linked Native people's supposed racial inferiority to their propensity for terrorism: "Inch by inch, the savagery that upon the American continent had, even from primeval times, kept pace with its crude though slowly developing intelligence, forced that intelligence into terrorism and decline." According to Brooks, terrorism was the natural result of what he determined to be Native people's inherent urge to commit violent acts, and thus turns the history of US expansion into a history of the triumph *over* terrorism.

The discourse of Indian terrorism long predates the "clash of civilizations" rhetoric that has dominated the twenty-first century War on Terror and shows that the racialization of "terror" as a struggle between civilization and barbarism has a much longer history, rooted, in part, in colonialism. The point is not to leap, crudely, from the Indian Wars to the War on Terror, but rather to situate the history of the evolution of "terrorism," as a discourse about violence, within Native American history, a connection that will come full circle in the final chapter of this book.

"THE INDIAN QUESTION WILL NOT LAST FOREVER"

In the final years of the nineteenth century, some of the US Army's most famous generals, including William Tecumseh Sherman and George Crook, championed the importance of the Indian Wars. These generals remembered their frontier service not just as a mythic national origin story, but as a crucial period of professional development, producing skilled soldiers with a wealth of expertise to draw on.[148] Brevet Major J. B. Babcock, in an 1891 essay arguing for the importance of field exercises and manuals to assist in the training of soldiers, complained that it was fashionable to underrate the Army's experiences in frontier warfare. Babcock maintained that it had been of great value in preparing troops, suggesting that future Army manuals should include lessons from "a century of Indian campaigning."[149] Other veterans of the Indian Wars during this period credited the Army's skill in marksmanship, horsemanship, and irregular warfare to lessons learned in conflicts with Native people.[150] Arthur L. Wagner, one of the foremost Army intellectuals in the early twentieth century, argued that there was little practical instruction in tactics prior to the Philippine-American War, and that the majority of officers "received the valuable actual experience afforded by the Indian campaigns."[151]

These celebrations of Indian fighting were not confined to the realm of nostalgia. During the 1891 *Baltimore* Crisis, a diplomatic incident involving the US and Chile, those who contemplated deploying troops to Chile recommended that Indian War veterans be sent. On October 16, 1891, in the midst of rising tensions between the two countries, angry Chileans killed two sailors from the USS *Baltimore*, injuring more than a dozen others. Cautioning against underestimating Chile's military, one military leader argued that in the event of war "an officer with a staff well educated in all the deceit and artifice of Indian warfare would be the most available and useful in a campaign against this people. The Modoc treachery and the Cibicu mutiny are incidents to be borne in mind when we have once put ashore on Chilean soil." There was even speculation that if President Benjamin Harrison decided to deploy troops to Chile he would send "famous Indian fighter" Nelson Miles, who had recently orchestrated the suppression of the Ghost Dance movement that resulted in the Wounded Knee massacre in 1890.[152] Ultimately, Harrison settled for an apology from the Chilean government, but the incident highlighted that experience in Indian warfare was not a professional liability at the end of the nineteenth century.[153] This was particularly true with racialized enemies, in this case Chileans, who were characterized as uniquely treacherous during the incident.

Against this positive characterization of the Indian Wars ran another current that looked forward to future "civilized" wars. In the 1883 issue of the *JMSI*, a US Army officer argued that "the idea that the Army only exists to keep the Indians in order should be pushed aside with a strong hand. It is fatal to any proper study and preparation, and before long the echo will return to plague us from Congress, for the Indian question will not last forever."[154] The US government had committed itself to resolving this "Indian question" through a blend of violence and colonial administration. A series of reforms in the late nineteenth and early twentieth centuries aimed at updating the US Army into a modern, civilized, intellectual, and professional institution.[155] Indian/fighting did not have a place in this institutional realignment. The experience of continental expansion did not disappear overnight, and veterans of the frontier had their experiences to draw on when shaping the Army's doctrine. But as a general rule, the Army's orientation was increasingly toward future "civilized" or conventional wars.[156] After all, the Indian question "would not last forever."

Army generals such as John Pope called the Indian Wars a "fleeting bother" and criticized their value in producing knowledgeable and professional soldiers.[157] Francis Lieber, author of the Lieber Code, wrote that "the fighting and slaying of the Indians is terrible to me; but their gradual extinction I consider desirable, and the quicker the better."[158] John Bigelow Jr., whose book *Principles of Strategy* was one of the few texts that seriously considered wars with Native people, also doubted the future utility of Indian-fighting.[159] Writing in 1884, Bigelow claimed that the "Indian problem" had been eliminated, with the Army reduced to a police force. This form of military occupation was ill-suited to preparation for impending wars, according to Bigelow, as "preserving the peace is not preparing for war."[160] As another officer argued in the pages of a military journal, "The days of savage warfare in this country are numbered; and now, in time of perfect peace and quiet, should the training of our forces be devoted to their use in modern civilized battles."[161] Hugh Lennox Scott, who served as superintendent of

West Point in the early twentieth century, recalled a series of training maneuvers in 1889 that "had the salutary effect of awakening a good many of us to the fact that the day of Indian wars was over and that we must fit ourselves for war with civilized peoples."[162] These calls to focus on civilized war influenced the reorganizations of the US military in the first decades of the twentieth century, even as soldiers in the Philippines continued to imagine themselves as Indian fighters engaged in a protracted counterinsurgency.[163]

Military training was undergoing something of a renaissance in the US Army at the turn of the century, and writers were quick to point out that prior to the Spanish American War and subsequent occupation of the Philippines most soldiers received the majority of their training "on the job" in wars with Native people. One retired officer even cautioned against the fetishization of "civilized war," arguing that "no troops have been successful in our service on Indian campaigns that have not been able to adapt themselves to the methods of their savage foes; on the contrary, the most serious disasters recorded in the annals of our Indian wars have been due to too rigid adherence to the tactics of civilized warfare."[164] Some argued that the Army must emancipate itself from dependence on foreign military theory, the ideal of civilized war, while bemoaning the lack of military literature focused on the wars of continental expansion.[165]

In 1894 the Infantry and Cavalry School at Fort Leavenworth was not teaching Bigelow's *Principles of Strategy*, Farrow's *Mountain Scouting*, or Marcy's *The Prairie Traveler*, each of which had set down an approach to the Indian Wars. Of the books on the curriculum, only Arthur Wagner's *Organization and Tactics* and *The Service of Security and Administration* discussed the Indian Wars at any length. *The Service of Security and Administration* emphasized the utility of using Indian scouts, albeit as an afterthought to the majority of the text. *Organization and Tactics* made brief mention of the Indian Wars, highlighting the value of mounted infantry to counter Native mobility. Wagner valued the developmental experience of the Indian Wars for the US military. He argued that "the Sioux, quite as well as the Prussian, teaches the lesson that nothing but constant practice in the real or simulated conditions of war can properly prepare the soldier for the duties of a campaign." A reading list on military history distributed to soldiers at Leavenworth, compiled by Wagner, included books on the wars with the Seminoles and the Sioux War of 1876–77 under the heading "Minor Wars." Wagner seemed to find useful historical lessons in the Indian Wars, but he was less enthusiastic about their future utility. He argued that these lessons would be "profitable in operations against a savage foe or partisan troops, but will rarely be advantageous in a campaign against regularly organized and trained forces." His focus was on the civilized wars of the future.[166]

To combat their characterization as a ragtag militia, America writers frequently emphasized the importance of "civilized war" modeled on the armies of Europe. Army generals such as George B. McClellan and Emory Upton, who played a key role in shaping the modern US military, sharply differentiated wars with Native peoples to "civilized war" and sought to build on (and eventually eclipse) the European military tradition. They argued that Indian warfare prevented the Army from preparing for its true function—defending the nation and projecting American power on a global scale.[167] Many officers worried that their role in what they called "constabulary operations"—those "small wars" in places like the American West—had made the Army inadequate for "conventional" warfare.[168] And while the Army's performance during the Spanish-American War has been criticized by some military historians, the *Gazette* article argued that European soldiers, who had long disdained the US Army, "woke up" to American military expertise as a result of the swift defeat of Spain.[169] To some in the US military it may have felt as though they had finally shed their characterization as little more than a ragtag militia.

As the nineteenth century came to an end, the *Army and Navy Journal* commended the War Department for sending generals with "experience in Indian Warfare" to the Philippines, writing, "It is gratifying to see that the apparent useless warfare in the Indian country years ago is bearing good fruit in these later days."[170] It is clear that many American soldiers at the turn of the century were drawing directly on their experiences with Indian/fighting, something elaborated on in the next two chapters. However, these comparisons could be tempered by a desire to emphasize the "civilized" accomplishments of the US Army. Elwell Otis, the top general in the Philippines, often characterized Filipinos as "Indians" while in the islands. However, Otis also emphasized the "civilized" nature of Filipino fighters, paradoxically criticizing those (including himself) who had argued the Filipinos fought "like Indians."[171] Other soldiers in the Philippines continued to characterize Filipinos as "savages" but argued that US Army maneuvers in the islands would have been just as effective against a "civilized" foe.[172] US soldiers felt pressure to highlight their "civilized" martial skills, even as the institutional memories of frontier warfare continued to exercise great influence. Over time, the differentiation of "savage" and "civilized" war would further marginalize the Indian Wars from the mainstream of US military doctrine. But first, many of the veterans would take their experiences across the ocean to the Philippines, to a new yet familiar arena of "savage war." There the history of the Indian Wars would be transformed in a new imperial context, the first step in the continual evolution of Indian/fighting as a definitive aspect of US militarism.

CHAPTER 2

Indian/Fighters in the Philippines

"WORSE THAN FIGHTING INDIANS"

During the initial campaigns of the Philippine-American War, General Elwell Stephen Otis was quick to argue that the war would soon be over.[1] He censored the press in the Philippines and manipulated the news coming from the islands.[2] Like many counterinsurgents that have followed him, Otis was proven wrong when the Filipino revolutionary forces launched a renewed offensive against the American occupation in the fall of 1899 that eventually shifted toward guerilla tactics.[3] Like the Tet Offensive sixty-nine years later, some elements of the counter-offensive were strategically aimed at eroding domestic support for the war to influence the US presidential election. Filipinos hoped to spur anti-imperialist sentiment and help defeat the reelection of William McKinley, a supporter of the US occupation. Filipino fighters scored some small victories, but they failed to prevent the reelection of Mc-Kinley, who defeated William Jennings Bryan.[4] The war continued, and impatient soldiers, journalists, and politicians called for the US Army to tap into the shadow doctrines of colonial violence forged during the previous century.

Lieutenant Colonel Edward M. Hayes compared conditions in the Philippines to Arizona during the Apache Wars, writing that "no wagon train could travel the plains unescorted without being attacked by the redskins, and so to-day are the conditions in the Philippines."[5] Writer Phelps Whitemarsh argued that the US commanders had conducted the

war in an "intolerably feeble and hesitant manner" and unless more
stringent measures were taken, the war would go on for years. Colonel
Jacob Smith, a veteran of the Wounded Knee Massacre, told reporters
that he had already adopted appropriate tactics for fighting "savages"
because fighting Filipinos was "worse than fighting Indians."[6] General
James Parker, in a letter to his mother, noted that "if these Filipinos
could ambush like our Indians, we would have a bad time; but they
have not the grit." And Secretary of War Elihu Root proclaimed that the
Army had to return to "methods which have proved successful in our
Indian campaigns in the West."[7] What did it mean for the Army to return to such Indian/fighting "methods"? This chapter sets out to answer
that question, exploring how aspects of the Philippine-American War
were influenced by the US military's experience with the Indian Wars.
Perhaps geographic distance has concealed temporal proximity, because
these connections have remained surprisingly elusive.[8] Rather than viewing 1898 as a caesura marking the separation between the continental
and global phases of American imperialism, this chapter examines the
translation of the Indian Wars into a shadow doctrine that influenced,
narrated, and validated US imperial violence in the Philippines.

Indian/fighting was not the only racializing discourse that US soldiers
were influenced by in the Philippines. Anti-Black racism and imperial
paternalism abounded, as did new forms of anti-Filipino racism.[9] But
the discourse of Indian/fighting exercised a potent imaginative power
that journalists, officers, and individual soldiers deployed to legitimate
and narrate US military action. Many of the top officers in the Philippines had experience in wars with Native people to draw on, and they
did, as this chapter will show. But a more subtle influence was exercised
on the younger US soldiers who had never fought against Native people
but who nonetheless were conscripted *into* a discourse of Indian/fight-
ing while in the Philippines.[10]

This chapter is thus attentive to both the material consequences of
the Philippine-American War and the discourses that shaped its participants. It is both a history of Indian/fighting as a mobile, imperial discourse, and a story about one of the earliest American experiences with
irregular warfare. In less than a decade the US military moved from the
1890 massacre of Lakota Sioux at Wounded Knee on the Pine Ridge Indian Reservation to the jungles and mountains of the Philippines. Many
of the same men who fought the Lakota, the Apache, the Cheyenne, and
the Ute now had to fight a war in the Philippines that was both familiar
and different.[11]

The Indian Wars resonated to the Philippines in the words of journalists who compared Geronimo to Filipino leader Emilio Aguinaldo, and in the justifications of politicians who compared the occupation of the Philippines to the reservations that Native people in the late nineteenth and early twentieth centuries were fighting to transform from government-controlled prisons into homelands. But the Indian Wars also traveled materially in the minds and actions of US soldiers required to fight a war against opponents they regularly labeled "insurgents."[12] Analyzing the Philippine-American War as a part of the history of US irregular warfare thus demands a critical analysis of how subjects are defined as "insurgent," a process that relied, in part, on comparing Filipinos to Native American people.

The bulk of this chapter focuses on the first year of the Philippine-American War, highlighting General Henry Ware Lawton and the scouting unit he created called "Young's Scouts." The time frame and geographic scale will be relatively narrow. Lawton operated on the island of Luzon, the largest island in the Philippines, from March 1899 until his death on December 19, 1899. He was present for the initial phases of the war, when the US assumed control of the islands from colonial Spain, betraying Filipino hopes for independence. American troops won several early victories against the Filipino revolutionary forces, but as the conflict transitioned into a protracted guerilla war, men like Lawton were increasingly imagined as "Indian fighters" that would be able to translate their experiences with colonial violence into success in the Philippines. Lawton and Young's Scouts would help set the tone for the increasingly brutal war and occupation of the islands, and their experiences would offer a wealth of material for journalists and writers seeking to connect US settler colonialism to the broader contours of US empire in the early twentieth century.

IMAGINING INDIAN/FIGHTERS

In the January 1900 issue of *Leslie's Illustrated Weekly*, writer H. L. Mencken published a poem titled "The Four-Foot Filipino." The first stanza reads as follows:

We have chased the slick Apachy over desert, plain and hill,
    We have trailed the sly Osagy through the bresh,
We have fullered Ute and Sioux all their blasted country through,
    When their liquor made them get a little fresh;
We have seen our share of fightin', we have stopped our share of lead,

> We have fought all sorts of fighters, great and small,
> But the four-foot Filipino, when it comes to doin' harm,
> Is the toughest proposition of them all.[13]

A cut out of the poem is included at the end of a scrapbook dedicated to the life of Henry Ware Lawton, assembled by his close friend and fellow soldier Robert G. Carter. The poem is not particularly remarkable for its racism nor for the connections drawn between Native North American peoples and Filipinos. The overseas expansion of US territory at the turn of the century was driven, in part, by a virulently racist paternalism that assumed nonwhite peoples were incapable of self-government. Much of this rhetoric drew on descriptions of the supposed inferiority of American Indians when describing the inhabitants of the Philippines. But the inclusion of the poem in a scrapbook dedicated to Lawton was not incidental. Lawton could have been the inspiration for the poem. He chased Apache people all over the Southwest, fought Lakota and Cheyenne on the northern plains, and worked to confine Ute people to their reservation in Colorado. Lawton ended his career in the Philippines, where his experiences in the Indian Wars formed a potent endorsement of his potential to defeat Filipinos. The crude caricature of the "slick Apachy" and the "four-foot Filipino" met, in Lawton, a lifetime of experience fighting against men and women working to preserve their independence from US political authority.

Born in Ohio in 1843, Lawton enlisted at the start of the Civil War and served throughout. After the war, Lawton studied law at Harvard but returned to the Army in 1866, serving in the Reconstruction South. In 1871, Lawton joined the Fourth US Cavalry in Texas and began an extended period of active duty against Native peoples on the plains and in the Southwest. Lawton fought in the 1871 expedition into Indian Territory, the 1872 expedition to the Staked Plains, in border fights with both Mexicans and Indians in 1873, and the Red River War in 1874. In 1874, Lawton was assigned to recruiting detail and took a short break from frontier service, but after the defeat of Custer and the Seventh Cavalry in 1876, Lawton requested and received permission to join the troops headed to the northern plains. There Lawton took part in General Crook's campaign against the Lakota, Cheyenne, and Arapaho. He was present for the destruction of Dull Knife's village of Northern Cheyenne in November of 1876 and was tasked with escorting the remaining Cheyenne to their reservation in Indian Territory. Lawton's regiment was then reassigned to Texas, but the ever-aggressive Lawton would again request reassignment to an active conflict zone in 1879 for the war with the Utes. Lawton even postponed his marriage so he could join his regiment when it was reassigned to Arizona Territory. Lawton remained in the Southwest until 1888, an integral part of the US military's ongoing war on Apache people.[14] At the outbreak of the Spanish-American War, Lawton was appointed a brigadier general of volunteers and he played an integral role in the invasion and occupation of Cuba before heading to the Philippines.[15]

Lawton's military career, particularly in the US Southwest, endowed him with an aura that followed him to the Philippines. His reputation in the Philippines was built on his Indian/fighting prowess, and the troops there had anticipated his arrival. Reverend Peter MacQueen recalled the following conversation: "'Wait till Lawton comes,' said a husky volunteer from the West; 'he'll rip this insurrection up the back.'"[16] Being a frontier-experienced regular carried a great deal of military capital with the soldiers in the Philippines, and no general had more than Lawton. He was "idolized in song and rhyme"—a mythical figure to journalists and the troops that served under him precisely because of his role in the Indian Wars.[17] That mythical status was supposed to translate into a tactical advantage over the Filipinos. Writers covering the war emphasized it as soon as he arrived in the islands. In an article for the *Saturday Evening Post*, Senator Albert J. Beveridge noted that the US troops in the Philippines were full of "hardened regulars who had seen service with the Indians for years."[18] None of these frontier soldiers was more celebrated than Lawton. An article in the *American Manila* from May 6, 1899, proclaimed "Lawton: Fighting Machine." The general was "as tireless as a wolf and can go a week without food or sleep." Lawton was "steady, rapid and remorseless," and for these reasons the general had been chosen to lead US troops in the Philippines.[19]

Foremost among Lawton's accomplishments was his role in the surrender of Apache leader Goyahkla (Geronimo): "It is the Geronimo incident—or rather the record of years in the West crowned by the Geronimo incident—which has sent him to the Philippines to command the American forces in the field." Some of the descriptions of Lawton even begin to slip into the realm of folklore, sounding more like Paul Bunyan or Johnny Appleseed: He can sleep for three days straight, he can drink anyone under the table, and he can eat two-dozen redbirds in one sitting. "It is not difficult to imagine him a pillar of steel, hurling his huge bulk through the lists or heading some heroic thunderous charge when a thousand spurs are striking deep and a thousand lances are in rest."[20] This was the literary Lawton that served as an endorsement for the actual military actions the real Lawton would undertake in the early campaigns of the Philippine-American War.

On May 1, 1898, the US Navy defeated the Spanish fleet in the Battle of Manila Bay, the first battle in the Pacific theater of the Spanish-American War. A month later, Filipino revolutionaries led by General Emilio Aguinaldo, who had been fighting the Spanish since 1896, declared their independence from Spain. In the ensuing months, Filipino forces would gain control of most of the country except Manila, surrounding the city. They erected a governing apparatus throughout the islands and appealed to foreign leaders for recognition. However, neither the United States nor Spain recognized Filipino independence, and Spain ceded the country to the United States in the Treaty of Paris, signed on December 10, 1898. Tensions would mount in early 1899 as Filipino troops continued to surround Manila. The US occupation, commanded by General Elwell Otis, was conducted with an imperial paternalism and increasing belligerency that served to heighten the tension, and fighting broke out the night of February 4 when Filipino troops confronted a group of US soldiers and shots were fired.[21]

US troops quickly pushed Filipino forces away from Manila in a series of violent clashes.[22] Otis, rejecting a conditional surrender, sought to capture Aguinaldo and destroy the Philippine Revolutionary Army, which was concentrated in the northern part of the island of Luzon under the command of General Antonio Luna. He naively believed that if he could eliminate the revolutionary leadership and capture Malolos, the capital of the Philippine Republic, most of the provinces would accept the "benevolent assimilation" of American rule. Otis's unrealistic assessment of the conflict extended to US troop levels; he had maintained that a force of twenty-five to thirty thousand was sufficient, despite the disagreement of his subordinate officers. Exacerbating the problem was that many of the American soldiers in the Philippines were volunteers, due to return home once the war with Spain was over.[23]

Shorthanded, but intending to cut the fractured revolutionary army in two, in mid-March Otis sent General Lloyd Wheaton southeast from Manila and General Arthur MacArthur north toward a fleeing Aguinaldo. These columns made limited gains, but the US advance quickly stalled, as commanders learned that occupying Manila and controlling the dense Philippines countryside were two very different endeavors.[24] The *Manila Freedom* reported that Filipinos were increasingly turning to "harassing tactics," unable to face US troops in pitched battles.

Hidden sharpshooters were picking off US soldiers and then running away before they could be engaged. The paper argued that these tactics were expected and were the reason that when sending for reinforcements the War Department "made it a point to send as many as possible of the regular troops, who had been used to Indian fighting in the bad lands of the west." Foremost among these was Henry Ware Lawton.[25]

Lawton arrived in the Philippines in March to great fanfare from the press, and a possibly jealous Otis kept the general in Manila for a month before sending him to attack the city of Santa Cruz southeast of Manila along the shores of Laguna De Bay, the largest lake in the Philippines.[26] As Lawton and his troops moved away from the urban areas around Manila their Indian/fighter pedigree became increasingly prominent in coverage of the war. One newspaper proclaimed, "Indian Tactics to be Adopted" in an article titled "In Pursuit of Rebels." The reporter, who likely spent time with Lawton or someone on his staff, wrote that "the tactics will be those of the old-time frontier fighting, and it is probable that the command will be divided into squads of twelve, under non-commissioned officers."[27]

Other journalists emphasized that Lawton's attack on Santa Cruz would be modeled on the "old Indian tactics" of mobile, smaller units. Of course, these tactics were hardly old. They were fresh from use in the US Southwest and on the plains, but journalists were quick to endow Indian/fighting with a nostalgia that sat awkwardly alongside the actual war they were covering. These tactics became "old Indian fighting" almost immediately, discursively closing off the colonization of North America as finished, complete, even as Native people were working to maintain their political autonomy on reservations. The campaign was a logistical nightmare, with Lawton's soldiers hampered by dense swamps and an amphibious strike force stuck in shallow water, but despite these difficulties US troops captured Santa Cruz on April 10 and nearby Pagsanjan on April 11. The expectation was that Lawton's command would continue to scour the region in smaller units, much as he had the mountains of Arizona. However, Otis recalled the expedition on April 15, against Lawton's wishes. Otis was concerned that he did not have enough troops to hold the territory Lawton had claimed, and he wanted to shift the Army's focus northward.[28]

After the Laguna de Bay campaign, Lawton's troops moved north from Manila on April 22 into central Luzon. The Philippine Revolutionary Army had fortified many of the railroads and river crossings in the region north of Manila, but friction between Aguinaldo and Luna threatened to fracture Filipino resistance to the American advance.[29] The plan was to coordinate with General Arthur MacArthur and catch the retreating Filipino forces in a two-pronged attack, targeting the towns of Calumpit, Baliuag, and Norzagaray.[30] Like Lawton, MacArthur had commanded troops in the Southwest during the Apache Wars, although largely as a garrison commander. Lawton and MacArthur's frontier service was useful for writers trying to project a hopeful image of the American advance. The *Army and Navy Journal* reported that "the strange country proved to have no terrors for such an old Indian fighter as Gen. Lawton."[31] Other writers highlighted the romanticism of frontier landscapes, such as the *National Magazine*'s Peter MacQueen. He described the campaign as full of "wild, romantic scenery and rich, abounding vistas . . . wild trails through unknown mountain tribes" which could not help but invoke the months Lawton spent in the Sierra Madre mountains.[32] The reality was that small groups of Apache warriors had, for years, eluded sustained efforts to confine them to reservations, continually outmaneuvering Lawton and other American soldiers in the US-Mexico borderlands. It was only through the use of Apache scouts that the US Army finally cornered Goyahkla (Geronimo) and his followers.[33]

MacQueen referred to Lawton as the "old Indian exterminator" and noted that while the general was strict about looting and plundering, he was "the very scourge of God" with armed Filipinos.[34] Emilio Aguinaldo was the prime target of the campaign, but he remained elusive despite the efforts of Lawton and his troops and was eventually captured in the spring of 1901.[35] The successes ascribed to Lawton in chasing down Geronimo were supposed to result in a similar success with Aguinaldo. A Massachusetts newspaper reprinted correspondence from a soldier with Lawton under the title "Tireless Lawton: He Will Follow Aguinaldo as He Did Geronimo—Officers on His Staff Have to Work Hard."[36] The *Washington Post* ran an article on Lawton that made a similar argument: "Just now he is using in the Philippines to excellent purpose the tactics and strategy he learned years ago against Naches and Geronimo in Apache land, in pursuit of Aguinaldo."[37] Clearly the press was invested in emphasizing the connection between Lawton's career in the Indian Wars and his campaign in the Philippines. But these were not simply imaginative linkages with little relation to on-the-ground decisions. As much as Lawton was the embodiment of the discursive aura of an Indian fighter, he also put into practice tactics that directly drew on his experience in the Indian Wars.

"OLD FRONTIERSMAN"

Very little of the US Army's experience with nineteenth-century frontier violence made it into training manuals or other military publications.[38] However, that did not mean that wars with Native people left no impact on American soldiers. At the end of the century, many soldiers believed their experience in the Indian Wars left them well-prepared for combat in the Philippines.[39] Military newspapers lauded the War Department for sending veterans of the Indian Wars to the Philippines, thankful that the "apparent useless warfare in the Indian country years ago is bearing good fruit in these later days."[40] Men like Lawton were the main repository for that sort of institutional knowledge. Their worldview was partly shaped by a racialized conception of savage warfare. Filipinos, like Indians, were "savages." On his way home from the islands, Major General Thomas Anderson noted that his experience had been "much like Indian fighting."[41] As a less clinical article in the *Santa Fe Daily* put it, "the woods must be full of savages."[42]

While the early phase of the US campaign in the Philippines emphasized defeating the Philippine Revolutionary Army, officers like Lawton also pursued strategies targeting Filipino noncombatants and their property.[43] Lawton also made frequent use of scouts, and he emphasized mobility, pushing his troops so far ahead of their supply trains that his northward advance out of Manila stalled out.[44] Although the role of Native scouts in the US military had been hotly debated for decades, with both supporters and critics, Apache scouts had played a critical role in the campaign to capture Goyahkla (Geronimo) in 1886.[45] Lawton had witnessed firsthand the advantages of mobile scouting units in pursuing and wearing down the enemy. A member of Lawton's staff even remarked that Lawton was "prosecuting an Apache warfare," and was held back by his superior, General Otis.[46] It would not take long for Lawton to organize an elite scouting unit that would reflect his desire for mobility and seek-and-destroy operations.

On May 3, 1899, as US troops pushed north from Manila, Lawton sent a telegram to the adjutant general with an unusual report: "I have organized a most efficient detachment of scouts, employing Mr. W.H. Young, an old frontiersman, prospector and scout, as chief— with 25 selected volunteers."[47] Who was this "old frontiersman," and why had Lawton given him control of a picked group of soldiers? The history of this elite unit exemplifies the shadow doctrines of Indian/fighting in the Philippines. Where Lawton was the soldier, Young was the *frontiersman*, a civilian who could operate at the bleeding edge of civilized warfare and military convention. "Frontiersman" evoked the settler-militias, trappers, mountain men, guides, prospectors, and criminals of the American West. An old frontiersman was just what Lawton felt he needed as he pushed farther into the island of Luzon, and he used Young to deadly effect.

Much of our information on W. H. Young comes from the diary of John B. Kinne, a member of the First North Dakota Volunteer Infantry. Kinne's first encounter with Young is entirely literary, a glimpse of the frontier mythos manifested in the jungle of the Philippines. "While watching the troops embark on the cascoes my attention was called to a fine, athletic looking individual in civilian clothes, leaning on his rifle. He was not taking any part in the preparations, but seemed to be an interested spectator of the operations. He reminded me of Leatherstocking, the hero of Cooper's Tales. Finally he went aboard the Wapidan with the scouts, and we afterwards learned that his name was William H. Young, of whose interesting career in action we will have considerable to tell later."[48] Nothing could be more indicative of the literary inflection of the Indian Wars, and US empire more broadly, than Kinne's immediate association of this frontier soldier of fortune, standing on the shoreline in the Philippines, with a hero from James Fenimore Cooper's famous novels. Here was a real-life Leatherstocking, a man whose deviation from the professional norms of the US military would ultimately make him the perfect tool. Born in Connecticut, Young had served as a scout under General Howard in the wars with the Nez Perce, had prospected in Montana, California, Korea, and China, and had served as a soldier in Korea and in Japan. He had made his way to the Philippines hoping to prospect, but instead found himself joining the fighting. Young gained quite a reputation with the US soldiers, particularly for his skill at countering the hated Filipino sharpshooters. His reputation was further amplified by his history as a frontier scout in one of the more famous conflicts of the Indian Wars. Much of his time was spent with the First North Dakota, and many of his scouts, including Kinne, came from that regiment.

The First North Dakota spent about a year in the Philippines, largely serving under the command of Lawton.[49] In May of 1898 the regiment was ordered overseas and moved west on the trains that had been so integral to the conquest of Native land on the northern plains, land these men's families had settled on. Where US empire had once expanded west in search of continental supremacy, now it pushed farther west in search of an ocean to cross, prairie settlers bound for San Francisco, Hawaii, and finally the Philippines. A few decades earlier an east-west movement meant an invasion of Native land, but in 1898 Kinne narrates the journey as a sober reflection on now-pacified Indian people. Rather than bison herds he notes that the bones of these animals had been collected by Natives and piled near the track for shipment to sugar refineries. Their train passes near a Blackfeet village in Montana, no longer a threatening presence but rather a curiosity, the Blackfeet waving blankets in answer to the shouts of the soldiers. Indian people are now met with cameras rather than guns. In Bonner's Ferry, Idaho, the North Dakotans took pictures and shook hands with three Indians, which Kinne calls "a little burlesque and seemingly solemn occasion" that he thoroughly enjoyed. Kinne seems to understand the staged nature of their interaction with these three nameless Native men.[50] For Kinne, Indian people are no longer the preoccupation of US imperialism but rather a remnant, a distraction and curiosity that precedes his deployment to the Philippines. The immense effort Native communities were exerting to transform reservations from prisons to homelands remains invisible, submerged by Kinne's imperialist nostalgia.[51]

Arriving in San Francisco at the start of June, the First North Dakota camped in what Kinne calls "an old Chinese graveyard." Now on the coast, the contours of US empire are larger, and the soldiers find themselves sleeping on the graves of people whose labor helped construct the railroad they had just traveled on. The initial disrespect of stationing soldiers on top of the graves was compounded when those graves were violated. Kinne noted that "in digging a sink the boys dug up two Chinese skeletons and had lots of amusement with the queues." After a month of drilling, Kinne's global tour of US empire continued on a boat to Hawaii, where he landed in early July. Docked in Honolulu, the soldiers threw coins in the water for Native Hawaiian divers to retrieve and stole from a food vendor. Kinne felt it was a shame to steal from such "simple and honest" people. After traveling farther across the Pacific the regiment took part in the capture of Manila, and then helped to garrison the city for the remainder of 1898. Kinne and the North Dakotans participated in the initial fighting of the war around Manila in early 1899.[52] Kinne casually recounts stories of "dead niggers," burned buildings, and wounded noncombatants in between the daily minutiae and entertainments of young soldiers: paddling canoes, the quality of the food cooked by their Chinese chef, and the appropriation of brass from an abandoned church to be sold for cash to fund gambling. The narrative alternates between fatigue, hilarity, boredom, and adventure, punctuated by episodes of violence.[53] Eventually Kinne would find himself in the company of Lawton's "Old Frontiersman."

Lawton first encountered Young on April 29, 1899, when he noticed a civilian walking ahead of the troops as they advanced toward the town of San Rafael.[54] Lawton summoned the strange man, intending to reprimand him and send him to the rear of the line, but Young apparently made quite the impression on the general. Young told Lawton he had been a scout in Indian campaigns and had made his way to the Philippines to "help the boys." The general was impressed, and he recognized Young's name as "one who had done some gallant work against the redskins." This was enough to earn the itinerant civilian a chance to work his way into the general's good graces: "Something in the man's bearing and appearance, made me change my mind, and I directed him to go to the front and bring me in a citizen that I might get definite information about the location of San Rafael."[55] Five minutes later Lawton heard three shots, and soon Young reappeared, carrying a rifle and a sack full of ammunition. He had encountered a Filipino outpost of eight men, killed one, and drove the others off. Impressed, Lawton had Young select twenty-five men to form a scouting unit. Most of the men had been sharpshooters or scouts in their respective regiments, uninterested in military discipline and protocol. One had served in the Spanish, English, and US navies before enlisting in the Army. A few had multiple courts-martial on their record. Private William Harris, one of the original scouts, recalled the men as informal and rugged, often heading into the countryside without permission to explore.[56]

The men chosen for Young's scouting unit fit a long history of ragtag soldiers who are allowed to escape military discipline by becoming particularly deadly frontline (or behind-the-lines) killers. These sorts of military units have become cultural tropes that often draw explicitly on "Indianness" to represent both their savagery and effectiveness. From Mel Gibson's bloody tomahawk in the film The Patriot to Brad Pitt's scalp knife in Inglourious Basterds, certain soldiers are allowed to exceed the boundaries of civilized warfare in the pursuit of US military goals. These men become irregulars in the service of liberalism and democracy, their mismatched clothing and guerilla tactics an alluring transgression of civilized norms. Often these men embark on suicide missions, a Cooper-esque twist in which they help to win a peace that they themselves can never enjoy.

"Young's Scouts," as the unit came to be known, were independent from the main body of soldiers. This independence was galling for some officers that had to interact with the scouts, but Lawton consistently backed them up in the face of criticism or discipline.[57] They advanced a half-day ahead, locating the enemy and sometimes engaging them. At this stage in the conflict the war was somewhere in between a series of pitched battles and the guerilla warfare that would later come to define the conflict. Young's Scouts allowed Lawton to disrupt the ability of Filipino revolutionary forces to maintain their day-to-day resistance to the US occupation. A set of orders Lawton issued to Young's Scouts could almost sound like they were setting out from a fort in the American West: "Chief Scout Young was instructed to proceed on the afternoon of the 4th with the entire detachment of scouts in a northeasterly direction covering the country between San Rafael road and the Maasin River, for the purpose of locating and destroying all magazines, storehouses and caches of insurgent subsistence or other supplies."[58] Travel light, acquire food as you go, and seek and destroy the enemy's supplies. Destroyed supplies and captured guns functioned as a quantifiable measure of progress against the so-called insurgency. And although Lawton's orders included cautions about respecting noncombatants and private property, looting and burning became hallmarks of the scouts and the US occupation of the Philippines in general. As an Indian Wars veteran, Young was the perfect vehicle for transmitting these shadow doctrines.

In what would become one of the primary occupations of the unit, Young's first "rice burning expedition" involved the scouts creeping, as Kinne puts it, "Indian fashion" through the Philippines countryside, thirty paces apart. They appropriated food from Filipino villagers, captured prisoners, and searched the buildings they came across. In one house they captured a Filipino officer and two soldiers and forced them to shed their uniforms. The next day, they discovered a series of rice beds, which they tore up and burned, drawing the attention of the locals, who proceeded to flee into the hills. In one storehouse the scouts reportedly found ten thousand bushels of rice, and later they found a cache with twenty thousand bushels of rice, fifty gallons of kerosene, one hundred gallons of coconut oil, five tons of sugar, as well as uniforms, cloth, sewing machines, and ammunition. Due to the large quantities of supplies they made camp and spent three days burning everything. The scouts then circled back toward Manila, floating down a river on a raft and cutting telegraph lines as they went. Lawton was happy with the expedition, which had resulted in destroyed supplies and several Filipino prisoners, and it had demonstrated that the scouts could operate independently and quietly in the countryside.[59]

In his subsequent report, Lawton offered a ringing endorsement of the scouts: "The services of these scouts have been from the beginning peculiarly valuable, and are daily increasing in value as a result of experience. The individuals detailed were in all cases men who had either lived for years on our Indian frontier, were inured to hardship and danger, and skilled in woodcraft and use of the rifle, or had demonstrated their service in these islands peculiar fitness for the work contemplated."[60] For Lawton, the Indian frontier was both a training ground and instrument of validation. It had produced men suited to these seek-and-destroy missions and discursively validated the scouts' existence. They were Indian/fighters—therefore they were effective Filipino fighters, effective counterinsurgents. Young certainly had experience in Indian warfare and put that experience into practice. But many of the men in Young's Scouts were too young to have directly fought with Native people. However, they came from North Dakota, from Oregon, from places recently taken from Native people. This history of conquest clung like an aura to these men in the Philippines. It turned soldiers into "old Indian fighters," even young men like Kinne, who became receptacles for the shadow doctrine of Indian/fighting. It also seemed to endow the scouts with a certain recklessness that resulted in several highly risky actions that would lead to Young's death and numerous Medals of Honor awarded to the unit.

Young's Scouts could move quietly and quickly through the Philippine countryside, but that does not mean they avoided fighting. As Kinne noted in his diary, the entire North Dakota Volunteers were eager to get into the fighting and resented not being on the front lines in the beginning of their deployment. Young's Scouts killed numerous Filipinos on their expeditions, occasionally noncombatants. Kinne's diary notes several noncombatant casualties, in one instance the death of a woman holding a baby.[61] One soldier even wrote home to a friend that "most of the boys say as the cowboys of our North American Indian: A dead Philipino [sic] is a good Philipino." This was not an empty threat—another soldier noted in his diary that "they caught a sharpshooter in the act of changing his uniform for a white suit and now he is a good Philipino [sic]."[62] References to "dead niggers" in Kinne's diary indicate that the war was influenced as much by anti-Blackness and anti-Filipino

FIGURE 3. Members of Young's Scouts attacking over a bridge in the Philippines, depicted in *Soldiers in the Sun*, a National Guard Heritage painting by Donna Neary, courtesy of the National Guard Bureau.

racism as it was Indian-hating. African American soldiers in the Philippines found themselves positioned between these foreign and domestic racisms, and were sometimes critical of their role in the exercise of US imperial violence. Kinne overheard one soldier from the all–African American Twenty-Fourth Infantry Regiment, newly arrived in Manila, remark as he encountered Filipinos on the street: "I ain't goin to shoot none of these here niggas [sic]." When ordered to move, this soldier, according to Kinne, sarcastically responded "Waal, have to take up de white man's burden" [sic].[63] Kinne's diary seems to have captured a moment of anti-imperial critique, although Kinne's quotation may be indulging in additional racist caricature. Regardless, the moment is telling, a Black soldier critiquing the racial dynamics of US empire.

On several occasions the Scouts threw themselves recklessly at the enemy (Figure 3). In mid-May, the Scouts helped capture two towns against overwhelming odds. At San Ildefonso the Scouts engaged in a daylong firefight with hundreds of Filipino soldiers. The next day, at San Miguel, the scouts charged a bridge into the city held by hundreds of Filipinos, scattering them in a sudden rush and then taking refuge in the church bell tower until reinforcements arrived.[64] While crossing the bridge at San Miguel, Young was shot in the leg. In his diary Kinne narrates Young's injury like a heroic last stand in a Frederic Remington painting or John Ford film: "As they reached the bridge in the center of the town, Young was hit in the knee with a Remington bullet and fell. He kept up the fire as long as he could see any niggers and then bound his knee. When they found him he was sitting up with his wound bound and surrounded by empty shells."[65] Another story of racial violence and bravery to amplify Young's reputation, with the mess of spent rifle shells being a potent visual for the sort of long odds the scouts' mystique was built on.

In a telegram praising Young and the scouts, Lawton noted that the wound was not life-threatening, likely to result in no more than a stiff joint.[66] Captain William Birkhimer, in his report on the fight, called the charge of the scouts "one of the rare events in war where true valor asserts itself against overwhelming odds."[67] High praise, but the captain was tired of the independent scouts, who were only supposed to reconnoiter the town, not attack it. Birkhimer gathered the scouts for a meeting and lectured them on military discipline and protocol, a speech that was not at all well received. Corporal Anders received instruction on the proper method of saluting a superior officer that was particularly unwelcome. Several of the scouts appealed to Lawton, who told Birkhimer to leave them alone. Ultimately Birkhimer and eleven of the scouts would receive the Medal of Honor for the charge at San Miguel, and Birkhimer's attempted interference was negated by the general.[68] The scouts would remain independent.

Lawton was confident that Young would return to duty, and predicted that "if we have guerilla warfare, he will be very useful," even if Young was forced to go mounted from then on.[69] As Filipinos turned increasingly to guerilla warfare in the latter half of 1899, Americans predicted that men like Lawton or Young would be essential "as we have found in our Indian warfare."[70] However, Young's injury became infected, and he died in Manila. The loss of their namesake certainly demoralized Young's Scouts, but the unit would continue to operate for the remainder of Lawton's northern expedition. The scouts, led by Young's replacement, Lt. J. E. Thornton, were instrumental in the capture of San Isidro, the then-current capital of the Philippine Republic, on May 16. At San Isidro, Lawton's campaign came to a halt. The general once more blamed Otis's timidity, but the reality was that Lawton's troops were suffering widespread illness, he had used up his supplies, and had no way to acquire more. Aguinaldo and the revolutionary government had eluded capture, and the Philippine Revolutionary Army, though battered, had not been destroyed.[71] By June of 1899, the worn-out soldiers of the First North Dakota were running out of steam, and they would soon board a ship to return to the United States. Kinne would end his diary describing a barbecue in a park in Fargo, but the war was far from over.

Lawton himself would remain in the Philippines until his death in December of 1899. His time there would continue to be described in terms that sought to position the general and his troops as Indian fighters, often in the face of increasing Filipino success in guerilla warfare. A June campaign led by Lawton southward from Manila toward the town of Cavite initially failed to engage a single Filipino fighter, the US soldiers defeated by swamps, mosquitoes, and weather. Nonetheless, the press, tightly managed by Otis, reported that the insurgents were fleeing from Lawton.[72] When Lawton did manage to engage Filipino forces, Otis told reporters that Lawton's troops had killed four hundred "Indians" in a battle, and one newspaper proclaimed: "Success of the Moment against Filipino Braves," but the reality was that hundreds of Filipino soldiers managed to elude Lawton once more.[73]

In the fall of 1899, Lawton and Otis would clash again when Secretary of War Elihu Root ordered the formation of scouting detachments of Filipino Macabebes, Spanish loyalists who were opposed to the Filipino revolutionary forces, over the protests of Otis. Lawton had spread the idea to his friends in Washington, which enraged Otis, but the idea of Native scouts would have appealed to Lawton, who had made such effective use of Apache scouts in the Southwest. The Macabebes eventually morphed into the Philippine Scouts, inaugurating a relationship between the Filipino and US militaries that continues to this day.[74] Indeed, a resonance of Lawton's experiences in the Apache Wars would catch up with him when he was shot by a sniper and killed in the Battle of Paye on December 19, 1899. The Filipino general in command was Licerio *Gerónimo*. And while this Filipino general did not do the actual shooting, his presence on the battlefield evoked the Apache leader Goyahkla (Geronimo), whom Lawton had played a role in convincing to surrender thirteen years before, a man still in US military custody at Fort Sill, Oklahoma.

Like the journalists that had covered the war, the obituaries commemorating Lawton's life emphasized his military career, particularly his role in the Indian Wars. According to these memorials it was Lawton's past as an Indian fighter that had made him such an effective general in the Philippines. As one speaker at Lawton's funeral put it, "Having fought it out with the insurrectionary tribes for fifteen years, he was the picked man of men to track the Apaches to their last lair and to wrest the southwest from the terror of Geronimo and his band." As another vividly said, "He hunted them off their feet." One of his obituaries noted that Lawton's experience with the Apache made him especially competent when dealing with Filipino insurgents, "whom it required chasing to catch." It was this tenacity in what the military termed "savage war" that made Lawton famous. One writer noted that he was "constantly in the field of action—here, there, and everywhere—moving rapidly and striking quick, decisive blows after the fashion which he had learned so well in the border wars of the west."[75]

The Army's inspector general went even further in his announcement of Lawton's death. Rather than jumping from the mountains of the American Southwest to the jungles of the Philippines, General Breckinbridge inserted Lawton into a centuries-old lineage of white militarism:

> The man of El-Caney is the man of the Mogollons, and the man of the Mogollons is the reincarnation of some shining, helmeted warrior who fell upon the sands of Palestine in the first crusade, with the red blood welling over his corselet and his two-handed battle sword shivered to the hilt. The race type persists unchanged in eye, in profile, in figure. It is the race which in all centuries the Valkyrs have wafted from the war docks, have hailed from the Helmgangs, or helmet strewn moorlands—the white skinned race which drunk with the liquor of the battle, reeled around the dragon standard at Senlac, which fought with Richard Grenville, which broke the Old Guard at Waterloo, which rode the old slope at Balaklava, which went down with the Cumberland at Hampton Roads, which charged with Picket at Gettysburg, the race of the trader, the financier, the statesman, the inventor, the colonizer, the creator, but, above all, the fighter.[76]

Lawton is presented as the inheritor of a Nordic and Anglo-Saxon martial tradition stretching from the Crusades to the wars of nineteenth-century Europe, to the Civil War (and noticeably, *both* sides of the Civil War). He is presented as a leader of the race of colonizers, and his prominence in both continental and overseas colonial violence made Lawton an ideal candidate, in both life and death, for writers wishing to draw a link between the conquest of Native people and the occupation of the Philippines. And as General Breckinbridge's obituary makes clear, this was a racialized connection.[77] Lawton was viewed as an expert in savage warfare, uniquely suited to subduing the Filipinos, just as he had the Apache. However, soldiers like Lawton were not simply exporting

North American racisms to the Philippines. As Paul Kramer reminds us, much of the racialized violence US soldiers directed at Filipinos was the product of distinct, localized processes.[78] But soldiers like Lawton *were* bringing with them a shadow doctrine of colonial violence that shaped both their attitudes and their practices, their investment in defeating Filipino independence and their tactical approach to combat with people they deemed racially inferior. The mobility of US colonialism had as much to do with how soldiers imagined themselves as it did with how they racialized their enemies.

THE LITERARY LAWTON

The Philippine-American War occurred amid widespread concern about race, gender, sexuality, nationality, and social class. Writers, educators, and politicians in both the United States and Britain warned that white racial superiority and masculinity were under threat, eroding in the face of industrialization, poverty, urban overcrowding, immigration, women's suffrage, and labor unrest. These fears were inseparable from America's imperial policies, producing what Amy Kaplan calls, borrowing the phrase from W. E. B. Du Bois, the "anarchy of empire." As some Americans pushed for an aggressive foreign policy to reinvigorate a nation forged in the "vanished" crucible of frontier expansion, others worried the resulting "anarchy" would trouble the hierarchical boundaries between different groups, dangerously entangling the foreign and domestic. In this context Lawton's eulogies celebrated him as a hero of white Anglo-Saxon militarism and masculinity, a bulwark against the complaints of timid anti-imperialists (Figure 4). These were themes that authors of turn-of-the-century fiction literature for children would amplify.[79]

Lawton may have died in the Philippines, but a literary version of the general would return home and enter the pages of several novels. Fiction literature in the late nineteenth and early twentieth centuries was inseparable from the expansion of US empire. Popular genres like historical romances and travel stories celebrated white masculinity while both amplifying and reflecting American political desires for global expansion.[80] Here I am concerned with a particular subset of this imperial literature, namely the children's adventure stories that became very successful in the late nineteenth and early twentieth centuries. Marketed largely to boys, these stories sought to mythologize the now "closed" frontier and offer narratives with new venues for masculine

FIGURE 4. A ghostly Lawton prevents anti-imperialist William Jennings Bryan from tearing down the US flag in Cuba and the Philippines. "Halt!" by Louis Dalrymple, Library of Congress LC-DIG-ppmsca-25471.

development, often taking place outside the United States. These stories typically featured boys roughing it outdoors while facing a variety of dangers.

The narrators in these adventures paradoxically reflect on the loss of wilderness while celebrating the effects of US expansion, urbanization, and development.[81] Readers learn the value of physical and moral strength as they traverse the newly forged networks of US empire. The stories emphasize white racial superiority and transform dangerous warzones like the Philippines into lighthearted arenas of American dominance. The boys in these stories are *learning* masculinity, and they do so through participation in US empire. Intended for the next generation of soldiers, many of these stories include details about the military occupation of the Philippines, and they often narrate the Philippine-American War as an "Indian War." As such, they transmitted a record of the conflict to an audience that would have been unlikely to receive more formal instruction as Indian/fighters if they entered the military.

In the aftermath of the war in the Philippines, the military largely failed to create any doctrinal record that would preserve institutional knowledge acquired during the occupation. Professional journals discussed the conflict sparingly, and the military censored several publications intended to transmit the lessons learned, likely due to the descriptions of harsh counterinsurgency tactics, the very measures that were currently under fire by anti-imperialist politicians.[82] As a result, the record of US counterinsurgency in the Philippines was ephemeral in the early twentieth century, and the children's literature I highlight here became an unlikely venue for the transmission of the conflict's history. Can children's literature tell us much about military doctrine? Perhaps not. But it can illuminate the contours of a broader imperial culture in which doctrine is developed, a culture in which race was linked to violence through the figure of the Indian/fighter. In these stories, the overtly racialized violence that the military attempted to downplay in more formal channels is refigured as a lesson in masculinity for young readers. Two prominent authors working in these genres were Elbridge Streeter Brooks and Edward Stratemeyer, both of whom wrote books about the war in the Philippines that featured Lawton prominently. In both authors' stories, young men become involved in Lawton's campaigns of 1899, where they interact with the general, Young's Scouts, and other members of the US military. Lawton may have been larger than life, but after his death a literary Lawton would continue to develop the mystique of the Indian/fighter.

Elbridge S. Brooks's *With Lawton and Roberts: A Boy's Adventures in the Philippines and the Transvall* was published in 1900 soon after Lawton's death. The story is a broad endorsement of empire, in which the US occupation of the Philippines is connected to European colonialism in southern Africa. The American and British generals, Lawton and Roberts (Frederick Roberts, a famed imperial general who commanded British Forces in the South African War), are introduced in the preface as "heroes of Anglo-Saxon blood." Their intertwined stories are meant to defend the cause of imperialism. Similar to politicians that sought to deny self-determination to colonized peoples, Brooks writes that "the Stars and Stripes in the Philippines, and the Union Jack in South Africa, are advancing the interests of humanity and civilization, and that untrammeled liberty to the barbarian is as disastrous a gift as are unquestioning concessions to a republic which has been a republic only in name."[83] This ambitious project is narrated through the story of sixteen-year-old Ned, a California schoolboy who, on a dare, stows away on a transport ship headed to the Philippines. The precocious Ned is swept up in the US campaign, fights alongside Lawton and Young's Scouts, and manages to play an integral role in the early months of the war in the Philippines. He then travels to South Africa before returning home a hero.

With Lawton and Roberts is a work of fiction aimed at adolescent boys, and men like Lawton become instructors for Ned, and by extension the reader. Foremost among Lawton's credentials: he is the hero of the Apache Wars. Ned discovers "that no work was too severe, no fighting too hot, no march too rapid, to baffle the man whom the Apaches used to call 'man-who-gets-up-in-the-night-to-fight,' and whom the Filipinos dubbed 'the sleepless one.'" Ned is also introduced to Young and his scouts, and together with Lawton they become a cautionary tale for the reckless teen. When he fails to follow orders and stumbles into a group of Filipino revolutionaries, barely escaping with his life, Lawton warns Ned that he has not had the same frontier experience. "Just you take a lesson from Young's scouts, lad, whom I am going to detail for service with Colonel Sinclair. They'll tell you that a woodsman knows before he feels. . . . You ought to hunt Apaches a little while, then you'd get schooled to cautiousness."[84] From Brooks's story we learn a few things. First, that Lawton and Young's Scouts were famous enough to justify an entire novel dedicated to their exploits. We also get a sense of how much the Indian Wars continued to influence cultural meanings around military violence in the early-twentieth century. Soldiers made sense of their actions in the Philippines by relating it back to the frontier. The same is true of the writers who translated the violence of empire into narratives for children.

Brooks does not confine himself to perpetuating a mythological frontier, transplanted to the Philippines. He is writing historical fiction, and Ned's adventure narrates Lawton's northern expedition, the push out of Manila into northern Luzon in the spring of 1899. Lawton is "the gray-haired giant of the piercing eye and the tireless tactics," swiftly taking town after town with the aid of Ned, whose experience of war is both lighthearted and exhilarating. Readers of Brooks's story embark on an adventure in which the US soldiers, particularly Lawton and Young's Scouts, form an invincible tide against which the routinely treacherous Filipinos can only flee. Filipinos are sent to the "happy hunting grounds," the stereotypical Native afterlife of westerns. "Grim Indian Fighters" outmaneuver and out-fight their opponents in the towns of Baliuag, San Isidro, and San Miguel. Ned is instrumental in these fights, which made the real Young's Scouts famous. He learns how to behave like "an old Indian-fighter," and is taught to have "little respect for savage or half-civilized 'hostiles.'"[85] In the story, even young boys like Ned can become old Indian fighters, endowed with a practiced frontier brutality. The overarching message is that violence is justified and necessary in the service of empire. Ned and his companions are continuously contrasted to the "savage" or "treacherous"

Filipinos, who are kept in check only through the efforts of men like Lawton.

At the end of the story, Ned travels to southern Africa, where he learns from a Filipino man that had also traveled there that Lawton had died. In a fit of rage, he mercilessly beats the man. Embarrassed, Ned is chastised by a British general for breaking camp discipline, who nonetheless commends Ned's love for the now-dead Lawton. In Africa, this Filipino soldier, who has opposed Ned throughout the story, is transformed into an ally. Removed from the defense of his own home and plugged into the global network of empire, his transformation is the final resolution of the story before Ned returns home: "'We may never meet again, my brother,' said the Filipino, as he stretched out a hand in farewell to the American. 'But you have done me a good service. I hated you as an American invader; I love you as an American brother, and I shall go back to my own dear Luzon to work among my fellows for what I now believe to be our best and surest interest.'"[86] By story's end, Ned has almost single-handedly converted this hardened insurgent into an enthusiastic booster for the US occupation. This was the final lesson from the literary Lawton, who earlier in the story had argued that the American way was to convert the Filipinos into friends rather than simply destroy them: "'We wish to reclaim your people and not to revenge ourselves. A dead Aguinaldo would not be so great a feather in our caps as a contented and friendly Aguinaldo.'" Ned fulfills Lawton's charge, ending the story with the ultimate counterinsurgency fantasy, a hardened enemy transformed into a friendly and loyal subject of US power.

Few readers will recognize the name Edward Stratemeyer. But what about Franklin W. Dixon? Victor Appleton? Carolyn Keene? Perhaps if you think back to the books you read as a child, these authors might ring a bell. Those names stand in for the ghostwriters of some of the most enduringly popular children's literature ever published, in *The Hardy Boys*, *Tom Swift*, and *Nancy Drew*, respectively. Edward Stratemeyer was the creator and initial author of all three of these characters, as well as numerous other popular series in children's literature. Through his Stratemeyer Syndicate he published more than a thousand books and helped to define the genres of children's literature and series fiction. And while Stratemeyer is mostly known for his sleuthing teenagers, his first successful hardcover novels were a series of stories about the Spanish-American War. Beginning with *Under Dewey at Manila*, Stratemeyer published six stories about the war in which young men are paired with top military leaders, including Lawton, MacArthur, and Otis. To prepare for the stories, Stratemeyer read military reports in an effort to be historically accurate. The fifth in the series, *The Campaign of the Jungle; or, Under Lawton through Luzon*, closely follows Lawton's "southern campaign" toward Laguna de Bay and his "northern campaign" toward San Isidro, primarily in April and May of 1899.

Like Brooks's novel, Stratemeyer's is an endorsement of US militarism in which Lawton's history as an Indian/fighter gives definition to his campaigns in the Philippines. In the preface, Stratemeyer writes that Lawton's northern campaign "was one of the most daring of its kind, and could not have been pushed to success had not the man at its head been what he was, a trained Indian fighter of our own West, and one whose nerve and courage were almost beyond comprehension."[87] The Lawton of Stratemeyer's story is larger than life, just as he was in media depictions of his actual military service. The narrator introduces Lawton as the captor of Geronimo and recycles the story that his Apache name was "man-who-gets-up-in-the-night-to-fight." The novel's main characters, Larry and Ben, are in awe of the general from the moment they see him. At one point Larry assures his companion that "'a soldier who has whipped the Apache Indians isn't going to suffer any surprise at the hands of these Tagals, no matter how wily they are.'"[88] Apache people remained the benchmark against which cunning and savagery were measured, and Lawton's success in the Southwest served as an endless endorsement of his ability to beat Filipino opponents. At one point Ben tells a fellow soldier that "'I never heard of such a campaign.'" His companion replies that "'General Lawton puts it down as a regular Indian campaign.'" Just a *regular Indian campaign*, one in which soldiers like Lawton and Young's Scouts, who also make an appearance in the story, base their ability to defeat insurgents on their experiences as Indian/fighters.

"SOUNDED SAVAGE ENOUGH"

On May 30, 1899, Kinne and the rest of Young's Scouts, recently returned to Manila after the end of Lawton's Northern Expedition, celebrated Decoration Day (the precursor to Memorial Day) by adorning Young's grave with flowers.[89] The flowers, scripture, and crisp new uniforms in which the scouts were photographed should not give the impression they had lost their rough edge. One of the first things they did upon return to Manila was head to a market and sell off a captured pony and cart for $250, which was divided among the men. The independent scouts seemed to take their cues from their namesake, even after his death. In the following pages of his diary Kinne recaps, with no small amount of admiration, Young's winding career, which took him from the North American plains to the Philippine islands.[90] It's hard to imagine a man more enmeshed in the overlapping networks of colonialism, imperialism, and global capitalism at the turn of the century. Young's tenure in the Philippines helps to connect the Philippine-American War to continental US colonialism in the nineteenth century. It demonstrates the persistence of Indian/fighting in a supposedly post-frontier US culture.

By June of 1899, John Kinne, the rest of the First North Dakota, and many of the other young men who had volunteered for the Spanish-American War were nearing the end of their service in the Philippines. However, the war was far from over, and the Philippines would remain a US colony until 1946.[91] Kinne and several of his fellows spent their final month on the outskirts of Manila attempting to root out persistent Filipino revolutionary forces on the Morong Peninsula. Many of the men in Young's Scouts had been reassigned back to their original regiments with assurances that they would get "special mention to the secretary of war." The soldiers of the First North Dakota who had been in Young's Scouts were promptly chosen as scouts for their old regiment, a clear indication that these men had built a reputation in just a few short months. For Kinne, this was a welcome assignment, as it promised relief from the more onerous guard duties and the opportunity for increased freedom. Kinne seems to have taken advantage. The final pages of his journal juxtapose a sometimes holiday-like atmosphere alongside a series of tense firefights. On several occasions Kinne goes duck hunting and canoeing on the nearby lake, but the scouts also lost their third commander of the war, J. H. Killian, during a skirmish in early June (Young's successor, J. E. Thornton, had been reassigned earlier).[92]

As the First North Dakota and other volunteer regiments prepared to return home to the United States, the War Department appointed J. Franklin Bell, a rising star in the Army, commander of the Thirty-sixth US Volunteer Infantry, the first of the new volunteer regiments in the Philippines. Bell was given permission to recruit officers and soldiers already in the Philippines, and Kinne notes on June 20 that "Bell came out from Manila [sic] looking for recruits for his regiment of sharp-shooters." It is likely no coincidence that Bell targeted the First North Dakota, a unit that had contributed several soldiers to Young's Scouts.

Bell was an offensive-minded officer who, like Lawton, was a veteran of the Indian Wars. He organized scouting units that performed reconnaissance, advanced ahead of troop columns, and conducted search-and-destroy missions.[93] Bell's later campaigns in the Philippines are celebrated by contemporary military historians as some of the most effective examples of counterinsurgency warfare in US military history, a lineage that grew, in part, out of Lawton's use of Young's Scouts.[94]

At least one of the men in Kinne's regiment that had also served in the scouts, James McIntyre, put in for a transfer to Bell's new regiment. Kinne, anxious to return home to North Dakota, chose not to. On June 22, after several more days spent duck hunting, Kinne narrates the final firefight of his time in the Philippines with a literary flourish:

> The next day a few of the scouts were out and shot at some natives who were crossing an opening, stirring up a regular hornets nest of them. The rest hurriedly went out to where they were and we got a few very good shots at the "Gugus." They dropped a few pretty close to us but none of us were hit. . . . We heard the war whoop of the Filipinos. It was a long drawn out oh—ah—oh, and sounded savage enough echoing and re-echoing among the hills and valleys around.[95]

It is clear when reading Kinne's journal that Indians were never far from his mind during his deployment to the Philippines, and this final skirmish fittingly ends with a savage "war-whoop" that echoes through the hills and valleys. The casual way in which he describes "shooting at some Natives" captures both the uncertainties of the guerilla warfare that was coming to define the conflict, and the dynamics of US imperial violence in which Filipino people, ostensibly the beneficiaries of the United States' benevolent assimilation, found themselves under a general threat of violence.

The "Oh—ah—Oh" that sent a shiver down Kinne's spine, that iconic marker of savage war through what Philip Deloria calls the "Indian sound," demonstrates one final time that US soldiers in the Philippines often narrated their experiences as an "Indian War."[96] Attention to the interaction between imperial culture and military violence allows us to see the connections between the violence of US continental expansion and the Philippine-American War. Indian/fighting was not the only lens through which US soldiers understood their time in the Philippines, but it was prominent and powerful, able to enmesh the soldiers in one of the United States' most enduring narratives about violence. Lawton's strategies and tactics, most prominently the creation of Young's Scouts, were the product of material conditions, institutional training, and these very cultural ideas about colonial violence. These are the narratives and stories that influence and define US militarism on the global scale. They have not gone away, and the war and occupation of the Philippines was one of the first conflicts that cemented Indian/fighting as an important structuring narrative capable of influencing US military violence.

CHAPTER 3

The Literature of Savage War

"SAVAGE WAR WAS NEVER MORE BEAUTIFUL THAN IN YOU"

Arizona Territory, November 1, 1874. Twenty-five or so men of the Fifth Cavalry are relaxing, trying to find some shade from the oppressive heat. They are chasing a group of Tonto Apache who ran off a herd of cattle and killed a settler before fleeing into the mountainous Black Mesa region near Sunset Pass.[1] Their leader, First Lieutenant Charles King, has reconnoitered ahead with some Apache scouts. The second in command, Lieutenant George Eaton, relaxes with a copy of James Fenimore Cooper's *Last of the Mohicans*, one of the iconic portrayals of Native people in American literature.[2] Cooper's novels, which center on the woodsman Natty Bumpo, otherwise known as Hawkeye or Leatherstocking, would have resonated with men like Eaton on the front line of the Indian Wars. At the center of Cooper's novels was an anxiety over the degeneration of white frontiersmen into uncivilized denizens of nature. Although such men were necessary to the colonial process, they were dangerous, too close to the undeveloped wilderness and the Native people that inhabited it. Cooper's frontiersmen could be admired for their Indian-like skills but had to step aside and make room for civilization.[3] As he reclined in the shade and read Cooper's story, Eaton may have imagined himself as the inheritor of Leatherstocking's legacy, a skilled warrior that had shed the rough buckskin of the frontiersman and replaced it with the professionalism of the modern Army, able to challenge Indian warriors on their own ground without sacrificing the trappings of civilization.

Perhaps Eaton was reading the passage where Native warriors, led by the novel's antagonist, Magua, ambush a column of British soldiers. Suddenly Eaton heard a few scattered shots from the direction King had taken, followed by an eruption of gunfire. He quickly gathered his troops and rushed toward the shooting, finding a badly injured King being carried, under fire, by Sergeant Bernard Taylor.[4] Eaton's literary repose had turned into the real thing. While scouting, King had, according to his and Eaton's version of the story, encountered the hostile Tonto Apache, who shot several arrows at King, one slicing the flesh near his left eye. Gunfire followed the arrows, which King answered, hitting one of the Apache hidden among the rocks. However, as King tried to reload, he was struck in the right arm and forced to make a haphazard retreat, his injured arm dangling uselessly at his side. Sergeant Taylor would eventually find the wounded King. Ignoring his superior officer's orders to leave him to his fate, Taylor struggled down the mountain where he was eventually met by Eaton and the rest of the command.[5] Apache Scout Mike Burns offers a different version of the story in which King is rescued by another scout named Bawnagoo, writing that King "made no effort to give any credit to the scouts for saving him."[6] Despite these diverging narratives, Taylor earned a Medal of Honor for his rescue, and King earned an injury that would trouble him for the rest of his military career.

Eaton's story about reading *The Last of the Mohicans* before an ambush blurs the line between the literary and the real. Out of moments like this the Indian Wars blossomed into an American mythology, proliferating in literature, film, television, video games, sports, and more.[7] Part of the reason that "Indian country" and the "savages" that inhabit it have shown up in almost every US conflict, from the Philippines, to Vietnam, to Iraq, is because of men like Charles King. King was both a soldier and chronicler of empire, and the ability of Indian/fighting to function as a shadow doctrine depended on the circulation of those ideas in the broader culture. King fought in the continental US and the Philippines and turned that experience into a collection of stories that influenced the Western genre. Through writers like King, Indian/fighting became one of the central images of US militarism, a discourse that has structured how the United States has viewed its enemies and its own soldiers. Charles King's writing is the vehicle for this chapter, the mechanism through which we will explore how US soldiers' ideas about

"Indians" became increasingly mobile at the end of the nineteenth century. A highly productive author during his time, Charles King deserves greater attention within the cultural histories of US empire.

Born into a military family in 1844, King graduated from West Point in 1866 and was stationed in New Orleans during Reconstruction. In 1874, King was transferred to the Fifth Cavalry and joined them in Arizona Territory, beginning a period of frontier service that would spawn his literary career.[8] King participated in General George Crook's campaigns against the Apache in the Southwest and later joined the general on the northern plains for the large-scale operation targeting the Lakota, Cheyenne, and their allies in 1876, the same campaign that resulted in the defeat of Custer's Seventh Cavalry. During that campaign, King witnessed his lifelong friend "Buffalo Bill" Cody in action as a scout for the Fifth Cavalry and participated in several famous battles, most notably the fight at Warbonnet Creek where Cody would claim he "took the first scalp for Custer" in a fight with Cheyenne warrior Heova'ehe.[9] In his narrative of that fight, King is rhapsodic in his description of the Native warriors he aims at with his rifle, writing "savage warfare was never more beautiful than in you."[10]

King often focused on what he called "savage warfare" throughout his literary career. In particular, he sought to defend the value of the service performed by American soldiers in their campaigns against those "savages," whether in North America or elsewhere. In *Campaigning with Crook* he included the "parting benediction" Crook issued to his soldiers, a statement that mirrors much of the sentiment in King's own writing: "Indian warfare is, of all warfare, the most dangerous, the most trying, and the most thankless. Not recognized by the high authority of the United States Senate as war, it still possesses for you the disadvantages of civilized warfare, with all the horrible accompaniments that barbarians can invent and savages execute."[11] The fight with the Tonto Apache in November of 1874 would leave King with a lasting injury to his arm, but he remained in the Army until 1879 when the pain finally forced him to retire. After his discharge, King joined the Wisconsin National Guard, taught military science at the University of Wisconsin, and began a writing career to earn extra money. However, his military service would continue in 1898 with the onset of the Spanish-American War, when he was commissioned as a Brigadier General of Volunteers and commanded a brigade during the early stages of the US occupation of the Philippines. In 1904, King returned to the National Guard and would remain involved until 1931 when he finally retired, two years before his death in 1933.[12]

During his life, King wrote hundreds of short stories, novels, essays, and articles for a range of magazines and military publications. His focus was primarily frontier violence, Army life, the Civil War, and the Spanish-American War. He was part of a cohort of US soldiers who published novels in the late nineteenth and early twentieth centuries that sought to trade on their experiences to render authentic wartime narratives. King was the most famous of these writers, and even found a market in Europe, with some of his novels translated into German (an audience eager for tales of cowboys and Indians).[13] King's writing has not entered the canon of great American literature, with its sometimes cumbersome focus on sentimental love stories and heroic soldiers. However, he contributed to the development of the western genre on both the page and screen. Owen Wister, largely credited as the father of the western, wrote that King "opened for us the door upon frontier military life." King's work is considered "the first series of western novels that was regarded as serious literature in their day."[14] Where writers like Wister mythologized the cowboy, King made the soldiers of the regular Army his focus, valorizing the men who fought in the Civil War, Indian Wars, and the Spanish-American War. Historian Michael Tate writes that King "probably did more than any single person to elevate the old army to a heroic position among the American people."[15] The *Army and Navy Journal* called King an advocate for the Army, "making it better known to civilians through the popularity of his works." They specifically thanked King for countering criticism of the Army, a task the author took up throughout his novels, which will be discussed later in this chapter.[16]

King also influenced the early days of film. In 1911, he sold the rights to several of his novels, and in the 1920s four more of his books were adapted to film. King even collaborated with the man most responsible for developing the mythological narrative of the American West, William Cody a.k.a. Buffalo Bill, on his series of Indian Wars films, serving as a screenwriter.[17] Cody pompously referred to King as a "splendid little officer, brave as a lion."[18] Through his writing, King helped cement the Indian Wars as an enduring literary construction. But unlike many who wrote about those conflicts King actually fought in them, and because he fought overseas in the Philippines his writing forms a bridge across which the mythologies of frontier violence migrated overseas (and back home). King was one of the most prominent examples of US soldiers narrating their overseas experiences as Indian warfare. In the previous chapter we saw how US soldiers in the Philippines were influenced by their prior experience in the Indian Wars. This chapter extends that analysis, showing how imaginative constructions of Indian/fighting could be used to explain and justify the broader US imperial project at the turn of the century.

IMAGINING THE APACHE

Unsurprisingly, King's fight at Sunset Pass, which led to the injury that forced him to begin a writing career, looms large in his canon. He first wrote about the fight in a short story in his collection *Starlight Ranch* and would later write an entire novel about an Apache ambush titled *Sunset Pass*. The Apache who fought on both sides that day at Sunset Pass became the focus of many of King's novels. King joined a body of writers, many affiliated with the Army, that sought to imagine, construct, and define the Native peoples of the Southwest borderlands.[19] In the stories of Charles King and these other writers, Apache people increasingly appeared as the specters that haunt the edges of American expansion. King typically narrates the Apache as invisible up to the moment they attack, shadows of violence that could manifest in actual Apache people but also in Mexicans and Filipinos. This was exactly how most American settlers in the Southwest characterized the Apache. They "ruled practically supreme by terrorism and robbery," maintaining their "arrogant dominance over an immense country."[20] King's stories set in the Southwest exist within a long history of fantasies about a dangerous and militarized border that continue into the present day.[21] The Indians of King's writing became increasingly abstracted over the course of his career, serving as flexible antagonists that could be transposed onto other groups of people and transported overseas, a literary companion to US empire. This abstraction was one aspect of a broader translation of sovereign Native nations into consumable representations in the late nineteenth and early twentieth centuries. As men like King conjured up imaginary Indians, the concerns of Native nations became increasingly invisible.[22]

Charles King first explored the fight that resulted in his injury in a short story titled "The Worst Man in the Troop," in the collection *Starlight Ranch*. The story features fictionalized soldiers that undergo a pursuit and fight nearly identical to the one King and the Fifth Cavalry experienced in 1874. In the story, King's Yuma Apache scouts are fearful and timid, unwilling to do their jobs and fleeing at the first sign of trouble. Perhaps they were simply unwilling to walk into an obvious ambush, but it allows King's narrative to focus on the exploits of the soldiers. The story is straightforward, with the Tonto Apache ambush suddenly revealed in the form of an arrow "photographed as by electricity on the retina." Mr. Billings, the fictional King, returns fire and sustains the same arm wound that interrupted King's real career. As he attempts to escape, the maligned sergeant O'Grady, the "worst man in the troop," rescues the fictional King and carries him down the mountain. Once they meet up with their reinforcements, the hostile Apache are swept away and the story ends. In the narrative the fight is largely a device that allows Sergeant O'Grady to put to rest his bad reputation and prove his worth. King's retelling of the fight is straightforward, but he would later resurrect the story in the form of a novel.[23]

In *Sunset Pass*, King utilizes his experiences fighting the Apache to develop a far more embellished narrative. The story centers on Captain Gwynne, a widower, and his children Ned and Nellie. The family is headed back east to Pennsylvania from Arizona Territory accompanied by their nurse "Irish Kate," their driver, an African American man known only as "Jim," a "swarthy Mexican" named Manuelito in charge of the mules, and a retired soldier named Pike. King's characters conform to the racist stereotypes of the day, the brave Captain Gwynne and Pike contrasting to the cowardly Manuelito, the crass "Irish Kate," and the lazy "darkey Jim." However, even the characters that King maligns in his writing get to stand together with the white settlers in their opposition to the Native threat. The small party is stalked and ambushed by a hostile group of Apache who force a final confrontation in a cave. Captain Gwynne and Jim barely manage to hold them off before they are rescued from their last stand by US soldiers.[24]

In *Sunset Pass*, King represents Apache people in a racialized literary form similar to how they were depicted by other nineteenth-century Americans. US soldiers had a respect for Apache martial skills mixed with a widespread belief in their racial inferiority.[25] Often these dehumanizing characterizations were animalistic in tone. Army officer Robert Evans called Apache people "swift as the eagle, cruel as the hungry wolf."[26] George Crook, celebrated as a particularly knowledgeable Indian fighter, referred to the Apache as "tigers of the human race."[27] In King's writing, these traits combined to begin to form the mythic image of the "Apache," a literary figure that would take on a ponderous cultural weight, overshadowing the experiences and struggles of actual Apache people. They became one of the quintessential and enduring figures of insurgency.[28] Apache successes in resisting the imposition of US authority in the southwest borderlands contributed to the longstanding animosity Spanish colonizers, Mexicans, and US settlers felt for the Apache. These struggles resulted in what María Josefina Saldaña-Portillo calls a racial geography of the *Indio bárbaro* or barbarous Indian that rendered militant Native peoples the threat against which the US and Mexico defended.[29] This is the discourse Charles King taps into through his novels and their depictions of the Apache.

King's Apache are at times dirty, then sleek. They are crafty and calculating, but they do not "have sense enough" to rush the cave and use their superior numbers to overwhelm the defenders. In the novel, "no human being on earth can follow an enemy like an Apache."[30] These expert trackers pin down Gwynne's party and capture Manuelito, whom they proceed to torture. They dance and sing a "devil-inspired chant," burning Manuelito with "jeering laughter and fiendish yells." Their "savage song" drowns out Manuelito's shrieks, after which they turn their attention to the trapped family.[31] Gwynne, Pike, and Jim spare their family a similarly barbaric fate by holding on until reinforcements arrive. Even Gwynne's young son manages to kill an Apache attacker, yelling "papa, I shot an Indian," and earning the admiration of the soldiers.[32] Several of King's stories make it clear that the Apache are a threat looming at the edges of civilization, but one that can be overcome by individual bravery and the constant presence of the US Army. Like most literary Indians these Apache are powerful, frightening, and positioned as the enemy. This would hold true, even when King left the continental US behind at the end of the nineteenth century.

INDIANS IN THE PHILIPPINES

In early 1899, Charles King returned from a short deployment to the Philippines, where he had served under Henry Ware Lawton and participated in some of the battles explored in the previous chapter. His health had forced the general to make an early exit from that conflict, and on his way home to Milwaukee he stopped off at Chicago and talked to a reporter from the *Chicago Daily Tribune*. King argued that the US should send an additional sixty thousand troops to the islands, a force that would enable General Otis "to crush out anything approaching organized opposition." Predicting a lingering guerilla conflict, King extolled the virtue of a particular subset of soldiers that had been under his command: "I want to say a word for the Western volunteers. Three regiments of them were in my command—the First Washington, the First California, and the First Idaho. Better soldiers the world never saw. They were uniformly cheerful in the face of most discouraging conditions, and never failed to show dash and gallantry."[33]

It is unsurprising that these westerners resonated with King, the author of so many works of western fiction. He complained publicly that there were not enough Indian War veterans in the Philippines at the start of the war, complaints that were echoed by other US Army generals. Those that were present—Otis, Anderson, Rucker, Lawton, and others—had, according to King, successfully used against the Filipinos tactics developed in wars with Natives in the American West. They were "as renowned for daring and devotion in Indian battle as . . . for skill, courage, and ability in action against insurgents in front of Manilla [sic]."[34] The mystique of Indian/fighting clung to these men, just like it had clung to the men in Young's Scouts, imprinted not just on the American military imagination but on their physical bodies.[35] King, recounting the fighting around Manila at the start of the conflict, remembered one officer, a Lieutenant Hawthorne, "who had already won a name for daring and skill in the face of a savage enemy. A Sioux bullet at the bloody fight at Wounded Knee eight years ago drove fragments of his watch through his body, but in no way impaired his efficiency or daunted his nerve."[36] Like his superior officer Henry Lawton, King expected his western soldiers to perform in the Philippines. They must have, for King would not only sing their praises in the press but continue his literary arc by penning several novels that take place in the Philippines, novels that continued his interest in western themes (Figure 5).

King's writing after he returned from the Philippines bridged continental US expansion and the overseas colonialism of the late nineteenth and early twentieth centuries. It also sought to legitimate the US occupation and justify the conduct of American soldiers in the Philippines.[37] In his novels, King emphasizes the Indian-fighting lineage of the soldiers who find themselves in the Philippines. These warriors had honed their skills "in the hardy, eventful and vigorous life of the Indian frontier."[38] In one of his novels, a group of American soldiers is caught in an ambush, and a frantic officer yells out "Those fellows have had no Indian campaigning or they'd have never got into such a box."[39] The literary King needed "Indians" to face his newly transnational Indian fighters. King was not solely preoccupied with transplanted "Indians," however.

FIGURE 5. A cartoon depicts Charles King gathering material for his next novel amid combat in the Philippines. Courtesy of the Carroll University Archives.

A variety of other racial characterizations circulating among imperial discourses at the turn of the century turn up in King's writing. In an article he wrote for the *Atlanta Constitution*, King reflected on the racial character of Filipino people, calling them "fanatical as the Turk," "more superstitious than the negro," sneaky, half child and half devil.[40]

King could, at times, push back against some of the prevailing stereotypes American leaders held of Filipinos, particularly regarding their ability to form a postcolonial government. In an article for the *Milwaukee Journal*, King wrote that "the capability of the Filipinos for self-government can not be doubted," going on to "rank" them higher than Cubans and African Americans. In a different article, he argued that "there is no reason in the world why these people should not have the self-government which they so passionately desire, so far as their ability to carry it on goes."[41] However, this mishmash of racist caricatures and patronizing affirmation was secondary to King's primary interest in Filipinos: their fighting prowess. And on that topic, King notes that Filipinos were "an enemy as utterly without conscience and as full of treachery as our Arizona Apache."[42] This was a comparative framework King would expand on. Indeed, Indians, and specifically the Apache, became a lens through which King's experiences in the Philippines were refracted when he composed his novels.

In *Found in the Philippines* (which he wasted no time on, beginning to write on the voyage home), which is largely concerned with a convoluted love story, King also narrates the beginning of the Filipino military resistance to the US occupation. As the first shots are fired around Manila, US troops faced "thickets of bamboo that fairly swarmed with Insurgents." They possessed an "Indian-like skill in concealment" that frustrates the US soldiers.[43] But King also began to consolidate and advance a new argument that was, according to Richard Slotkin and others, actually very old: that soldiers themselves could be caught up in the imaginative world of colonial representation. King denigrates Filipinos and calls them "little brown men," and thinks of the so-called "insurgents" as Indians. But King noticed—and imagined—the ways that US soldiers were *also* beginning to assume an imagined "Indianness," to "play Indian" in the midst of combat.[44] During a tense battle near the end of *Found in the Philippines* a group of US soldiers is pinned down by Filipino fire. They attempt to charge the Filipino position, "yelling like Apaches," and the story's hero (whose father once commanded at Fort Apache in Arizona) is lost in the chaos, sustaining an injury that he barely notices in the fury of the attack.[45] "Apache" had become an increasingly flexible descriptor in King's writing, appropriate for limited use to describe the more audacious actions of US soldiers.[46]

This connection between continental expansion and the war in the Philippines was based in King's lived experience. He commanded troops in both contexts, and understood his time in both arenas as linked. In the Philippines he was a brigadier general in the First Brigade of the First Division, serving under Henry Ware Lawton. King celebrated Lawton as "our famous Indian campaigner," someone that the "old frontier cavalry swore by."[47] King's troops were volunteers and militia from western states like Colorado, the Dakotas, Montana, Nebraska, Kansas, and more, men who had lived through conflicts and wars with Native nations.[48] King even saved a newspaper article about his service in the Philippines that made that connection explicit: "Captain Charles King's heroes fought Sioux, Apaches, and other barbarous foes, always against powerful odds, and always with triumph. The accounts from Manila indicate that he can enact the fighting parts he has been so fond of creating on paper."

The article relays an episode during the Battle of Manila (1899) in which King led an assault similar to what the officers in another of King's novels, Comrades in Arms, hoped to unleash: "The dark-skinned Natives, who outnumbered his brigade, were not unlike Apaches or Sioux, and General King was not unlike the fighting heroes of his books. He charged the Filipinos and drove them into the Pasig river."[49] This was a battle in the earliest stages of the war that took place February 4–5 on the outskirts of Manila. The battle was one of the bloodiest of the entire conflict, resulting in a decisive US victory that set the Filipino Army of Liberation on their heels.[50] For many US soldiers the decisive American victory seemed to validate their racist assumptions about the Filipinos; at the same time, it contributed to the Filipino revolutionary leadership's eventual transition toward guerilla warfare.[51] As the newspaper account makes clear, the Indian Wars were the imaginative frame through which Americans interpreted the service of men like King while they fought in the Philippines. King later remembered the fight as a short and violent affair in which "little mercy was shown" to the overrun Filipinos where the fighting was hottest. Many Filipino soldiers were driven into the river to drown or be shot in the back. Hundreds of Filipino soldiers were killed, hundreds more captured, and a surrendered general told King that the Americans were relentless in a way that the Filipino soldiers were unaccustomed to. The battle launched King, Lawton, MacArthur, and the rest of the US soldiers in the Philippines into the aggressive initial campaign, a campaign that would come under increasing criticism after King left the islands.[52]

King seems to use frequent references to the Indian Wars to make the patterns of guerilla warfare in the Philippines feel more familiar to his readers. In *A Conquering Corps Badge, and Other Stories of the Philippines*, Filipino tactics and the Army's response are compared to what King calls "the old time Indian business." An aging officer named Major Bellingham, returning from a scout through the countryside, is ambushed by Filipino revolutionaries who surround the Americans and shoot them to death. At this point King gives the readers a familiar, and oft-criticized, pattern from nineteenth-century military policy on the frontier: "Then came the old time Indian business over again. Cross went out to 'pursue and punish'; gave the poor mutilated remains Christian burial; sent a scrawl to Coates bidding him break the news to Mrs. Bellingham, that the major's remains would hardly bear transportation, and to look sharp to his own sentries lest the Tagals give him a touch of the same treatment."[53] The "old Indian business" refers to the frustrations of frontier officers, who viewed themselves as caught between encroaching settlement and Native peoples, forever reacting to Native attacks with punitive columns of soldiers.

These complaints betray a deeper effect of settler colonialism—the tensions between elimination and incorporation embodied in the military's multiple roles on the frontier. Military policies thus occurred in a liminal space between waging war and punishing infractions, King's "old Indian business" of forever chasing after Native ambushers and raiders. In an 1869 letter from General Philip Sheridan to one of his subordinate officers, Benjamin Grierson, Sheridan complains about Comanche, Kiowa, and Kiowa-Apache raids into Texas. He instructs Grierson to hang anyone guilty of murder and arrest those guilty of robbery and offers an appraisal of Indian policy: "The trouble heretofore with Indians has been caused by the absence of all punishment for crimes committed against the settlements. No people, especially those in a savage state, can be expected to behave themselves where there are no laws providing punishment for crimes."[54] This is the sort of attitude King is tapping into in *A Conquering Corps Badge*—the colonizer's frustration at being unable to enforce an imperial normalcy combined with an unwillingness to concede the martial legitimacy of Native resistance. There is, according to King, nothing else to do but bury the bodies and once more chase down the duplicitous "Amigos" who feign sympathy with the American occupation only to rise up at the slightest opportunity.

King plays with and reinforces some of the gendered aspects of colonialism in his Philippines stories. He contrasts the wives of US Army
officers with Filipino men as a mechanism of racialized emasculation in
A Conquering Corps Badge. When a US-occupied town faces the threat
of Filipino revolutionary resistance, Miss Bellingham, the focus of the
story's love triangle, is more than prepared for Filipino violence: "Army
girls, frontier bred as are most of them, have seen too much of the
American savage to scare easily at the puny Malay. Bessie Bellingham
had been one of the best shots with a little Smith & Wesson in old days
at Fort Custer. She had a heavier pistol now and well knew how to use
it."[55] Native "savages" are used as a contrast to the Filipinos of King's
story. And while the white women in his novels tend to conform to the
gendered norms of the period, largely serving as passive love interests
for his fictional soldiers, King does not hesitate to mobilize their participation in military settler-colonialism to further racialize Filipino men as
cowardly, diminutive, and weak, a common feature of the gendered and
sexualized characterizations of Filipinos.[56]

In another story, King instead characterizes Filipino men as sexually threatening to white women. He links this depiction to the threat
that Indian men supposedly held for white womanhood, which found
its way into *Captured: The Story of Sandy Ray*. In the story, Gertrude,
a white woman, is threatened with the possibility of being captured by
Filipinos. Her companion, the soldier Sandy Ray, watches as "in her di-
lating eyes there came a look of infinite horror, of dread unspeakable."
As their enemies draw closer, Gertrude throws herself at Sandy's feet
and begs him for a knife. Confused, the soldier protests that he could
never take on that many men with a single knife. "Oh, can't you understand. . . . Mrs. Blake told me—your regiment—never let a woman fall
into the hands of the Indians. Isn't this as—as horrible? Oh, you will
not! You shall not!"[57] The infinite horror—the sexual threat of nonwhite men, serves as a linkage in King's story between continental expansion and the occupation of the Philippines. In both contexts, the
presumed racial inferiority of Native people and Filipinos justified US
expansion and occupation, and specifically justified colonial violence.
Filipino sexuality as a threat would in turn refract *back* to the United
States in the twentieth century. Anti-immigrant violence against Filipinos on the West Coast, particularly men who had relationships with
white women, was driven in part by the "racial-sexual threat" that Filipino men supposedly posed. Amy Kaplan has shown how the "anarchy
of empire" causes disruption and change in the metropole as much as it

does on the colonial periphery, but King's writing narrates this process as a three-step transference, where frontier racism travels overseas only to travel back to the continental United States, reformulated through overseas colonialism.[58]

USING THE INDIAN WARS TO JUSTIFY TORTURE

Even the most controversial violence of the Philippines campaign is filtered through a frontier lens in King's writing, namely the use of torture by US soldiers and allies. To briefly summarize a complex history, the "conventional" phase of the war lasted from February 1899 through the fall of that year, when the Filipino fighters switched to guerilla tactics. By the end of 1899, frustrated US soldiers and their Filipino allies began to use torture to extract the location of firearms and the identity of guerillas hidden among the local population. Beatings, property destruction, firing on noncombatants, and other punitive measures saw increasing use despite official prohibitions from top American generals. The use of torture varied widely and seemed to depend on the lower ranking officers in charge on the ground. As reports of torture and other atrocities filtered up the chain of command, higher-ranking officers issued orders prohibiting torture, often referring to the Lieber Code for guidance, but they had a difficult time restraining their subordinates. Indeed, many cited Lieber's code as a justification for their harsh tactics. Torture, particular the "water cure," which will be discussed further on, continued to be used, and anti-imperialists in the United States began to use the issue to attack the war.[59] By 1902, a series of prominent courts martial, congressional hearings, and newspaper articles brought US conduct in the Philippines out into the open for most US citizens. The Army mostly defended the conduct of its soldiers, arguing that atrocities were rare, and usually in response to the "savage" conduct of Filipino guerillas, who, they argued, fell outside the legal protections of "civilized war." The investigations and hearings embittered many soldiers, including King, who filtered that resentment through his writing.[60]

King's novels that take place in the Philippines serve, in part, as a defense of US conduct. In *Comrades in Arms* the story follows a group of soldiers from their posting near the Standing Rock Sioux Reservation in 1897 to the Philippines. Once overseas, the men encounter the "savage" violence that they no longer find in the West. As the soldiers in *Comrades in Arms* work to justify the increasingly harsh measures they employ, the reader is reminded that they traveled overseas from a territory marked by exceptional violence that had effectively ended Native resistance. Indeed, *Comrades in Arms* turns into an impassioned defense of the more brutal elements of the US occupation.

Comrades in Arms chronicles the transition from the initial, more conventional campaign of the US troops in the Philippines to the guerilla warfare that began in late 1899 and spread throughout the islands. King participated in the initial campaign, but he observed the later years of the occupation from a distance. He uses the story in *Comrades in Arms* to address the charges of excess, torture, and illegality that slowly began to filter into the American press. Ultimately the story becomes a defense of torture and American counterinsurgency policy, a defense that King undertakes through a comparison to continental colonialism and the Indian Wars.

The Army worked hard to censor the press in the Philippines, and largely succeeded in keeping descriptions of torture, murder, and property destruction away from the American public until 1902, when the war (or at least the official version of the war) was nearly over.[61] Anti-imperialist groups and politicians made sporadic efforts to document abuses and disseminate them, but President McKinley, and later President Theodore Roosevelt, along with Secretary of War Elihu Root, vigorously defended the US military's conduct in the Philippines.[62] In February of 1902, Root informed the United States Senate Committee on the Philippines that most reports of atrocities had been either "unfounded or grossly exaggerated."

Root went on to justify what he argued were sporadic instances of illegal conduct by US troops by attacking Filipino conduct during the war:

> The war on the part of the Filipinos has been conducted with the barbarous cruelty common among uncivilized races, and with general disregard of the rules of civilized warfare. . . . That the soldiers fighting against such an enemy, and with their own eyes witnessing such deeds, should occasionally be regardless of their orders and retaliated by unjustifiable severities is not incredible. . . . The War in the Philippines has been conducted by the American army with scrupulous regard for the rules of civilized warfare, with careful and genuine consideration for the prisoner and the noncombatant, with self-restraint, and with humanity.[63]

Root is attempting to have it both ways, arguing that US troops had conducted themselves legally and with restraint, but even if there *had* been instances of "unjustifiable severities" they were, in fact, justified by the barbarous nature of the Filipinos. His choice of the word "barbarous" is calculated. Root attached a copy of General Orders 100 to his report to the Philippines Commission, the document that governed the conduct of US soldiers during war. Known as the Lieber Code, the document was careful to differentiate between the civilized warfare of the European tradition and the "barbarous armies" of "uncivilized people," and allowed for retaliation against the "barbarous outrages" that US troops might face.[64] Root was not the only person to criticize Filipino conduct as a way to disarm anti-imperialists' critiques. American soldiers justified their own harsh conduct as a response to Filipino "savages." The *Army and Navy Journal* criticized the "venomous attacks" of anti-imperialists on the conduct of US troops, and found it unsurprising that the patient Americans "finally let their gall run over at the treacherous tricks played upon them."[65]

By April of 1902 the pressure on the administration began to mount as the number of courts martial and testimony alleging torture by US soldiers increased. One soldier in the Philippines called the rising tide of criticism "warfare against the military." He dismissed the idea that "civilized war" should even be applied in the Philippines, arguing that "Our so-called 'little brown brother,' is not our equal and cannot be, and it seems absurd to attempt to successfully apply at once to these half civilized Malays methods and laws which suit an entirely different and enlightened race of people."[66] These were sentiments shared by many soldiers, who were angered by the anti-imperialists' critiques.[67] King channeled that resentment in his stories. In *Comrades in Arms*, which was published soon after the war was officially ended, King blames the press and anti-imperialist politicians for the protracted guerilla warfare that followed the initial successes of the campaign in the Philippines. According to King, criticism of the war and the conduct of US soldiers had emboldened the Filipino resistance to the occupation. His writing echoes the frequent complaints of the frontier army and predicts the more hawkish discourses of the Vietnam War.[68] The press, humanitarians, and a meddlesome government stood in the way of victory for the US military: "Then campaign orators and anti-administration papers denounced and disowned the deeds of the soldiery; revived and restored the spirit of rebellion, and the misguided natives, hearing and permitted to hear only these treasonable vaporings, believing the nation spoke and not a bigoted few, took heart and arms again, and in many a province and many a distant isle fell upon the far-separated detachments, ofttimes with fatal effect."[69]

Here the story is mirroring reality, as Filipino revolutionaries had tried, unsuccessfully, to intensify the war in order to influence the election of 1900, which pitted the incumbent pro-imperialist William McKinley against the anti-imperialist populist William Jennings Bryan. According to *Comrades in Arms*, these criticisms had "incited the Filipino to renewed and desperate effort." King even blames anti-imperialists for the death of Henry Lawton, who died in battle in December of 1899: "Lawton had died in December, pierced by a bullet, as he himself had expressed it, that might as well have been aimed by one of his own people."[70] These excoriations of anti-imperialist sentiment are combined with racialized descriptions of Filipino guerillas as "a screaming, screeching, triumphant host."[71] Just like the American generals who fought the war, the officers in King's story decide to intensify the occupation.

In his novel, King relates criticism of the Army directly to the frequent complaints officers in Indian country made about eastern newspapers and reformers. For soldiers like King, the enemy was not only Indians (or Filipinos), but a hostile press, meddlesome religious activists, and government intrusion into military affairs.[72] As the Philippines campaign intensifies, a soldier in the novel cautions his superior officer to rein in his more aggressive impulses. "'You know the orders, sir,' said his staff officer dryly. 'I used to think we were up against the press, the pulpit, the people, and the Indians, too, when we had our annual run for the scalp dancers, but that was a simple proposition as compared to this.'" "It's like the orders we used to get long days ago at Laramie, when the Sioux had scalped our herders," the officer responds. "'Make every effort to arrest the murderers, but be sure to do nothing to excite the Indians.'"[73] For these soldiers in King's story it is the Army against everyone else, called upon to do a difficult job but then criticized when they attempt to do it correctly. This was a pervasive attitude in the frontier military, one King was intimately familiar with and sympathetic to. The soldiers were willing but held in check by half-measures.

It is hard to fathom the massacre at Wounded Knee, which King references earlier in the story, as being a half-measure.[74] Nonetheless, King's fictional soldiers long for the opportunity to strike out at their Filipino enemies as they used to on the frontier. King himself longed for that opportunity. In a letter to his daughter while stationed near Manila, he wrote that US soldiers had orders to avoid all conflicts before the war broke out in early 1899. King clearly found those orders frustrating, telling his daughter that "I dare say these little Filipinos think they've got the Yankees scared half crazy—when the fact is it is galling . . . to keep our own tempers and our men from rushing the insurgent lines and 'eating them up.'"[75] Racial superiority drove this frustration. References to Filipino men as diminutive and cowardly, along with a variety of racial slurs, fueled the desire of US soldiers to conduct an aggressive campaign. King's desire to "eat them up" is an early iteration of the United States' military hubris, the faith that overwhelming firepower, technology, and strength can easily overwhelm any foe, a belief that guerilla fighters have been challenging since the war in the Philippines and continue to do so.

Particularly frustrating for the novel's soldiers are the dynamics of the US occupation in which Filipino guerillas move through the country unseen, embedded in the general population. US soldiers were forced to constantly patrol through the countryside, uncertain of the hostility of the Filipinos they encountered. King's soldiers again understand their frustrations in terms drawn from their experiences in Indian country: "You are trying to carry out your orders, but you can't, because of your instructions—the one blocking the other just as the War and Interior Departments used to keep us between two fires on the Indian frontier. You know there are hundreds of Mausers and thousands of Mauser cartridges cached somewhere in that village. You know that presidente knows all about it, too, but the only way you can prove it is to rip things to pieces until you find them, and you are forbidden to rip."[76] In King's narrative it took actual Indian Fighters to resolve this quandary, just as real-life generals like Lawton, MacArthur, Chaffee, and King himself aggressively pursued an end to Filipino resistance. Near the end of the story the American occupation intensifies: "Then at last there began a new dispensation. New district commanders stepped into the field, some from the regulars, some from the national volunteers. They were men chosen because of certain traits of strenuous, vehement energy that had marked them in other sections and at earlier stages of the game." Colonel Langham, the story's hero, is one of these "vehement and strenuous men," molded in frontier service and happy to "rip." Now the Philippines campaign had the men it needed, men who "belonged to the heroic age when results, not means, were of first consequence." And freed from restraint, Colonel Langham and this new cohort of strenuous men clamp down on the Filipino population in a way similar to the escalation that happened in the real Philippines war, complete with widespread destruction, death, and torture.

King describes Langham as the man who "swept the big island from end to end until he had scourged it clean," surrounding and occupying town after town, capturing insurgent leaders and using the water cure to reveal the location of weapons caches. This was the pattern of much of the war from late 1900 to 1902.[77] In one episode Langham's men occupy a Filipino town and demand intelligence from a local leader. The soldiers administer the "water cure," a torture technique that involves forcing an excessive amount of water down a prisoner's throat until their stomach becomes distended, and then applying sudden pressure to the abdomen. The victim feels as if they are drowning and experiences pain in the stomach and internal organs from the pressure of the water.[78] King goes out of his way to make the torture seem benign: "The tube of the funnel went into his mouth; cool water into the bowl of the funnel, and the presidente had either to swallow or choke. It didn't hurt; it was simply inconvenient.[79] "Cool water" and the mere "inconvenience" of the water cure in King's retelling attempt to portray the practice as far more benign than it was.

The water cure was hardly a gentle procedure. It was a mechanism of torture designed to inflict pain and coerce information, and in addition to the damage to the stomach and internal organs, could result in teeth getting knocked out and slashes and trauma to the limbs as the victim was held down.[80] Testimony offered by Herbert Yenser related an instance of the water cure at the town of San Pueblo in Laguna Province. Members of the Seventh Cavalry captured a Filipino revolutionary soldier while sleeping. Yenser crept into a loft overlooking the guard house and through cracks in the boards saw a Maccabebe scout attached to the Seventh Cavalry administer the torture. According to Yenser: "First a pipe was placed in the Victim's mouth and then water poured in until his abdomen became much distended. Then the men jumped with both feet upon the victim's stomach with such force that the water spurted from his mouth over three feet in the air. The second time this operation was performed blood also came out with the water."[81] King's downplaying of the severity of the water cure was consistent with others who defended the conduct of American soldiers in the Philippines. Indeed, Langham is a heroic figure in the story precisely because he is willing to do what it takes, including even the "inconvenient" torture.

Langham's methods convince the presidente to talk, and word begins to spread about these increasingly aggressive tactics: "The story went swiftly from town to town that at last the Americans were led by an officer who couldn't be fooled, and who carried a funnel." During the proceedings of the court martial, King once more suggests that the victims of the water cure had "been no more than temporarily inconvenienced," the aggrieved Langham being the victim of jealous subordinates eager to bring about his downfall.[82]

King paints the members of the court martial as largely sympathetic to Langham and his tactics, veterans of Indian country themselves that understand the demands of savage war: "Some of them, West Pointers and Indian fighters of the line, chosen, because of their energy in that line, to command volunteer regiments against the Insurgent Islanders, had been heard to say that the only way to thrash Indians or Islanders was to tackle them Indian or Island fashion, which was not with gloves, or close observance of a General Order devised for use in battling a civilized and not a savage foe."[83] King's story is a forceful defense of Army tactics, torture, and the necessities of "savage war." When fighting Indians or Filipinos, the Army was justified, according to these men, in removing their gloves and exercising a severity beyond that allowed by the formal rules of war. It is a defense that echoes the justifications of President Theodore Roosevelt, who argued in 1902 that "the army, which has done its work so well in the Philippine islands, has . . . been cruelly maligned even by some who should have known better. . . . The temptation to retaliate for the fearful cruelties of a savage foe is very great, and now and then it has been yielded to."[84] King's (and Roosevelt's) frequent references to savagery are more than just a reference to a central question of military law: whether the enemy's actions justify an extreme response. They show the ongoing influence the cultural discourse around "savagery" had in determining US military action. Indians lurked even in the shadowy recesses of military law, a potential indictment that more often was invoked as a justification. Against the savage the exception became the rule.

King turns criticism of Army conduct into a ringing denunciation of anti-imperialists, Indian sympathizers, and civilian interference with military policy. In *Comrades in Arms* the overwhelming majority favor aggressive tactics to subdue "savages" but are drowned out by a loud minority that controls the press and the halls of government. One of Langham's superiors, and the father of his love interest, offers a forceful defense of Army tactics in the Philippines, but to no avail.[85] Protocol prevails and Langham is punished:

Belden's plea was eloquent and forcible, but—orders are orders. No matter that our people, soldier or civilian, were shot from ambush, boloed in cold blood, trapped in pit-falls, flayed, flogged, and tortured to slow and cruel death; no matter that officials, sworn to loyalty, should give refuge to assassins, should conceal them, their arms, and their supplies—should laugh and lie in the face of the officers sent in search—the law and the prophets, the press and the pulpit held that only by the rules of civilized war should even savages be handled.[86]

King clearly feels betrayed, just as he and his fellow officers in Indian country felt betrayed in their nineteenth-century wars with Native people. "Just as in the days of the Indian wars the good folk farthest removed from the scene were loudest in denunciation of the troops at the spot. To these latter it was death if they lost, and defamation if they won. The men who put an end to the most savage and intractable side of the insurrection were summoned in turn to take their punishment."[87] Langham becomes a sacrifice to the demands of savage warfare, a hero willing to use extreme tactics in pursuit of ends that, according to King, justify the means.

King's description of torture in *Comrades in Arms* mirrored the unfolding of the controversy in real life. The rise of torture by US forces corresponds to the moment in King's narrative when the men of "strenuous, vehement energy" took over the occupation and proceeded to "rip" their way through the Filipino countryside. By 1901 the water cure was widely used, most infamously by Major Edwin F. Glenn, likely one of the inspirations for the court martial of Langham in *Comrades in Arms*. Glenn commanded a mounted intelligence unit that went from town to town administering the water cure to extract information. Somewhat paradoxically, Glenn had a law degree and expertise in the rules of warfare, which he used to justify the use of the water cure.[88] In his testimony Glenn did not deny administering the water cure but argued that it was humane and justified, a necessary element of the counterinsurgency campaign that hastened the war's end. Ultimately Glenn was convicted, receiving the sort of light sentence common for American soldiers convicted for their conduct during the war. A defiant Glenn complained that he was blamed for doing exactly what his commanding officers wanted in the Philippines.[89]

Some officers, such as Glenn and Jacob "Hell Roaring" Smith, famous for his orders to turn the island of Samar into a "howling wilderness" and kill every Filipino male over the age of ten, did face prosecution or censure. But the criticism of the military's conduct was not restricted to strident anti-imperialists in the United States. The Army's top general, Nelson A. Miles, a fellow Indian fighter who had done his fair share of complaining about civilian criticism of military conduct, himself criticized Army abuses in the Philippines. Miles toured the islands in 1902 and published a report focused on the dispersion of US troops, their condition, the progress of the war, and other concerns. A special section of Miles's report addressed the accusations of US atrocities in the Philippines, accusations Miles found credible. He detailed several meetings with Filipino community leaders and was introduced to people that had been tortured with the water cure. In one community, he met local leaders and was informed that fifteen people from the area had been tortured with the water cure; one man had been tortured and then confined to a burning building, where he died. Miles saw burned-out fields, destroyed towns, and heard stories of US officers known for their extreme tactics.[90]

Miles's report was criticized within the military. The editors of the *Army and Navy Journal* dismissed his claims as "gossip" and called him a friend to the anti-imperialists. Critics of Miles highlighted the general's history as a famous Indian fighter. They argued that he should have known better than to criticize soldiers engaged in a savage war: "General Miles is a soldier of large experience, he has learned in his warfare against Indians and others how difficult it is to reconcile the severity which is imperatively required in dealing with an armed enemy to the philanthropic conceits of men who know nothing of military necessities."[91] Just like the characters in King's stories, the real-life critics of anti-imperialism based their argument in the Indian Wars. These conflicts had taught the US military that savagery required severity. Torture may have been an excessive expression of that "severity," but the state of exception in which the laws of war operated sanctioned severity as an antidote for savagery.

Miles responded to the editorial directly, claiming his evidence that was dismissed as mere gossip was the result of interviews with multiple Army officers, as well as Filipino civilian leaders. In a twist to the familiar script, Miles used Indian "savagery" as a way to defend his critique of the conduct of US troops: "For a hundred years the Army has been waging war against savage Indians—and there is no namable atrocity that at some time some Indians did not commit—but retaliation in kind and violence towards captive and surrendered Indians have always been prohibited."[92] Miles was incorrect that retaliation and violence toward captives was not engaged in by American soldiers during the Indian Wars. Regardless, he felt comfortable invoking the Indian Wars as a defense of his own criticism of American troops in the Philippines. If frontier soldiers had controlled their behavior in wars with "savages," then soldiers in the Philippines should be able to do the same. Other soldiers echoed Miles's sentiment, accusing the press of printing lies and questioning "why have we treated with humane consideration Apache and Cheyenne prisoners only to break loose with almost savage vindictiveness upon the Filipino?"[93] Only a decade removed from the massacre at Wounded Knee and the Indian Wars were remembered as "gentle." Those wars were now used to refute charges of American atrocities on another continent.

The Miles Report was only one example of the widespread backlash to US atrocities in the Philippines, and King's writing in *Comrades in Arms* is a clear attempt to counter such criticism. King's writing joined the chorus of US soldiers angry over criticism of their conduct in the Philippines. The Roosevelt administration managed to contain most of the fallout from the torture scandal, and the president declared the war officially over on July 4, 1902. Like most occupations, Filipino resistance continued, particularly in the majority Muslim regions in the southern part of the Philippines. But the Philippines commission passed the Brigandage Act in November of 1902 that defined remaining resistance to US authority as "banditry" and "ladronism," categories even more delegitimizing than insurgency. This attempt to inject a colonial normalcy in the islands was furthered by the establishment of the Philippine Constabulary, a police force under Commission control that Paul Kramer calls "a colonial army in police uniform." When the US assumed control of the Philippines, they had turned anticolonial resistance into an insurrection; the creation of the Constabulary now turned insurgency into mere criminality. The majority of US troops returned from the islands, having suffered minimal consequences from the torture scandals King so vociferously critiques in *Comrades in Arms*.[94]

The Philippine-American War has been largely forgotten in US historical memory. That amnesia has extended, in part, to the US military. In the aftermath of the war, the military neglected to develop doctrine that would preserve lessons learned during the occupation. In the years after the war soldiers at places like the USAWC or the new school at Fort Leavenworth received little instruction in guerilla warfare, even though that type of combat had defined the war in the Philippines.[95] Military professional journals discussed the conflict sparingly. First Lieutenant Louis M. Hamilton, in an article titled "Jungle Warfare," for the *JMSI*, complained that the most recent (1904) version of the Infantry Drill Regulations did not include tactics developed in the Philippines. The recent British infantry regulations had included a section on "savage war," and Hamilton argued that US tactics in the Philippines deserved to be recorded in US Army manuals.[96] However, it was precisely the "irregularity" of much of the American military experience in the Philippines that prevented its institutionalization in Army doctrine, which was increasingly oriented toward future conventional wars.[97]

Soldiers reporting on their service in the Philippines, much like the previous generation that had served in the Indian Wars, were acutely aware that their duties on the islands included a large number of "civic duties" beyond the traditional mandate of the soldier. They were tasked with "winning hearts and minds" and governing Filipinos through military channels, a precursor to the sort of counterinsurgency that David Petraeus would popularize in Iraq one hundred years later.[98] As this and the previous chapter have made clear, racial antagonism motivated many US soldiers in the Philippines. But not all. Some saw it as an impediment to their counterinsurgency mandate. One soldier in the Philippines bemoaned the lack of Army discipline in the islands, complaining that he had heard many of his peers say "kill them off," referring to Filipinos, an argument he found comparable to those who said "the only good Indian is a dead Indian." To this soldier's mind, an increase in discipline was a necessity due to the "great many civil duties forced upon them" in the context of the occupation.[99] Recent discussion of counterinsurgency has focused on the contradiction between "kinetic" military force and the desire to "win hearts and minds," and clearly this is a paradox with antecedents that go back to the nineteenth century.

An official history of the war was commissioned by the government, written by Captain J. R. M. Taylor and titled *The Philippine Insurrection against the United States*. However, it was repeatedly censored by Secretary of War Taft and other government officials, for fear that it would harm the ongoing colonial relationship that the US had with the Philippines. US politicians also worried the book would reignite the debates over US war crimes in the conflict.[100] Taylor's study included analysis of the reconcentration of Filipinos in "zones of protection," concentration camps that opened up those outside US surveillance to violence. Outside the protected zones, American soldiers destroyed crops, torched buildings, and fired on Filipinos who were assumed to be insurgents.[101] Taylor also covered the destruction of Filipino food, supplies, and houses, and the "right of retaliation"; the execution of Filipino prisoners American officers believed was sanctioned by General Orders 100.[102]

Taylor placed the blame for the viciousness of the conflict on Filipino guerillas, writing, "If war in certain of its aspects is a temporary reversion to barbarism, guerilla warfare is a temporary reversion to savagery. . . . Guerilla warfare means a policy of destruction, a policy of terror." He went on to argue that guerilla warfare is an inherently self-defeating strategy that ends in inevitable defeat: "Guerilla warfare is like privateering—it causes damage, it sometimes causes irreparable damage, but never yet has it changed defeat to victory."[103] Native peoples, the archetypal savage guerillas, seem to hover over Taylor's writing. His broad claim about the self-defeating nature of guerilla tactics is sketchy at best. Guerillas contributed to the defeat of Napoleon in the Peninsular War, the conflict that birthed the very name "guerilla."[104] Native guerillas (as well as confederates) certainly gave the US Army trouble during the nineteenth century. However, Taylor, just like Charles King, was a chronicler of empire. These men inhabited a world in which savagery and guerilla tactics slid together, and they viewed the United States as a sometimes-unwilling expert in savage warfare. The irony is that their conflation of guerilla warfare with savagery hampered the development of military doctrine. The history of these "savage wars" was an ugly history, one that military institutions were hesitant to record.

The Philippines Insurrection was not the only casualty of political censorship following the war. Very few lessons from the Philippines were incorporated into Army training or education, although some have more recently been resurrected during the War on Terror.[105] In 1902, Captain M. F. Davis compiled a collection of telegraphic circulars issued by General James Franklin Bell, regarded as one of the most successful US generals in the Philippines, who commanded troops in the provinces of Batangas, Laguna, and Mindoro. A record of Bell's strategy was in high demand from soldiers anxious for a guide to irregular warfare. In his introduction to the pamphlet, Davis noted that frequent requests from Army officers, both those who had served under Bell and others, led to his compiling the documents for distribution. The orders covered in detail Bell's approach to counterinsurgency, including the reconcentration of Filipino populations; the destruction of food, supplies, and dwellings; the treatment of prisoners; and the execution of insurgents.[106] The document was never distributed outside of the Philippines, likely due to the descriptions of harsh counterinsurgency tactics and the fear of a possible backlash, the very measures that were currently under fire by anti-imperialist politicians.[107]

Bell was aware of the discomfort counterinsurgency warfare engendered in civilian observers, and even some of his soldiers. In an address to his officers when he took command of Batangas, Bell noted that he much preferred a policy of conciliation but warned that they would "unquestionably be required, by a sense of duty, to do much that is dis-agreeable."[108] Ultimately Bell's circulars never saw widespread distribu-tion nor application, and they have only recently been revived by the Combat Studies Institute at the United States Army Combined Arms Cen-ter (CSI) and published in a series of strategic essays during the War on Terror. Army historian Andrew Birtle calls the *Telegraphic Circulars* a lost "gem" of counterinsurgency theory, similar to George Crook's *Resumé of Operations against Apache Indians*, another proto-counterinsurgency document that failed to make inroads into US military doctrine.[109] The resurrection of Bell's *Telegraphic Circulars* in the context of the War on Terror is somewhat ironic given his prescient analysis: "Judging from experience in this war, a much greater length of time is always required to settle claims and outstanding obligations of the government, after a campaign is concluded, than is required to successfully conclude the cam-paign itself."[110] Clearly this has been an elusive lesson for the US military, a reminder of the imperial hubris that encouraged George W. Bush to declare "Mission Accomplished" in Iraq in 2003.

"THE OLD FRONTIER CAVALRY"

In August of 1899, following Charles King's return to the United States, Henry Lawton wrote the following letter to the general:

> I cannot express to you how much I regret the necessity for your return to the United States at the time you did. I want to say to you that you are the only General officer whom I know who possesses that peculiar faculty or that magnetism which attracts men to him; you are the only one of all the General officers who has excited among the men of his command any great amount of enthusiasm. I remember when you left your launch to come aboard the gunboat just before the attack on Santa Cruz, that a cheer went up from all the men in the transports; and you seem to possess that peculiar dash and spirit which carries men who follow you along with you with enthusiasm.[111]

King reciprocated Lawton's enthusiasm, writing years after the gener-al's death that Lawton was "a glorious soldier, and we of the old fron-tier cavalry swore by him."[112] Recall the earlier report in which Lawton lauded Young's Scouts for their "peculiarly valuable" service. The word *peculiar* functions as a coded signifier for Indian/fighting, and seemingly links to the more modern usage of *irregular*. *Peculiar* serves to remove that fighting into a state of exception in which "savage" tactics can be used to defeat savages and institute colonial controls. King's familiar use of the word *old* traffics in the nostalgia for Indian warfare that clearly was not really nostalgia but rather a material fact of developing US counterinsurgency strategy. Soldiers like King and Lawton thought fondly on their "old" Indian/fighting days even as they translated that experience into a coherent program to defeat Filipino revolutionaries. Nostalgia masked the continuities at work in military strategy. The reputation of both men was built on their role in the conquest of Native people in the continental United States, which informed their subsequent history as soldiers, writers, and objects of a frontier mythology that became infused into the US military.

Yes, both Lawton and King fought Native peoples and Filipinos. But when you dig into their histories, a more complicated process of cultural formation emerges. Lawton, King, and their peers from the frontier army moved overseas to the Philippines and in the process made Indian/fighting a structuring narrative of US military violence. This narrative was capable of transmitting shadow doctrines that could influence military practices on the ground. And, as we see with Charles King, Indian/fighting could also influence the defense of those practices in the literary archive of US empire. Soldiers like Lawton and King were discursively positioned as Indian fighters, and they willingly filled that role, narrating their time in the Philippines as an Indian war, and in King's case further cementing that connection in a body of written work that played a significant role in the development of the western genre. Charles King glorified savage warfare even as writers in the twentieth century increasingly looked toward the "civilized" wars of the future.

Savage and Civilized War

REMEMBERING AND FORGETTING

From 1929 to 1931, soldiers at the US Army Infantry School at Fort Benning (now Fort Moore) conducted a training exercise focused on an imagined enemy, the "Reds." The instructional materials located the operation in the American Southwest and described the Reds as "one of the most warlike tribes of Indians in America." An obvious reference to the history of militant Apache resistance to US colonialism, the Reds were "a hardy and courageous people . . . agile, fleet of foot, and extremely cunning." Soldiers were cautioned that the Reds "avoid open combat with regular troops, unless their villages and farms are threatened, when they fight with tenacity, employing guerilla tactics." Several of the Indian/fighting strategies discussed in this book were included in the exercise. The soldiers were accompanied by Indian scouts, the focus of the maneuvers involve taking away the Reds' mobility, and the troops, initial orders were to "attack and destroy" a village of Reds engaged in the planting of crops. The remainder of the exercise involved the soldiers moving through the terrain and engaging the remaining Reds, bringing artillery to bear, and driving the fictional Indians from the field, ending their "revolt."[1]

Despite the myth of the "vanishing Indian," Native people did not disappear in 1890 after the Wounded Knee massacre.[2] Neither did the structures of colonial dispossession, out of which Native nations continue to carve out spaces of sovereignty.[3] But the US military focused less and less on Indian/fighting after 1890, making the exercise against the Reds somewhat anomalous. Films, novels, and traveling shows told stories about the end of the Indian Wars.[4] "Savage war" was relegated to the past, and "civilized war" became the preoccupation of a modernizing military that largely declined to preserve a specific doctrine of Indian warfare that could be applied to future conflicts. That does not mean the Americans stopped thinking about Indian/fighting entirely. As time passed, the Army's experience in the Indian Wars became increasingly difficult to untangle from the frontier mythologies that proliferated in popular culture during the twentieth century.

If our focus is narrowed to formal doctrine, it is clear the Indian Wars were largely left behind in the nineteenth century.[5] But the discourses of informal doctrine and American popular culture tell a very different story. Soldiers and civilians celebrated the United States as a nation of Indian fighters. This included the well-documented potency of the frontier as a national mythology.[6] But it also included articles, stories, and examinations of the Indian Wars, and the subsequent Philippine-American War, that celebrated the value of Indian/fighting as a crucible that had molded American soldiers into warriors capable of meeting the demands of colonial violence. A narrow focus on formal doctrine will miss out on this history.

The training exercise against the "Reds" noted above is representative of these discursive entanglements. Just like the fictionalized Indians of settler nightmares, Indian warfare lurks at the edge of US military doctrine, emerging in unexpected ways as a shadow doctrine through which Americans have reckoned with their expanding imperial power and its limits. This chapter examines the period in the late nineteenth and early twentieth centuries where the threads of continuity between the Indian Wars and ongoing US militarism grew even more thin than they were in the Philippine-American War. As military writers advocated for a civilized, modern military, they increasingly pushed what they understood to be "savage" warfare to the margins. And yet, American writers, observing an increasingly imperial world, could not stop talking about Indian/fighting. Whether examining their own history, observing European colonialism in Africa, debating the ethics of ammunition, or preparing for the first World War, Americans simultaneously dismissed and glorified their relationship to colonial violence. By midcentury, Indian/fighting was a readily accessible discourse to narrate the fighting of World War II. It could stand in for the absences in US military doctrine, pulling together the intertwining histories of settler mythology and colonial violence. When the façade of civilized violence slipped, Indian/fighting was there to fill in the blanks.

This chapter tells the story of this simultaneous *remembering* and *forgetting*, examining the way in which Americans at the turn of the century celebrated their experience with "savage war" even as they pivoted away to a focus on "civilized war." This pattern mirrors Lisa Lowe's discussion of the "economy of affirmation and forgetting" that structures liberal narratives of freedom (and the attendant inequalities that are the conditions of possibility for those freedoms).[7] Borrowing Lowe's terminology, the currents of American militarism both *affirm* and *forget* the histories of colonial violence that are the conditions of possibility for US empire, a phenomenon particularly visible in this chapter. These debates formed part of the larger discussions over race, class, gender, sexuality, and nation that circulated in US political discourse during the early twentieth century.[8] During this period white masculinity was challenged by the shifting currents of labor unrest, women's suffrage, immigration, and imperial expansion. An aspect of this history that deserves great attention is the way in which these debates, particularly those focused on imperial violence, were repeatedly framed through references to Indian/fighting. Americans told themselves two stories: they should not be fighting Indians, and they were *good* at fighting (or fighting like) Indians. Over time these stories continued to coalesce as a shadow doctrine that could help make sense of the violence that continuously exceeded an imagined "civilized" norm.

"THE WORLD'S TUTOR IN MODERN WARFARE"

Many readers probably think about the hugely popular *Call of Duty* videogame franchise when they hear the phrase "Modern warfare." Given Indigenous people's persistent association with all things premodern, it may come as a surprise that a book written in 1901 comparing the British and American militaries called American Indians "the world's tutor in modern warfare."[9] This was a somewhat astonishing assertion that runs counter to the standard narrative of US military history. The Indian Wars are widely considered to have been a diversion from "civilized war" that made little to no doctrinal impact.[10] However, as we saw in the previous chapters, there was a moment at the end of the nineteenth century when US soldiers were increasingly aware of their expertise in the forms of warfare now variously referred to as "small wars," "irregular war," "guerrilla war," and "counterinsurgency."

Soldiers writing in the venues of informal doctrine at the turn of the century celebrated a particularly *American* approach to irregular war based on their experiences in the Indian Wars. This was certainly true in the Philippines, as the previous two chapters documented, but there were other examples that caused some Americans to compare their military history to that of the British Empire.

American observers of the South African War (or Second Boer War, 1899–1902) often characterized the conflict as a validation of the American military tradition. The conflict pitted the Dutch settler-colonial states of the South African Republic and the Orange Free State against Great Britain, whose imperial influence was growing in southern Africa. The Dutch settlers, or Boers, maintained an organized militia of "commandos," mobile guerilla units that proved highly successful against the regimented British Army.[11] The British high commissioner in South Africa supported harsh measures because the Boers "as guerillas are carrying on a resistance which is illegitimate and do not hold themselves bound by recognized rules of civilized warfare," which sounds a great deal like Custer's description of the Cheyenne in 1869.[12] Ultimately the British prevailed in the South African War, and some attributed that success to counterinsurgency measures similar to what the US was employing at the same time in the Philippines—concentration camps and the targeting of civilian populations directly with forms of collective punishment like the burning of farms.[13] One American observer even compared the British campaign to Philip Sheridan's winter war on the Cheyenne in 1868, locating the origin of Britain's increasingly indiscriminate approach in one of the more devastating campaigns the US Army undertook against Native peoples after the Civil War.[14] The conflict was a colonial and imperial war in multiple dimensions, causing both Americans and British to grapple with their evolving relationship to empire.[15]

If British successes in South Africa occasionally evoked US Army tactics in the American West and the Philippines, Boer resistance seemed to validate the other side of American warfare—the savagery, individualism, and guerilla fighting that has continuously existed in tension with "civilized" violence.[16] The British defeat at the Battle of Colenso in 1899 was called "the apotheosis of the Indian fighting style" by the *Army and Navy Journal*. Observers compared the British soldier's inability to match Boer mobility, use of cover, and sharpshooting to defeats they suffered years earlier at the hands of colonists and Native peoples in North America. Writers routinely compared the Boers to Native people, arguing that they used "exactly the tactics of the Indian of

America in the past." These comparisons extended to American colonists. Many accused the British of underestimating the individualistic guerrilla tactics of the Boers, just as they had the Americans.[17] By the late nineteenth century the much-maligned individualism of American warfare was sometimes understood as a valuable trait, a discourse that linked together the Cooper-esque frontiersman, the Indian warrior, and the militiamen of the American Revolution.

US Army Captain A. H. Russell, extolling Americans' tradition of guerilla individualism, claimed that "the Armies of all nations have now copied the freedom of our old irregular troops, learned in the Indian wars, and made it into a system."[18] According to Russell and others, it was this individualism that had helped American soldiers defeat Filipino insurgents and Boer commandos challenge the might of the British Empire. Russell may be overselling the scale on which other nations copied the American Indian/fighter, but the British did deploy their own Indian scout in the form of Frederick Russell Burnham, an American fortune seeker and Indian Wars veteran who served a variety of roles in colonial southern Africa, mostly notably as chief of scouts during the South African War. Burnham certainly carried the shadow doctrine of Indian/ fighting with him to Africa and was used by the British to counter the "savage" Boers during the South African War. Burnham was very much enmeshed in this inter-imperial understanding of savagery and civilization; he compared Africans to "red Indians" and Boer settlers to "the great Sioux chiefs who were [his] boyhood enemies," ultimately concluding that trained scouts were a necessary component of the Anglo-Saxon imperial project. Writing to Robert Baden-Powell, founder of the youth scouting movement, Burnham advocated for scout training because "it is the good strong hand of the white man above that holds this empire."[19]

The South African War prompted some observers to go even further in their comparisons between US frontier violence and the fighting in southern Africa. Archibald's *Blue Shirt and Khaki*, the aforementioned book that called Indians "the world's tutor in modern warfare," juxtaposed the rugged frontier tradition of the US soldier to the prim professionalism of the British. Archibald concluded that while the British had the advantage in logistics and funding, the Americans had the advantage in tactics. What set Americans apart, according to *Blue Shirt and Khaki*, was precisely that which US soldiers advocating for increased professionalism had long worried about: the experience of the Indian Wars. Archibald, contrasting American to British youth, argued that the first toys of American boys were guns, used in games in which they "play Indian," shooting and scalping their sisters. Archibald traces this tradition out of frontier conflicts and settler's proximity to American Indian youth, whose constant use of guns during childhood "made the North American Indian not only the most formidable fighter in the world, but also the world's tutor in modern warfare."[20]

Archibald's argument would have gratified an entire generation of US military officers. For a long time, American soldiers lived in the shadow of the professional European military tradition, anxious over their characterization as an "amateur organization, suitable for fighting frontier Indians, but useless for practical warfare," as one journalist put it.[21] Archibald's book was just one example of late nineteenth- and early twentieth-century writers who compared the imperial experience of the United States and Great Britain. These writers often cited the American experience with Native peoples and compared that history to British imperial history. For example, William Booth, founder of the Salvation Army, compared Britain's Criminal Tribes Act of 1871, which criminalized and confined a number of South Asian groups, to the methods "adopted with great success in dealing with the Red Indians."[22] In the parlance of Kipling, both were engaged in a series of "savage wars," and this discourse was one piece of larger discussions around race, gender, and empire at the turn of the century.[23] What did it mean for Euro-American nations to seize and govern colonies, and how did this encounter with difference impact hierarchies of power back home? How did ideas about race change the ways warfare was prosecuted and imagined? In these debates the Indian Wars often served as the reference point for the United States' imperial violence.

As the "world's tutor in modern warfare," Indians were the benchmark for success against an opponent waging guerilla warfare. Euro-Americans could adapt Indians' martial skills while jettisoning the savagery, and *individualism* functioned as the code word for this translation. In an analysis of the British military, US Army officer Frank Geere argued that the South African War had finally convinced the British to abandon the stifling, machine-like quality of their military training in favor of a more flexible, individualistic approach: "They learned their lesson fighting the Boers, we learned ours fighting 'frontier Indians.'"[24] Geere went on to argue that a uniquely *American* individualism is what made the US Army successful in wars with American Indians, Filipinos, and Chinese during the Boxer Rebellion, exercising "civilized humanity" in the face of "unwarranted barbarity." He even emphasized the specific, proto-counterinsurgency qualities of these conflicts, which were undertaken "with the sword in one hand and the school book in the other."[25]

With "the school of frontier Indian fighting" now closed, Geere called on these lessons in individualism to be fully incorporated into the training manuals and drill yards of the US Army, arguing that they were prerequisites to success in "the demands of civilized war."[26] The tactics of nonwhite soldiers made them savages; those same tactics, redefined as the individualism exercised by Euro-Americans, made them successful in wars with those very "savages." This was the latest example of a familiar story about frontier warfare. Anglo-American men could occupy a space adjacent to, but distinct from, Native people. They could deploy the savage violence of frontier warfare in the service of conquering that very frontier.[27] Military observers at the turn of the century inscribed this discourse into their observations of imperial warfare. However, Geere's call for the incorporation of Indian/fighting in the US military's formal doctrine went unfulfilled. Individualism and Indian/fighting would ultimately be submerged by an emphasis on "civilized war."

SAVAGERY, CIVILIZATION, AND IMPERIAL VIOLENCE

In the late nineteenth and early twentieth centuries the US military worked to update its instructional institutions for the conflicts they might face in the future. An analysis of the Infantry and Cavalry School at Fort Leavenworth in the pages of a military journal argued that "the absence of real field service in the army of late, renders it necessary to provide a simulation of it. While there is no better school for testing young officers and giving them self-confidence than the Indian scouting of former years, instruction should be on the lines of civilized warfare."[28] Army officers consistently looked past the Indian Wars to future conflicts. Calls to focus on "civilized war" tapped into a discourse that had followed the US military from the country's very beginnings. American colonists found themselves between the highly polished British military and supposedly "savage" Native nations, many of whom contested continued US expansion into their territories. Eager to justify their position as a member of the civilized European fraternity, military leaders such as George Washington balked at characterizations of the US Army as an undisciplined militia and sought to build up an Army modeled on those of Europe's empires.[29]

While some in the US military looked at the wars in the Philippines and South Africa as validation of their experience in irregular war, others cautioned against celebrating the value of these conflicts. For these writers, *irregular* did not solely describe the form of the conflict; it described their future probability as well. US Army Major James Chester singled out for specific criticism the "military prophets" claiming that the experience of the British in South Africa and the Americans in the Philippines would "change the art of war." He argued that "abnormal" campaigns were always occurring. The South African War and the Philippine-American War were both "irregular in the extreme" but that did not justify a change in US military doctrine. The danger, according to Chester, was that "irregular war drifts towards barbarism," normalizing deception, falsehood, and conquest. He cautioned that civilized warfare was plenty horrible without contaminating it with the savagery of irregular war.[30] Euro-Americans had long worried about "contamination" in the wars of colonization. Chester's criticisms illuminate the way in which their concerns shifted in the twentieth century, increasingly couched in the language of military professionalism rather than frontier mythology.[31]

Some writers explained the British Army's difficulties in the South African War by arguing that their military had been similarly contaminated by wars with "savages." In an article comparing the South African War and the Philippine-American War, the *Army and Navy Journal* criticized the British for being overly rigid in their approach to that conflict and argued that their military had experienced a sort of colonial atrophy resulting from the wars of empire: "England has not met a civilized foe in nearly half a century, and meantime her ideas of war have been demoralized by too long an experience with enemies always inferior to Europeans in weapons, in staying fighting qualities, or in both."[32] Wary of similar issues on the American side, the *Journal* advised that the British experience should offer a warning for the still-ongoing war in the Philippines. It also celebrated the American expertise in both savage and civilized war and encouraged the War Department to continue to send generals similar to General Otis to the islands able to operate in both venues: "Americans like Otis have been trained in the two schools of savage and of civilized war, and are able to quickly adapt themselves to either."[33]

In the early twentieth century both the British and Americans talked regularly about savages and savage warfare.[34] Both were fighting with racialized populations throughout their imperial holdings. Military writers on both sides of the Atlantic were quick to note that they had plenty of experience in guerilla warfare, albeit not a written record that could translate that experience from conflict to conflict. The British were faster to rectify that problem, with the emergence of prominent texts like T. Miller Maguire's *Guerilla or Partisan Warfare* and Charles Edward Callwell's *Small Wars*. A review of *Guerilla or Partisan Warfare* for the *Journal of the US Cavalry Association* noted that "of this kind of warfare, we may remark, both England and the United States have had much, and their military history, if not text books, their experience, if not their curricula, make it tolerably familiar."[35] Maguire's writings eventually fell out of circulation, but Callwell's *Small Wars* has remained a foundational text on irregular warfare, enjoying a surge of interest (no pun intended) during the War on Terror. These works compiled the British experience with small imperial wars to a degree that no American text would until the Marine Corps published *Small Wars Operations* in 1935.[36]

Callwell and other British writers, like their American counterparts, believed that war with "savages" required specific approaches.[37] Callwell was aware that these conflicts could turn nasty, with tactics like burning villages liable to shock "humanitarians."[38] He even drew on the history of US continental expansion in *Small Wars*, utilizing the Indian Wars as a frequent example in his text, calling them "the desultory warfare of the United States troops against the nomad Red Indians."[39] Like previous American writers, including Bigelow and Farrow from chapter 1, Callwell advocated offensive strategies against Indians that prioritized relentlessness, mobility, and the elimination of property and food.[40] Callwell was not the only British writer to address the "small war," and when other British writers took up the topic at the turn of the century and failed to mention American military experience, US soldiers could get angry. An American review of *Tactics for Beginners* by British soldier Cuthbert Montague De Gruythe noted with some disgust that the section on savage warfare was lacking: "The author seems never to have heard of American Indians or Moros, his lessons are not specially useful to us."[41] Much of this comparative imperial thinking took place in the informal doctrinal venues featured in this chapter, and one of the most prominent discussions concerned the use of certain kinds of ammunition.

EXPANDING BULLETS AND IMPERIAL CONNECTIONS

An early twentieth-century debate over military ethics served to highlight the sharp differentiation between savage and civilized war in both

American and British discourse. This debate was driven by the violence that accompanied Euro-American imperial expansion, which resulted in the colonization of nearly five hundred million people in the late nineteenth and early twentieth centuries.[42] It centered on the morality of firearms and the bullets they discharged, in the process revealing the inter-imperial solidarities between the United States and Great Britain at the turn of the century. These discourses bound together race and military technology. A familiar narrative about modernity explores the advances in military technology that led to the bloodbath of World War I. But in the late nineteenth and early twentieth centuries British and Americans sought to turn advances in military science to the particular needs of "savage warfare," and then proceeded to debate how those savage wars differed from civilized war.

Rapid-firing machine guns began to appear during the nineteenth century, developed by inventors Richard Gatling and Hiram Maxim.[43] Although infamous for the slaughter they unleashed on the battlefields of World War I, these early machine guns often saw a diverging kind of use. Critical appraisals of the machine gun noted their use in savage warfare in places like the Philippines, but soldiers wanted confirmation of their use in civilized war before signing off.[44] John H. Parker, who famously commanded a US Army Gatling Gun (early machine gun) unit during the Spanish-American War, delivered that endorsement in a book he published in 1899 titled *Tactical Organization and Uses of Machine Guns in the Field*. Commenting on the history of the gun, Parker noted that they "were used in savage warfare by several countries with good results, but all nations waited for the test of civilized war before adopting them as an integral arm of the service."[45] One of those examples of savage warfare cited by Parker was the Bannock-Shoshone campaign of 1878, where he describes cavalry tactics that utilize machine guns appropriate "in either Indian or civilized warfare." Another early machine gun, the Hotchkiss Gun, was used in the massacre at Wounded Knee in 1890, a tragedy many American settlers considered to be the end of their continental "savage wars."[46]

Parker believed the machine gun suitable for both savage and civilized war. Reviewers of his book were not so sure. A writer in the *Cavalry Journal* noted that Parker's sole example of "civilized war" was the Spanish-American War, the other examples being "campaigns against irregular troops or savages, viz: the Turcomans, the American Indians, and the Dervishes of the Soudan." In critiquing Parker's book, the reviewer wrote that "the machine gun has been eminently useful in campaigns of this character against barbarians—either fearless horsemen who fight in the open, superstitious fanatics who attack in dense masses, or savages ignorant of the value of intrenchments. . . . But it would seem that in the offensive use of machine guns in civilized warfare, the writer allows his enthusiasm to run away with his good judgment."[47] The lines drawn between civilized and savage war resulted in a reticence about the machine gun that sits awkwardly alongside its prominent use in the major conflicts of the twentieth century. The gun's performance against "savages" was simply not enough to earn a universal endorsement, at least from this reviewer.

Debates over the utility of machine guns were marginal in comparison to the controversies over "expanding" or hollow-point bullets at the turn of the century. Firearm technologies advanced rapidly during the nineteenth century. Over time, single-shot muzzle-loaded guns were replaced with increasingly sophisticated rifles that were deadlier, more accurate, and could fire repeatedly without reloading. Massive armies were outfitted with these new guns, and colonial powers failed to maintain a monopoly on the new technologies as Native warriors raced across the North American plains with the latest repeating rifles.[48] Advances in ordnance kept pace during this period, and by the 1860s Russia was experimenting with exploding bullets, which prompted the 1868 Declaration of St. Petersburg banning their use in war.[49] Bullet calibers continued to get smaller with the invention of full metal jackets, and eventually a preoccupation with "stopping power" emerged as a concern, particularly in the colonial outposts of the British Empire. In the late 1890s, experiments at the Dum-Dum Ordnance Factory in India resulted in a bullet with exposed lead at the tip. This caused the bullet to "mushroom," or expand upon impact, opening up deadlier wounds in the body. British troops began using the bullet in India and Africa, where it gave "the necessary stopping power" against "savage" opponents.[50]

Discussion of the new expanding bullets by both the Americans and the British was explicitly racialized. British imperialists spoke of the need for "stopping power" when dealing with "savage tribes." Members of the British Army Medical Service concurred, writing that modified bullets were required when facing a "fanatical Asiatic" and that "no purely humanitarian sentiments, therefore, need interfere with the use of bullets of a destructive nature by civilised nations when at war with people of this class."[51] Their American colleagues seemed to agree. Writing in the *British Medical Journal*, US Surgeon-Major-General J. B. Hamilton detailed the history of the "Dum-Dum" bullet. He noted that the bullet was developed for its "stopping power" and that in "European warfare this was of comparatively little consequence, as "civilised man is much more susceptible to injury than savages. As a rule when a white man is wounded he has had enough, and is quite ready to drop out of the ranks and go to the rear; but the savage, like the tiger, is not so impressionable, and will go on fighting even when desperately wounded."[52] Other writers in the *British Medical Journal* echoed this assessment, noting that non-expanding bullets had been "found to be ineffective in stopping rushes of such determined fighters as we have recently encountered in both India and Egypt."[53] This was a technology understood to be linked to the race war of empire.

The debate over expanding bullets came to a head at the Hague Convention of 1899, an international conference on the laws of war. At the convention, rules were adopted that drew inspiration, in part, from the Lieber Code, a document that itself differentiated between civilized and savage warfare.[54] One provision specifically banned the use of expanding bullets, targeted primarily at the British "dum-dum" bullet. The British delegation opposed the rule, arguing that there was "a difference in war between civilized nations and that against savages" that necessitated the use of an expanding bullet.[55] The proposal was ultimately adopted by all but the British and US delegations. Captain William Crozier of the US delegation proposed a more general amendment to the original proposal that would ban "the use of bullets which inflict wounds of useless cruelty." Crozier felt the original proposal was too narrowly targeted at the British dum-dum. This proposal was rejected. In his report on the conference, Crozier was careful to note that his dissatisfaction with the initial proposal should not signal the United States' opposition to "a proposition of humanitarian intent," and that the United States had no plans to adopt an expanding bullet in the future.[56]

Despite Crozier's insistence that the US military had no plans to adopt an expanding bullet, there were some Americans who advocated for its use in the Philippines. This was, after all, America's latest savage war that ran parallel to Britain's imperial conflicts at the turn of the century. And like their British counterparts, American soldiers advocated for better "stopping power" for their wars with "savages." Major S. D. Rockenbach, a leader of the Philippine Scouts, claimed that sensitivity to the shock of being struck by a bullet increased as the "culture" of the individual became increasingly civilized. When discussing his preferred ordnance in the Philippines, he noted that "a wound that may stop and incapacitate for further aggressive action a civilized man, may only increase the fury and efforts of a savage to destroy his enemy."[57] It is clear that the differentiation between savage and civilized war in the early twentieth century cut across multiple categories, from the legal, to the cultural, to the scientific. Soldiers like Rockenbach viewed these technologies of savage warfare as a necessary aspect of empire.

Rockenbach published an article speculating about different ammunition types and their relative "stopping power," and issued a warning to those who would complain about the ethics of savage warfare: "Self-preservation is the first law of nature. Against the savage with kris, head knife, spear or arrow, the so-called humanitarian should either come and practice his theories, or keep quiet; should he come without police protection (a cool protector with a stopping weapon) the theorist will succumb to the fittest."[58] Writing in the aftermath of the controversies over US atrocities in the Philippines, Rockenbach's frustration is palpable in his dismissal of "humanitarians." And while the reference to the "kris," a dagger used by Moro warriors, places Rockenbach's savage war in the Philippines, the reference to spear or arrow cannot help but evoke the Indian Wars. These complaints fit neatly alongside similar critiques leveled at "humanitarians" in the nineteenth century by soldiers and settlers in the American West. Settlers in particular felt victimized by a meddlesome federal government and the reformers that sought to soften what they viewed as a struggle between the civilized and savage where leniency had no place.[59]

Rumors even floated around that US troops in the Philippines had been equipped with, or were modifying, their bullets into expanding ammunition. Consider Henry Labouchère's satire of Kipling's poem "The White Man's Burden," titled "A Brown Man's Burden." In one stanza Labouchère writes:

> Pile on the brown man's burden;
> And if ye rouse his hate,
> Meet his old-fashioned reasons
> With Maxims up to date.
> With shells and dumdum bullets
> A hundred times make plain
> The brown man's loss must ever
> Imply the white man's gain.[60]

Labouchère was a British anti-imperialist who sharply criticized the South African War and the treatment of the Boers, and his poem is a clear signal that dum-dum bullets circulated among the comparative imperial discourse of the United States and Britain at the turn of the century.[61] These debates about dum-dum bullets also entered the controversy over US conduct in the Philippines. During congressional hearings before the United States Senate Committee on the Philippines in 1902, Richard O'Brien testified that he witnessed torture, sexual violence, and other atrocities while serving in the Twenty-Sixth Infantry Regiment. O'Brien had first made the allegations in an interview with *Irish World*, and during his testimony he accused American officers of using the water cure on captives, misappropriating supply funds, and issuing orders to "take no prisoners."[62]

In perhaps the most surprising part of his testimony, O'Brien claimed he had been issued dum-dum bullets. While unsure of whether they were expanding or explosive in nature, O'Brien claimed they inflicted abnormally grievous wounds, and he had seen them "hit a man in the back of the ear and lift the whole of his head off" and also "a man hit in the abdomen and it would lay his whole front bare." He also claimed they did not bear the same markings as their standard-issue ammunition. O'Brien brought several of these suspicious bullets to this second day of testimony, and they were examined by William Crozier, the Army's chief of ordnance and a US representative at the Hague Convention in 1899. Readers will recall that Crozier had objected to the specifics (if not the spirit) of the resolution that banned Britain's dum-dum bullet. In the hearings, Crozier examined O'Brien's bullets and declared them standard issue, neither exploding nor expanding. Crozier conceded that if tampered with by removing metal from the tip, a bullet could be turned into an expanding bullet, and noted that he had heard rumors that explosive bullets were being used by US soldiers in the Philippines, Cuba, and China, but he explained away those rumors as people mistaking the "pop" of a gun passing near their head for an explosion.[63] Crozier's explanation was accepted by the senators at the hearing.[64]

In addition to Crozier's rebuttal, O'Brien's other "explosive" allegations came under criticism. His answers to senators' questions became increasingly convoluted, and some of his claims were repudiated by other witnesses with documented evidence. One of the witnesses who testified in rebuttal to O'Brien was Bishop James M. Thoburn, a missionary who spent decades in Asia. Explaining the spread of American empire as the will of God, Thoburn was challenged by Senator Thomas Patterson, who asked whether God led "great powers to subjugate "semi-civilized people," later asking, "If the British shall in the end subjugate the Boers, will that, in your opinion, be done in the Providence of God?" This exchange angered other senators and derailed the hearing, and after the interruption Senator Beveridge cut short the testimony. The exchange is striking, and it reveals, once more, the imperial connections that were envisioned (sometimes controversially) between the United States and Great Britain, and the way in which those comparisons circulated through ideas about savage war.

O'Brien was ultimately charged with perjury for his testimony, although he maintained his innocence and went on to a successful career as an actor.[65] Crozier continued to insist that no expanding dum-dum or exploding bullets had been manufactured by the United States or distributed to its soldiers. And yet the persistence of these rumors highlights the parallel discussions around race, warfare, and empire that were taking place in the United States and Britain at the turn of the century. Many agreed that "savage war" required particular technologies suited to an opponent's racial differences.

References to "stopping power" continued to show up in the US military's sources for informal doctrine in the early 1900s, notably with regard to the lingering conflict in the Philippines. By 1902, much of the conflict in the Philippines had subsided outside of the Muslim-majority islands in the south, Mindanao, Jolo, and Sulu. There the Moros continued to resist the imposition of US authority in conflicts that perpetuated the references to Native Americans, the exoticism perhaps exaggerated by the addition of Islam.[66] Just as they had in the nineteenth century with regard to Native peoples, American soldiers and politicians spoke of a "Moro question," with, again, some predicting it would "be settled in the same manner as the Indian question, that is by gradual extermination."[67] Moro fighters, called "juramentados," became another example of the racialized fighter whose violence challenged the norms of civilized war. Wielding swords and fighting in close-quarters, Moro warriors became another "savage" that required particular kinds of colonial ordnance. A writer for the *Chicago Tribune* noted that American officers worried their Krag–Jørgensen rifles would "prove of little avail in stopping a headlong rush of crazed juramentados. They advocate arming the troops in Sulu with Springfield rifles or furnishing them with the dum-dum bullet as absolutely necessary in a warfare against fanatics."[68] Clearly, US soldiers and the journalists who told their stories were scared of the abilities of Moro fighters, a fear driven, in part, by a racialized belief that they would refuse to stop if hit by a bullet, a fear that ran parallel to the fears of British colonial troops.

American soldiers in the Philippines criticized the restrictions on expanding bullets adopted at The Hague. In an article titled "The Stopping Power of a Bullet," First Lieutenant G. C. Lewis complained about the use of the smaller caliber .38 revolver with reference to the fighting with Moros. Similarly to the British, Lewis drew a sharp contrast between "savages" and "civilized men," particularly with regard to their differential abilities to withstand wounds. He wrote that "even the most sanguine anti-imperialist should pause at the prospect of an argument with an energetic juramentado" when equipped with inadequate firepower." Lewis even criticized The Hague directly, writing that "the .38, conceived in a spasm of humanitarianism, designed by a Hague peace conference as an initial step in disarmament, required to be carried in a holster, which is a source of satisfaction to only the juramentado and the anti-imperialist, has proven a bloody trial to all troops equipped with it."[69]

This heightened rhetoric about savage Moros likely contributed to the severity of some of the US Army's conduct during the occupation of the Moro provinces. The most dramatic example was the battle at the Bud Dajo volcano on the island of Sulu in 1906, the same year Lieutenant Lewis complained about the inadequacy of small caliber bullets for stopping "juramentados." Leonard Wood, who twenty years earlier played a key role in the final surrender of Goyahkla (Geronimo), was military governor of Moro Province at the time. Wood was a proponent of a harsh military policy toward those Moros unwilling to accept US authority, many of whom gathered at Bud Dajo. In early March, eight hundred US soldiers marched on the volcano and over the course of four days killed approximately six hundred to one thousand Moros, including women and children, in a slaughter one US soldier described as "ghastly." Machine guns proved especially deadly in the fighting.[70]

The killing at Bud Dajo became a controversy, and pictures of dead Moro men, women, and children, disturbingly similar to pictures of the aftermath of the Wounded Knee massacre in 1890, were published in the United States. President Roosevelt defended Leonard Wood against the criticism, and the occupation of Moro Province continued.[71] US soldiers in Moro Province continued to dismiss criticism of their conduct and they did it using the now familiar reference to continental expansion. As Captain C. C. Smith put it: "Those who do not know the Moro or his country should be sparing in their criticism of an officer who with his party falls into an ambuscade. The Apache Indian in the old days of Arizona was not so difficult to come up with and fight as is the Mohammedan fanatic of the Philippines."[72] In short, this was savage war.

Critics simply did not understand—just as critics of the Indian/fighting Army had failed to understand—that savages required a particular form of violence.

"SAVAGERY MUST CEASE"

Despite all this talk of savage war, the United States' colonial conflicts were viewed as relics of the past that would be superseded by an increasingly civilized world. Charles Woodruff, a surgeon in the Army, published an extended study of the supposed racial inferiority of "Malays," or Filipinos, that made this point explicit. According to Woodruff, "Acts which we abhor are perfectly normal for these Malay people, on account of their savage brain." Woodruff went on to claim that "the welfare of civilized people demands that savagery must cease throughout the world. It must be safe to travel or do business wherever our needs compel us to go, and all people must abide by civilized rules, whether they like it or not."[73] Woodruff's views were not unique, and the preponderance of these ideas, particularly from those in the military, should indicate that "civilized" and "savage" were not neutral descriptors for the form of combat, but were bound up in the ideological baggage of empire. This was baggage that Americans increasingly hoped to transcend as they modernized their armed forces.

In the first decade of the twentieth century many Americans worried the country had fallen behind the rest of the "civilized world" in the development of tactics, weapons, mobilization, the maintenance of a national guard, and other key aspects of militarization. The *Army and Navy Journal* cautioned that "the other civilized nations of the world have recognized the absolute necessity of keeping pace with the advances in military science, and we alone are laggards in this respect."[74] Younger officers such as Arthur Wagner and John Bigelow Jr. published books and manuals intended to correct these deficiencies, and the pages of military newspapers and journals during this period were full of discussions about the need for reform in American military institutions. Military ideas were increasingly standardized, and there was a shift away from belief in an innate military "genius" toward a conviction that military skills could be imparted by an institution.[75] As the wave of professionalization crested, there were some who held the Indian Wars and other "savage" conflicts responsible for impeding the development of a modern military. These conflicts might have "played havoc" with the judgment of younger officers tasked with defeating enemies like

Filipino insurgents, leaving them unprepared for the realities of modern warfare against a "civilized" enemy.[76]

This was particularly (and unsurprisingly) true for the cavalry. In 1912, a panel of high-ranking Army officers discussed the need to update the organization of the cavalry for modern warfare. These included men like J. Franklin Bell and Leonard Wood, veterans of both the Indian Wars and the Philippine-American War. The various officers argued that the US cavalry was badly antiquated relative to Europe's modern armies, a consequence of Europe's "long experience" in civilized war, something the US had not fought since the Civil War. They advocated a reorganization of the US Army's cavalry regiments along "modern lines" that would make it more suitable for future "civilized" wars, with some holding up the recent Russo-Japanese War as a model. Several of the officers placed the blame for the cavalry's antiquated organization on the Indian Wars. They argued that the spread-out frontier posts required a proliferation of junior officers able to oversee all these small detachments. However, the organization of this antiquated "Indian police" was no longer relevant to modern warfare.[77] In his concluding remarks to the panel of officers, Captain Charles Fenton argues that "the days of the Indian wars are passed . . . and there would seem to be no further need for maintaining an obsolete troop organization that has long been discarded by modern armies."[78]

The push to reorganize the Army in preparation for civilized warfare crested in the years leading up to World War I. In 1912, the War Department issued the *Report on the Organization of the Land Forces of the United States*. This document outlined a plan for meeting the "emergency of modern war," focusing on the organization, distribution, and size of the US military, which was the smallest of the global powers.[79] The authors argue that the political conditions of the United States had fundamentally changed since the 1890s, but that the US military had failed to keep pace with these changes:

> Until quite recently our people have been almost wholly occupied with the task of overrunning our continental possessions and taking full possession of them. The Regular Army has been the forerunner of this movement, and has been organized, distributed, and trained for the requirements thus involved. This has kept the bulk of the Regular Army scattered in small units in our western country. Conquest and settlement have been fairly completed now, however, and the civil authorities are capable of maintaining orderly conditions as well in one part of our country as in another.[80]

With frontier duties now finished, the military had to prepare for a world depicted as sliding toward inevitable global conflict. The document makes clear that these imagined future conflicts will look nothing like the Indian Wars, the occupation of the Philippines, or Pershing's recent expedition into Mexico.[81] These would be modern wars, fought with modern weapons such as heavy artillery and machine guns. They required a modern military, updated beyond that of a frontier police force.[82]

In his annual report the following year, Secretary of War Henry L. Stimson argued even more explicitly that the Indian Wars and the counterinsurgency campaign in the Philippines had impaired the military's development. In particular, the Army had been "virtually a number of scattered groups of constabulary rather than an integral organization, which prevents the proper training and teamwork of a national army."[83] Stimson and other military officials would continue to advocate for reforms to the Army's reserve system up until US involvement in World War I made an expansion of the military's size a necessity. In 1913, Army Chief of Staff Leonard Wood worried that "long service in petty operations of a police character" had left the US military woefully unprepared for future conflicts: "We must remember that we have never yet been engaged in war with a first-class power prepared for war under conditions in any way approaching the conditions of military preparedness which exist among civilized nations to-day."[84] Somewhat ironically, Wood voiced this concern when discussing the need to update the cavalry, itself an increasingly antiquated branch of the Army, but similar concerns about preparedness to face a "first-class power" were raised by his successor, William Watherspoon, the following year.[85]

As US military officers observed the beginning of World War I, any celebration of the Army's history with irregular warfare faded away. Heavy artillery and machine guns, the weapons of modern warfare, became the focus.[86] The rising pressure to reform the US military's structure resulted in the National Defense Act of 1916, which made many of the demanded improvements to the National Guard while expanding the Guard and the Army. President Woodrow Wilson encouraged Congress to pass other laws that further militarized the United States on the eve of entering World War I. Chief of Staff Hugh Scott had pushed for these reforms over the objection of dubious politicians who doubted whether the United States needed a large military.[87] Scott expanded on the sort of manifest-destiny rhetoric of the nineteenth century, arguing that the

United States was an "enlightened civilization," the most advanced nation in the world and the caretaker of "alien races" overseas. Somewhat paradoxically, this colonial obligation meant that the US had a duty to bring its military up to date for civilized war, despite the savagery of "unenlightened races." Colonial expansion had made the US a world power, skilled in savage war; that reality made it incumbent on them to modernize the military to maintain their position as a global leader.[88]

The following year, the United States would enter formally into World War I. Reflecting on the massive mobilization that resulted, Secretary of War Newton Baker wrote that the United States was operating under a new, modern paradigm: "It was understood at the outset that war under modern conditions involved not only larger armies than the United States had ever assembled, but also more far-reaching modifications of our ordinary industrial processes and wider departures from the peacetime activities of the people."[89] This was a paradigm shift. It was the first step toward a military buildup that would intensify during World War II and further cement the US as a global power. The US military's focus would be on the modern, and there was no room for Indians in the modern. This did not mean, however, that there was no room for Indians in the modern *imagination*. The very ideologies that constructed an idea of "modern" or "civilized war" helped to refigure Native peoples into a fluid military discourse that would find increasing mobility as the twentieth century passed. As Americans turned a blind eye to the concerns of existing Native nations, "Indians" proliferated in the imaginations of soldiers all over the world, including those who served in World War I.

INDIAN COUNTRY OVERSEAS

For all the emphasis on "civilized war," World War I carried over a handful of imaginative resonances of the Indian Wars. US troops charged the German trenches yelling "war whoops," the stereotypical call of Native warriors.[90] Canadian troops, themselves no strangers to histories of colonialism, carried out similar displays. During the Battle of Flers–Courcelette, a handful of Canadian soldiers reportedly got drunk and began yelling "red Indian war cries and other wild whoops." German soldiers advancing over No Man's Land "suddenly heard frightful bloodcurdling sounds. It was as if the tribes of the Blackfeet had come out upon the warpath yelling as they swung their tomahawks and dancing round with scalps of their victims." The news article describes the

Germans turning and running as if "all the devils of hell were upon them."[91] This story is not the only example of the fear German troops held specifically for Native soldiers. German popular culture had cultivated a widespread romanticization of American Indians, particularly due to the writing of prolific author Karl May, and German soldiers worried about facing them on the battlefield and sometimes specifically targeted them with sniper fire. One US officer even suggested nighttime raids be made in full Native regalia.[92]

Thousands of Native soldiers served in the American Expeditionary Force during World War I even though most were not US citizens. They were fully integrated into Army units unlike African Americans soldiers, who continued to serve in segregated units. American propaganda trumpeted the martial value of Native soldiers, and tribes renewed ceremonies that had long been repressed by the American government, particularly those related to warfare.[93] Native soldiers enlisted for a variety of reasons: a strong warrior tradition, patriotism, a belief that the war would preserve global democracy, pressure from Bureau of Indian Affairs officials, the encouragement of organizations like the Society of American Indians, the opportunity to escape harsh economic conditions, and a desire for travel and adventure. Some enlisted to defend their treaty rights; for example, the Iroquois independently declared war on Germany, and Haudenosaunee people enlisted in large numbers on both sides of the US-Canadian border.

Native soldiers performed a variety of roles, including the transmission of messages in their Native languages. Many experienced a particular sort of racism in Europe that drew on long-standing depictions of Indians as uniquely suited to certain kinds of warfare.[94] They were often assigned dangerous scouting and reconnaissance missions, for example. This meant that the wartime accomplishments of Native soldiers were typically overshadowed by racial stereotypes.[95] One correspondent reported that "the American Indians in France quickly adjusted themselves to the conditions of the country. They soon became just as cunning as in their native haunts."[96] Lieutenant John Eddy attempted to organize all-Native scout battalions. He distributed a questionnaire throughout the service that asked officers about the performance of Native soldiers. The responses included racialized ideas about the physical attributes of Indian men, their supposed "bloodthirst" and "inherent bravery," and their ability as scouts.[97]

Native soldiers in Europe thus were often viewed through the frontier mythologies that had characterized nineteenth-century perceptions of Indians.[98] These resonances of frontier violence had the power to shape both US and German perceptions of Native soldiers during World War I, and in turn, to shape their tactical responses, whether that meant deploying Ojibwe men as nighttime scouts, or tasking German snipers with specifically targeting anyone that looked "Indian."[99] This linkage between racial perceptions and tactics would continue throughout the twentieth century, as Indian country became an ever-expanding battlefield on which America waged war.

"IT IS ALL A MEMORY NOW"

By the mid-twentieth century the Indian Wars were a fleeting presence in US military discourse. Such "irregular" concerns were overshadowed by the conventional warfare of an increasingly mechanized world.[100] There was still the occasional mention of Indian/fighting in informal doctrine. In 1932, Marine Corps Captain Maurice Holmes published an analysis of Custer's defeat at the Little Bighorn that compared the war on the northern plains to the many interventions, police actions, and wars waged by the US Marine Corps in Central America and the Caribbean in the early twentieth century. Holmes identifies many similarities between the Indian and the "Banana Native," and advised Marines to draw a number of lessons from Indian fighters, most of which dealt with overcoming the interference of civilian administrators (Indian Agents and "Bamboo Americans").[101] Similarly, US Army Major E. S. Johnson critiqued the Army's *Field Service Regulations*, a core manual, as outdated and narrow. He worried specifically that the emphasis on civilized war was resulting in blinders that obscured the continuous existence of small wars relative to the large conflicts that were the Army's focus: "Our *Field Service Regulations* was designed for war against a modern opponent, on the assumption that this would suffice for any minor emergency. Unfortunately, this theory is not correct. Braddock's defeat, our Indian wars, the British South African War, and many other examples testify to the contrary."[102] Braddock's infamous defeat, the Indian Wars, and the South African War here serve as another cautionary tale about forgetting the lessons learned in irregular warfare. Johnson directly confronted perhaps the greatest contradiction of the US Army's focus on modern warfare: viewing large-scale conflicts as the norm, when, in fact, these conflicts were the exception. Small wars, interventions, counterinsurgencies, policing operations—these sorts of mission far outnumbered the large-scale conflicts envisioned whenever a twentieth-century military theorist talked about "modern war" or "civilized war."

The mythologies of cowboys and Indians were far more visible: on baseball jerseys, movie screens, and the games of children. An institution called the Order of the Indian Wars played an important role in transitioning frontier soldiers from fighters to mythmakers. Founded in 1896 by Colonel B. J. D. Irwin, the Order of the Indian Wars served to "perpetuate the memories of the services rendered by the military forces of the United States in their conflicts and wars against hostile Indians within the territory or jurisdiction of the United States."[103] A military society with elaborate ceremonies and traditions, the organization met yearly to induct new members, honor those that had passed away, and to listen to papers delivered on relevant historical topics. The tone of the meetings was largely nostalgic; nowhere in the record of proceedings does the discussion situate the Indian Wars in relation to twentieth-century conflict. In his address at the 1921 meeting, Charles King declared that "it is all a memory now, but what a memory to cherish!"

Although the order continues into the present in a reduced form, the 1941 meeting was the last in which a major address was given and published. As recorded in the proceedings,

> Before they were to meet in session again—and none knew the next meeting was to be the last—the United States was to enter into World War II after an attack on Pearl Harbor, Hawaii. The end of an era had been long in coming. The Indian fighter was no longer the subject of hero worship by the young, of admiration by the middle-aged and of envy by his peers. The remaining Order of Indian Wars membership—by virtue of a sneak attack—became *ancient* history, and no longer *just* history. . . . It was an unfitting death of an image so long loved, admired and respected by Americans.[104]

For the Order, the Indian Wars were the stuff of nostalgia and myth, the translation of the real experiences of the Order's members into a heroic narrative about US history. The tone is almost petulant, the attack on Pearl Harbor becoming the final nail in the coffin of public interest in the lingering nostalgia for the frontier, the racialized "sneak attack" refigured as a hallmark of Japanese aggression rather than Indian treachery. For the Order, an era was over, but the Indian Wars had penetrated most aspects of American popular culture and were still present in the military, baked into the language of conflict in persistent ways that came out with increasing frequency during World War II.

CHAPTER 5

Fighting Indian Style

A WAR BONNET FOR MACARTHUR

In early 1943, at a hotel on the Upper West Side of Manhattan, the Indian Confederation of America honored General Douglas MacArthur, Supreme Commander of Allied Forces in the Southwest Pacific Area, as the "greatest example of an American warrior in 1942."[1] In a ceremony, Mohawk ironworker Paul Horn presented a feathered war bonnet to Lieutenant General Hugh Drum, who accepted on MacArthur's behalf. The ICA was a Native American cultural organization that provided support for Native people in New York City, particularly newcomers trying to find work in the huge metropolis.[2] During World War II, hundreds of Native people worked defense industry jobs in the city. Many, including ICA leaders such as Horn, worked at the Brooklyn Naval Yard where Mohawk men continued their long tradition of iron working. With the honoring of General MacArthur, the ICA was continuing a tradition that began the previous year when they awarded a similar war bonnet to Soviet leader Joseph Stalin for the Red Army's successful repulsion of the German advance at the end of 1941, and continued the following year when they gave the same award to General Dwight D. Eisenhower.[3]

General MacArthur cabled his appreciation for the honor, noting that "many successful methods of warfare in use today are based on those the Indian warrior evolved centuries ago." He went on to remark that the tactics of Indian warfare had been applied "in basic principle to the vast jungle-covered reaches of the present war." Newspaper coverage of the ceremony commended the ICA for their choice, noting that it was "no small honor" to be designated as a warrior by American Indians.[4] It is not surprising that MacArthur and the press appreciated the award, given American culture's strong association of Native peoples with military prowess. MacArthur's second claim—that US troops island-hopping across the Pacific toward Japan were employing "American Indian fighting tactics"—is more interesting. During World War II, Americans in and out of the military advocated for Indian/fighting as a counter to Axis Power aggression. This was particularly true for soldiers engaged in irregular warfare—the commandos, rangers, and operatives that were the precursor to the modern-day special forces.

MacArthur's message to the ICA was not the only time during World War II that someone claimed US troops were engaged in Indian/fighting. On the night of August 14, 1944, members of the joint US-Canadian First Special Service Force stealthily paddled rubber boats to the shore of two small islands off the southern coast of France. Their mission was to capture German defensive positions that could interfere with Operation Dragoon, the Allied invasion of southern France that took place two months after the invasion of Normandy (D-Day). On one of the islands, Levant, the soldiers scaled steep cliffs and captured 850 German soldiers, although the expected German artillery were just wooden decoys. On the other island, Port-Cros, German resistance lasted a couple days before they too surrendered. The capture of these islands helped the Allies gain access to ports through which supplies could be moved into France, supplies that contributed to Germany's eventual downfall.[5]

Newspaper coverage of the operation took on a more imaginative tone. The *New York Times* reported that the soldiers had reverted to "Indian-style warfare" in their stealthy movements on the island. Faces camouflaged, the "black-face commandos" clambered up the cliffs, moved silently through dense underbrush, and took the Germans by surprise.[6] The newspaper seemed to argue that the Allied soldiers had tapped into a uniquely North American mode of violence to defeat the Germans: the history of the Indian and the Indian/fighter. *Both* the Indian and the Indian-fighter, the vagueness of "Indian-style warfare" simultaneously signaling Native military skill and the Euro-Americans who conquered them. A closer look at the soldiers' uniforms would have confirmed that lineage. Their shoulder patch was a red arrowhead, powerfully evocative of Native warriors. Similarly, for their branch service insignia the First Special Service Force had inherited the crossed arrows worn by US Army Indian Scouts, those Native soldiers who had served in the Army in the late nineteenth and early twentieth centuries.[7] These Americans (and Canadians) in World War II were, according to the *New York Times* and many others, redeploying the history of North American colonial violence as an antidote to twentieth-century fascist aggression.

The global upheavals that brought the United States into World War II were followed by a massive mobilization that transformed America's military. World War I introduced the horrors of mechanized modern warfare, with its emphasis on combined operations that integrated infantry soldiers with deadly, oil-fueled machines on land, sea, and air.[8] These lessons were haltingly incorporated during the interwar period, and with greater intensity once the United States entered the war in late 1941.[9] This revolution of tanks, bombers, and aircraft carriers did not, however, drive Indian/fighting out of US military discourse. During World War II, "Indian country" was increasingly deployed as a signifier for enemy territory by soldiers. Similarly, both civilians and soldiers called for the US military to embrace Indian/fighting as a particularly *American* way of war. For some, the challenges of World War II demanded a return to the Indian/fighter, a catch-all for the harder-to-quantify qualities many believed made soldiers effective: toughness, elusiveness, and individualism, qualities contrasting the mindless fascist automatons portrayed in US propaganda like the War Department's *Why We Fight* film series.

Americans now began to reconfigure the symbolic meaning invested in colonial violence into a blueprint for the modern soldier. They talked a bit less about savages, exceptions, and states of quasi-war, relative to other conflicts, instead focusing on honing the abilities of individual soldiers to meet the Axis war machine. Proponents of Indian/fighting during World War II combined the martial prowess of the Indian and the Indian fighter. They also combined the freedom so intrinsic to American identity: the mythologized freedom of the Native that tragically fell away, and the settler freedom that replaced it. Such a soldier would be able to defeat fascist aggression and Japanese imperialism. The cultural meanings invested in Indian/fighting as a blueprint for the ideal soldier compensated for the lack of doctrinal continuity between the Indian Wars and World War II. This chapter thus demonstrates the ability of discourse to influence the meanings attached to violence in ways that exceed strict definitions of military doctrine.

INDIAN COUNTRY FOREIGN AND DOMESTIC

World War II was a global conflict, and narratives of Indian/fighting were similarly global. They traveled with the Native Americans who enlisted, with the soldiers who referred to enemy territory as "Indian country," and with the journalists who captured readers' imaginations with references to the violence of earlier conflicts. In a war identified with crumbling empires and new totalitarianisms, invoking these resonances allowed Americans to reframe the violence onto familiar terrain. In a curious bit of discursive colonialism, the war was in some ways Americanized *through* Native Americans, both their participation in actual fighting and through language such as "Indian country."[10]

References to Indian country could be found in both major theaters of the war. US Navy officers referred to Japanese-patrolled waters in the Pacific as "Indian country," and journalist Allan Nevins characterized American hatred for the Japanese as "emotions forgotten since our most savage Indian wars." The Patrol Torpedo (PT) boats the Navy used in the Pacific Theater were even dubbed the "Indian fighter of the sea" for their agile work intercepting enemy ships, often at night.[11] The Pacific theater of World War II was characterized by a brutality that seemed to exceed, for many observers, the other campaigns US soldiers participated in. Racial animosity, on the part of both Americans and the Japanese, drove some of this violence. References in the Pacific Theater to Indian/fighting, the United States' first and most lasting experience with race war, are perhaps unsurprising given this context, although clearly racial, ethnic, and religious hatred was not confined to the Pacific Theater of World War II.[12]

The race war in the Pacific emerged domestically in the United States through the internment of Japanese and Japanese Americans. As we have seen throughout this book, the architectures of US colonialism are consistently repurposed in the service of new imperial ventures in ways that erode the boundary between the foreign and the domestic.[13] This was true during World War II, with internment camps taking the form of what Juliet Nebolon calls "settler militarism," the mutual investment in land acquisition and colonial dispossession shared by settler colonialism and military expansion, each process sometimes obscuring the other.[14] Many of the Japanese internment camps were located on Indian reservations, land previously used to confine the Native peoples now fighting to assert the sovereignty of their homelands.[15] These "domestic" camps were joined by a transnational network of bases, internment camps, and prisoner of war camps throughout the Pacific, an important reminder that the internment of civilians was not confined to the continental United States.[16]

The injustice of the Japanese internment reprised the appropriation of Native land, and the infrastructure of ongoing US colonialism played a role in enabling it. Schools in the camps were staffed by individuals who had worked as teachers and missionaries on Indian reservations. The Office of Indian Affairs supervised thousands of internees. John Collier, head of Indian Affairs, and other bureaucrats sought to "guide" Japanese internees toward a more democratic political identity, citing as precedent their efforts to "uplift" Native Americans and integrate them into Anglo-American society.[17] Japanese internment was built on the history of US colonialism, embodied most clearly in the career of Dillon S. Myer, who served as director of the War Relocation Authority that oversaw the camps. After his stint as director of the WRA, Myer ran the Bureau of Indian Affairs during the 1950s and pushed the catastrophic "termination" policy, which attacked tribal sovereignty while accelerating the loss of tribal land and resources.[18] Myer's BIA deployed the techniques of repression honed during Japanese internment to disrupt tribal efforts to resist termination.[19] Japanese internment, enabled by US colonialism, thus contributed to the dispossession of Native American lands in the war's aftermath as US government bureaucrats continued to refine their approach to the governing of racialized populations. World War II impacted a variety of "Indian countries," foreign and domestic.

References to "Indian country" and Indian/fighting were also invoked in the European theater.[20] An issue of the military magazine *Yank: The Army Weekly*, reported that "there were so many roving bands of Germans loose in the area that it was like running the stagecoach through Arizona in Apache days."[21] The image of Indian warriors menacing a stagecoach remained a potent image of threat in the mid-twentieth century, exaggerated by the popularity of western films, most obviously John Ford's 1939 film *Stagecoach*, which made the omnipresent threat posed by Apache people the central focus of the film.[22] In the European theater of the war, German soldiers replaced the Apache as the threatening presence, rendering visible the increasing mobility of "Indian country." Some of World War II's biggest events were narrated through US colonial mythologies. One journalist described the aftermath of the D-Day landings as "a 20th century version of the winning of the west." American tanks were the "bluecoats of old Indian war times" hounding the Nazis through "Indian territory." The lawlessness of German-occupied Europe was given meaning through these comparisons, and the article looked forward to a future when the "covered wagon" truck convoys would no longer need protection while moving through German "Apache country."[23]

These resonances were not confined to American usage. Thanks to Hollywood, dime novels, and other forms of popular culture, European soldiers once more imagined themselves to be in "Indian country," much as they had in World War I. A German newspaper article on aerial reconnaissance from 1944 explained that a skillful pilot "employs the tactics of the Indian" when engaged in a stealth mission.[24] German battalion commanders, reflecting on the invasion of the Soviet Union, argued that the conflict relied increasingly on stealth maneuvers, tactics in which Red Army soldiers apparently excelled: "The fact must be emphasized that in this Indian-type warfare the Russians were far superior to the Germans. They were truly masters in devising means of camouflage."[25] Other German writers compared the Russians to Apache warriors, who remained the quintessential "enemy" for all sides of this conflict far removed from Apache homelands in the American Southwest.[26]

Hitler and the Nazis also drew on America's colonial history in fashioning their own imperial policies. In 1928, Hitler admired how the US had "gunned down the millions of Redskins to a few hundred thousand, and now keep the modest remnant under observation in a cage." Other Nazi leaders referenced US continental expansion when discussing German colonialism to the east, the policies of lebensraum or "living space."[27] That so many of the participants in World War II made reference to Native peoples emphasizes the global saturation these mythologies attained in the twentieth century. Of course, World War II was not just the arena of these imagined "Indians." Native soldiers played a key role in defeating the Axis powers, from the beaches of the Pacific to the forests of Europe.

Native American participation in World War II is a reminder that these imaginative "Indian countries" run the risk of submerging the experience of living Native peoples, particularly Native veterans. By the end of World War II, Native Americans represented, proportionally, a larger portion of the US armed forces than any demographic group. The most celebrated are perhaps the Navajo Code Talkers whose unbreakable code played a crucial role in the Pacific theater of the war. However, many other tribes contributed code talkers to the war effort, and Native soldiers won numerous awards, including the prestigious Medal of

FIGURE 6. Members of the "Filthy Thirteen" apply war paint before the invasion of Normandy. National Archives photo no. 5957435.

Honor.[28] As in World War I, Native soldiers enlisted for a variety of reasons. Chester Nez, one of the original Navajo Code Talkers, enlisted out of a desire to experience life outside his reservation, in addition to wanting to "serve and defend" his country." Other Native soldiers served in the war because they were drafted, out of patriotic duty, to protect their homelands, and because of their community's warrior tradition.[29]

Some of these Native soldiers were larger-than-life figures, such as Jake McNiece, a paratrooper of Choctaw heritage who served in the 101st Airborne Division. McNiece was a member of the so-called "Filthy Thirteen," a unit infamous for its lack of discipline who became the inspiration for the film *The Dirty Dozen*. In his own telling, McNiece was adept at mobilizing his Native identity as he maneuvered through the Army, whether that meant getting out of unwelcome briefings or inspiring his soldiers with the visual markers of Indian prowess. McNiece outfitted his unit in Mohawk haircuts and "war paint" before parachuting into Normandy on D-Day, a moment that was captured in another iconic World War II photograph (Figure 6).[30]

Native soldiers faced their share of struggles after the war. Ira Hayes was one of the Marines who famously raised the American flag over the island of Iwo Jima in the now iconic photograph. After Iwo Jima, Hayes toured the US promoting the sale of war bonds (see Figure 7), but he struggled with alcoholism and died young, a tragic story historian Tom Holm characterizes as emblematic of America's treatment of Native veterans. Hayes went on to become a symbol for the service of Native veterans in America's wars.[31] Stories of Native veterans coping with postwar life are mirrored in some of the greatest works of Native American fiction, including Leslie Marmon Silko's *Ceremony* and N. Scott Momaday's *House Made of Dawn*.[32]

Representations of Native peoples in American culture have been consistently tethered to ideas about violence, primitiveness, and savagery.[33] Racialized depictions of Indians contributed to the American public's fascination with stories about Native soldiers. This racialization also impacted the way many of those soldiers experienced combat. During World War II, Native soldiers were often tapped for dangerous scouting missions, much as they had been in World War I. Officers continued to assume that these soldiers had an inherent advantage in scouting, marksmanship, and woodcraft. Celebrating the high enlistment rates for Native Americans, Secretary of the Interior Harold Ickes wrote that Indians had "endurance, rhythm, a feeling for timing, co-ordination, sense perception, an uncanny ability to get over any sort of terrain at night, and better than all else, an enthusiasm for fighting."[34] These expectations seemed to be confirmed by the Native soldiers who enlisted in new, specialized units like the US Army Rangers, where they performed admirably in the sort of stealthy combat in which they were assumed to have natural abilities.

These Native American Rangers were men like Kenneth Scisson, Robert Stabler, and Sampson One Skunk. They were decorated soldiers who were celebrated in the American press as perfect guerilla fighters. One newspaper article proclaimed Kenneth Scisson to be the winner of a contest in his Ranger unit to see who could kill the most Germans; in one battle in North Africa Scisson had cut ten notches into his rifle. A magazine profile on Sampson One Skunk quoted his superior officer as saying, "This is just child's play to him. He's probably known how to sneak right up on a chipmunk since he was six years old."[35] That readers assumed Native Americans would be uniquely skilled at certain kinds of warfare is unsurprising given the trajectory of depictions of Native peoples in American culture discussed in this book. However, during

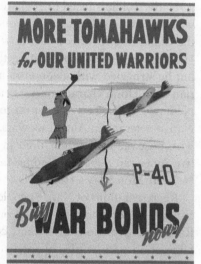

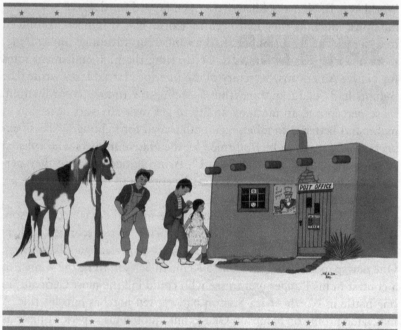

FIGURE 7. Posters encouraging the sale of war bonds made by students at the United States Indian School in Santa Fe, New Mexico. Hennepin County Library no. MPW00311.

World War II, commentators in and out of the military began to call for *all* American soldiers to be trained as Indian/fighters. The history of colonial violence in North America was occasionally reconfigured as a blueprint for preparing soldiers for combat, one that drew on both the history of anti-Indian violence *and* the prowess of the Indian warrior.

THE ART OF INDIAN WARFARE

Throughout World War II, both soldiers and civilians encouraged the US military to train troops as Indian/fighters. This included everyone from newspaper correspondents to high-ranking US military officers. These calls to train Indian/fighters were largely abstracted from formal military training and doctrine, demonstrating the ways that US colonial history saturated the American understanding of violence. As in the Philippines, being in proximity to colonial violence could legitimate American soldiers while situating them within a familiar script for violence. However, there are glimpses of shadow doctrines that will emerge throughout this chapter that linked colonial violence to guerillas, commandos, and other irregular fighters during the conflict in more material ways. For example, Colonel Arthur Trudeau, a deputy director of military training for the Armed Service Forces, juxtaposed an imagined frontier military tradition to the new brutality of fascist conquest. The US military was facing opponents who were "bred on hate, greed, and egotism." Trudeau worried that freedom-loving American boys raised to respect their fellow man would be unable to match the cruelty demanded by a fascist enemy. Trudeau turned to a familiar figure from American history in crafting his response: "To instill the discipline to control men in battle; to fill them with the will to fight, to kill, to die if need be—all with the cunning of the Indian—is an Herculean task."[36] Soldiers like Trudeau seemed to reference Indian/fighting in relation to military training because they believed only those American soldiers able to strike with the cunning of the Indian would be able to match the German, Italian, and Japanese soldiers. Young Americans, trained to skirt the edges of savage warfare, could defeat Fascism abroad without permanently damaging the inherent moral superiority of the American way of life.

Training soldiers as Indian/fighters was often linked to particularly hostile environments: dense forests, steaming jungles, or the rigors of combat during winter. As early as 1939, an instructor at the US Army Command and General Staff College (CGSC) advised soldiers they would find the "Indian fighting style most appropriate" to combat in wooded terrain. This reference to "Indian fighting" was inserted at the end of a list of instructions for fighting in the woods, a shorthand that summarizes complex procedures into the mythic "Indian fighting style."[37] Writers outside the military would similarly link Indian/fighting to particular environments. In November of 1942, the *Chicago Tribune* urged the US military to hire civilian instructors in the arts of "forest or jungle fighting." Criticizing, inaccurately, the Army for not using such "American woodsman" in World War I, the paper emphasized that the war with Japan would require a "special kind of Indian fighting."[38] For centuries, Anglo-American colonialism connected Native peoples, forests, and violence. The racial animosity that animated the Pacific Theater of World War II reconfigured forest-dwelling Indians into Japanese soldiers hidden in jungles. The solution: a special kind of Indian/fighter.

As they observed the ongoing conflict in Europe, Americans readily accessed the Indian Wars as a lens through which to view this new World War. The brutality of the fighting seemed to demand a soldier be prepared for unique hardships. One instructor at Fort Leavenworth contrasted the German army's lack of winter-preparedness during its invasion of the Soviet Union to the US Army's practice of attacking Native villages during the vulnerable winter months. During the decisive battle over the city of Stalingrad, Lieutenant Colonel William F. Britten argued that the Germans, just like the American Indians, had believed their training sufficient to offset extreme climatic conditions. The Germans, like the Indians, "were beaten by a succession of campaigns conducted in mid-winter, under climatic conditions which they proved unable to withstand." To offset such challenges Britten encouraged the US Army to train its soldiers to be physically and mentally tough, to make them Indian/fighters: "Our program must include the training of every American soldier, or at least all members of combat units, to be physically and mentally tough. We have plenty of historical precedent. The original settlers, the pioneers, the frontiersmen, the Indian fighters—these were a tough breed. . . . However, with the more intensive settlement of our country, the breed has become scarce. Today we must train our individual soldier, in order to re-create the frontier type."[39] The "Indian fighter" offered here is a colonial abstraction reconfigured as an instructional template. Such men had been forged into hardened soldiers in the crucible of colonial violence, but "intensive settlement" had caused that well to run dry. Here is Frederick Jackson Turner's frontier thesis reformulated as a story of military decline.[40] The solution proposed was to "re-create the frontier type," to build on that history in order to win World War Two.

The most obvious effort to develop these Indian/fighters during World War II were the Ranger units formed in 1942. US Army Rangers trace their lineage back to men like Puritan soldier Benjamin Church, who led a mixed group of settler and Native fighters during King Philip's War, and Robert Rogers, who led Rogers' Rangers during the French and Indian War. These men incorporated the guerilla tactics of frontier warfare and became the archetypal "Indian fighters" of American mythology, fighters who navigated the boundary line between civilization and savagery.[41] Disheveled individualists that ranged through the forests, hills, and rivers of the "New World," their role in the conquest of Native territory cemented their legacy, one that endures in the US military. Rogers's "rules of ranging" are still published at the beginning of the US Army Ranger Handbook. Rule one reminds rangers to "don't forget nothing," while the final rule encourages rangers to let the enemy come to them before "finishing him up with your hatchet." The Ranger Handbook calls the techniques of Rogers' Rangers "an inherent characteristic of the American frontiersmen," and the particular *Americanness* attached to ranger combat has cast a long shadow over the irregulars, specialists, and elite units that make up the ranger tradition in the US military.[42] This is a tradition of Indians, Indian/fighters, and frontier violence.

America's World War II Rangers were based on the British Commando units formed in 1940, which were used to strike back at the Axis Powers in advance of a full-scale invasion of Europe that would not come until 1944.[43] The Commandos were elite units that conducted hit-and-run attacks on oil refineries in Norway, German ports in occupied France, and Italian fortifications in North Africa. Exciting imaginations across the Atlantic, American journalists described the Commandos as "super-guerillas, the modern Apaches of the British Army."[44] Indeed, to American observers raised on a steady diet of western films and Cooperesque frontier novels such as John Ford's *Stagecoach* (1939), the Commandos must have seemed more American than British.[45] Reports of a raid on the Italian-held port at Bardia in North Africa claimed that Commandos were striking fear into Axis soldiers through their adoption of Indian/fighter tactics: "There have been unconfirmed rumors of terror among German coastal garrisons inspired by sudden sorties of grim men in rubber-soled sneakers who stalk and slay Nazi sentries in a manner reminiscent of American Indian warriors."[46] American culture's long association of Indians with irregular warfare made such narratives an irresistible way to describe the British Commandos. Such rugged specialists captured the imagination even as they failed to capture the attention of US generals far more concerned with massed armies of regular troops. However, with the advent of the Commandos it seemed possible to revive the Indian/fighter as a modern warrior. With the encouragement of high-ranking officers and politicians, that is what happened.

The development of the US Army Rangers was influenced by the intertwining histories and forms of popular culture that translated colonial violence into a quintessential American story. Rogers' Rangers, the legendary scouts who fought in the French and Indian War, enjoyed a resurgence of interest in the years leading up to World War II. A novel by Kenneth Roberts based on Rogers titled *Northwest Passage* was published serially in 1937 and became a bestseller, reprinted seventeen times in its first year. A similarly popular film adaptation premiered in 1940. Moviegoers watched actor Spencer Tracy bring the original ranger to the screen in a fictionalized account of Rogers's violent raid on an Abenaki village during the French and Indian War.[47] An Armed Services Edition was later printed during the war and read by American soldiers all over the world, but the history of Rogers' Rangers would move from imagination to reality as the US military contemplated their own version of Britain's Commandos.

The first Ranger units were formed in the spring of 1942 on the orders of US Army Chief of Staff George C. Marshall. Under pressure to involve US soldiers in the European theater of the war, Marshall saw the British Commando program as an opportunity to get soldiers into combat where they could gain crucial experience. It was hoped that this experience would filter through the ranks.[48] Colonel Lucian K. Truscott was sent to Britain to organize American units to participate in British raids. Led by Major William O. Darby, the new battalion drew more than five hundred volunteers from a cross section of American units already stationed in Britain. Truscott and Darby sought soldiers with a blend of athletic ability, martial prowess, and independence. Scouts, expert marksmen, and demolition experts were prized. Organized in Northern Ireland, the battalion was named the First Ranger Battalion.[49]

When initially conceiving of the battalion, Truscott and General Dwight Eisenhower wanted an alternative to the British *commando*, something uniquely American, and they settled on *rangers*. Truscott recalled that he "selected 'Rangers' because few words have a more glamorous connotation in American military history. In colonial days, men so designated had mastered the art of Indian warfare and were guardians of the frontier." Truscott went even further, noting that the ranger tradition had filtered throughout US military history as a check on the lawlessness of a global frontier: "On every frontier, the name has been one of hope for those who have required protection, of fear for those who have lived outside the law." These connections would have been highly visible in 1942 given the recent success of *Northwest Passage*. In the fight against fascism these new rangers would be the latest iteration of an American military tradition.[50] Indeed, these historical resonances were impressed upon the new Rangers. When the First Army Ranger Battalion was officially activated, Darby told the men that their name was "honored in American military-history annals, since it was first used by Rogers' Rangers of Indian war fame." The message was clear: this new ranger battalion would carry on the tradition of the frontier scouts, Indian fighters, and elusive revolutionary guerillas. As one Ranger recalled, the men took it as "a stern challenge to measure up to the highest standards and demands that modern war can impose on the individual."[51]

As the First Ranger Battalion began training with the British Commandos, American journalists immediately recognized that *rangers* was a reference to Rogers' Rangers, with an Associate Press correspondent noting they had taken their name from those "crafty Indian fighters." Ranger training conducted by British Commando instructors was intense. The men endured long hikes over wild terrain; received instruction in weapons, hand-to-hand combat, and wilderness survival skills; and drilled with live ammunition. They were being "taught to kill with the cunning of the Indian and the ruthlessness of the gangster," as one journalist who observed the program put it.[52] That same journalist could not help but note that many of the ranger recruits were westerners, with all the symbolic meaning attached to that geography. There was even one Native man, Private Sampson One Skunk, a former bronco buster at local rodeos who received several awards for his service.[53]

The Rangers would see their first action in *Operation Jubilee*, a raid on the port of Dieppe that began on August 19, 1942. Only fifty men of the First Ranger Battalion participated alongside a force of Canadian troops and British Commandos. The operation was designed to test German defenses in Europe and practice amphibious operations, but foul weather, faulty intelligence, and an unimaginative frontal assault resulted in a fiasco, with three thousand four hundred casualties from the approximately five thousand participants, nineteen hundred of which became prisoners of war. Some defended Dieppe as a necessary precursor to the Normandy invasion two years later, a source of valuable intelligence. Critics alleged that large numbers of Allied soldiers were killed, injured, or captured for little to no gain. For his part, Truscott, the organizer of the new Ranger battalion, called it "an essential though costly lesson in modern warfare." Regardless, the fact that a handful of Rangers had participated in the raid excited observers back in the United States. American soldiers had finally fought directly with Germans, and wildly overblown newspaper headlines declared "U.S. and Britain Invade France." Journalists described participants in the Dieppe battle as "Indian fighters" who carried on the tradition of Rogers' Rangers, hopeful that this seeming throwback to frontier warfare could advance the cause of the Allies.[54]

THE ORIGINAL COMMANDOS

Despite their dubious initial foray into battle, the Rangers had captured imaginations in ways that eroded the lines between how Americans imagined violence and how they exercised it. More and more, the history of Indian/fighting functioned as a "shadow doctrine" that intruded on practical military training. Less than a month after the Dieppe raid, the *Boston Globe* profiled Massachusetts State Guard troops at the First Service Command Tactical School in Sturbridge, Massachusetts, who were being taught guerilla warfare by veterans of Britain's Commando training program.[55] This school built on the excitement generated by US participation in the Dieppe attack and focused on training the state-level forces that replaced the newly federalized National Guard.[56] This guerilla training filtered throughout the various State Guards across the United States as soldiers from around the country attended the Massachusetts school.[57] The program was the brainchild of Lieutenant Colonel John K. Howard and H. Wendell Endicott, who, in 1941 before the United States even entered World War II, envisioned something similar to Britain's Home Guard, a citizen militia that prepared for a German invasion of the British islands. The men spent time in Britain studying the Home Guard and composed a confidential report for the US War Department that advocated training state defense forces in guerilla warfare in anticipation of a possible German invasion of the United States.[58] With enthusiastic support from the War Department, Howard and Endicott set out to prepare New Englanders for Wehrmacht paratroopers falling out of the sky.

At the Tactical School, which began at Concord before moving to Sturbridge, soldiers hailing from all over the United States received a crash course in guerilla warfare. Instructors trained their pupils in what one observer called "modernized Indian warfare."[59] One of the instructors, Bert "Yank" Levy, was the author of a recent book titled *Guerilla Warfare* that made a similar claim about the influence Native Americans exercised on modern warfare: "The Red Indians of North America defended their country against the pale-face invader by guerilla tactics. These Red Indians were of course savages, but they also happen to be the inventors of modern warfare. They gave the British forces sent against them such an unpleasant time that those British forces had to unlearn a great many things, and learn many new things before they could be much use. Stiff English units all trained to move like clockwork soldiers on parade were always running into Indian ambushes."[60]

A Canadian-born World War I veteran and soldier of fortune who participated in the Mexican Revolution and the Spanish Civil War, Levy eventually found himself instructing the British Home Guard after the outbreak of World War II. While in Britain he published *Guerilla Warfare* and developed a reputation as an expert and advocate for that form of warfare. Levy argued that modern warfare had "brought back guerilla fighting" and believed Allied soldiers in World War II would benefit from waging irregular warfare. In 1942, he moved back across the Atlantic at the invitation of US Secretary of State Cordell Hull to train US troops, an indication of the premium put on his expertise.[61]

Levy's genealogy of guerilla fighting in North America located the origins in the tactics of Native peoples and in the adaptation of those tactics by the frontiersmen who used them against both Native and British enemies during the American Revolution. His instructions on guerilla combat made several references to the tactics of American Indians, references that likely would have resonated with New Englanders surrounded by references to Pilgrims, Puritans, and other monuments to the history of colonial Early America.[62] The school's location in New England certainly called to mind the tradition of frontier warfare for observers. The soldiers were "modern minute men" engaged in training "exciting as the Indian games." Some even envisioned a modern Indian war against potential German invaders. A profile on the school for the *Boston Globe* concluded with this prophecy: "If an enemy ever gets in they'll have the devil of a time getting out. We'd go back to the violent Indian warfare. From every roof and from every rafter and behind every rock outraged Americans would gather. And then, like a great swarm of angry bees, they'd sting."[63] Similar scenarios were envisioned by other publications. *Life* magazine imagined a German invasion that renamed the United States "New Prussia" and confined Americans to an "American Reservation" in the Southwest.[64] Ultimately these home-grown guerillas would not have to face German soldiers in the forests of New England. But the school also trained US Army soldiers that served overseas, including members of the segregated 366th Infantry Regiment, which included future US senator Edward Brooke, who spent time at Sturbridge in a training course with "emphasis on infiltration behind enemy lines."[65] The school indicated a growing acceptance of irregular warfare on the part of the US military, an acceptance driven, in part, by a belief that Indian/fighting offered a path to victory.

It was not just in the State Guards that Americans advocated for training soldiers as Indians/fighters. In early 1943, as the Ranger program was in full swing, celebrated journalist Damon Runyon wrote an article titled "This Army Takes a Lesson from the Indians" that commented on the similarities between Ranger training and the history of the Indian Wars. Runyon, who continued to use the British term *commando* to describe these soldiers, noted that "the poor Indian was forgotten until the commando business came along." He described "redskins" as the "forerunners of the commando school of this war" whose "methods were similar to those taught our commando soldiers today, except, of course, the cruelty that the Indian warriors practiced."[66] Of course, the immediate influence on the US Ranger program was the British Commandos, and the tactics Runyon describes were a basic element of Commando training, including stealth, ambush, and toughness. Commandos and Rangers had to learn to move silently through terrain, take enemies by surprise, and function under incredible stress. But Runyon's writing makes these tactics into something more, something both uniquely *American* and *colonial*. And this is precisely the point—Indian/fighting functions as the shadow doctrine of US militarism, giving form to otherwise commonplace tactics and reframing them as part of a narrative of colonial violence. In Runyon's telling, these tactics originated in the frontier violence of North America's past, and for this reason Americans made "natural commandos."

"PREACH INDIAN TACTICS"

The Rangers served throughout World War II in multiple theaters. They played important roles in several campaigns, including the invasion of Normandy in 1944 when members of the Second Ranger Battalion famously scaled the cliffs at Omaha Beach. Other specialized units similar to the Rangers were formed during the war, including Marine Corps Raider battalions operating in the Pacific, and the First Air Commando Group in Burma. Many in the US military disliked the idea of "elite" units (and the publicity they received), and most were reassigned or disbanded at the end of World War II. However, these units laid the groundwork for the US Special Forces.[67] One of the Americans who served in Asia with these specialized units (and who played a role in publicizing their exploits) was Major James Bellah. During the war, Bellah spent time with the Chindits, special operations units of the British and Indian armies, as well as with the First Air Commando Group. An accomplished author, Bellah published numerous novels, short stories, and nonfiction pieces during his lifetime, including pieces that celebrated the ranger-style units he served in during the war.[68] After the war, Bellah wrote that US soldiers had "an American native instinct" for the unconventional warfare they undertook in places like the jungles of Burma, a natural talent for "irregular jungle fighting."[69]

Perhaps more than anyone in this chapter Bellah exemplifies the blurring of the lines between colonizer mythmaking and practical military instruction. He encouraged the US military to train soldiers as Indian/fighters while composing many of the stories that encouraged that very impulse. In an essay for the *Military Review,* Bellah encouraged instructors of military intelligence to "preach Indian tactics, ingenuity, alertness, caginess." Soldiers should be trained to move soundlessly and execute enemies at close range with knives and garrotes, proficient in the sort of ambushes central to the mythological idea of Indian warfare.[70] Bellah's ideas about military training were driven as much by colonizer nostalgia as by an actual doctrinal history. But Bellah clearly took this method seriously. He went on to prepare a training manual for the Army focused on military intelligence that made similar arguments for the utility of "Indian warfare" when training soldiers.

A key figure in Bellah's manual is George Washington. Early in the text, Bellah argues that the best way to train a new intelligence officer is to "tell him the story of Will Washington's boy George, who learned how to fight Indians as a lieutenant in the Virginian Militia." Bellah uses the first president of the United States as a cautionary tale, referencing an incident from 1755 during the French and Indian War in which Washington, while serving as an aide to British General Edward Braddock, recalled that he warned Braddock about the liklihood of an attack by French and Native troops while Braddock's soldiers moved through the "Mountains and covered country" of modern-day Pennsylvania.[71]

Washington's advice was ignored and his fears came true, with the Battle of Monongahela resulting in a British defeat at the hands of a French, Canadian, and Indian attack as the British marched toward Fort Duquesne. Indian warriors firing from hidden positions among the trees proved the decisive element of the battle. General Braddock lost his life, and the British failed to capture Fort Duquesne.[72] According to Bellah the lesson is clear: "Because General Braddock didn't listen to George, an appalling number of red-coated soldiers got themselves killed, while George looked on from behind a tree. . . . After that George not only knew how to fight Indians, but he also knew how to fight Englishmen."[73] Bellah's manual mythologizes Washington into the originary Indian/fighter whose experience enabled the American Revolution, and uses him as a template for military intelligence, a paradigmatic example of the blending of colonizer fantasy and concrete military doctrine found throughout this book.

Bellah's text is not just a history book, but a series of specific training exercises for soldiers. He argues that "the keynote of the Intelligence schools should be a return to Indian fighting methods." Bellah references the history of the Indian Wars as a blueprint for the sort of guerilla tactics he describes, encouraging soldiers to revisit a history that existed in American military culture more as myth than doctrine: "We haven't so far to go back to them in this country. Go back!"[74] In this training program mythology intrudes *into* doctrine through calls to train soldiers as Indian/fighters. Bellah argues that soldiers should be trained to move soundlessly, kill enemies at close range with knives, and infiltrate enemy positions at night. Soldiers must be "as ingenious in the use of cover as a Comanche Indian." Perhaps most importantly for Bellah, soldiers must be trained to "know the difference between the minds of soldiers who serve in the armies of countries with a mission of conquest—and the mind of the soldier of the United States Army."[75] This juxtaposition between the free American and the conquering Axis found in Bellah's manual reconfigures the United States' history of conquest into a prescription for stopping the onslaught of the Axis Powers. The Indian/fighters of history, as well as the Indian/fighters of the screen and the novel, became an anti-Nazi blueprint. This mélange that simultaneously celebrated Native people *and* their conquest was, during World War II, increasingly conceived of as a blueprint for modern warfare.

These repeated calls to train soldiers as Indian/fighters certainly impacted the US military during World War II, most obviously in the formation of the Rangers and similar units. The mythology of American colonial violence masked the fact that the US military did not, in fact, fully remember how to fight "Indian Wars," at least as far as formal military doctrine was concerned. But the mythology was good enough, or at least good enough to validate forms of violence beyond the mechanization of tanks, bombers, and aircraft carriers. This is not to say that guerilla fighting played nearly as important a role in defeating Germany or Japan relative to the United States' decisive economic mobilization that enabled the successes of conventional units on land, sea, and in the air.[76] It certainly did not. However, the Rangers and other units like them came into being, in part, thanks to the linkage American culture formed between irregular warfare and colonial violence. The history discussed in this chapter demonstrates that these discourses, by the mid-twentieth century, had the power to blur the lines between discourse and doctrine. They show that Americans still imagined themselves as Indian/fighters, and they would continue to do so after Germany and Japan surrendered, particularly as counterinsurgency became a focus under the Kennedy administration.

After the war, James Bellah became a prominent architect of frontier nostalgia, writing numerous westerns, many of them short stories published in the *Saturday Evening Post*. Some of these stories were adapted into films, including all three movies in John Ford's famous "Cavalry Trilogy," *Fort Apache*, *She Wore a Yellow Ribbon*, and *Rio Grande*.[77] Bellah's stories are rich in description of rugged western battlefields; they are also full of dangerous, reviled Indians. Bellah's Indians smell "salty and rancid"; they had "a childish curiosity and the excitability of terriers." If the soldiers in Bellah's stories were not careful, those Indians could defeat them on the battlefield, as they did in the story "Massacre," which became the basis for the film *Fort Apache* starring John Wayne.[78] During World War II, James Bellah believed the US military should train soldiers in the shadow doctrine of "Indian fighting methods," as did other soldiers and civilians that sought an answer to the threat posed by the Axis powers. They wanted soldiers who embodied the fantasy propagated by cultural texts like those written by Bellah. Men who were brave, shrewd, tireless, crafty, elusive, and dangerous. Men who were Indian/fighters. It is no surprise that this desire was particularly focused on the Rangers and other specialized units that sprang up during the war. Indian/fighting is central to American violence, but particularly with regard to irregular warfare, a linkage that would be further cemented during the Cold War.

Indian Country and the Cold War

"GOOD INDIANS"

On September 2, 1945, less than a month after atomic bombs were dropped on the Japanese cities of Hiroshima and Nagasaki, US military leaders including General Douglas MacArthur and Admiral Chester Nimitz hosted a Japanese delegation on the USS *Missouri*, a battleship anchored in Tokyo Bay. The Japanese, led by Foreign Minister Shigemitsu Mamori, were joined by representatives from China, the Soviet Union, Australia, Canada, France, the Netherlands, and New Zealand. At 9:02 a.m. MacArthur began a twenty-three-minute ceremony, voicing his hope for a future in which "a better world shall emerge out of the blood and carnage of the past." He assured the Japanese that the Allied occupation would be conducted with "justice and tolerance," after which representatives of each nation signed the surrender documents.[1] World War II was over. The seeds of future conflicts were already germinating, but people throughout the Pacific Theater could begin the difficult work of rebuilding fractured nations, communities, and families.

Three weeks after the surrender, Americans relieved at the end of World War II would have opened their morning newspaper to a scathing critique of the United States' occupation of Japan. Journalist Gordon Walker, channeling a sentiment he believed was commonplace throughout a vengeful US population, worried that the occupation was being conducted with "kid-gloves." Instead of punishing the Japanese for their war of aggression, Walker argued that US officials were pursuing a "soft" policy. Japanese war criminals were still at large, demobilization of the Japanese military was moving slowly, and American leaders seemed tentative about enforcing the dictates of the occupation. In summarizing the viewpoint of those officials he argued were being "soft," Walker noted that this policy was based on a belief that Japan's defeat was so profound, so devastating, that it had "made 'good Indians' out of those who wanted war." According to this line of thinking, the Japanese were no longer a threat. They were good Indians. Walker was not so sure.[2]

The remainder of this chapter looks beyond World War II to the evolution of US empire during the Cold War, with an emphasis on counterinsurgency and the war in Vietnam. In the aftermath of World War II, with the Cold War looming on the horizon, journalists like Gordon Walker debated whether the devastation unleashed on Japan in the final months of the war had made the Japanese "good Indians." Would victory in the Pacific be as complete as mainstream narratives of US history rendered the defeat of Native peoples? Were the Japanese completely pacified? What did it mean to occupy a country, and how could those under occupation be transformed into the "good Indians" that inhabited settler fantasies, the chastened savages who could either disappear or integrate into liberal-democratic governments and capitalist economies?[3]

Of course, the Red Power movement and Native nations' efforts to claim increasing sovereignty during the Cold War, movements that challenged the very notion of "good Indians," ran parallel to the ferment of global decolonization as movements for national liberation replaced colonial rule and challenged US efforts to dictate the terms of global politics.[4] In 1945, Gordon Walker worried about whether the US had succeeded in making the Japanese "good Indians." In the decades that followed, American efforts to produce a variety of "good Indians," both at home and abroad, would involve the continuing translation of Indian/fighting into a method for managing and imagining Cold War decolonization.[5] Framing the decolonizing struggles of the Cold War as Indian War–style insurgencies racialized global revolutionary activity as dangerous, backward, and savage.

As US counterinsurgency developed under Presidents Truman and Eisenhower, and expanded under President Kennedy, a central tenet was that so-called insurgencies had to be the result of external foreign influence—in most cases from the USSR.[6] This effaced the presence of a local political culture contributing to revolutionary upheaval. Such disavowals have been a consistent element of colonial militarism going back to the Declaration of Independence, which blamed King George III for inciting the "merciless Indian savages," rather than acknowledging that the colonists posed a grave threat to the sovereignty of many Native nations.[7] The conscription of Cold War–era counterinsurgency into a frontier mythology revived that particularly American fantasy of the not-quite-Indian warrior, "who combines the amoral pragmatism and technical expertise of the gunfighter with the skill in handling natives that belongs to the 'man who knows Indians.'"[8] Slotkin demonstrates this primarily through readings of cultural texts such as films. But it was not just in the culture industry that the United States' Indian-fighting pedigree was celebrated. As the violence of the Cold War spread, Americans, as always, could reassure themselves that they were good at fighting Indians.

SECURING THE NEW FRONTIER

The United States emerged from World War II a global superpower.[9] Geographically cushioned from the devastation wrought in Europe and Asia, American families, institutions, and infrastructure suffered far less than other belligerents.[10] The Soviet Red Army was arguably the world's single most unstoppable fighting force in 1945, but the US economy stood alone in productive power. To this economic dominance was added the atomic bomb, a weapon utilized with terrifying results in the final days of the war. The US national security state expanded dramatically in the decades after World War II, militarizing American culture in ways that continue to influence the nation's policies. Race played a large role in this military buildup. The US disavowed state-sanctioned racism even as the expanding mechanisms of national security targeted racialized populations at home and abroad.[11] With its network of bases, massive fleet, and fearsome military, the US was poised to step into the geopolitical void left behind by the tired, decolonizing empires of Europe.[12] As postwar Europe divided between the liberal-democratic capitalist states and the Soviet Union, tensions rose between former allies. Soon the world seemed poised between the United States and the Soviet Union.[13]

The Cold War may not have been inevitable, but a series of diplomatic decisions that radiated outward from World War II caused the world's superpowers to slip toward increasing polarization. Winston Churchill warned of an "iron curtain" descending over Eastern Europe, and Soviet leader Joseph Stalin sought a buffer of client states to prevent future invasions. In 1947, the United States committed to supporting the Greek government in its war against leftist fighters, and President Harry Truman outlined the "Truman Doctrine," a commitment to prevent the spread of communism through support for "free peoples who are resisting attempted subjugation by armed minorities or by outside pressures." Anticommunism would be a cornerstone of US foreign policy for the next four decades.[14]

None of the Cold War presidents managed to invoke a grand narrative of US history quite like John F. Kennedy and his "new frontier." A slogan for the 1960 presidential campaign, Kennedy introduced his New Frontier at the Democratic National Convention that year:

> I stand tonight facing west on what was once the last frontier. From the lands that stretch 3,000 miles behind me, the pioneers of old gave up their safety, their comfort and sometimes their lives to build a new world here in the West. . . . Today some would say that those struggles are all over—that all the horizons have been explored—that all the battles have been won—that there is no longer an American frontier. But I trust that no one in this vast assemblage will agree with those sentiments. For the problems are not all solved and the battles are not all won—and we stand today on the edge of a New Frontier—the frontier of the 1960's—a frontier of unknown opportunities and perils—a frontier of unfulfilled hopes and threats.[15]

Kennedy's message was one of peril, possibility, and the weight of history. The battles were "not all won," and the US had to develop (or remember) a particular kind of warfare that had emerged during westward expansion. A central element of the "new frontier" foreign policy was an emphasis on counterinsurgency as a means to contain the Soviet Union and the revolutionary struggles underway all over the globe.[16]

Kennedy's invocation of the frontier is a reminder that settler colonialism is the United States' first discourse on security, a justification for expansion through dual claims of danger and control. Americans did not, however, *solely* want an endlessly expanding frontier that is continually transcended, the vision laid out by Frederick Jackson Turner at the end of the nineteenth century and since reformulated by later studies of the "frontier."[17] Americans have also desired the security of a *contained* frontier, what Stuart Schrader calls "a police posture in foreign relations."[18] The contained frontier is never fully transcended, but rather enables the expansion of US power outward while maintaining the hierarchies of difference that define that expansion. And perhaps this signals an unresolved tension in our use of *frontier* to describe the spread of US empire (or perhaps any empire). The interplay between the "foreign" and "domestic," the external and internal, and the gray areas that exist at the margins of imperial geography, remind us that colonialism and empire are never *totalizing* but are in fact built on the management of that very lack, that inability to fully realize the imperial vision. The same could be said for settler colonialism, which often requires a more "standard" colonialism of management (rather than elimination).[19]

For scholars interested in continuities between the period of US continental expansion and the twentieth century, Kennedy's New Frontier is a flashpoint, the most overt statement that the metaphors that animated frontier violence persisted in American culture.[20] It would be inaccurate, however, to say that Kennedy revived a discourse that had been in hibernation since the Spanish-American War. A decade before presidential candidate John F. Kennedy declared the 1960s to be a "new frontier," members of the US military were conceiving of the growing conflict with the Soviet Union as an Indian War. Recall Arthur Trudeau, who, in the previous chapter, encouraged the US Army to train soldiers during World War II with the "cunning of the Indian." In 1951, Trudeau, now a brigadier general and deputy commandant at the USAWC, conceptualized the places where Soviet influence was expanding as a frontier:

> You know full well the stories of the massacres and depredations on our frontiers during our westward push in the nineteenth century. Today, there is another vast and vital frontier wherever the prongs of communism infect the peoples of the world. One segment of this frontier is in the United States Zone of Germany, where 100,000 American troops, together with at least another 150,000 American civilians representing the 48 states and territories, stand guard as an outpost against a threat that would make an Indian attack seem innocuous and gentle. Behind them are the peoples of the Western World.[21]

American settlers regularly portrayed their invasion of Native lands as a defensive struggle, a proto-security discourse in which territories are defined as threatening in order to justify intervention in (or colonization of) those territories. In Trudeau's twentieth-century update to this potent mythology the entire globe becomes a dangerous frontier. In this version the United States and its allies are holding back the threat of Soviet expansion, the "prongs of communism" that threaten to overwhelm the Western world. However, before we can identify the Soviet Union as equivalent to American settlers, Trudeau flips back to the familiar script: the United States is an outpost under constant threat of "massacres and depredations" analogous to, but far worse than, any Indian attack. For soldiers like Trudeau, communism was the twentieth-century equivalent to the existential threat posed by the "Indian," the archetypal threat to US security. This was an alternate *red* menace. Trudeau was not the last US soldier to frame the Cold War as an Indian War. As Americans mobilized to intervene in decolonial conflict in the jungles of Southeast Asia, many were quick to argue that they already had experience in this sort of war—experience in Indian/fighting.

COUNTERINSURGENCY AND THE COLD WAR

The Rangers detailed in the previous chapter certainly captured imaginations and contributed to the Allied war effort during World War II. Their institutionalization in the US military was more fleeting. Most Ranger units were swept away in the demobilizations that reduced the US Army from a wartime high of eight million troops to nine hundred eighty thousand by 1947. The unique skills employed by Rangers and other special operations troops during World War II made little imprint on US military doctrine in the war's aftermath. Institutional distaste for unconventional units served to once more bury, temporarily, US military expertise in irregular warfare.[22] This recurring amnesia would not last long. Truman and Eisenhower committed to stopping the spread of communism, and US soldiers found themselves engaged in irregular warfare in places like Greece, Korea, and French Indochina, often serving as military advisors.[23] Counterinsurgency doctrine continued to stagnate, however, with soldiers guided by pre–World War II manuals and a set of common approaches among the officer corps. In the early 1950s, manuals on guerrilla warfare emerged that largely focused on the experience of World War II. The manuals cited historical examples such as the Indian Wars, the South African War, and the Philippine-American War, among others.[24] There was additional doctrinal development during the 1950s, but it would take Kennedy's vision of a "new frontier" to bring counterinsurgency to the forefront of the US military. The parallel visions of containing communism and supporting "development" in the decolonizing world guided this new emphasis.[25]

The Cold War was not the first time that civil/military tools had been mobilized by the United States to shape the development of entire populations. As discussed in the first chapter, US Army officers often complained that their soldiers were asked to engage in "duties foreign to their military training" during the Indian Wars. And, despite the frequent acrimony between the Army and civilian officials tasked with overseeing Indian affairs, US settler colonialism mobilized a network of civil and administrative controls backed by military force.[26] Cold War policy makers were aware of this history. In a 1952 address, Department of the Interior official Vernon Northrop noted Interior's origins in "the undeveloped West of the 1850s." Northrup linked that history to the Cold War, explaining that the department was now involved in "the underdeveloped areas of the free world of the 1950s," what he called "the opening of this new frontier."[27] Similarly, the 1958 Draper Committee report on US military assistance overseas, an important document on Cold War policy initiated by President Eisenhower, argued that "the object of policy is focused more directly on what it is we are trying to construct, and to defend while we are constructing it, rather than merely upon reaction to Communist encroachments." According to the Draper Committee, the US military could be used to construct an anti-communist world through internal development backed up with military force.[28] The committee's report cited US continental expansion as a historical precedent. The report argued that "the use of military resources in economic or other nonmilitary fields is not in violation of the traditions or policies of the United States. Many less developed countries, now recipients of our aid, are confronted with conditions resembling our post–Revolutionary War days." With colonization had come exploration, infrastructure, political institutions, and development supported by military force. Just as the US Army had played an integral role in the colonization and development of the West, the Cold War military would commit to developing the world. US colonialism would be a historical precedent for Cold War foreign policy.[29] These aspects of the Draper Committee report would be expanded under President Kennedy.[30]

John F. Kennedy was enamored with both development and counterinsurgency, and he filled his administration with social scientists and other academics eager to shape the trajectory of the decolonizing world.[31] He became the thirty-fifth president of the United States immediately after Soviet premier Nikita Khrushchev publicly declared the Soviet Union's support for "wars of national liberation." Khrushchev's speech was a direct challenge to US foreign policy that Kennedy took personally.[32] This was a challenge Kennedy was familiar with through his visits to French Indochina, where he saw firsthand France's futile efforts to combat the efforts of Vietnamese revolutionaries. Guerrilla warfare captured Kennedy's imagination, and he spoke about it in near-romantic terms. He told a graduating class at the US Military Academy,

"This is another type of war, new in its intensity, ancient in its origins—war by guerillas, subversives, insurgents, assassins."[33] Kennedy even penned the introduction to a US Army publication on "special warfare" that outlined the Army's shifting orientation toward counterinsurgency, calling guerrilla warfare "a militant challenge to freedom" that had to be met with a "full spectrum" military that combined combat with civil action.[34]

As the decolonial liberation movements of the twentieth century became increasingly enmeshed in Cold War politics, counterinsurgency moved further into the forefront of US foreign policy. The Special Group (Counter-Insurgency) (or SGCI) was convened by the Kennedy administration in 1962 to oversee US efforts "in resisting subversive insurgency in friendly countries."[35] A White House memorandum on the SGCI characterized it as part of an effort to address "a gap in our national security posture to defeat communist-inspired indirect aggression or subversive insurgency," another example of the forgetting/remembering cycle of irregular warfare in US history.[36] Convening the SGCI was the initial step in a broader emphasis on counterinsurgency that would reframe civil and military Cold War policies over the next few years.[37] The Kennedy administration viewed counterinsurgency, particularly the civil components, as the necessary response to the appeal that leftist politics had for people emerging from under colonial oppression. Walt Rostow, one of Kennedy's advisors, called communists "the scavengers of the modernization process." In contrast, Rostow called for US intervention that would guide decolonizing societies toward integration into the liberal-capitalist order.[38] Famous counterinsurgents like Edward Lansdale, an Air Force officer and later CIA operative who oversaw US counterinsurgency efforts in Asia, were tasked with playing a crucial role in this process.[39] In just a few decades the US Army Special Forces grew in prestige, immortalized in films like *The Green Berets*.

Development, aid, policing, and covert action increasingly became the tools with which the US intervened in a changing world. Indeed, Jordan Camp, Stuart Schrader, Joanne Barker, and others have documented the deep links between overseas counterinsurgency and domestic policing during the Cold War. A mix of violence and assistance sought to woo (or coerce) the Third World away from Soviet influence even as movements for liberation contested the entrenched inequalities within the United States.[40] The promotion of internal stability and development became the tools mobilized against any revolutionary movements that had so much as a whiff of leftist politics. This program was made official by the Kennedy administration's formal statement on counter-insurgency, "U.S. Overseas Internal Defense Policy." Influenced by Rostow's theories on modernization and development, the document made counterinsurgency a keystone of US foreign policy, promising to "safe-guard and assist less developed societies in fulfilling their aspirations to remain free and to fashion ways of life independent from communism or other totalitarian domination or control."[41] The document, evoking the Indian Wars of the nineteenth century, sought to blend civil and military capabilities in its recommendations for making counterinsurgency the keystone of US national security. On the flip side, critics of modernization, development, and foreign aid programs could also reference the treatment of Native peoples. Political scientist Edward Banfield, a conservative critic of foreign aid, argued that "democracy and freedom" were too foreign to "backward peoples": "The American Indian, for example, has had extensive aid for decades, but he is in most cases far from belonging to the modern world."[42] Despite such criticisms, counterinsurgency and related programs of foreign aid emerged as a key part of the US military's Cold War playbook during the Kennedy administration, and the military had to get up to speed.[43]

The military's top generals were not as interested in counterinsurgency as Kennedy. The new administration was pushing for a serious realignment of military priorities away from nuclear retaliation and a conventional showdown with the Soviet Union on the plains of Europe, a war of tanks, aircraft, and massive armies.[44] The chairman of the Joint Chiefs of Staff claimed the new administration was "oversold" on the threat posed by guerrilla warfare. Other generals believed current military doctrine was perfectly capable of handling guerrillas, and the realignment envisioned by Kennedy was unnecessary. There seemed to be a particular distrust of Kennedy's emphasis on civil, rather than military, operations, a reoccurring conflict in the history of the US military's relationship to counterinsurgency. General Maxwell Taylor told military historian Andrew Krepinevich in an interview that the Army treated Kennedy's interest in counterinsurgency as "something we have to satisfy. But not much heart went into [the] work."[45] Despite this lack of enthusiasm, by 1965 counterinsurgency was increasingly visible in the US Army's educational instructions and professional journals.[46]

The US military was hesitant to embrace Kennedy's emphasis on counterinsurgency. There were, however, a few who seemed more willing, and most narrated that willingness through references to the United States' history of colonial warfare. Retired US Army Colonel R. W. Van

De Velde argued that the majority of US military officers had little to no knowledge of guerrilla warfare and a hesitancy to study it. He located this hesitancy in the political dynamics of guerrilla warfare, and its association with decolonial liberation movements. Rather than shy away from the political nature of guerrilla combat, Van De Velde advocated that the US military embrace that aspect, arguing that all war is political to some degree. Van De Velde situated guerrilla warfare in the ever-familiar civilized/savage binary that had been structuring the United States' approach to irregular warfare since the late nineteenth century. In an evocative critique, he claimed that "the object of war among civilized states is not to bring home heads or scalps," thus positioning the United States as a third option between the revolutionary politics of Marxists and the supposedly apolitical barbarism of Indians and other racialized enemies.[47]

While some in the military approached counterinsurgency with hesitancy, others noted that the United States had a long history of counterinsurgency warfare that had become obscured. This included top advisors to Kennedy and high-ranking military officers. Even if US military doctrine did not draw explicitly on the Indian Wars, at the highest level, those conflicts were invoked as a historical precedent for Cold War counterinsurgency. The US Army publication *Special Warfare*, which outlined the Kennedy administration's emphasis on counterinsurgency, included articles from a selection of high-ranking civilian and military leaders (including the president himself, who wrote the introduction). In the foreword, Secretary of the Army Elvis Stahr Jr. emphasized the importance of special warfare as a tool against communism, writing that he expected "commanders to draw upon this material in their training."[48] A mix of history, theory, and tactics, *Special Warfare* repeatedly reminded readers that the Indian Wars were a precedent for current US foreign policy.

Several of the articles in *Special Warfare* mention Braddock's defeat by a combined force of Native and French warriors at the Battle of Monongahela in 1755, the same battle several previously mentioned writers used as a cautionary tale about American irregular warfare. Given its repeated invocation by several generations of soldiers throughout this book, it seems that Braddock's defeat has gone down in history as one of the definitive examples of "new world" guerrilla combat overcoming the stodgy formality of European warfare. American soldiers cannot stop narrating imaginary conversations about George Washington and Braddock, whose failure to take Indian-style warfare seriously continued to serve as a cautionary tale for later generals of counterinsurgents.[49] Captain Thomas Collier's article for *Special Warfare*, "Guerillas: A Formidable Force," opened with a scene from Braddock's defeat. Narrating an imagined conversation between a disinterested soldier and his patient superior officer, Collier writes, *"Yeah, that Braddock was stupid. Old George Washington knew what to do, but the Redcoats wouldn't listen to him."* "No, Braddock was not stupid," Collier replies. Instead, the British had listened to American colonists describe "a bloody tale of scalp-taking" and had done nothing to prepare themselves. Collier warns his readers to not make the same mistake: "World War II and the violent years of peace since have shown you more guerilla fighting than all three centuries of the Indian wars. And yet, how much do you know *today* about guerilla warfare?" Collier goes on to describe the rise of leftist guerrilla armies and the steps needed to counter them. He then concludes by once more narrating Braddock: "As General Braddock lay dying in the wreckage of his command, he gasped, 'Who would have thought it? We shall better know how to deal with them another time.' For Braddock and hundreds of his men, there was no other time. For you and your men, the time is now."[50] Collier's message is explicit. US soldiers have a long history of Indian/fighting on which to draw, and they needed to stop ignoring it lest they fail in the challenges posed by the Cold War. The mythologies of American colonialism continued to creep into the informal doctrine of the US military.

The Army's chief of military history, Lieutenant Colonel Hugh Gardner, offered an even more extensive history lesson in guerrilla warfare that focused on wars with Native people. Like Collier he used Braddock's defeat as a cautionary tale, noting that "to combat the Indian guerilla forces, the British formed ranger units capable of employing the same battle tactics as the Indians."[51] These were, of course, Rogers' Rangers, who "proved extremely valuable in the performance of special Indian fighting missions." Gardner dwells at length on the Indian Wars in his submission to *Special Warfare*. American soldiers in the process of being inculcated with the US military's new focus on counterinsurgency would have learned that the US Army was "almost continuously engaged in counterguerilla warfare as it sought to protect the western borders from Indian depredations." They would have learned that fighters like Robert Rogers were the originators of a counterinsurgency legacy the military hoped to build on. They would have learned that Indian fighters like George Crook had "outstanding success" in defeating Native peoples through mobility, the use of Indian scouts, and campaigning in winter, in addition to Crook's supposedly unique understanding of and sympathy for Native peoples, a topic I'll return to in the next chapter.[52] In short, Gardner exhorted his readers to draw on this long history of American expertise in counterinsurgency:

> The earliest colonists were forced to resort to counterguerilla operations to gain a foothold and expand westward on the American continent. . . . For nearly 100 years—from 1790 to 1885—the U.S. Army was engaged in fighting the most fanatical and dedicated guerilla forces the world has ever known—the American Indian. . . . Since the first settler in the New World dodged the first Indian arrow, we Americans have adopted and used guerilla tactics to seek out, defeat, and destroy our enemies. A long record of victory in guerilla and counter-guerilla warfare is a bright part of the heritage of today's modern Army."[53]

Gardner's (and others') insistence on the Indian/fighting "heritage" of the modern Army shows clearly that casual references to "Indian country" or "Indian warfare" during the Cold War were not solely the result of soldiers raised on western films. At the upper echelons of the US military the message was clear—victory had been achieved against Indians, and so too could victory be achieved in twentieth century decolonial warfare.

Another author of informal doctrine that contributed to *Special Warfare* was Lieutenant Colonel Donald Rattan, an instructor at the CGSC. Rattan held up George Crook as a model for Cold War counterguerrilla operations. He claimed that Crook's "antiguerilla methods could be modified to utilize current materiel with equally effective results against any present-day guerilla force." In Rattan's view, the current counterinsurgency doctrine used by the Army was entirely consistent with Crook's approach to wars with the Apache. In an article for the *Military Review* he juxtaposed excerpts from current doctrine alongside analysis of the Apache Wars and concluded that "disregarding the time element with regard to General Crook's operations against the Apaches, one might easily conclude that he had attended one of the recent courses at the College."[54] In fact, the line between George Crook and 1960s counterinsurgency doctrine was twisted, convoluted, and ephemeral, as this book demonstrates. But the fact that Crook and other examples from the Indian Wars were repeatedly held up as precedents for current doctrine indicates that we cannot simply dismiss these as casual resonances. As US military leaders worked to formulate a program for Cold War counterinsurgency, they repeatedly referenced the Indian Wars as precedent on which to draw.

Kennedy's top advisors were making similar criticisms of America's attempts to relearn its counterinsurgency history. These included Roger Hilsman, who had fought as a guerrilla during World War Two, first as a member of Merrill's Marauders, and then as an OSS operative. Hilsman would later serve the Kennedy and Johnson administrations as an advocate of counterinsurgency.[55] He encouraged policy makers to embrace counterinsurgency and noted that "it is ironic that we Americans have to learn this military lesson again in the 20th century. Have we forgotten that we were the ones who had to teach the British regulars 'Indian fighting' back when we were still a colony? Have we forgotten that we taught the British regulars another kind of lesson in 'Indian fighting' during our own Revolution?"[56] Colonialism cannot be separated from counterinsurgency in American military history, and the amnesia Hilsman identifies around counterinsurgency occupies a space similar to the invisibility of ongoing colonialism. American culture has rendered colonialism both invisible and hyper-visible, hidden as an ongoing reality but amplified as a national mythology.[57] This dynamic extends to the military, who, as we have seen throughout this book, fight imagined "Indians" but have to consistently relearn the supposed "lessons" of those wars.

Nowhere was this amnesia more apparent than in Vietnam, a conflict that would come to define the United States' sometimes-futile attempts to control the process of decolonization. In the aftermath of the defeat of French colonial forces in 1954, the US committed to supporting the South Vietnamese government in opposition to the communist North Vietnamese. This support would begin with military advisers to the South Vietnamese Army. To fight what US Army Captain Richard A. Jones called a "forgotten enemy," the guerrilla, the Military Assistance Training Advisor Course was quickly developed at Fort Bragg. Its purpose was to "give combat arms personnel a quick resume in lessons learned from guerilla wars of recent years." Writing about the quick development of a counterinsurgency training program for Vietnam, Jones notes that soldiers were schooled in Vietnamese culture, history, language, and politics, an admission that the military problem faced in Vietnam extended far beyond outmaneuvering the enemy on the battlefield.[58] This meant dredging up the US Army's counterinsurgency history, which was a colonial history: "Virtually within weeks and with some degree of skill, soldiers who had spent years and careers thinking in terms of armored divisions and Honest Johns were advising in tactics which had been in our military limbo since the Indian wars of the late 1800's."[59] Captain Jones declared "the nationbuilder" to be "the soldier of the 1960's." In Vietnam this nation-building mission would be accompanied by increasing references to the Indian Wars. This is unsurprising given that trainers such as Captain Jones invoked those conflicts as the foundation on which they trained soldiers bound for Vietnam.

INDIAN COUNTRY IN VIETNAM

As Jimmie Lambert's patrol boat passed through a dangerous stretch of river known as Heart Attack Alley near the Vietnamese port city of Da Nang, one of his fellow soldiers called out, "From here until we get to CAG-II [the USS *Canberra* missile cruiser] it's all Indian country. Stay sharp!" The patrol boat and its nervous crew managed to make it back to their base of operations without incident, and a relieved Lambert recorded that "I had just completed my first waterborne combat patrol. We had not seen nor made contact with Charlie but I'm sure he had seen us and decided to give us a free ride."[60] For Lambert the expectation was that "Indian country" meant potential violence from "Charlie," slang for NLF fighters that opposed the United States military. Similar moments played out over and over during the Vietnam War, by land, air, and sea. Platoon leaders in the Marine Corps impressed on their troops the seriousness of stepping outside the perimeter into "Indian country." Cobra helicopter pilots talked about night raids in which "we would go out into some of the known Indian Territory, and we go out and I'd fly in the low Cobra, and we'd got out looking for the fight." Soldiers hiking through the countryside would assume a village "wasn't friendly because we were in cowboy-Indian country this time."[61] Frontier references such as "Cochise," "Crazy Horse," Daniel Boone," and "Kit Carson" abounded, both on the ground in Vietnam and back home in American pop culture.[62]

The violence of the Cold War, at least for US soldiers, was defined in part by references to continental colonialism. Nowhere was this more evident than in Vietnam.[63] Vietnam was dangerous, and references to Indians was a shorthand for soldiers to communicate that danger as they engaged in the "search-and-destroy" missions that characterized much of the conflict.[64] It was common for US soldiers in Vietnam to refer to enemy territory as "Indian country," a pattern one literary critic calls "the compulsive recollection of America's frontier experience."[65] Even journalists, novelists, and poets, many of them critical of the war in Vietnam, invoked similar references to the history of US colonial violence. This was only one dimension of a conflict intersected by the

United States' history of colonialism, anti-Black racism, and race-war in Asia during the Philippine-American War and World War Two.[66] Questions of race were a part of day-to-day life during the war in Vietnam. Take the following exchange during the Dellums Committee Hearings into war crimes in Vietnam. In response to a question from the congressional panel about the effect of anti-Vietnamese racism on the race relations among US soldiers, Gary Battles relates a story that occurred while he was pinned down in a foxhole with two other soldiers, one a Black man, the other a Native man from Arizona:

> Mr. Battles: It so happens that I was with a guy from Arizona, who was an Indian, and this colored person and I were in the same foxhole, the three of us, and things were pretty bad and we felt we were going to be wiped out.
>   So we got down into some conversation like, "You black bastard, what's going to happen now?" He sort of hit me on the shoulder and the Indian says, "Look, you both came to my country."
>
> Mr. Burton: What was that last part?
>
> Mr. Battles: The Indianhead said, "Look, you both came to my country." I'll tell you, I'm not a bit proud that I am white. But it is a racist war.[67]

This Native soldier, who is reduced to an "Indianhead" in the story (a likely reference to Indian sports mascots), manages to leverage a critique against both US colonialism and the war in Vietnam, binding the two together: "Look, you both came to my country." The full dimension of the colonial entanglements at play in that foxhole are perhaps lost on Mr. Battles, who nonetheless is aware of the degree to which racial ideas shaped his experience of Vietnam with both his fellow soldiers and the enemy. During the congressional investigation of the My Lai massacre, Colonel K. B. Barlow similarly referred to "Indian country" as the area "where most everyone is enemy and the US forces dealing more directly with the guerillas and local NLF forces that habitually operate in the areas occupied by the civilian populace."[68] Indian country was the realm of ambushes and hidden enemies, the place where the rules of war slackened in favor of Indian/fighting, what Samuel Moyn calls "the everyday excesses of a counterinsurgent war."[69]

The relationship of America's colonial history to the violence in Vietnam was most visible after the controversy over the My Lai Massacre, the killing of hundreds of Vietnamese noncombatants by US Army soldiers on March 16, 1968.[70] Dee Brown's bestselling history of the Indian Wars, *Bury My Heart at Wounded Knee*, was published shortly after the news of the killings at My Lai were made public, and many readers linked the violence they read about in that book, particularly the 1890 Wounded Knee Massacre, to the violence in Vietnam. Kiowa author N. Scott Momaday reviewed the book for the *New York Times* and wrote that "having read Mr. Brown, one has a better understanding of what it is that nags at the American conscience at times (to our ever-lasting credit) and of that morality which informs and fuses events so far apart in time and space as the massacres at Wounded Knee and My Lai."[71] In the forword to the thirtieth anniversary edition of *Bury My Heart at Wounded Knee*, historian Hampton Sides recalled those link-ages: "Here was a book filled with hundreds of My Lais."[72] Roxanne Dunbar-Ortiz, describing a newspaper article that published pictures of Wounded Knee and My Lai side by side, noted that "had they not been captioned, it would have been impossible to tell the difference in time and place."[73] In the poem "Hatred of Men with Black Hair," Robert Bly wrote, "Underneath all the cement of the Pentagon / There is a drop of Indian blood preserved in snow," once telling an audience at a reading, "I think the Vietnam war has something to do with the fact that we murdered the Indians."[74] The cultural climate of the late-1960s seemed to shrink the distance between Wounded Knee (as a stand-in for the various atrocities of continental expansion) and My Lai for these ob-servers, the violent resonances overcoming geographic, temporal, and historical differences.

It was not just critics of US foreign policy that connected My Lai specifically to the Indian Wars. Resonances of the Indian Wars are malleable and could serve as a validation of the excesses of US mili-tary policy in patterns similar to the Philippine-American War. One US Army major compared My Lai to the Marias Massacre, the killing of hundreds of Piegan Blackfeet people in 1870. At Marias, the US Army attacked the "wrong" group of Blackfeet people resulting in investiga-tions and criticism of Army conduct. Major David Perrine, reviewing a book on the massacre in 1970, likened the controversy that followed Marias to the press coverage of My Lai: "Interesting to note is the pub-lic hue and cry raised over the affair. Newspaper headlines blared out 'massacre'—acting upon reports from nonparticipants of the engage-ment. Both Generals William T. Sherman and Philip H. Sheridan, under heavy political pressure, remained calm, investigated the affair, and ex-pressed confidence in Major Baker and his men."[75]

Comparing press coverage of My Lai to that of the Marias Massa-cre, Perrine writes that "the story is not without parallel even 100 years later" and leverages a common complaint: that civilians had no right critiquing the conduct of combat soldiers, and that the press rushed to judgment. US soldiers were clearly aware that their use of *Indian country* as a descriptor for Vietnam could be turned against them, linking criticism of US continental expansion to Cold War militarism. Careful examination of *how* soldiers deployed the term *Indian country* offers an answer to why they did so: references to the Indian Wars in Vietnam were often linked to the conflict's most violent moments.

FREE-FIRE ZONE

A survey of the memoirs, oral histories, and studies of the Vietnam War emphasizes that *Indian country* became a pervasive descriptor for Vietnam, particularly those areas deemed dangerous or outside of US or South Vietnamese control. I am certainly not the first writer to comment on this phenomenon. Journalists during the war frequently invoked the violence of US continental expansion in their war reporting.[76] In the Pulitzer Prize–winning *Fire in the Lake: The Vietnamese and the Americans in Vietnam*, Frances FitzGerald calls the frequent invocation of "Indian country" no more than a figure of speech that placed the war in a mythology of American conquest. Journalist Michael Herr noticed a similar pattern in his book *Dispatches*, calling the Vietnam War "where the Trail of Tears was headed all along."[77] Richard Drinnon argues that "it was as if Cowboys and Indians were the only game the American invaders knew," the terminology touching everything from the names for military operations (Operation Crazy Horse) to the conduct of individual soldiers ("like scalps, you know, like from Indians. Some people were on an Indian trip over there).[78] In contrast to FitzGerald and other writers, I see these references to the Indian Wars as more than casual utterances. "Indian country" meant not only the potential for violence, but a space in which US violence was given free rein. What if we were to take the phrase *Indian country* as an informal description of tactical thinking? What if, more than a simple metaphor, *Indian country* named the intertwining of ideology and tactics, a shadow doctrine, that animated US conduct in Vietnam? We can see this most clearly with the so-called "free-fire zones."

In August of 1968 a river convoy in the Mekong Delta made up of troops from the Ninth Infantry Division was hit with rocket-propelled grenade fire from the riverbank near the city of Can Tho and responded, in the words of one soldier, by shooting back "with everything they had," including 105 mm howitzers and flamethrowers. The incident precipitated a minor controversy when the press got word of the battle, and subsequent investigations placed the Vietnamese civilian death toll at seventy-two, with 240 wounded and more than 450 homes damaged or destroyed. It was one of the worst incidences of civilian casualties to that point in the war.[79]

General Jack Merritt, who commanded the Thirty-Fourth Artillery in the Ninth Division and participated in the fight firsthand, worried that his career in the Army might end as a result of the political fallout from the engagement. In describing his troops' approach to river patrols Merritt noted, "We hadn't really established the kinds of rules of engagement that we probably should have had. We had been living in Indian territory most of the time, and it's not the first time we've ever been attacked from the bank, and we did exactly what we always did." A survey of Army generals in Vietnam found that only 29 percent thought the rules of engagement (ROEs) were clearly understood prior to the My Lai massacre in 1968. Only 19 percent thought the ROEs were carefully followed. Enforcement was limited, and at least one historian highlights the Mekong Delta as a place where the worst abuses of the ROEs occurred. In this confusion, shorthand ROEs such as *Indian country* filled the void.[80]

Unhappy with the civilian casualties and worried about the political fallout, General Merritt composed a more detailed "rules of engagement" in the aftermath of the incident, and his superior officer Joe Wallace defended the Army's conduct, saying, "Look, this was a combat response. Now, maybe it was somewhat more vigorous than you would wish. This is a combat response to an attack on a column, and it was more vigorous than you'd wish, but we also learned some lessons about it as we went along."[81] It seems that the US military made at least a public effort to wrestle with the question of what the rules of engagement should be in Vietnam. Top generals, including William Westmoreland, demanded that US soldiers be exposed to the rules of war. However, it also seems clear that "Indian country" was functioning precisely *as* a set of rules of engagement; an informal set of rules attached to a descriptor for the environment soldiers occupied, an environment where the rule was "do what you want to do."[82] The river convoy under Merritt's command had been living in "Indian territory" which meant they were under constant threat and ready to unleash on the enemy. They responded to the incident near Can Tho according to the rules of Indian country. This was not a moment of excess, so much as it was a moment when ideology and tactics were intertwined. Over time, the Ninth

Infantry Division's conduct in the Mekong Delta would grow increasingly controversial, particularly the high number of civilian casualties generated by their efforts to pacify the Delta, which focused on producing "body counts."[83] These controversies mirrored broader patterns of US conduct in Vietnam, as the civilians US troops were supposed to be protecting became targets of American violence.[84]

Merritt was not the only officer in Vietnam to lead troops into "Indian country." Captain Robert S. Salzer described his command as "sort of like cavalry coming to the rescue of the fort besieged by Indians, or rather with the Indians already in."[85] US Navy Captain Clarence J. Wages echoes Merritt's description of Indian country as a "free-fire zone" in an oral history interview:

> Jerry Wages: Again, we went down the Saigon River and fired H&I (harassment and interdiction) fire one night, but that was, it was uneventful. You went down there to the Indian Country and had a sector that you fired H&I fire, but there was nowhere—
>
> Laura Calkins [Interviewer]: Again, for someone who doesn't understand that reference, can you spell it out?
>
> JW: Harassment and interdiction fire. They keep the trails from exciting the—if the enemy moved along certain trails at night or kept them up at night or whatever. Yeah, you weren't—
>
> LC: Just so they couldn't get a—
>
> JW: It was indirect fire. You were just shooting out at the area.
>
> LC: Right. Just so in case there was someone out there who shouldn't be.[86]

The heart of this exchange concerns "harassment and interdiction fire," discharging weapons in a general area to create fear and uncertainty. According to Army veteran Andrew Krepinevich, H&I was "often fired routinely, with no particular purpose in mind other than to keep the enemy on edge." In descriptions like this it could not be clearer that *Indian country* functioned as a descriptor for those zones in which indiscriminate firing was not only acceptable but common. In the nineteenth century, being "off reservation" made Native people susceptible to violence. The translation of "Indian country" to Vietnam manifested in a similar military strategy.

In an interview with Vietnam veteran Michael Sweeney, the rules of engagement are addressed even more explicitly in the following exchange that jarringly juxtaposes "Indian country" to actual indigeneity:

> Richard Verrone [Interviewer]: What were your rules of engagement there?

Michael Sweeney: Everything was Indian. It was all Indian country. There really were no civilians other than a few indigenous. Oh gosh, I've forgotten what we called them.

RV: The Montagnards?

MS: Yes, Montagnard folks back in there. We'd find a little Montagnard settlement once in a while. We tried not to bother them and they didn't bother us.

RV: How much interaction did you have with them?

MS: Very little, very little. They'd run like hell when they saw us in the area.[87]

Here we can see clearly that *Indian country* is literally shorthand for rules of engagement in which anything can be fired upon. "Everything was Indian" means that everything can be shot. Everything is killable, everything is a threat, and everything poses a danger both of the immediate physical sort (they might shoot you) and the ideological sort (they opposed American power).

"GETTING IN TOUCH WITH MY TRIBAL ROOTS"

What is most interesting about the above interview is the reference to the "Montagnards," a French word for Vietnam's Indigenous peoples concentrated in the heavily forested central highlands. The Montagnards, generally speaking, opposed both the North Vietnam communists as well as the South Vietnam government. Montagnards were routinely scorned as *mọi* (savage) by other Vietnamese, but many became staunch allies of the US, particularly the US Army Special Forces troops (known colloquially as Green Berets) operating deep in the Vietnamese countryside.[88] Montagnards occupied a contradictory position in the American imaginary of Vietnam. Many Americans in Vietnam compared the Montagnards to American Indians. In a 1965 edition of Rowland Evans and Robert Novak's syndicated column, they describe the US Special Forces enlisting the Montagnards as if "during our own Civil War the North had asked a friendly foreign power to mobilize, train, and arm hostile American Indian tribes and lead them into battle against the South."[89] Other writers would similarly compare the Montagnards to American Indians, but Montagnards seemed to reject that comparison, instead identifying with the rugged Special Forces soldiers or the cowboys of the western films that were so popular during the period.

Former Special Forces soldier George "Sonny" Hoffman, who served in Vietnam alongside the Montagnards, centers their indigeneity in his description of them: "They are the locals; the Vietnamese are the new kids on the block. The Yards viewed the arrival of Orientals much as the American Indian viewed the arrival of white men." This indigeneity generated an affinity between Hoffman and the so-called "Yards." He reflected that "my grandmother on my father's side was a full-blooded Cherokee, born on the reservation at Pine Ridge, NC. Being part Cherokee has always been a source of pride. I have exaggerated my American Indian heritage and down-played the three-quarters of me that is German. I saw getting in tight with the Yards as getting in touch with my tribal roots." In his initial meeting with the Montagnards, Hoffman remembered, "I pointed to the beaded bracelet worn on my left wrist and said, 'Do you know Indian, American Indian?' I made a sign like shooting a bow and arrow, placed feather fingers up the back of my head, and made a stupid whooping sound by slapping my palm against my open mouth. When they showed signs of recognition, I said, 'I am Cherokee Indian—American Indian, same Montagnard.'"[90]

What had probably been an obvious comparison for Hoffman "went over like garnet toilet paper." He learned that the Montagnards identified not with American Indians but with cowboys: "The reason Yards identify with cowboys is because John Wayne is a cowboy, and John Wayne is a Yard." The Montagnards were already predisposed to favoring cowboys over Indians, given the prevalence of westerns during the 1950s and 60s, films that portrayed Indian people as savages and cowboys as heroes. According to Hoffman, the Montagnards loved movies, and he speculates somewhat facetiously that they only fought alongside US troops in order to have access to them. Movies were everywhere in Vietnam, and even the smallest outpost had a projector for screenings. Montagnards became so invested in the films that "they'd shoot up the wall we projected the movie on trying to save the settlers from the circling redskins. Camps that couldn't or wouldn't want to disarm their Yards had to invent screens that would reflect light but allow bullets to pass through and go safely down range. Bed sheets or bleached mosquito netting stretched between poles over the concertina wire worked well. Some piled sand bags behind a plywood screen."[91] Montagnards clearly had their own ideas about where they fit within American popular culture. Most westerns from this period identified Indians with enemies. Given their alliance with US soldiers, and given those soldiers' clear identification of "Indians" with the "enemy" in Vietnam, it is perhaps unsurprising that Montagnards picked the side of John Wayne. Indeed, one group of Montagnards reportedly claimed Wayne as one of their own.

FIGURE 8. John Wayne signs a soldier's helmet during a visit to Vietnam, 1966.
National Archives photo no. 532442.

While visiting Vietnam in 1967, John Wayne was presented with a
bracelet by a (Rhade) Montagnard strike force fighting alongside US
soldiers. The bracelet can be seen on his wrist in several movies filmed in
the late 1960s.[92] Hoffman writes that John Wayne's visit (Figure 8), and
subsequent role in *The Green Berets*, cemented him as a Montagnard
icon that was explicitly opposed to American Indians: "After the Duke
starred in the Green Berets and accepted membership into the 'Rhade'
tribe by wearing their bracelet, it was a done deal. When the Yards saw
the movie, and saw the Duke wearing their bracelet, he was elevated to
the status of a God. VC were Indians. VC country was Indian country.
The Duke hates Indians. Nuff said!" Hoffman notes that he followed
suit, ditching his Indian bracelet and instead wearing a brass bracelet of
the Koho tribe. "I became a cowboy."[93]

While Hoffman learned not to compare the Montagnards to Indians,
he did not stop viewing them through the lens of indigeneity. They reminded him of "little Cherokees," whose "entire world was alive" with
spirits: "Like Cherokees, they were part of the world they worshiped

and that world had a plethora of taboos." At one point he underwent a ceremony similar to "the blood brother ritual of the American Indian," receiving a brass bracelet like the one given to John Wayne, which he interpreted as conferring membership in the Koho tribe. Hoffman admired Wayne's dedication to the bracelet, writing, "John Wayne took his vow seriously. In every movie after *The Green Berets*, you can see his bracelet. From *True Grit* to *The Shootist*, the Duke was a Rhade. I understand, he wore it to his grave."[94]

Hoffman was similarly dedicated to his bracelet, never removing it. In 1975 as South Vietnam fell, he served as an interpreter for Immigration and Naturalization Services on the island of Guam. He met more than a hundred thousand Vietnamese refugees, but only one Montagnard, who told "a grim tale of genocide against the helpless, friendless Montagnards." In 1977, Hoffman suffered an accident while teaching demolitions, losing his right arm when the timer on a block of TNT malfunctioned. His first words to his commanding officer once he was able to talk were "Did anyone find my bracelet?" Soldiers searched the demolitions range but found no trace, and Hoffman concludes his story by writing "I have this nagging feeling that the last Koho died on January 21, 1977." Fenimore Cooper's shadow emerges once again as Hoffman narrates a classic "last Indian" story, the colonial resonances blending with the deep affection soldiers like Hoffman held for the Montagnards. There is a sizeable population of refugee Montagnards in the United States, many of whom settled in North Carolina with the assistance of the Special Forces Association, a veterans group, near Fort Bragg, which houses the US Army Special Forces.[95]

John Wayne cast a large shadow over the US troops in Vietnam, both for his contemporary roles in films such as *Green Berets* and his image as the iconic cowboy, forever opposed to Indians.[96] Indeed, Wayne pushed for the making of *The Green Berets*, writing to the White House that the film would counter portrayals of the United States as an imperial power. Instead, Wayne wanted to demonstrate that "it is necessary for us to be in Vietnam."[97] One soldier from the 101st Airborne Division who served under Charles "Charlie" Beckwith, the famed Special Forces officer and creator of Delta Force, could not help thinking of John Wayne in his first meeting with Beckwith: "He was a legend before we ever heard about him or ever saw him. We didn't know, 'What does this guy look like? Is he ten foot tall? Does he look like John Wayne?'" Beckwith, in this soldier's memory, seemed to live up to the hard-nosed reputation of the characters John Wayne portrayed in film.

INDIAN SCOUTS

References to Indian people could become even more confused for men that served alongside Native soldiers, thousands of whom served in Southeast Asia. Many Native soldiers were critical of the war, identifying colonial parallels between their own struggles and the struggles of the Vietnamese. Others supported the war and situated the conflict within a long tradition of Native military service.[98] The familiar story of Native soldiers serving as scouts seems to have held true in Vietnam. Many Native veterans reported that they were often asked to walk at the head of patrols, and they believed those assignments to be motivated by race.[99] One platoon leader, Bill Paris, recalled that his unit "had a couple Indians," including one, "an Indian kid, he was a Piute. His name was Cesspooch. He was an excellent scout and so I put him up front."[100] Like many of his peers this Native soldier scouted ahead of his platoon and performed well according to the recollection of his platoon leader. Cesspooch was not the only Native soldier that served under Bill Paris. He recalls another incident when his platoon was doing base security during a scheduled Miss America USO event. The company commander called Paris over and told him that he was "nervous that Miss America is coming with all these women and I quote, 'I don't want Paris and his God damn Indians all over those women. They're here to do a show and we're going to represent the 1st of the 12th as gentlemen.'" Paris seems to have had a habit of waking up his commanding officer in the middle of the night, which partly accounts for his exile during the USO event, but clearly the presence of Native men in the unit also led to anxieties about the propriety of them being around (presumably) white beauty pageant contestants.[101] Paris was chewed out by his commanding officer on several occasions about "his Indians," which seemed to be the scapegoat for all unruly behavior.[102]

Paris, despite serving alongside Native men, described Vietnam as Indian country. In his description of the Tet Offensive, he remembers an air assault that responded to a sighting of "some Indians running along a river" who are subsequently destroyed in a firefight. At other moments he refers to dangerous areas as "Indian country."[103] Like others, Paris also uses the term as a shorthand for the loose rules of engagement that prevailed in Vietnam:

> Well, we were invariably out in Indian country so rules of engagement were pretty generous. I mean, we were—in the buildup areas you had to have an identifiable target and none of this just shooting people because they

run. When you got out in the operational areas it was like, hey, if you saw them you killed them. You didn't give a shit. Of course, if you took fire any time you could return fire but you tried to hold down on the nonsense. So I thought the rules of engagement were, you know, pretty sound. I had no problem with them.[104]

The threat of Indian country even extends to one of the grimmer sections of this interview, namely a discussion of soldiers that contemplate suicide to avoid being captured. Paris declines to comment in detail due to the highly personal nature of the subject, but he does reference a poem that originated among the cavalrymen serving in the Indian Wars titled "Fiddler's Green." "The last line in Fiddler's Green is, 'So when the situation's getting bad, my boy, and there's nothing but Indians to be seen, you put your revolver to your head and you go to Fiddler's Green.' It's there. The Fetterman Massacre, 1866, almost half of the officers killed themselves. Custer, at Little Big Horn, several of the officers killed themselves."[105] Rather than discuss the possibility of capture in his own experience Paris instead explains that the US military has always faced the reality of suicide over capture and relates that directly to the Indian Wars. The experiences of US Cavalry troops on the northern plains becomes the mechanism through which he discusses the most intimate elements of his service in Vietnam. The most famous of those US soldiers that died on the northern plains was certainly George Armstrong Custer, the villain/hero of the Battle of the Little Bighorn, or Battle of the Greasy Grass. Custer and his famous "last stand" also made an appearance in Vietnam.

CUSTER'S LAST STAND IN VIETNAM

One US soldier in Vietnam anticipated his unit's dangerous deployment to the A Shau Valley through references to the famous defeat of the Seventh Cavalry by Lakota warriors and their allies: "So I'm getting, our first action, we got up and we were getting ready to go into the A Shau, we'd been talking about it for a long time, we'd heard A Shau, A Shau, A Shau. It was like to me, it would have had the same ring as going to the Little Bighorn with Custer. We were going to the A Shau Valley. I mean this was this real bad place out there and everybody referred to it as Indian Country."[106] It is unsurprising that John Wayne and Custer would be linked together. Each represents a key piece in the ongoing representation of US colonial violence. Custer was the martyr of US expansion, the victim of Indian militarism so effectively reconfigured from national defense into savage threat. John Wayne was the twentieth-century continuation of that image. In movies like *The Searchers* he represented the sort of hard-nosed masculinity that may have been uncomfortable but was ultimately necessary to carve out the boundaries of the United States.

Another soldier referenced Custer when discussing the pressure US troops were under to produce body counts. Retired Major General Neal Creighton, who commanded troops in Vietnam, remembered, "As I look back at it from future years the body count and I still have great qualms about that because I never really considered it to be that accurate. . . . I'm just now studying the Indian wars with Custer and those things like that. I think they had the same problems with body counts." Creighton ultimately concluded that body counts, which were used as a measure of US progress in Vietnam, were unreliable: "Body count became very important. I think what some of it was, it was kind of almost a competition and people were judged on their body count and things like that. . . . My view was that the body counts were highly inaccurate."[107] Creighton's distrust of body counts lines up with much of the scholarship on the Vietnam War. His distaste for the practice, and the way he connects it to the Indian Wars, hints at the influence America's colonial history exercised on those aspects of the Vietnam War soldiers found discomforting.

Custer, the martyr of the Indian Wars, was an evocative reference for American soldiers in Vietnam.[108] A US Navy pilot who led an attack into North Vietnam that encountered heavy antiaircraft fire told a reporter, "I felt like Custer going into Indian country."[109] Even journalists got in on the Custer comparisons. A *Washington Post* column from 1968 critical of US responses to the Tet Offensive argued that "Many observers feel that the United States might have done better if Westmoreland had forgotten all he learned in World War II and studied the Indian Wars instead." In fact, because of having failed to learn lessons from the Indian Wars, the author argued, "Our troops find themselves operating from fortified strongholds into hostile country, just as the cavalry did in Sitting Bull's day. The parallel is heightened by the Marines at Khe Sanh, who must know how Custer's troops felt at the Little Big Horn."[110] Vietnam reporter William Eastlake's novel *The Bamboo Bed* includes a scene in which a dying soldier confuses his circumstances with those of Custer: "All I remember is that I was with Custer's Seventh Cavalry riding toward the Little Big Horn and we were struck by the Indians. . . . No. I must have my wars confused. . . . That was another time, another place. Other Indians."[111] One nervous journalist experiencing a taste of combat remarked that the battle seemed "less like Dunkirk and more like Custer's Last Stand," juxtaposing the British retreat from France in 1940 to the destruction of the Seventh Cavalry.[112] For those soldiers that felt betrayed by their country's increasing distaste for the war in Vietnam, identification with Custer, a martyr of the American military, would have been alluring. But as Eastlake's novel reminds us, Vietnam and the plains of present-day Montana are not the same place, and it is the ability of these Indian War resonances to bridge those divides in sometimes contradictory ways that has made colonial violence such an enduring aspect of both American culture and American violence.

"40 MILES IN INDIAN COUNTRY"

In the aftermath of the US withdrawal from Vietnam, President Richard Nixon promised that America would continue to support its allies through its nuclear umbrella, as well as the provision of aid and assistance, but it would avoid deploying large numbers of ground troops. This "Nixon Doctrine" was interpreted by some as a repudiation of Vietnam, specifically the commitment of large numbers of ground troops pursuing counterinsurgency. Nixon's policies resonated with many Americans, who were eager to avoid similar conflicts in the future.[113] At the same time, withdrawal from Vietnam precipitated a backlash to perceived US weakness, the "Vietnam syndrome." There were many who believed that Vietnam was a defeat of policy, not of the armed forces. They claimed the US military lost the war but was never defeated on the battlefield.[114] In cultural venues, the *Rambo* film franchise and magazines like *Soldier of Fortune* celebrated a particular brand of white masculinity some believed was under threat, a masculinity that would right the perceived wrongs of defeat in Vietnam.[115] More extreme manifestations of this backlash included the rise of racist extremist groups who saw the Vietnam War as a betrayal of the military by a corrupt government. This Vietnam War story helped fuel the rise of the white power movement that culminated in the Oklahoma City bombing carried out by Timothy McVeigh.[116] As Americans debated the legacies of the Vietnam War, members of the military deliberated over what lessons should be drawn from the conflict. This was particularly true for the role of counterinsurgency warfare.[117]

Given the commitment to not replicate Vietnam, some in the US military argued that there was no longer a need to train soldiers in counterinsurgency. The armed forces had spent millions on research into counterinsurgency "to accumulate tons of reference material which no one knows how to use," as one officer put it. However, these were not universally held opinions. Lieutenant Colonel James R. Johnson, addressing the aftermath of Vietnam, countered such arguments with a simple history lesson: "Since its inception, the American Army has experienced at least 21 years of direct participation in revolutionary warfare (not including the Indian campaigns, the Moro suppressions, or punitive expeditions into Mexico) compared to some 12 years in conventional war and no years in nuclear war. There is little reason to suspect that the future will bring substantial changes in ratio."[118] We might quibble with Johnson's numbers. Twenty-one years falls far short of the mark if we count the ongoing occupation of Native nations. Nonetheless, what Johnson correctly points out is that the US military has a long history of irregular warfare. These were the savage wars, the uncivilized wars, the wars of guerrillas, insurgents, and ambushes. It was not a foregone conclusion that this history would be continually forgotten and then relearned, but the ebb and flow of US foreign policy, marked by a consistent expansion outward, meant that the guerrilla continually appeared as an opponent.

Despite the call for no more Vietnams, the United States waged or supported numerous counterinsurgency wars in the final decades of the Cold War. Many of these were in Latin America, where the Reagan administration sought to "roll back" communism through opposition to left-wing governments and revolutionaries.[119] Vietnam was certainly not the last time the term *Indian country* was deployed in the twentieth century. On February 18, 1991, Marine Corps General Richard I. Neal addressed the media in his role as deputy for operations during Operation Desert Storm. Responding to a reporter's question regarding the rescue of a downed F-16 pilot, Neal casually remarked that "it was as I said 40 miles in Indian country and they did a superb job and there was one happy camper of a pilot when he got back to a safe base." In the main part of his briefing Neal referred to the rescue as occurring in "enemy territory," but his off-the-cuff reference to "Indian country" during the Q&A touched off a minor controversy when the National Congress of American Indians demanded an apology for the remark.[120] When questioned, a spokesman for the US military explained that *Indian country* was a term for enemy territory during the Vietnam War, going on to say that "if you think in common sense terms, where might it have come from? From the days of the wild West and something like that." The

Pentagon declined to comment except to say that *Indian country* did not have an official definition in any military manuals.[121]

By the end of the twentieth century, it was commonplace for US soldiers to refer to enemy territory as "Indian country," something that is obvious in the casual way General Neal used the phrase. Occasionally these utterances, unremarkable in military circles, made headlines, with subsequent demands for an apology. Wayne Ducheneaux, president of the National Congress of American Indians, called General Neal's comment "ignorant and insensitive." However, the Pentagon's claim that *Indian country* was not defined in any military manuals was true. As the US military emerged from the wars of continental expansion at the end of the nineteenth century, it focused on future "civilized wars," leaving Indian/fighting to mostly disappear from military doctrine. However, this did not prevent *Indian country* from being redeployed to describe a range of twentieth- and twenty-first-century conflicts. Given the persistent hold that "Indian country" has held on military imaginaries, it seems that there has been an even longer counterinsurgency waged against Indians both real and imagined, and the various Fort Apaches of Arizona, Vietnam, New York, and Iraq exemplify that history. Irregular warfare keeps dragging Indian country to the forefront of US military discourse. Indeed, in some cases it seems that defining a population as "Indians" is a prerequisite for prosecuting such a war. This history would repeat itself during the War on Terror. More than ever, American soldiers would imagine the world as Indian country and seek to apply the history of the Indian Wars to the War on Terror.

CHAPTER 7

Relearning the Indian Wars

"INSURGENT WAR REMAINS THE SAME"

Indian Wars everywhere? In a 2011 monograph completed at the USAWC, Lieutenant Colonel Michael G. Miller reflects on the similarities between the Indian Wars and the War on Terror:

> It's not a stretch when looking at an early photo of military officers sitting in a circle with Indians having council or "pow-wow" over some grievance; just as we have seen young officers doing in Afghanistan with the local tribal elders. The times, places, names and combatants are different, but the human nature of the conduct of insurgent war remains the same. Clearly then, Red Cloud's War and the Indian Wars in general can provide us with many lessons learned to help in the fight against insurgents of the 21st Century.[1]

Miller proposes a striking visual continuity: the frontier soldier transplanted to the mountains of Central Asia, dual images that evoke the colonial nostalgia of continental expansion and the imperial ambitions of the War on Terror (Figures 9 and 10). This has proven to be an attractive comparison, one that Miller and many other US soldiers, strategists, and historians have made in the years since the terror attacks of September 11, 2001, and the subsequent invasions of Afghanistan and Iraq. These writers reimagined the War on Terror as an Indian War in an effort to (re)learn how to fight a counterinsurgency.

In this chapter I will explore how and why the Indian Wars continue to be an alluring object of study for contemporary military professionals,

FIGURE 9. Geronimo and other Apache Indians meeting with General George Crook, 1886. Science History Images / Alamy Stock Photo.

FIGURE 10. Soldiers meeting with Afghan elders, 2005. Photo by SGT. Andre Reynolds, National Archives photo no. 6677501.

both as a source of strategic insight and a set of mythologies that help soldiers to make sense of warfare. In the nineteenth century, the US Army developed a largely informal approach to Indian/fighting that combined indiscriminate violence with efforts to control Native life. However, as this book has shown, the continuities across time that would link the Indian Wars to the War on Terror are more fleeting. The US military spent much of the twentieth century disavowing the importance of savage/irregular war, even as soldiers continued to remind themselves that they inherited a history of Indian/fighting that could be applied to those conflicts that exceeded the boundaries of more traditional military practice. It was during the War on Terror that Indian/fighting emerged more fully back into the venues of US military doctrine.

The invasions of Afghanistan and Iraq began with swift military victories that degenerated into protracted occupations. Unprepared to fight multiple counterinsurgencies, the US military scrambled to update its doctrine. Irregular warfare had been out of vogue since the Vietnam War, an institutional scar so deep that the armed forces worked to forget what they had learned (and not learned) in Southeast Asia.[2] In the effort to (re)learn counterinsurgency, the Indian Wars became a potent well of knowledge to draw from. Baghdad, Kandahar, and other zones of the War on Terror became "Indian country," and the Indian Wars became the focus of study at places like the CGSC and the USAWC. The colonial violence of US continental expansion has always circulated through the US military, but in the decade after 9/11 this history moved increasingly to the forefront.[3] At its core, this chapter is an examination of how the United States' ongoing history of colonialism informs its military present. When we go looking for strategic continuity between the nineteenth and twenty-first centuries, we find that irregular warfare is as much about a cultural attitude toward those defined as enemies as it is about applying a technical form of warfare. And those attitudes have colonial roots.[4]

ONCE MORE INTO THE INDIAN COUNTRY

As First Sergeant John Kurak's transport zoomed across the border from Kuwait into Iraq in April 2003, a voice crackled over the radio: "Boys, we are in Indian Country now." Perhaps Kurak and the other members of G Troop sat up a bit straighter, hands tightening on the grips of weapons. After all, the US military has long used *Indian country* to denote particularly dangerous wartime environments. And, although

Kurak entered the country just days before President Bush declared an end to combat operations, he would soon find himself in the city of Fallujah, a place he characterized as "total chaos and civil unrest." At the end of Kurak's deployment to "Indian country" he would reflect that his regiment had not been adequately trained to conduct stability and support operations, one of the many modern military terms for irregular warfare. Sounding very much like a US Army general during the Indian Wars, Kurak explained that he and his fellow soldiers had learned a hard lesson: they were not simply tasked with killing enemies, but responsible for governing, negotiating with, and controlling an often hostile civilian population. Indian country was a lot more complicated than their training had prepared them for.[5]

In response to the terror attacks of September 11, the United States invaded Afghanistan on October 7, 2001, followed by the invasion of Iraq on March 20, 2003.[6] When American troops deployed to Afghanistan and later Iraq, their movement was accompanied by the now familiar invocations of Indian country.[7] Moving through Indian country meant danger, heightened awareness, and often violence. A series of oral histories titled Operational Leadership Experiences in the Global War on Terrorism published through the CSI offers many examples. Like Sergeant Kurak, other soldiers described the rising sense of danger when they moved across the Kuwaiti border into "Indian country." Lieutenant Colonel George Akin, who commanded a transportation battalion during Operation Iraqi Freedom, described crossing the Kuwait/Iraq border as "going into Indian country." As they approached the border, military trucks drove much faster than the standard forty-five miles per hour to present a more difficult target. Transportation convoys learned to function as combat maneuver units, constantly ready for attack. As Akin told an interviewer, "You were never secure. If you were on an Iraqi road, you were never secure. That was the bottom line."[8] The same was true in Afghanistan. Air Force Major Jerry Kung, who served in Afghanistan during Operation Enduring Freedom, reported that "there was the threat of improvised explosive devices (IEDs) out there. You're still driving out there in Indian country, so to speak, and there was the potential for vehicular ambushes and that type of stuff."[9]

Special Forces Major Shawn Carden recalled his 2002 deployment to Kandahar in southern Afghanistan as one of ever-increasing risk: "It was still Indian country." After flying across the Atlantic to Germany, the soldiers switched planes and loaded their weapons. As they flew over Kandahar, small arms fire greeted their transport. They quickly exited the plane, which immediately took off again. Carden would continue to characterize Kandahar as "Indian country." Shots echoed on the perimeter of the base, mortars fell out of the sky, and the soldiers quickly learned to have backup plans for their backup plans.[10] Soldiers in both Afghanistan and Iraq often described moving off-base as moving into Indian country. Major Matt Johnson told an interviewer that "once you're inside Iraq, whether you're on a FOB or not or in what you think is kind of a safe house or patrol base, there is always a potential for a drive-by shooting, a mortar, a rocket—something. . . . Whenever you have troops outside the wire you obviously constantly worry or think about that. It kind of never goes away. Once you get on the road it is more increased when you're out in what we call 'Indian country.'" Leaving behind Indian country seemed to bring a comparative relief. Major Johnson remembered that "when we pulled out of country after the first deployment and pulled into Kuwait it literally felt like a weight was lifted off my shoulders."[11]

A hallmark of the American occupations in both Afghanistan and Iraq was the convoy. US troops moved through cities and the countryside in armored vehicles, weapons at the ready, wary of ambush or attack by IEDs. IEDs accounted for a large number of US casualties in Iraq. They could be buried along roads, inserted into parked cars, or loaded onto moving car bombs.[12] They were a hated daily reality, and became representative of the threats present in "Indian country." Major Daniel Benz, who commanded a 115-vehicle company during the combat phase of Operation Iraqi Freedom, was primarily responsible for the secure movement of fuel trains. He became very familiar with the dangers of convoy travel in Iraq. Major Benz described Bagdad's "Green Zone" as "you're kind of getting in Indian country . . . we had a number of close calls. One time an IED put the window out of one of our vehicles. . . . A lot of times you see cars parked all over the side of the road. Is this the IED that's going to blow us up? Shit's just happening constantly." The constant danger of "Indian country" took a toll on US troops. Major Benz, while denying any long-term post-traumatic stress disorder, explained that after his second tour of duty he initially hesitated any time he saw a car parked on the side of the road.[13]

Just like in Vietnam, soldiers in Afghanistan and Iraq used "Indian country" to describe those areas with fewer constraints on their own violence. Major Donald Sapp, an infantry commander who served in Iraq from 2005 to 2006, appreciated a last-minute change in his deployment to the more dangerous Ramadi area: "Once I got out there and

I started to understand the area I felt kind of fortunate. The area was still a lot of Indian country so it was easier to go in there as an infantry-man with the background I have and the type of training I've had over time. I was able to go in there on raids and stuff like that." Rather than rebuilding infrastructure and engaging in the "hearts and minds" aspects of counterinsurgency, Major Sapp was in an area "full of bad guys" that required a more "heavy-handed" response from the US military.[14] He described executing raids every night, and attributed his success to that aggressive orientation: "With my area, I was out there working the AO [Area of Operations] all the time. We were keeping pressure on the bad guys and that was keeping them off balance."[15]

Some American soldiers grew frustrated at the transition toward counterinsurgency. They wondered how their training to engage with and kill the enemy would translate to a strategy that required "drinking *chai*, handshaking, being political," as one soldier in Iraq put it to jour-nalist David Finkel.[16] Like Major Sapp, they longed for more "kinetic" duties that avoided the complexities of counterinsurgency. They longed for the Indian country of the Vietnam War. The free-fire zone, the fron-tier, the Wild West. As one Marine Corps Lieutenant explained his time in Iraq: "I love being here. It's the new version of the Wild West, minus the booze, the whores, and the fun, of course. But we do have Indians in Iraq—good Indians and . . . very, very bad Indians."[17] Invoking "In-dian country" was commonplace for soldiers fighting the War on Terror. Journalist Robert Kaplan experienced the phrase as routine, claiming that "'Welcome to Injun Country' was the refrain I heard from troops from Colombia to the Philippines, including Afghanistan and Iraq. To be sure, the problem for the American military was less fundamental-ism than anarchy. The War on Terrorism was really about taming the frontier."[18]

"Indian country" remained a potent way for American soldiers (and civilians back home) to imagine the War on Terror. These imaginative gestures toward Indian country would intensify as the wars in Afghani-stan and Iraq transitioned into counterinsurgency. They would become a part of the technical language of war—a history on which to shape current strategy. In short, after more than a century of shadowy circula-tion within the formal venues of the US military, the Indian Wars were once more considered fully relevant. A central argument of this book is that these frontier metaphors were never *just* metaphors. They were the subtle embedding of Indian/fighting within the shadow doctrines of an ever-evolving military. And as the US started to take irregular warfare seriously again, so too did the military's strategists begin to study the Indian Wars with increasing intensity. The rest of this chapter will examine how the Indian Wars circulated through the US military's embrace of counterinsurgency.

COLONIALISM AND COUNTERINSURGENCY IN US MILITARY DOCTRINE

In a prescient analysis, a 1995 Master of Military Arts and Science thesis completed at the CGSC warned that "the Army's next adversary may very well be much like the plains Indians. . . . One of the problems of today is that our military is convinced that there is no one in the world that can match our military. The leaders of the Indian Wars thought the same thing."[19] Ten years later, if you were to peruse the strategic writing coming out of the various US military command schools, the prediction would seem to be confirmed: the military's next adversaries *were* just like Indians, and the United States had once again underestimated the enemy's ability to confound the nation's seemingly overwhelming military power. As soldiers in Afghanistan and Iraq talked about the dangers of Indian country, strategic publications, conferences, and research coming out of places like the USAWC, the Naval Postgraduate School, the CGSC, and the CSI were suddenly paying increasing attention to the United States' history of colonial violence. Soldiers and historians could no longer complain that the Indian Wars had been ignored in US military doctrine. Indians were everywhere, and it had everything to do with the shift in focus toward irregular warfare.

In 2006, the US Army and Marine Corps published Field Manual 3-24, *Counterinsurgency*. Designed to address a twenty-year doctrinal gap, the manual was a frank admission of the failures of the War on Terror. It acknowledged the US military's long history of excellence in conventional warfare and simultaneous unwillingness to address the unique demands of irregular warfare, a blanket term for the various interventions, occupations, and small-scale conflicts that have been the quiet and continuous subtext of US military history. In his forward to the published edition, Lieutenant Colonel John A. Nagl acknowledged that "the sad fact is that when an insurgency began in Iraq in the late summer of 2003, the Army was unprepared to fight it." The enemy in Iraq "waged war from the shadows" and confounded a military more equipped for large-scale conventional warfare against organized armies.[20] The military was unprepared not because this was an entirely new form of warfare, but because of an institutional amnesia and partial rejection of irregular warfare.

In Nagl's view the Vietnam War was to blame. The Army had "purged itself" of irregular warfare in the aftermath of Vietnam, unwilling to incorporate the lessons of that conflict. This had left the United States unprepared for the wars in Afghanistan and Iraq as the military scrambled to update everything from strategies to basic equipment. This included one of the military's primary institutions of doctrinal development and higher education. The Combined Arms Center at Fort Leavenworth rushed a temporary counterinsurgency manual out in 2004, and in 2005 Lieutenant General David Petraeus returned from a celebrated tour in Iraq to assume command of the CAC and oversee US Army doctrinal development. This may have seemed like an odd posting for a general fresh from the front lines whose star was on the rise, but it demonstrated the military's commitment to developing an updated approach to counterinsurgency warfare.

Petraeus and his Marine Corps counterpart General James Mattis moved quickly to produce an updated counterinsurgency field manual, involving civilian academics and workers at nongovernmental organizations (NGOs) in the process. The result was Field Manual 3-24, *Counterinsurgency*. The manual touched a nerve, and was downloaded millions of times when first made available online, although the manual (and the broader emphasis on counterinsurgency) was not without its critics.[21] The University of Chicago Press released a commercial edition featuring an expanded introduction by academic Sarah Sewall, who called the manual an unprecedented collaboration between military and civilian thinkers, noting its emphasis on human rights.[22] The interest in the new manual was part of a broader outpouring of academic and military writing on counterinsurgency. The history of Euro-American colonialism loomed over much of this writing but was often unacknowledged or invisible. The manual obliquely referenced (but did not reckon with) this history in the overview of section one: "For more than two centuries, the United States military has been called upon to defeat insurgencies like the Whiskey Rebellion in the eastern United States, the Native Americans on the western plains of the United States, the Boxer Rebellion in China, Pancho Villa in Mexico, Augusto Sandino in Nicaragua, and the Viet Cong in Vietnam."[23] In spite of this lengthy history, the manual argued that America's counterinsurgency skills had atrophied and the lessons of this centuries-long history of irregular warfare had been forgotten. The failures of Vietnam loomed large, a scar on the collective memory of Americans. It was in this context that a usable history of counterinsurgency drawn from the Indian Wars and the war in the Philippines emerged as the counters to Vietnam; lessons in irregular warfare that could serve as a blueprint for the War on Terror.

An example of this usable history is the continued attention given to British general Edward Braddock, whose defeat and death at the Battle of Monongahela in 1755 has recurred throughout this book. During the War on Terror, Braddock was once more dredged up as a cautionary tale for irregular warriors, his failures both real and imagined serving as a warning. William Flavin, a member of the faculty at the USAWC, argues in a 2011 report for the Peacekeeping and Stability Operations Institute that Braddock's defeat resulted in the adaptation of the British military "to deal with the challenges of the North American continent." These adaptions were not sustained, however, and Flavin argues that by abandoning the lessons in guerrilla combat learned in the forests of North American the British set themselves up for defeat just a few years later during the American Revolution. Flavin then compares this history to the US military's failure to preserve the lessons learned in Vietnam, before pondering whether the military will commit the same mistake in response to the wars in Afghanistan and Iraq, once again failing to balance the institutional attention given to conventional and irregular warfare. Flavin does not seem optimistic.[24] Other military writers during this period deployed what we might call the "Braddock analogy" as a warning for the War on Terror. Braddock serves as a through-line for the history of US irregular warfare, a cautionary tale, and a set of lessons to be learned. The remainder of this chapter digs further into these "lessons," of which Braddock is only one example among many.[25]

"THE PAST IS PROLOGUE"

The United States Army Combined Arms Center (USACAC) at Fort Leavenworth, Kansas, is the "lead organization for lessons learned, doctrine, training, education," and a host of other responsibilities related to US military education, training, and doctrinal development.[26] A central component of the USACAC is the Combat Studies Institute (CSI), which publishes original works for the US military. The motto of the CSI is "The Past Is Prologue," and many of their publications are historical studies intended to refine military doctrine. These include the Staff Rides, studies that serve as guides to in-person (or virtual) examinations of famous battlefields. The CSI has published multiple staff rides focused on the Indian Wars, many of which find lessons that can be applied to the War on Terror. A staff ride focused on the Nez Perce War emphasizes the importance of "cultural awareness," a counterinsurgency buzzword that is treated at greater length later in this chapter. The CSI's *Atlas of the Sioux Wars* is even more explicit about these connections, encouraging soldiers to uncover the "threads of continuity" between the Indian Wars and the War on Terror.[27]

The demands of the counterinsurgency campaigns in Afghanistan and Iraq clearly inspired some of these publications. The *Cheyenne Wars Atlas* explains that there is a "firm commitment" within the CSI that the Indian Wars hold particular relevance to the twenty-first century US military: "Today's soldiers find themselves, as did the frontier regulars of the 19th century, on an asymmetric battlefield with an enemy whose culture and fighting styles are vastly different from their own. A study of the Indian Wars offers the opportunity to compare, contrast, and discover the threads of continuity linking the Indian campaigns with the unconventional warfare of the 21st century."[28] It is hardly surprising for military institutions to examine past conflicts to glean lessons for the future. However, the Indian Wars carry a unique historical weight. These were wars of conquest, a conquest that remains forever unfinished as the settler colonialism of modern America continually rubs against the sovereignty that Native nations work to preserve. The *Atlas of the Sioux Wars* concludes with the Wounded Knee Massacre, the "end of organized Indian resistance."[29] Of course, Wounded Knee did not mark the end of the US military's involvement with the Oceti Sakowin. Nor, arguably, their *war* on the Oceti Sakowin, evidenced by the Army Corps of Engineers' involvement in the damming of the Missouri River and the forced construction of the Dakota Access Pipeline.[30] And this is precisely the unresolved issue with how the US military seeks to learn lessons from the Indian Wars. The United States continues to occupy Indian country, even as it moves into "Indian country" overseas.

Beginning in 2004, the CSI issued a series of papers on the Global War on Terror, some of which explored the links between Indian/fighting and the wars in Afghanistan and Iraq. These publications found much to offer soldiers fighting the War on Terror in the history of US continental expansion. The study *In Search of an Elusive Enemy: The Victorio Campaign* by Kendall D. Gott makes this connection explicit. The introduction to the text, which deals with the US Army campaign to capture or kill Apache leader Victorio and his followers, argues that the case study has extreme relevance for the contemporary Army: "The commanders of the 9th and 10th US Cavalry Regiments faced a skilled adversary who used unconventional tactics and methods as well as an international border to seek sanctuary. However, it could just as easily have featured the stories of Osceola, Aguinaldo, Pancho Villa, or Osama bin Laden. The similarities to challenges that US and coalition forces face in Afghanistan and Iraq are striking."[31] Gott's study sketches a long history of US counterinsurgency, which stretches from the Seminole Wars of the early nineteenth century to the Apache Wars, the war in the Philippines, violence on the border with Mexico, all the way to the hunt for Osama bin Laden. While the comparison to bin Laden in part evokes the contours of war in the rugged environments of Afghanistan, it also traffics in the image of the Apache war leaders as intractable and particularly vicious enemies of the United States, a connection that was similarly recycled in 2011 when bin Laden's code name was "Geronimo" during the operation that accomplished his death, much to the frustration of Apache people.[32] Gott attributes American successes against Victorio to core counterinsurgency principles: separating insurgents from civilian populations, relentless pursuit, the use of Indigenous scouts, and the control of food and water. He concludes by arguing that "the cavalrymen fighting Victorio showed a tactical agility, including the ability to reach beyond the capabilities normally assigned to them. Today's army continues this tradition in Iraq and Afghanistan."[33]

One of the more devastating weapons that the US Army used against Native peoples during the Indian Wars was field artillery. These weapons, most often the M1875 mountain gun, required multiple mules to transport, but they could deliver a two-pound percussion shell that was deadly when the Army managed to fix highly mobile Native peoples in place. Put simply, field artillery was often a tool of massacre wherever the Army trained its guns on Native noncombatants.[34] Another of the Global War on Terror papers published by the CSI acknowledges this reality. In "Field Artillery in Military Operations Other Than War," Larry Yates proposed ways the US military could use artillery in the irregular wars then ongoing in Afghanistan and Iraq. He acknowledged that artillery was prone to inflicting "collateral damage" on Native noncombatants but nonetheless argues for its utility in what the paper refers to as "military operations other than war" (MOOTW), a category that includes the Indian Wars and the counterinsurgency phases of the wars in Afghanistan and Iraq. Conventional thinking was that there was little need to discuss the use of artillery in MOOTW, since you stopped firing your biggest guns once the main stage of combat ended.[35] Challenging this assumption, Yates looks to the Indian Wars for an example of the effectiveness of artillery in MOOTW, which should perhaps elicit more reflection given the brutal history Yates cites.

There are probably many reasons why contemporary soldiers should not look to George Armstrong Custer for inspiration. Yates's study notes a very particular example: Custer did not believe in using artillery when fighting Native peoples. Yates, like many of his contemporaries, views the Indian Wars as primarily offering precedents for irregular warfare. As such, *Field Artillery* asserts that the successful use of artillery during the Indian Wars provides a template for the use of artillery during the War on Terror. Yates outlines several recommendations for military doctrine that he traces out of the Indian Wars: artillery is effective when unconventional forces are massed together; it can serve as a deterrent, a form of "firepower insurance"; and artillerymen can and should be expected to serve a variety of other duties in support of a mission besides firing their guns. These conclusions, offered in the neutral language of military strategy, carry an unresolved conflict. Yates's study accepts that the use of artillery on concentrated populations can result in noncombatant casualties. Indeed, he cites examples, including the death of Modoc women and children as the result of artillery fire during the 1873 Modoc War. Nevertheless, the study argues that artillery can prove effective in counterinsurgency "when hostile, unconventional forces have come together in mass to fight or to seek the protection of a fortified position."[36] The potential for noncombatant casualties, "collateral damage," is apparent in this recommendation. It points to one of the contradictions the US military has grappled with throughout the War on Terror; the tension inherent in trying to "win hearts and minds" at gunpoint.

Many of the GWOT oral histories published by the CSI that discuss the dangers of Indian country were done with soldiers involved in transportation. It seems that soldiers who faced the daily threat of driving through Afghanistan or Iraq were particularly inclined to imagine themselves in "Indian country." These histories evoke the images of harried stagecoaches making their way through Apache territory in films like *Stagecoach*. A more strategy-minded example of this resonance can be found in another publication in the Global War on Terrorism series titled "Circle the Wagons: The History of US Army Convoy Security." Focused on the rise of attacks on transport convoys in Iraq, the author, Transportation Corps historian Richard Killblane, sketches a history of US Army convoy security with a focus on the lessons learned (and then forgotten) in Vietnam. But Killblane's title, "Circle the Wagons," is not a casual metaphor, and he spends a portion of the study on the Army's experience in the Indian Wars. Killblane shows how Native attacks on convoys, the archetypal "ambush," became a recurring American trope. "Circle the Wagons" went from an Indian-fighting tactic to a figure of speech. The threat posed by Native peoples fighting off invading settlers was refigured into a rallying cry. Killblane argues that this was how "Indian country" became such an enduring descriptor for enemy territory: "Before and after the Civil War, the Army fought a guerrilla war against Indians on the prairies and deserts of the western and southwestern United States. From the moment the wagon train left the fort's security, it faced the constant threat of ambush by hostile war parties. From then on, 'Indian country' has referred to a contested area without any secure rear area."[37]

Killblane offers a convincing history for the origin of Indian country's enduring appeal for soldiers, and just as "Circle the Wagons" draws a comparison between the Indian Wars and the Iraq War, so too did "Indian country" become a common way to describe the increasingly hostile landscape of the War on Terror, particularly Iraq. In a presentation at the 2006 CSI Symposium, at which Petraeus was the keynote speaker, Lieutenant Colonel Peter Newell discussed the efforts to build up the Iraqi Security Forces and remarked, "I can't tell you how many of my own soldiers, my Iraqi soldiers, were ambushed on the way home for relieve, or on their way back to work, only because they lived out in what we considered Indian country."[38] Conceptualizing enemy territory as Indian country was nothing new. What changed in the years after 9/11 was the degree to which Indian country, and the Indian Wars more broadly, were taken up in military-intellectual spaces like Fort Leavenworth. These papers from the Global War on Terrorism Series are just one example of the military's newfound interest in the Indian Wars, an interest driven, in part, by the need to develop a workable strategy for the ongoing occupations of Afghanistan and Iraq. The most extensive examples of this effort are the monographs and thesis projects that officers rising in the ranks have produced at the military's various institutions of higher education. The remainder of this chapter will focus on these documents.

MASTERING THE INDIAN WARS

The Fort Apaches of Iraq, the Geronimos of Pakistan, and the transportable Indian countries surround US troops wherever they go in the world, validated by strategic writing that has rediscovered the always-insurgent Indian as a mechanism through which to understand the War on Terror. These include thesis projects written by US military officers at places like the CGSC, the USAWC, and at similar schools run by the other branches of the military. These projects represent the academic and professional interests of rising officers in the US military and thus offer a window into the historical, theoretical, and practical concerns of military leaders.[39] Consistent with the broader military discourse around the War on Terror, recent projects often emphasize irregular warfare, particularly counterinsurgency. Indians both real and imagined figure prominently in these texts.

In the years since September 11, the volume of projects that consider US continental expansion and wars with Native people has increased. Hundreds of master's theses in military art and science completed at the various officer schools mention the "Indian Wars," and do so at a much higher frequency than in prior decades. This dynamic emerges more clearly if we focus just on the monographs written by students at the School for Advanced Military Studies, a program for higher-ranking officers that produces top military planners. Since 9/11, the number of monographs at the SAMS that mention the phrase *Indian wars* was sixty, compared to just fifteen in all the years prior to 2001.[40] This mirrors the increase in projects that discuss counterinsurgency warfare more generally at military command schools.[41]

I do not want to give the impression that every student at the US military's command schools is writing a thesis focused on the Indian Wars. In fact, topics vary widely. The point is that American soldiers have sharply increased their interest in the Indian Wars with the advent of the War on Terror. Like the counterinsurgency field manual, these projects acknowledge the challenges posed by the Global War on Terror and argue that the Indian Wars contain valuable lessons for the modern military. My analysis of some of these thesis projects is cautiously critical (given that they are produced by students), and that is because these papers are some of the best evidence that for the US military the "Indian Wars" function as more than just a metaphor. I read them as such: sources that offer a window into how contemporary soldiers see their current duties in relation to America's colonial history, but not sources that should be evaluated the same as peer-reviewed journals or books. The remainder of this chapter will focus on several characteristics that are common to these studies: an uncritical use of the word *insurgent* that positions Native people as the always-insurgent foils to the

United States; an emphasis on historical lessons that paradoxically render counterinsurgency ahistorical and apolitical; and a form of counterinsurgency "culture talk" in which simplistic readings of insurgents as primitive or tribal supposedly offer special insight into counterinsurgency, best exemplified by widespread interest in the (in)famous Indian fighter George Crook.

ARE INDIANS INSURGENTS?

In many ways, Indians have always been insurgents to the settlers of North America. Hundreds of years before the words *guerrilla* and *insurgent* saw widespread use, the Native peoples of North America were described by European colonists as skulking, elusive, and savage, language that predicted the way in which various insurgencies throughout history have been characterized. Often portrayed as internal threats to an already-established US sovereignty, Native people were the specters at the edges of colonial expansion, a constant menace both material and existential. Settlers described Native peoples in these ways to mask the ongoing reality of Native sovereignty. Settlers are "at home" everywhere, and their desire for security thus manifests as expansion. The homeland is always surrounded and permeated by threats that must be neutralized.[42] Indians-as-insurgents is a key feature of US settler colonialism. It remains so today, and this is true for military writing on the War on Terror.[43]

It is no coincidence that depictions of violent Indians both predate and predict the terms in which later insurgents have been described. "Insurgent" is, or at least should be, a highly contested category. The technical definitions of *insurgency* applied by governments and militaries fall woefully short of describing the complicated cultural and political dynamics of rebellions, anti-colonial movements, civil wars, military occupations, and the host of diverse conflicts lumped together as "insurgencies."[44] But that is precisely the point—if Indians were some of the first insurgents, then "insurgent" must be a deeply colonial concept that is normalized as a neutral descriptor, just as the ongoing colonialism of the United States is normalized at the expense of Native sovereignty.

Insurgency typically involves competing claims to political authority, often combined with the imposition of foreign imperial power. My point here is not simply that we should challenge the word *insurgent* for political reasons (although that may often be a valuable project); it is that the history of this category, particularly as used by the US government and military, emerges in part from the process of continental expansion and carries with it colonial logics. Now, more than ever, Indians are uncritically rendered as "insurgents" in military writing, particularly writing that attempts to apply historical lessons to the War on Terror. The term does not have to be nuanced, massaged, or argued for. Ongoing Native sovereignty, the reality of conquest, and the historical obfuscation of Native independence and political superiority at different points in history are submerged when Indian = insurgent.

As one writer put it in a thesis submitted to the USAWC less than a year after September 11, "As the United States engages in the war on terrorism in Afghanistan, it is prudent that military leaders relook [sic] the lessons of America's Indian Wars. . . . If insurgency is becoming the predominate [sic] form of warfare for third world countries, American senior leaders must understand its nature."[45] The increasing preoccupation with insurgency drove these officers to seek out historical examples to apply to Afghanistan, Iraq, and the broader War on Terror. Scholars have noted the ways in which *terrorist* became at once an increasingly broad and narrow term after the September 11 attacks, applicable to a range of different groups and individuals reduced down to "Islamic terrorist."[46] The same could easily be said of *insurgent*, which became a shorthand for those contesting US occupations. These writers, then, were not only looking for historical examples of counterinsurgency warfare; they were looking for historical examples of insurgents.

Many of the US Army's noncommissioned officers were educated at the Sergeant Major Academy (USASMA), now the NCO Leadership Center of Excellence, located at Fort Bliss, a military post established in the 1850s to assert US control over Native peoples in the Southwest. A common recent assignment for soldiers at the academy is a compare/contrast paper focused on insurgency. There are numerous examples of these papers in the Sergeant Major Academy's digital library. Unsurprisingly, the Indian Wars have been a popular subject for this paper during the War on Terror. In these papers, soldiers stationed at a military installation founded during the Indian Wars are prompted to compare and contrast two counterinsurgency campaigns and to "synthesize the insights gained from your analysis that soldiers can apply to the Global War on Terrorism."[47] Many of these officers see themselves as the inheritors of a two-hundred-plus-year history of American experience in counterinsurgency warfare. They hold up the Indian Wars as the foundation of that experience, a model that can be applied to the War on Terror. One officer argues that the "essential paradigm" of the War on

Terror is identical to nineteenth-century American settlers: "Us (the attacked) against them (the attackers)—was no less essential to the mindset of white settlers regarding the Indians, starting at least from the 1622 Indian massacre of 347 people at Jamestown, Virginia."[48]

The Indian Wars seem to have played such a large role in how twenty-first-century soldiers conceptualized the War on Terror that some students at the USASMA overestimate how much of a doctrinal impact they made. One paper comparing the "insurgencies" of the Indian Wars and the Philippine-American War argues that "over the years the lessons learned from these campaigns have been successfully utilized to achieve victory in numerous conflicts."[49] As this book has shown, it is difficult to argue that the Indian Wars directly influenced how American soldiers fought the wars of the twentieth century. There are connections, but those connections are circuitous, the "lessons learned" often manifesting as shadow doctrines that make imaginative gestures toward "Indian country." Despite this, the repeated references to applying the lessons of the Indian Wars to the War on Terror seems to have created a climate in which those conflicts appear to have always been central to American counterinsurgency strategy.

The same soldier is equally optimistic about how the Indian Wars can inform the present: "Some of the valuable lessons learned in the conflicts discussed in this paper are being utilized with success in today's contemporary operating environment. The policy of attraction and chastisement has proven successful over the years and is proving itself again in Iraq where it is achieving success against a cunning and aggressive foe."[50] Like much of the military writing that conceives of Native people as insurgents, these compare/contrast papers are a blend of concrete military analysis and racialized characterizations of enemies. Such racializations were a common element of the War on Terror more often applied to Muslims, Arabs, and others, and were certainly not restricted to members of the military.[51] Descriptions of specific military tactics sit alongside references to "cunning and aggressive" foes. Native peoples are difficult to disentangle from the harmful ways in which they have been represented in American culture. This is certainly true within military writing. "Insurgent" is not a neutral category. It was produced within patterns of colonialism and empire, and Native peoples play an outsized role in how American soldiers conceive of insurgency.

A thesis completed at the CGSC a year after the surge of troops into Iraq in 2007 explicitly connects contemporary insurgency to Indigenous resistance to colonialism.[52] The officer argues that insurgency defined the entirety of North American colonization: "From the first European settlers to set foot on the North American continent, the conflict with Native Americans was a counterinsurgency war that ran parallel to the development and westward expansion of the United States. It was not just a conflict that was defining the American experience; it was a key formative experience for the US Army during the first 115 years of its existence."[53] This argument normalizes the conquest of North America by situating Native people as insurgent to colonial invasion from the moment settlers set foot on the continent. Defining Native peoples as insurgents is a practice that sits alongside manifest destiny; the doctrine of discovery; and the various legal, political, and ideological structures that divested Native people of their land.[54] These are persistent, indeed; persisting concepts that continue to legitimize the occupation of Native land. This thesis, and many like it, is not simply historical but comparative. It attempts to glean a usable history from colonialism for application to the War on Terror. In the process, many of these writers are simply recycling colonizer mythologies.

Military historians spent the twentieth century lamenting that the Indian Wars made little to no doctrinal impact on the US military. Yet this surge of strategic writing focused on the Indian Wars effortlessly resituated the Indian Wars as America's counterinsurgency past, present, and future. As one officer put it in their thesis for the CGSC: "The United States government still manages the consequences of it [the Indian Wars] today through the United States Department of the Interior's Bureau of Indian Affairs. While Native American tribes may no longer have the capacity to fight a protracted insurgency against the United States government, significant issues still occur, even as late as 2016, demonstrated by the large-scale protests of the Dakota Access pipeline by the Standing Rock Sioux."[55] This writer frames ongoing colonialism as a counterinsurgency, and the extreme, militarized response to the Standing Rock protests supports this conclusion, at least from the perspective of US government and capital interests. As scholars have shown, global empire always "comes home," and so, it seems, does counterinsurgency.[56] The lines of militarized SWAT police officers facing down water protectors at Standing Rock reinforced this reality.

AHISTORICAL HISTORY LESSONS

CSI publications open with the phrase The Past Is Prologue!—a motto that encapsulates an institutional desire within the US military to apply historical examples to contemporary conflicts.[57] As the 2006 *Atlas of the Sioux Wars*, published by the CSI, argues, "While historical analogies are always fraught with danger, many of the difficulties faced by US soldiers fighting today parallel the tactical and operation dilemmas faced by soldiers fighting during the Indian Wars. Our goal is to learn from the experiences of 19th-century soldiers."[58] This is a desire echoed by most military graduate theses that discuss the Indian Wars. They seek to retranslate the Indian Wars back from an enduring cultural trope into a usable military history.

The Indian Wars are a ready example on which to draw, viewed, for the most part uncritically, as a success. They offer up seductive comparative frameworks to wars in places like Afghanistan or Iraq: deserts, mountains, and tribes. The Indian Wars become case studies; they offer historical examples that can be applied to the present. Critically, the "case" almost always has to do with perceived tactical or cultural similarities divested of political and historical context. In other words, these are historical case studies *outside of history*. As Laleh Khalili shows in her careful historiography of Western counterinsurgency doctrine, counterinsurgency rejects politics and history, turning insurgency into a series of technical problems to be solved.[59] To Khalili's analysis I would add "culture" as an object of counterinsurgency problem solving, a problem some have declared unsolvable, at least in Afghanistan.[60] The ready comparison that strategic writing makes between Arizona and Afghanistan, between the northern plains and the streets of Baghdad, has more to do with cultural ideas about Native people and the Indian Wars than it does actual history. It betrays the ways in which cultural depictions of Indians structure the American discourse around insurgency.

A thesis completed at the CGSC argues that "the history of the United States provides many examples, which yield fruitful insight into the very nature of Irregular Warfare, perhaps none more so than the struggle to subdue the Native Americans in the American West."[61] The author, like many other modern counterinsurgents, elevates the Indian Wars to the primary example of irregular warfare in US history. Many analogous thesis projects use a similarly simplistic compare-and-contrast formula to offer recommendations for the War on Terror, peppering their highly technical accounts with words like *tribal*, *civilized*, and *primitive*. These words traffic in a long history of Native representation that serves to collapse the distance and difference between nineteenth-century North America and twenty-first-century Afghanistan:

> In both the Indian Wars and Afghanistan, the United States has been far superior in numbers, technology, and wealth. The enemy in each case was cunning and ruthless, and seemed to adroitly counter our main advantages in a manner that suited their strengths. The enemy in both cases was a tribal based society with a warrior ethos that put a premium on fighting ability. . . . The United States government took a similar approach in each case by attempting to apply western models of governance, when in reality those models would never work. These tribal societies were primitive, and existed for hundreds, if not thousands, of years without a semblance of an organized governing body.[62]

These reductive comparisons between Native people and the various anti-US forces in Afghanistan rely on erroneous understandings of tribal societies. Indeed, the above-quoted passage does not cite any secondary literature for the conclusions drawn about the inherently warlike societies of Afghans and Native peoples in North America. Perhaps the most telling claim is that "tribal societies" exist without organized political leadership, a claim that is insupportable.

I am not proposing we hold a master's thesis project to the same standards as a published piece of scholarship. However, this mode of comparative analysis is consistent across much of the literature on counterinsurgency, not just student papers but also in published works. These writers, COINdinistas as they are often known, tend to flatten out the diverse histories and motivations of groups that have found themselves defined as insurgent to US authority. In the above example, the invasion and conquest of North America is invisible, as is the complicated colonial history of Western and Soviet influence on Afghanistan. Instead, the differences are rendered as cultural; insurgent tactics emanate from a societal warrior ethos. These depictions of Native people were amplified by the deluge of movies, television series, novels, art, and other cultural representations that have proliferated images of violent Indians in US culture. Similar amplifications of representations of Muslim and Arab terrorists proliferated after 9/11, and these dual images seemed to reinforce each other, fueling the War on Terror's mobilization of a sense of danger that justified the outward projection of power.[63] As Hannah Gurman argues, a perception of threat, criminality, and potential for violence, relative to US interests, functions as the true barometer for insurgency in much of the literature on counterinsurgency.[64] And Native people are the original, enduring threat in the colonial imaginaries of the United States.

The historical lessons that officers attempt to glean from the Indian Wars are not only an academic exercise. They are studies undertaken by soldiers with combat experience, who pursue their master's research with an eye toward lessons applicable to future deployments. This is the approach taken by a 2009 master's thesis written at the Naval Postgraduate School titled "The Future of Raiding: Lessons in Raiding Tactics from the Indian Wars and Law Enforcement." In this study the Indian Wars and police techniques for disrupting street gangs are used as historical examples relevant to the War on Terror. The author had combat experience, having deployed for forty months in both Iraq and Afghanistan from 2001 to 2007 in conventional and Special Forces operations. The study was therefore personal for this officer: "One aim of this thesis is to explore raiding techniques that may be used in specific situations to help units like the ones to which I have been assigned."[65] The author continued to be involved in the Army's developing counterinsurgency programs. These included the Security Force Assistance Brigades, designed to provide advice and assistance in the development of security forces in partner nations.[66] This particular thesis thus offers a window into how an officer involved in the ongoing development of US counterinsurgency doctrine understood the Indian Wars in relation to the War on Terror.

"The Future of Raiding" draws a number of lessons from the Indian Wars that center on acceptable limits for military violence. The author grapples with many of the same questions that nineteenth-century Army officers and politicians had to face. In the process, they arrive at similar conclusions that reframe the logic of defensive conquest into a modern biopolitical security discourse: US foreign interventions make the world safer, not more violent. Just as nineteenth-century writers elevated Native people to a physical and existential threat that served to justify the invasion of Native land, the War on Terror has mobilized discourses of security to justify invasion, occupation, and the suspension of the rule of law in places like Guantanamo Bay, while simultaneously framing counterinsurgency around questions of development, aid, and "winning hearts and minds."[67] In the global discourse of the War on Terror, violence is pursued not solely to defeat enemies, but to make the world safe; you kill so that all may live:

We should always look to historical cases to find ways to improve our current techniques. It may be necessary to kill a large number of one's enemy in order to defeat his will to fight. . . . It is also important to treat civilians as well as captured enemy personnel with humanity. Taking family members captive, as the Plains Indians did so frequently, may be a logical and humane way to force terrorists to surrender (while this method may be called into question by current international laws of war). Finally, the ruthless cavalry techniques used against the Indians may be justified in some cases when it is required to kill your enemy and defeat his way of life in order to preserve your own.[68]

In this fascinating passage the writer flirts with captive taking as a counterterrorism measure but ultimately dismisses it as a likely violation of the rules of warfare. However, we might question whether captive taking was restricted to the Plains Indians (it was not) or whether the United States refrained from a modern analog to captive taking (it has not). However, the interesting portions of this argument deal with killing. Specifically, the necessity of killing large numbers of the enemy, and the related claim that it may be required to kill large numbers of the enemy to preserve one's own way of life. In moments like this, an implicit logic underlying counterinsurgency comes to the forefront: that despite calls to "win hearts and minds" counterinsurgency campaigns deemed "effective" have often utilized harsh, even brutal, measures.[69]

The offered history lesson is that increasing brutality may be the only way to handle insurgents. The author argues that "the Indian wars offer an underutilized wealth of information concerning how governments should handle outlaw groups," and later concludes that "killing Indians in sufficient numbers and with increasing brutality after the Civil War did eventually break the will of most nomadic tribes, and caused them to move to reservations and live under United States protection and rules."[70] Examples including the Sand Creek massacre and the attacks on Lakota and Cheyenne during the winter of 1876 are used to demonstrate the effectiveness of this counter-raiding strategy, in which Native populations were targeted directly with violence. The author concludes that the indiscriminate violence of the Indian Wars "should never again seem to be necessary, but in dealing with people who believe their atrocities are justified by a higher power, such as Salafi jihadists, this may be more applicable than most Americans realize."[71] The enemies of the various wars under the umbrella of the War on Terror cannot be reduced to Salafi jihadists, and the consistent refrain of "terrorist" functions as a racializing move that helps to resolve the tension between liberal norms of government and illiberal practices such as indefinite detention and extrajudicial killing.[72] Racialized enemies can be subjected to exceptional forms of state violence in the service of protecting an amorphous global population, a discursive move that relies on simplistic notions of culture.

COUNTERINSURGENCY CULTURE TALK

In a 2005 issue of the *Military Review*, the professional journal of the US Army, anthropologist Montgomery McFate lamented that "once called 'the handmaiden of colonialism,' anthropology has had a long, fruitful relationship with various elements of national power, which ended suddenly following the Vietnam War. The strange story of anthropology's birth as a warfighting discipline, and its sudden plunge into the abyss of postmodernism, is intertwined with the US failure in Vietnam." In the conclusion to that same article, McFate argues that the "DOD yearns for cultural knowledge, but anthropologists en masse, bound by their own ethical code and sunk in a mire of postmodernism, are unlikely to contribute much of value to reshaping national security policy or practice."[73]

It may sound strange to hear a scholar of anthropology, a discipline that is no stranger to theory, bemoan the "abyss of postmodernism" and complain about the decline of social scientific collaboration with the US military. However, intimately connected to the US military and the network of think tanks, private contractors, and policy groups that permeate America's militarized culture, Montgomery McFate is something of an outlier among twenty-first-century anthropologists. McFate contributed to Field Manual 3-24, *Counterinsurgency*, and helped develop the US Army's Human Terrain System, which placed social scientists inside military units.[74] The HTS ended in 2014 and was a source of continuous controversy, including a 2007 statement from the executive board of the American Anthropological Association calling the program incompatible with disciplinary ethics.[75] A longtime participant and advocate for social scientific collaboration with the US military, McFate's efforts to incorporate "cultural knowledge" into the War on Terror and the occupations of Afghanistan and Iraq was one element in a surge of what we might call "cultural thinking" in the US military since 2001.

In the same 2005 article, McFate argued that coalition forces in Iraq "have been fighting a complex war against an enemy they do not understand. The insurgents' organizational structure is not military, but tribal. Their tactics are not conventional, but asymmetrical." The answer, according to McFate, was increased attention to culture as a key military focus: "Countering the insurgency in Iraq requires cultural and social knowledge of the adversary. Yet, none of the elements of U.S. national power—diplomatic, military, intelligence, or economic—explicitly take adversary culture into account in the formation or execution of policy. This cultural knowledge gap has a simple cause—the almost total absence of anthropology within the national-security establishment."[76] McFate was not alone in calling for increased attention to culture as a key component of the burgeoning counterinsurgency revolution in the US military, even if she may have been a minority among academic anthropologists. This preoccupation with culture would be enshrined in the counterinsurgency field manual published in 2006, which declared that "cultural knowledge is essential to waging a successful counterinsurgency."[77]

The military's increasing attention to culture as a key component of warfare was not without critics, both within the military and without. In 2007, a group of anthropologists formed the Network of Concerned Anthropologists, which, similarly to the aforementioned statement from the American Anthropological Association, questioned the ethical and academic implications of anthropologists participating in US military operations. Dubbed "mercenary anthropology" by some, it was, according to renowned anthropologist Marshall Sahlins, "a planetary strategy of research and destroy."[78] Anna Simons took aim at both "parachute anthropologists" and "concerned anthropologists" in a 2011 article, decrying the former for overselling the usefulness of anthropology to counterinsurgency warfare and the latter for having a political axe to grind, too caught up in theoretical "navel gazing."[79] Anthropologists and other academics have a long history of collaboration with the national security apparatus of the United States, and the War on Terror reignited these debates given the emphasis placed on "cultural understanding" as a key that would unlock success in Iraq and Afghanistan.[80]

These controversies over the use of anthropology in US military strategy provide some context for my focus in the remainder of this chapter: military writing that emphasizes the importance of cultural understanding in both the Indian Wars and the War on Terror. Culture has been an attractive concept for the counterinsurgency experts of the War on Terror. If violence can be understood in cultural terms, it allows strategists to downplay or ignore the historical context of the various organizations, military and paramilitary forces, and resistance movements that are positioned as insurgents to the United States and its allies. It comes as no surprise, then, that Native American peoples, the archetypal "savage" of the Western colonial imaginary, have proved to be such an attractive comparative framework for analyzing the cultural aspects of the War on Terror.

These arguments, couched in the language of military strategy, engage in what Mahmood Mamdani calls "culture talk." These are discourses that depoliticize and de-historicize entire groups of people, focusing instead on a supposed "cultural essence" that serves to explain any number of actions, including terrorism. Culture talk tends to position populations as either premodern or anti-modern, tribalists and fundamentalists opposed to a "modernity" that is code for US global hegemony.[81] Two of the most visible originators of culture talk are Bernard Lewis, who coined the phrase "clash of civilizations" in his 1990 article "The Roots of Muslim Rage," and Samuel Huntington, who, expanding Lewis's argument, wrote in his 1993 article "The Clash of Civilizations" that "the fundamental source of conflict in this new world will not be primarily ideological or primarily economic. The great divisions among humankind and the dominating source of conflict will be cultural."[82]

The infusion of social scientific thinking into the US military approach to counterinsurgency is its own form of culture talk. In the strategic turmoil that resulted from the growing resistance to the occupation of Iraq, culture was elevated to a near-mythical key to counterinsurgency success, both as a method to "win hearts and minds" and to better deploy military violence in the complex environments of the War on Terror. Whereas Mamdani's "culture talk" is the stuff of international studies and public policy, the culture talk of counterinsurgency has attempted to transplant academic discourse into the blood, sweat, and violence of the War on Terror. The counterinsurgency field manual includes extensive discussion of culture, race, ethnicity, and other categories of social organization and difference. But despite celebration of the field manual's academic rigor, scholars have questioned just how scholarly the document's deployment of social scientific thinking really is. David Price has noted numerous instances of the manual's authors directly quoting academic work without using quotation marks and the widespread use of unacknowledged source materials.[83]

This simplistic regurgitation of anthropological concepts does little more than legitimate military occupation: critiques of colonialism, empire, and power can be discarded, and basic instruction in local manners and customs is translated into a more effective form of conquest and occupation.[84] The culture talk of counterinsurgency, unsurprisingly, has served as a popular way to connect the Indian Wars to the War on Terror in recent military writing. North American colonialism is the first and most enduring conquest that the US military has ever been involved in, and perhaps no group of people has had their diverse cultures subjected to investigation, critique, and mythologizing than Native people.

Characteristic of these arguments is the idea that improved cultural understanding will translate into success in warfare. This is how culture talk divests analysis of political and historical context. According to a 2013 study titled "Savages in a Civilized War: The Native Americans as French Allies in the Seven Years War, 1754–1763," "the modern army officer can learn much from the study of the French and Indian War. We find that knowledge of culture, of understanding your allies, and the very nature of warfare in your environment is key."[85] This study examines the French army's cooperation with Native allies during the conflict, allies who wage a form of "savage frontier warfare" that French officers often found distasteful. The author compares this history to contemporary partner forces in places like Afghanistan, who are deemed, through comparison to Native people, to be similarly savage, requiring a unique approach that begins with cultural understanding. The author argues that "understanding an irregular force's culture is crucial for success."[86] This is another way of saying that irregular warfare is a cultural practice, a primitive practice. Irregular warfare is "cultural," it is backwards, and it requires special understanding that focuses on culture and not political context.

Much of the counterinsurgency culture talk deals with so-called "tribalism." For these writers, tribalism *creates* irregular warfare; in other words, insurgency emanates from the tribal social structure of enemies in places like Afghanistan. The "tribalism" of Native peoples and groups in Afghanistan and Iraq forms the basis for these comparisons. As one study argues, "The American Indian Wars share some similarities with the Global War on Terror. The vast number of Indian tribes is comparable to the variety of terrorist groups that make up Al-Qaeda, as well as those groups not affiliated with Al-Qaeda. Additionally, the diversity of the tribal cultures of Indians is similar to the cultural differences faced throughout the Muslim world. Just as a Sioux is not a Cheyenne, Cherokee, or Apache, neither is an Arab the same as a Persian, Malaysian, or Balkan Muslim."[87] At no point in this study is *tribe* or *tribalism* defined through reference to other scholarship. The reference to tribal diversity has the opposite effect, "tribalism" itself being far more important than actual differences between Cheyenne and Apache (or Arab and Malaysian Muslims). Another study, titled "There Shall We Be Also: Tribal Fractures and Auxiliaries in the Indian Wars of the Northern Great Plains," elevates conflict with "tribes" to a central component of US military history. The author argues that the United States has a continuous history of dealing with so-called tribal societies: "From its beginning in the American Revolution to its current conflicts in Afghanistan and Iraq, the United States (US) Army has had to deal with tribal societies. In order to succeed in tribal societies it is essential that the US Army understand tribal structures and the fractures in tribal societies that present opportunities and possible solutions."[88] According to this study the Indian Wars offer perfect examples of tribal warfare to draw on: "The Indian Wars on the Great Plains from 1865–1890 clearly demonstrated that natural fractures and structures of tribal societies provide opportunities for the use of tribal auxiliaries."[89]

The author arrives at the conclusion that tribes are fractured and therefore open for exploitation through their lack of cohesion. This is consistent across many of these documents that discuss culture, particularly in the research that examines the use of Native scouts by the US Army. According to the author, tribes are defined by their fractured nature, a lack of cohesion that the counterinsurgent can exploit: "One has to look no further than the conflicts in Iraq and Afghanistan to see that tribes play a significant role in current operations. Tribal rivalries and competition play a critical role as each tribe decides to support either the insurgency or the United States (US). A common technique developed in both Iraq and Afghanistan is the use of tribal auxiliaries or militias to assist in providing security and stability."[90] This mirrors the frequent incredulity with which US settlers viewed Native resistance: in other words, how come Native tribes do not unite against us?[91] This sort of viewpoint divests Native people (and all tribal people) of complicated motivating factors based on politics, economics, and more. To be clear, not all US military appraisals of Afghanistan's tribal structure were lacking in scholarly engagement or thoughtful complexity. The point, rather, is that all the discussion of "tribes" proved a ready mechanism for the history of Indian/fighting to be inserted into the American military thinking.[92]

The emphasis on tribalism within counterinsurgency led some officers to argue that tribes are the future of warfare: "The preponderance of conflicts in our nation's future will be against foes of a tribal nature. As such, it is not likely that these tribes will possess the assets or size of a nation-state. Understanding the tribal foe, their culture, and unique identity will be critical to strategic success for the United States."[93] These tribes are understood to be outside of time, history, and politics: "Tribes operate outside modern political, economic, and military systems."[94] For this author, tribes exist at the fringes of a modernity they oppose. The argument is that the US military simply has to understand why tribes do what they do, no matter how irrational or barbaric it may be: "One of the issues the nation clearly has difficulties with is seeing things as our enemies see them. This is not to say that we should lower ourselves to their 'barbaric' standards (though that is an option). Rather we should attempt to understand why they do what they do. It is hard to be empathetic with a group that hunts down and tortures members of another group—particularly when both groups have the same language and similar customs and rituals."[95] Given that these tribal peoples supposedly operate outside the confines of politics or economics, the author attempts to apply a cultural frame of analysis to their "barbaric" practices. One is left to wonder where that metric leaves the United States. History tells us that killing and torture are not restricted to America's "primitive" enemies.[96]

Some of these military documents take seriously Native resistance to colonialism and acknowledge the pressures that resulted from conquest. The writer of a thesis titled "Uncomfortable Experience: Lessons Lost in the Apache War" is an example of this, noting, for instance, the influence that the reservation system had on Nazi Germany. But attention to conquest only goes so far. While discussing the invasion of Apache land in the Southwest, the author argues that if US officials had understood Apache culture better, the Apache may have willingly accepted removal from their homelands. Culture becomes another way to get around talking about conquest. It is unlikely that greater understandings of Apache culture would have prevented Apache resistance to invasion. This sort of analysis is applied to the occupation of Iraq, and similar conclusions are drawn: "At the highest levels, the United States' removal policy shares many parallels with the Bush administration's decision to implement de-Ba'athification and disband the Iraqi national army in Iraq following Operation Iraqi Freedom. In both instances, the government failed to recognize the implications of their decisions, which were based on gross over-simplifications of cultural understanding."[97] On one level this is a compelling analysis of how occupying powers can damage their attempts to restore political stability through ignorance. However, one is left to wonder whether the presence of several anthropologists in the Bush administration would have resulted in a different geopolitical trajectory. It seems unlikely. But the pervasive idea that "cultural understanding" can minimize missteps in warfare shows just how deeply rooted counterinsurgency culture is in the legacy of colonialism. Simplistic discussions of culture narrow the frame, reducing largescale questions of imperialism and conquest down to communities and individuals. The question becomes "how can we keep them from resisting?" rather than "why are they resisting?"

THE MAN WHO KNOWS INDIANS

No frontier officer gets more credit for understanding Native culture than George Crook, a US Army general who served all over the United States during the Indian Wars. The editor of Crook's autobiography calls the general "the acknowledged master" of Indian warfare. Robert M. Cassidy, a veteran of the wars in Afghanistan and Iraq, refers to Crook in his 2008 book *Counterinsurgency and the Global War on Terror* as "the quintessential counterguerrilla leader."[98] Crook has proven to be a popular topic for US military officers that study counterinsurgency. He is the focus of more research projects completed by officers than any other topic from the Indian Wars and is mentioned in several of the publications in the Global War on Terrorism series from the CSI. Crook has become something of a counterinsurgency legend.

A study from 2001 titled "General Crook and Counterinsurgency Warfare" argues that "General Crook was one of the few senior officers who spent the majority of his military career conducting counterinsurgency operations. He left a written record of that history, a record that did not make its way into doctrine."[99] Due to this lack of doctrinal continuity, more than a historical lesson, Crook is rendered as the precedent for contemporary counterinsurgency warfare. That same master's thesis claims that "the antecedents of how the U.S. Army conducts its stability and support operations in the present day can be directly related to how the military conducted operations against the Indians in the nineteenth century. The current emphasis in stability operations on mobility, continuous operations, small unit leadership, and self-sufficiency are all directly related to the U.S. Army's experience fighting the Indians. This continuity of experience needs to be understood by the military."[100] But are they directly related? This entire book has focused on how the Indian Wars, while exercising a powerful and continuous hold on the US military, failed to make a lasting impact on military doctrine during the nineteenth century. This "continuity of experience" did not receive broad acknowledgment in the US military until the twenty-first century. Crook even wrote up a detailed "resume of operations" that outlined his approach to Indian warfare, defending both his use of Apache scouts and his actions during the campaigns against Geronimo and the Chiricahua Apache. However, the military refused to publish the *Resumé*. They recognized that it was Crook's attempt to legitimate his actions and were unwilling to aggravate an already bitter debate over Crook's and Nelson A. Miles's responsibility for ending Apache military resistance.[101] Crook ultimately self-published his *Resumé of Operations against Apache Indians, 1882–1886* in limited quantities, but it has remained a scarce item, and certainly never entered formal US military doctrine.

Nevertheless, contemporary counterinsurgency thinkers hold Crook up as a crucial part of America's counterinsurgency legacy: "Whether it is MacArthur on Luzon or Pershing in Moroland and Mexico, one can see the outline of Crook's techniques in these successful campaigns. A generation of officers served with Crook in the southwest, where they gained an appreciation of the complexities of combating an insurgency and the knowledge on how to solve those complexities and gain success in a counterinsurgency environment. This is the legacy that Crook left the United States Army."[102] It is reasonable to assume that officers like MacArthur and Pershing carried an influence from Crook's southwestern campaigns with them across borders and overseas. Many of the officers who served under Crook and Miles in the Southwest went on to lead the US Army during the Spanish-American War, the Philippine-American War, and World War One. But once these officers left the military, Crook's knowledge would have left with them, so we can question just how much of a legacy Crook left behind. It is more accurate to say that interest in George Crook is maintained through the persistent connection made between Native people and irregular warfare, interest driven by Crook's reputation as a frontier officer who understood Native people.

Take, for example, this analysis of Crook in a master's thesis completed by a Marine Corps major titled "Redskins in Bluecoats: A Strategic and Cultural Analysis of General George Crook's Use of Apache Scouts in the Second Apache Campaign, 1882–1886":[103] "During General George Crook's Second Apache Campaign (1882–1886), his unique approach to the use of Apache scouts and his culturally sensitive leadership were so misunderstood by his contemporaries that it eventually led to his resignation of command and the imprisonment of all Chiricahua Apache scouts who faithfully served the US Army following General Nelson Miles' successful completion of the Apache campaign."[104] The author's emphasis on "culturally sensitive leadership" evokes the sort of culture talk discussed in the previous section. Understanding "culture" provides the basis for Crook's attractiveness as a historical example of counterinsurgency. According to this study, and others, Crook *understood* Apache people, at least more than his peers, making him the ideal counterinsurgency example for the War on Terror. As the author notes, this sort of cultural sensitivity is essential in a war with "indigenous peoples" with whom the US military alternates between combat and the provision of humanitarian assistance: "The military, as an organization, is more understanding of the cultural dimensions of warfare today and how this makes a huge impact on the success of its current campaigns."[105]

The bulk of the study focuses on Crook's success utilizing Apache scouts in his operations. Crook did not attempt to turn Apache warriors into US soldiers; rather, he utilized their unique skills in tracking in the arid Southwest, and they proved extremely effective in enabling the US Army to track down and engage resistant Apache groups.[106] The Army's use of Native scouts generated plenty of resistance, but Crook consistently defended the practice, and ultimately he was vindicated by the integral role Apache scouts played in the final surrender of Geronimo in 1886. As Crook argued in his *Resumé of Operations*, "There has never been any success in operations against these Indians, unless Indian scouts were used either as auxiliaries or independent of other support."[107] At the very least, Crook was able to convince Apache individuals to enlist in the military and serve effectively, a cross-cultural step that many of his contemporaries balked at. Crook's use of scouts is given particular weight for the supposedly "cultural" effect they have. As the thesis "Major General George Crook's Use of Counterinsurgency Compound Warfare during the Great Sioux War of 1876–77" argues, "A highly skilled conventional force fighting an insurgency will often face significant cultural, ethnic, linguistic and physical challenges. An irregular, indigenous force can fill the gap and meet many of these challenges by working in concert with the conventional force."[108]

Crook is celebrated as one of the more Native-friendly US generals, which, at least comparatively speaking, has some basis in reality.[109] For example, when he resumed command of the Department of Arizona in 1882 he issued a general order that, among other directives, proclaimed that "officers and soldiers serving in the department are reminded that one of the fundamental principles of the military character is, justice to all—Indians as well as white men—and that a disregard of this principle is likely to bring about hostilities, and cause the death of the very persons whom they are sent here to protect." Crook also ordered his officers to observe "the strictest fidelity" and to address Native complaints quickly and fairly.[110] He certainly respected Apache prowess, evidenced by his insistence on using Apache scouts. Crook argued that in borderlands warfare the Apache "is more than equal of the white man, and it would be practically impossible with white soldiers to subdue the Chiricahuas in their own haunts."[111] Like most Army officers, Crook was not single-mindedly genocidal in his rhetoric, which was often enmeshed in the "state of quasi war" that defined frontier violence.

But we should not exaggerate Crook's cultural sensitivity. Like many Anglo-American settlers, soldiers, and politicians, Crook often depicted Apache people in bestial terms. In his *Resumé of Operations* he calls the Apache "savage and brutal by instinct" and "tigers of the human race."[112] Similarly, in an article for the *JMSI*, Crook, in multiple places, compares the Apache to wolves and coyotes: "The Apache can be compared most aptly to the wild animal he fittingly calls his cousin—the coyote. The civilized settlements are his sheep-folds, and even supposing that a toilsome campaign results in destroying forty out of a band of fifty, the survivors are as much to be dreaded as ever, until the very last one can be run down, killed or got under control, and taught to labor for his bread."[113] Crook certainly was not the only American in the late nineteenth century to denigrate Apache people in racialized, bestial language. The persistent dehumanization of Apache people as animals was commonplace and resulted in excessive patterns of violence and mutilation by settlers in the Southwest. Crook was typical in that regard, no matter his reputation as a scholar of Native culture and a defender of Indian rights.[114] And that is precisely the point: counterinsurgency culture talk, whether in the nineteenth or twenty-first century, does not necessarily translate into empathy, respect, or an erosion of racist caricatures and depictions. And this is a crucial reminder that conquest when prosecuted with greater cultural awareness *is still conquest*. Strategy is not the same as ethics, and cultural understanding does not necessarily translate into empathy.

According to the contemporary counterinsurgents that lionize Crook, it is the general's adaptability and cultural understanding that led to his success, a blueprint for the modern military: "General George Crook's ability to adapt to his enemy, and his understanding of the nuance and context required to fight a war against an unconventional foe, in what amounted to a true clash of civilizations, are the lessons that are as applicable to the modern United States military as they were on the American frontier."[115] Another study offers greater detail, emphasizing Crook's ability to overcome tactical and cultural barriers posed by differences in language, culture, social organization, government, and religion.[116] But even these more technical descriptions are combined with similarly racialized cultural moves. In a 2003 USAWC Strategy Research Project titled "Lessons Learned from MG George Crook's Apache Campaigns with Applicability for the Current Global War on Terror," we get a particular kind of cultural comparison: "Both the historical and current enemies have cadres of fighters who believe death in battle is to be sought out and embraced. These fighters make no distinctions between military forces and unprotected populations except to seek out vulnerable populations and to avoid pitched battles. Both enemies seek to fight a technologically simpler fight, and to do so in a manner that seeks to minimize the strengths of US forces."[117] The lesson is that understanding Apache people, represented here as death-obsessed obstacles to progress, will lead to a smoother form of conquest. This analysis reduces the invasion of Apache land to a clash of cultures, with Crook positioned as an expert on Apache people. In George Crook the proponents of the humanitarian violence of counterinsurgency find a historical precedent.

TOMAHAWKS IN AFGHANISTAN

Indian country, Indian Wars, Indian country, Indian Wars . . . perhaps at times this chapter has felt like a vinyl record locked into a single groove, endlessly repeating the same loop. I have emphasized this litany of Indian War resonances (seen again in Figure 11) in order to explore the ways in which colonial violence continues to structure American counterinsurgency culture. Permit me two more utterances from these endless Indian Wars. The first comes from Allan R. Millet, a retired Marine Corps colonel. In 2001, referring to the difficulties of conducting military operations in the mountainous terrain of Afghanistan, he argued that "It's like shooting missiles at Geronimo. . . . You might get a couple of Apaches, but what difference does that make?"[118] Here is a juxtaposition of the United States' absurd technological superiority and the disposable life of the Apache/Afghanis. Each Tomahawk cruise missile costs more than one million dollars, so why bother launching

FIGURE 11. Soldiers in Afghanistan commemorate the 66th anniversary of the D-Day invasion by giving each other mohawk haircuts and donning war paint, a reference to the "Filthy Thirteen." Photo by Spc. Tracy R. Myers, June 2010, photo 302831, Defense Visual Information Distribution Service.

them into the mountaintops if all the US military has to show for it are a few enemy casualties, particularly if Geronimo/bin Laden continues to escape? The arithmetic of colonial necropolitics allows for such calculations, and Indian people remain the rubric through which US imperialism imagines such hostile terrains, impenetrable even to the destruction of flying tomahawks. This is Indian country as the place of imperial intervention, a site of violence and danger, forever the frontier of US militarism.

This chapter has been almost entirely focused on the ways in which non-Natives have twisted and shaped images of Indian people and histories of colonialism to serve the imaginative needs of US empire. It seems appropriate to end with a Native voice, in this case a Native veteran named Sergeant Eli Painted Crow, who served twenty-two years in the US Army, including a final tour in Iraq. The following is an exchange with journalist Amy Goodman on the news program *Democracy Now!* from 2007.

Amy Goodman: How did you end up becoming a peace activist, Sergeant Painted Crow?

Sgt. Eli Painted Crow: Well, this is very important for me, because being Native, I don't see this as a war, number one. I see this as an invasion that's committing a genocide to a nation, to a people. I see that we are over there, and we are doing the same thing that we did here with the indigenous people of this land, calling it democracy, calling it freedom. Well, it isn't freedom if it's imposed. And what I learned about the Iraqi people, while I was there, was they're very much like the indigenous people here. They have clans, they have circles, they have their ceremonies, they have their drum. There are so many similarities, and it just really hurt me to realize that here I'm a survivor of this attempted genocide on my people—and I say "attempted," because we're still here, even though they want to say we're not, we're erased, we're not even in the history books—and here I am over there doing the same thing that was done to me, and so I—

Amy Goodman: You said that in the military they refer to Iraq as "Indian country"?

Sgt. Eli Painted Crow: Well, they referred to—what they said in the briefing, they called enemy territory "Indian country." And I'm standing there, just listening to this briefing, and I'm just in shock that after all this time, after so many Natives have served and are serving and are dying, that we are still the enemy, even if we're wearing the same uniform. That was very shocking for me to hear.[119]

Sergeant Painted Crow's story about standing in a briefing and hearing the phrase "Indian country" says more than any amount of analysis could. What must it feel like for Native soldiers to hear the phrase "Indian country" while deployed, describing the very territory in which they risk life and limb? Historians of North American colonialism often talk about "facing east from Indian country," inverting common narratives of US history in an attempt to capture the perspective of Native people facing a settler invasion.[120] Native soldiers serving in places like Afghanistan and Iraq face Indian country *from* Indian country, and they are uniquely positioned to recognize these imperial geographies for what they are: sites of invasion and conquest.

Twenty-first-century writing on irregular warfare has often invoked comparisons between the Indian Wars and the War on Terror. Native people have been positioned as the eternal insurgents of US empire, the savages at the gate from whom counterinsurgency warfare supposedly keeps the world safe. These are comparisons that perpetuate colonial narratives of US history and legitimate racialized forms of violence. However, Sergeant Painted Crow twists these comparisons in her description of Iraq. Her list of similarities between Native North Americans and Iraqis—clans, circles, ceremonies, drums—serves as a critique of the US invasion and occupation, rather than a blueprint for more effective conquest. Iraq is not like Indian country because it is full of savages, guerilla fighters, rugged terrain, and recalcitrant tribal peoples. Iraq is like Indian country because both have experienced the full force of the United States' militarized imperial power. Sergeant Painted Crow articulates a resonance of Indian country not as an invocation of empire, but as a critique. In her telling, Indian country is the place where the United States military should *not* be, the site of invasion, of conquest, of an unbroken colonial legacy.

Conclusion

Counterinsurgency in Indian Country

Twenty sixteen was a year of visceral and violent political moments, but few matched the historical intensity of the Dakota Access Pipeline protests carried out by the Standing Rock Sioux and their allies. Videos and images, many disseminated on social media, showed groups of water protectors repeatedly targeted by police and paramilitary security forces with "less than lethal weapons." The images evoked the so-called "Indian Wars" of the nineteenth century, and they were a reminder of the ongoing violence of US settler colonialism. Resistance to the pipeline forged networks of transnational Indigenous solidarity even as the treaty claims of the Standing Rock Sioux were at times flattened by an environmentalism discourse that obfuscated Native sovereignty.[1]

The camps housing water protectors attracted people from all over the world, including hundreds of US military veterans. In a public ceremony on December 5, 2016, following a temporary break in the protests, a group of veterans issued a public apology to Native elders: "We came. We fought you. We took your land. We signed treaties that we broke."[2] Acutely aware of the role that the US military played in the conquest of Native people, these veterans sought to acknowledge that history and received a message of forgiveness from Lakota spiritual leader Leonard Crow Dog. After this brief reprieve in December 2016, the resistance continued into early 2017, when the protest camps were finally closed down following an executive order from newly elected president Donald Trump.[3] In June of 2017 the pipeline began transporting oil.

Colonialism in the United States defies temporal boundaries, requiring analysis that can move fluidly between the past and the present. The #NODAPL protests offer a window into the ongoing Indian Wars of the twenty-first century. The veterans who apologized at Standing Rock were likely focused on the military's role in nineteenth-century conflicts. But there were contemporary resonances as well. One Native veteran who attended the forgiveness ceremony noted that most veterans had received training in the sort of crowd suppression techniques used by law enforcement on the protesters at Standing Rock, linking domestic repression to the counterinsurgency tactics of the War on Terror: "We know that everyone on the other side of that has that training, so they know exactly the damage or the pain that they are inflicting."[4] Active-duty members of the military also took note of the historical continuities at Standing Rock. As one officer at the CGSC put it: "The United States government still manages the consequences of it [the Indian Wars] today through the United States Department of the Interior's Bureau of Indian Affairs. While Native American tribes may no longer have the capacity to fight a protracted insurgency against the United States government, significant issues still occur, even as late as 2016, demonstrated by the large-scale protests of the Dakota Access pipeline by the Standing Rock Sioux."[5] This officer frames ongoing colonialism as a perpetual counterinsurgency, and the extreme, militarized response at Standing Rock is evidence that Indigenous sovereignty claims will continue to be met with violence. And while this writer mentions Standing Rock, the focus is US counterinsurgency strategy on a global scale. The main thrust of his argument is that the Indian Wars offer valuable strategic insight into the War on Terror: "The lessons the Indian Wars provide are still salient and must not be lost to posterity, especially for professional military study."[6]

It is not coincidental that a Marine Corps officer would be connecting Native people, Standing Rock, and counterinsurgency in the year 2017. The US military has spent much of the twenty-first century preoccupied with counterinsurgency in response to the wars in Afghanistan, Iraq, and elsewhere. As officers scrambled to relearn and update the counterinsurgency tactics long relegated to the fringes of US military doctrine, the Indian Wars emerged as a historical "success," an example on which to draw. These conflicts have always exercised a powerful cultural hold, particularly in the military. Enemy territory has often been "Indian country," from the Philippines, to Vietnam, to Iraq.[7] US soldiers have imagined their enemies as "Indians" and imagined themselves as

"Indian fighters," inheritors of the shadow doctrines that continually drive US imperial power. But in the last fifteen-plus years, at places like the CSI and the USAWC, "Indian country" went beyond a series of discursive resonances as officers offered recommendations for the War on Terror that attempted to draw strategic lessons from wars with Native people. The contemporary military discourse on counterinsurgency warfare now situates continental expansion as the earliest, and one of the most effective, examples of this form of warfare.

This complex web of colonial histories played out at Standing Rock: veterans of the wars in Afghanistan and Iraq apologizing on treaty lands as paramilitary forces deployed counterterrorism measures against Indigenous water protectors, many of whom were themselves veterans. Temporal boundaries seemed to blur as if America's long counterinsurgency had come full circle. Private security firm TigerSwan, hired by pipeline builder Energy Transfer Partners to disrupt the protests in coordination with law enforcement, utilized a range of counterinsurgency tactics against what internal memos described as "an ideologically driven insurgency with a strong religious component," elsewhere noting that the resistance to the pipeline "generally followed the jihadist insurgency model while active," and that "we can expect the individuals who fought for and supported it to follow a post-insurgency model after its collapse."[8]

Indeed, internal TigerSwan communications referred to future antipipeline protests as budding insurgencies that had to be met with counterinsurgency efforts: "While we can expect to see the continued spread of the anti-DAPL diaspora . . . aggressive intelligence preparation of the battlefield and active coordination between intelligence and security elements are now a proven method of defeating pipeline insurgencies." *Pipeline insurgencies.* It would be easy to dismiss TigerSwan's rhetoric as alarmist hyperbole, but these are categorizations made by a company full of War on Terror veterans, soldiers serving the interests of both state and capital. In a disturbing blending of public and private interests, TigerSwan intelligence memos were regularly shared with state and federal law enforcement, and contractors met with investigators from the North Dakota attorney general's office and collected evidence that would aid in the prosecution of water protectors.[9]

As the water protectors left the protest camp in February 2017, TigerSwan continued to exaggerate the threat of violence. A memo from TigerSwan to the pipeline company, Energy Transfer Partners, warned, "The threat level has dropped significantly. This however does not rule out the chance of future attack. . . . As with any dispersion of any insurgency, expect bifurcation into splinter groups, looking for new causes."[10] Warning of an "anti-DAPL diaspora," one TigerSwan report predicted a flowering of insurgent cells similar to the aftermath of the anti-Soviet jihad in Afghanistan: "The archetype of a jihadist post-insurgency is the aftermath of the anti-Soviet Afghanistan jihad. While many insurgents went back to their pre-war lives, many, especially the external supporters (foreign fighters), went back out into the world looking to start or join new jihadist insurgencies. Most famously this "bleedout" resulted in Osama bin Laden and the rise of Al-Qaeda, but the jihadist veterans of Afghanistan also ended up fighting in Bosnia, Chechnya, North Africa, and Indonesia, among other places."[11] Portraying pipeline protesters as terrorists was not surprising to anyone that has followed the criminalization of animal rights and environmental activists. The repression and surveillance of so-called "eco-terrorists" in the years after 9/11 was widespread, and included the Animal Liberation Front, the Earth Liberation Front, Greenpeace, the Sea Shepherd Conservation Society, PETA, and others.[12]

TigerSwan and other law enforcement groups readily grouped the #NODAPL movement within the "eco-terrorist" umbrella, and company leaders continued to compare anti-pipeline protesters all over the United States to Islamic terrorists.[13] If the conduct of TigerSwan, other private security firms, and both local and federal law enforcement during anti-pipeline protests is any indication, "counterinsurgency" is becoming one of the dominant paradigms through which law enforcement views domestic protest and civil disobedience, particularly in Indian country. More than a year after the end of the #NODAPL protests, in September of 2018, the Department of Justice held an anti-terrorism training in Montana, likely in preparation for possible Native-led protest of the Keystone XL oil pipeline. Montana law enforcement agencies and state officials also worked with their counterparts in North Dakota to learn how to combat Indigenous water protectors and their allies.[14] Perhaps we have entered the era of pipeline insurgencies. The state-issued permit for the Line 3 pipeline in Minnesota included a clause specifying that "the Permittee, the permittee's contractors and assigns will not participate in counterinsurgency tactics or misinformation campaigns to interfere with the rights of the public to legally exercise their Constitutional rights," although activists claim those conditions have been violated.[15]

At this point it is appropriate to return to a passage from the introduction to this book. To once more quote a US Army officer, writing in

2003: "Both the Apaches and the Islamists possess a charismatic group of leaders. The Apaches were led by Cochise, Natchez, Victorio, Geronimo and others, names that still echo throughout the world. Today the leaders include Osama bin Laden, Mullah Omar. . . . All these historical and current leaders preach a fantasy ideology that seek[s] to have the US depart from 'their' territories and for 'the people' to return to an imagined life that is forever gone."[16] Comparisons like these point to the enduring hold that Native people have on US culture as the always-enemies haunting the edges of the American imaginary. But they also call attention to the role settler colonialism played in the development of proto-counterinsurgent ideologies that disavow Indigenous sovereignty in favor of a biopolitical claim of ownership over Native lives. The existence of Native nations is branded a fantasy ideology, and Native life, divested of its indigeneity, is claimed by the state. It is the persistence of such attitudes toward Native people that this project has tried to push back against, flipping "counterinsurgency" from a definition to a mode of critique that can account for the material and discursive effects of US colonialism. Counterinsurgency as a form of critique works to show how the US government and capital have a vested interest in continuing the centuries-long process of eroding and eliminating Native sovereignty.

In contrast to such blatant disavowals of Native sovereignty, the water protectors at Standing Rock attempted to mobilize their own biopolitical discourse through the slogan "water is life," insisting, as Joanne Barker writes, "on the vitality and viability of Indigenous governance, territorial integrity and cultural autonomy."[17] These assertions ran headlong into a far more entrenched biopower embedded in the colonial mechanisms by which the US continues to regulate the lives of Native peoples. A similar relationship exists between the assertion that "Black Lives Matter," and the response from police and politicians that "security and capital matter more" (to say nothing of the slogan "Blue Lives Matter").[18] Native lives and entire Native populations have been rendered, at different times, as killable, changeable, disposable, invisible, and hyper-visible, subjected to particular forms of state violence.

In contrast, #NODAPL and Black Lives Matter seem to both invoke what Michael Hardt and Antonio Negri call a "power of life by which we defend and seek our freedom," a biopolitics not of control, but of emancipatory potential, of the production of alternative subjectivities unbound by regimes of discipline, security, and repression. For Hardt and Negri, biopolitics is a site of struggle, and not a totalizing force.[19]

FIGURE 12. Indian Wars everywhere . . . "Air Apache" insignia of the 345th Bomb Group of the Fifth Air Force Bomber Command. Somewhere in the Pacific Theater, 1945. National Archives photo no. 204989436.

At stake in these competing discourses are the political meanings and values attached to "life." Water protectors defend the increasingly precarious role that natural resources play in sustaining human beings.[20] Black Lives Matter challenges the violence of entrenched anti-Black racism. In contrast, the normalization of counterinsurgency and other forms of irregular warfare, at home and abroad, has further embedded biopolitics in the mechanisms of war, policing, and social control.[21] "Life" under counterinsurgency is both under threat and under control; counterinsurgency mobilizes threats to life as a justification for the violence of security, and targets life as the object of military intervention. Under counterinsurgency, war not only makes the world safe, it *makes the world*, attempting to shape individual subjectivities, populations, and environments.[22] In this world, water matters less than capital, and Black lives remain threatened by the United States' racialized systems of control. As the archetypal "savages" of the Western colonial imaginary, Native people have been integral to the security discourses that define the world as dangerous, in need of intervention. "Indian country" is the United States' first security discourse, and Indian/fighting has been the mechanism for achieving that security.

It is appropriate that I would conclude this book with a discussion of #NODAPL and the repression at Standing Rock. The population-centric warfare deployed in Iraq and Afghanistan was reduced under the Obama administration, which saw an expansion of special operations under the Joint Special Operations Command and an increase in drone warfare, a further mechanization of warfare that stood in stark contrast to the intimate, community-based counterinsurgency championed by Petraeus and other COINdinistas during the Bush administration and the early part of the Obama administration. Instead of committing to large-scale developmental warfare and long-term deployment of troops, President Obama's counterterrorism strategy combined drones, legal experts, and Special Forces, with an emphasis on foreign partnerships and a more "humane" war. This meant working "by, with, and through" the governments in the countries in which the United States sought to intervene, a practice Laleh Khalili calls indirect rule, a common feature of imperial counterinsurgencies during the twentieth century.[23]

And, for all the "America First" rhetoric about travel bans and border walls, the Trump presidency largely continued the outward-facing imperialism of indirect rule while expanding the military's ability to conduct air strikes and drone attacks.[24] A survey of recent articles from places like the US Military Academy and the USAWC indicates that a familiar anxiety about "forgetting" counterinsurgency and other forms of irregular warfare is once again circulating in military circles. These fears have intensified in the aftermath of the US withdrawal from Afghanistan, coinciding with anxieties about large-scale conflict with Russia or China.[25] Perhaps Americans will once more "forget" counterinsurgency as they simultaneously forget their own imperial history. In a now ironic speech regarding Middle East policy given in Cairo in 2019, Trump's secretary of state, Mike Pompeo, declared that "those who fret about the use of American power, remember this: America has always been, and always will be, a liberating force, not an occupying power. . . . When the mission is over, when the job is complete, America leaves."[26] The United States only recently left Afghanistan after twenty years, and it is hard to argue that the job was "complete." Of course, the true hypocrisy of Pompeo's claim resides in Indian country, an occupation that numbers in the hundreds of years.

It remains unclear where American warfare is headed. It is possible the strategies championed by the counterinsurgency field manual will fade away in the face of technological advances and "great power" rivalries. However, similar arguments were made in the 1990s, and that did not prevent the US military from deploying large numbers of troops to sustained occupations in Afghanistan and Iraq. Which brings us back to Standing Rock and other sites of resources extraction, as well as the movements for racial equality that continue to push for the reform, if not outright abolition, of American police forces.[27] Given the violence against protesters enacted by police and federal agents in the aftermath of the murder of George Floyd in May 2020, and the continued repression of water protectors, perhaps we know exactly where the long history of US irregular warfare is headed: once more into Indian country, into the police departments of American cities, and into the ranks of private security firms promoting the interests of capital, empire, and resource extraction.

Notes

INTRODUCTION

1. Douglas Little, *Us versus Them: The United States, Radical Islam, and the Rise of the Green Threat* (Chapel Hill: University of North Carolina Press, 2016), 202–3.

2. Karl Jacoby, "Operation Geronimo Dishonors the Indian Leader," *Los Angeles Times*, May 10, 2011, articles.latimes.com; Kevin Bruyneel, *Settler Memory: The Disavowal of Indigeneity and the Politics of Race in the United States* (Chapel Hill: University of North Carolina Press, 2021), 132–35; Winona LaDuke and Sean Aaron Cruz, *The Militarization of Indian Country* (East Lansing: Michigan State University Press, 2013), 17.

3. Thomas King, *The Inconvenient Indian: A Curious Account of Native People in North America* (Minneapolis: University of Minnesota Press, 2013), 25–26.

4. C. Richard King, *Unsettling America: The Uses of Indianness in the 21st Century* (Lanham: Rowman & Littlefield, 2013), 57.

5. Aaron O'Connell, "Moving Mountains: Cultural Friction in the Afghanistan War," in *Our Latest Longest War: Losing Hearts and Minds in Afghanistan*, ed. Aaron O'Connell (Chicago: University of Chicago Press, 2017), 12; Jodi A. Byrd, *The Transit of Empire: Indigenous Critiques of Colonialism* (Minneapolis: University of Minnesota Press, 2011), xviii; Jasbir K. Puar, *Terrorist Assemblages: Homonationalism in Queer Times* (Durham, NC: Duke University Press, 2007), xxiii–xxv; Mahmood Mamdani, *Good Muslim, Bad Muslim: America, the Cold War, and the Roots of Terror* (New York: Pantheon Books, 2004), 15–16; Samuel Moyn, *Humane: How the United States Abandoned*

Peace and Reinvented War (New York: Farrar, Straus and Giroux, 2021), 4; Spencer Ackerman, *Reign of Terror: How the 9/11 Era Destabilized America and Produced Trump* (New York: Penguin, 2022), xvii.

6. Evelyn Alsultany, "Arabs and Muslims in the Media after 9/11: Representational Strategies for a 'Postrace' Era," *American Quarterly* 65, no. 1 (March 1, 2013): 161–69; Manu Vimalassery, "Antecedents of Imperial Incarceration: Fort Marion to Guantánamo," in *The Sun Never Sets: South Asian Migrants in an Age of U.S. Power*, eds. Vivek Bald, Miabi Chatterji, Sujani Reddy, Manu Vimalassery (New York: New York University Press, 2013), 350–53; Puar, *Terrorist Assemblages*, xxiii–xxv.

7. Mamdani, *Good Muslim Bad Muslim*, 17–19; Derek Gregory, *The Colonial Present: Afghanistan, Palestine, Iraq* (Malden, MA: Wiley, 2004), 249; Amy Kaplan, *Our American Israel: The Story of an Entangled Alliance* (Cambridge, MA: Harvard University Press, 2018), 8, 239–40; Joanne Barker, *Red Scare: The State's Indigenous Terrorist* (Oakland: University of California Press, 2021), 16–18.

8. Alex Lubin, *Never-Ending War on Terror* (Oakland: University of California Press, 2021), 20; Mark Cronlund Anderson, *Holy War: Cowboys, Indians, and 9/11s* (Regina, SK: University of Regina, 2016), 2–3; Nikhil Pal Singh, *Race and America's Long War* (Oakland: University of California Press, 2017), xii. See also: María Josefina Saldaña-Portillo, *Indian Given: Racial Geographies across Mexico and the United States* (Durham, NC: Duke University Press, 2016).

9. Stephen Biddle, quoted in Alexandra Zavis, "A Huge New U.S. Symbol In Iraq," *Los Angeles Times*, July 24, 2007; Robert D. Kaplan, *Imperial Grunts: The American Military on the Ground* (New York: Random House), 4; Elliot Ackerman, quoted in Brian Castner, "Afghanistan: A Stage without a Play," *Los Angeles Review of Books*, October 2, 2014, https://lareviewofbooks.org/article/afghanistan-stage-without-play/.

10. On the history of naming military helicopters after tribes, see "Why Army Helicopters Have Native American Names," US Department of Defense, November 29, 2019, https://www.defense.gov/News/Inside-DOD/Blog/Article/2052989/why-army-helicopters-have-native-american-names/.

11. Paul C. Rosier, *Serving Their Country: American Indian Politics and Patriotism in the Twentieth Century* (Cambridge, MA: Harvard University Press, 2009), 3. "Indian Country" was first used by King George III in the Royal Proclamation of 1763, which forbade settlement west of the Appalachians. Since then, the phrase has taken on a variety of meanings. See Mahmood Mamdani, *Neither Settler nor Native* (Cambridge, MA: Harvard University Press, 2020), 42.

12. King, *The Inconvenient Indian*, 21–22.

13. The idea of a "colonial present" is borrowed from Derek Gregory, and then filtered through the literature that explores how setter-colonialism is not a thing "in the past" but an ongoing set of structures, relationships, and ideas that perpetuate the colonization of indigenous peoples. See Derek Gregory, *The Colonial Present*. For settler colonialism see Patrick Wolfe, *Settler Colonialism and the Transformation of Anthropology: The Politics and Poetics of an Ethnographic Event* (New York: Cassell, 1999), 1–2; Audra Simpson, *Mohawk Interruptus: Political Life Across the Borders of Settler States* (Durham, NC:

Duke University Press, 2014), 10–12; Kevin Bruyneel, *Settler Memory*, 8–10; Rita Dhamoon, "A Feminist Approach to Decolonizing Anti-Racism: Rethinking Transnationalism, Intersectionality, and Settler Colonialism," *Feral Feminisms* no. 4 (Summer 2015).

14. While I owe a substantial debt to Slotkin and Drinnon, the frontier is an incomplete formulation for describing the continuous reproduction of "Indian/fighting" in US history. The frontier implies a process that is continually transcended, as the frontier line is pushed farther west, and the civilizing process goes through its successive stages. In fact, the colonial process is forever incomplete, and the settler-state needs to continually enact those colonizing pressures to maintain itself. This book also pays more attention to military sources than either Slotkin, Drinnon, or Byrd. See Richard Slotkin, *Gunfighter Nation: The Myth of the Frontier in Twentieth-Century America* (New York: Atheneum, 1992); Richard Drinnon, *Facing West: The Metaphysics of Indian-Hating and Empire Building* (Minneapolis: University of Minnesota Press, 1980). Other works that consider the resonances of the Indian Wars include Tom Engelhardt, *The End of Victory Culture: Cold War America and the Disillusioning of a Generation* (Amherst: University of Massachusetts Press, 2007); Stephen W. Silliman, "The 'Old West' in the Middle East: U.S. Military Metaphors in Real and Imagined Indian Country," *American Anthropologist* 110, no. 2 (June 2008): 237–47; Singh, *Race and America's Long War*; Katharine Bjork, *Prairie Imperialists: The Indian Country Origins of American Empire* (Philadelphia: University of Pennsylvania Press, 2018).

15. One of the ways this book expands on Byrd's argument is by showing that the expansion of US empire has deployed Indian/fighting not just to describe "others," but also as a way for US soldiers to imagine themselves. Byrd, *The Transit of Empire*.

16. I am not the first to argue that the Indian Wars are "everywhere." D'Arcy McNickle's history of Native resistance in the twentieth century referred to an "Indian war that never ends." See D'Arcy McNickle, *They Came Here First: The Epic of the American Indian* (New York: Harper & Row, 1975).

17. There are several examples of excellent scholarship that cite the Indian Wars as an early example of counterinsurgency without thoroughly examining exactly how those conflicts influenced later doctrine. See Laleh Khalili, *Time in the Shadows: Confinement in Counterinsurgencies* (Stanford, CA: Stanford University Press, 2012; Singh, *Race and America's Long War*; Jordan T. Camp and Jennifer Greenburg, "Counterinsurgency Reexamined: Racism, Capitalism, and US Military Doctrine," *Antipode* 52, no. 2 (March 2020); Moyn, *Humane*.

18. Indian/fighting is shorthand for bringing together two literatures, one that explores racialized forms of military violence, and the other we might call "playing Indian," or the ways settlers have performed indigeneity for a variety of reasons. For racialized warfare, see Paul A. Kramer, *The Blood of Government: Race, Empire, the United States, and the Philippines* (Chapel Hill: University of North Carolina Press, 2006); Singh, *Race and America's Long War*. For "playing Indian," see Richard Slotkin, *Regeneration through Violence; the Mythology of the American Frontier, 1600–1860* (Middletown, CT: Wesleyan

University Press, 1973); Philip Joseph Deloria, *Playing Indian* (New Haven, CT: Yale University Press, 1998).

19. My concept of "shadow doctrines" is informed by what David Fitzgerald calls "informal doctrine," the conversations about military doctrine carried out in less formal venues such as professional journals. These forums allowed for the transmission of institutional knowledge (such as Indian/fighting) not codified in strategic manuals and other locations of "formal doctrine." See David Fitzgerald, *Learning to Forget: US Army Counterinsurgency Doctrine and Practice from Vietnam to Iraq* (Stanford, CA: Stanford University Press, 2013), 15–16. See also: Janine Davidson, *Lifting the Fog of Peace: How Americans Learned to Fight Modern War* (Ann Arbor: University of Michigan Press, 2011), 40–44.

20. Of the different branches of the US military, this book pays the most attention to the Army, in large part because the Army was primarily responsible for fighting the Indian Wars. Military history has paid increasing attention to the cultural dimensions of warfare since the 1960s. See Wayne E. Lee, "Mind and Matter-Cultural Analysis in American Military History: A Look at the State of the Field," *Journal of American History* 93, no. 4 (2007): 1119.

21. James M. Suriano, "Lessons Learned from MG George Crook's Apache Campaigns with Applicability for the Current Global War on Terror," Strategy Research Project (USAWC, 2003), 1.

22. Odd Arne Westad writes: "From its inception the United States was an interventionist power that based its foreign policy on territorial expansion." See Odd Arne Westad, *The Global Cold War: Third World Interventions and the Making of Our Times* (Cambridge: Cambridge University Press, 2005), 9. See also Megan Black, *The Global Interior: Mineral Frontiers and American Power* (Cambridge, MA: Harvard University Press, 2018); Manu Karuka, *Empire's Tracks: Indigenous Nations, Chinese Workers, and the Transcontinental Railroad* (Oakland: University of California Press, 2019), xii; Jodi Kim, *Settler Garrison: Debt Imperialism, Militarism, and Transpacific Imaginaries* (Durham, NC: Duke University Press, 2022), 68–73; Moon-Ho Jung, *Menace to Empire: Anticolonial Solidarities and the Transpacific Origins of the US Security State* (Oakland: University of California Press, 2022), 8–9.

23. Robert F. Berkhofer, *The White Man's Indian: Images of the American Indian from Columbus to the Present* (New York: Knopf, 1978); Gerald Vizenor, *Manifest Manners: Postindian Warriors of Survivance* (Hanover, NH: Wesleyan University Press, 1994), 6. See also Deloria, *Playing Indian*; King, *The Inconvenient Indian*; Bruyneel, *Settler Memory*.

24. Kim, *Settler Garrison*, 26; Laduke and Cruz, *The Militarization of Indian Country*, 18–19.

25. For rates of Native enlistment in the military, see Alexandra N. Harris, *Why We Serve: Native Americans in the United States Armed Forces* (Washington, DC: National Museum of the American Indian, Smithsonian Institution, 2020). 6–9.

26. For a definition and history of the term *irregular warfare*, see Paul J. Tompkins Jr., *Irregular Warfare: Annotated Bibliography, Assessing Revolutionary and Insurgent Strategies* (Fort Bragg, NC: United States Army Special Operations Command, 2011), 1–4.

27. James W. Cook, Lawrence B. Glickman, and Michael O'Malley, eds. *The Cultural Turn in U.S. History: Past, Present, and Future* (Chicago: University of Chicago Press, 2008), 3–58.

28. My definitions here are drawn from Aaron B. O'Connell, *Underdogs: The Making of the Modern Marine Corps* (Cambridge, MA: Harvard University Press, 2014), introduction; Amy Kaplan, *Our American Israel*, 3; and Mary A. Renda, *Taking Haiti: Military Occupation and the Culture of U.S. Imperialism, 1915–1940* (Chapel Hill: University of North Carolina Press, 2001), introduction.

29. Philip J. Deloria and Alexander I. Olson, *American Studies: A User's Guide* (Oakland: University of California Press, 2017), 6–9.

30. Renda, *Taking Haiti*, 17–24; Nan Enstad, "Fashioning Political Identities: Cultural Studies and the Historical Construction of Political Subjects," *American Quarterly* 50, no. 4 (December 1, 1998): 746; Melani McAlister, *Epic Encounters: Culture, Media, and U.S. Interests in the Middle East Since 1945* (Oakland: University of California Press, 2005), 307.

31. Ronald V. Dellums, *The Dellums Committee Hearings on War Crimes in Vietnam: An Inquiry into Command Responsibility in Southeast Asia* (New York: Vintage Books, 1972), 53.

32. For a fuller accounting of American massacres in Vietnam, see Nick Turse, *Kill Anything That Moves: The Real American War in Vietnam* (New York: Picador, 2013).

33. Singh, *Race and America's Long War*, 1–4; Andrew J. Bacevich, *Washington Rules: America's Path to Permanent War* (New York: Metropolitan Books, 2010), 225; Derek Gregory, "The Everywhere War," *Geographical Journal* 177, no. 3 (September 1, 2011): 238–39; O'Connell, "Moving Mountains," 11–12; Simeon Man, *Soldiering through Empire: Race and the Making of the Decolonizing Pacific* (Oakland: University of California Press, 2018), 185; Moyn, *Humane*, 7.

34. Andrew J. Birtle, *U.S. Army Counterinsurgency and Contingency Operations Doctrine, 1860–1941* (Washington, DC: Center of Military History, 1998), foreword; Fred Anderson and Andrew Cayton, *The Dominion of War: Empire and Liberty in North America, 1500–2000* (New York: Penguin, 2005), x. Brian McAllister Linn argues that the US Army grew accustomed to imposing "government, law, and order" during the Indian Wars, and not just defeating Native warriors on the battlefield. See Brian McAllister Linn, *The Echo of Battle: The Army's Way of War* (Cambridge, MA: Harvard University Press, 2007), 70. For the history of US interventionism, see Westad, *The Global Cold War*, 406–7.

35. Linn, *The Echo of Battle*, 70.

36. Monica Rico, *Nature's Noblemen: Transatlantic Masculinities and the Nineteenth-Century American West* (New Haven, CT: Yale University Press, 2013), 165; Gretchen Murphy, *Shadowing the White Man's Burden: U.S. Imperialism and the Problem of the Color Line* (New York: New York University Press, 2016), 1–2; Daniel Immerwahr, *How to Hide an Empire: A History of the Greater United States* (New York: Farrar, Straus and Giroux, 2019), 94. For imperial paternalism, see Stefan Aune, "American Empire," in David Kieran and Edwin A. Martini, eds., *At War: The Military and American Culture in the*

Twentieth Century and Beyond (New Brunswick, NJ: Rutgers University Press, 2018), 37–38.

37. Colin G. Calloway, *The American Revolution in Indian Country: Crisis and Diversity in Native American Communities* (Cambridge: Cambridge University Press, 1995), 293; Byrd, *The Transit of Empire*, xxi–xxii.

38. Max Boot, *The Savage Wars of Peace: Small Wars and the Rise of American Power* (New York: Basic Books, 2014); David Fitzgerald, "Warriors Who Don't Fight: The Post–Cold War United States Army and Debates over Peacekeeping Operations," *Journal of Military History* 85, no. 1 (January 2021): 167.

39. Ben Anderson, "Population and Affective Perception: Biopolitics and Anticipatory Action in US Counterinsurgency Doctrine," *Antipode* 43, no. 2 (March 1, 2011): 205–36; Leerom Medovoi, "Global Society Must Be Defended: Biopolitics without Boundaries," *Social Text* 25, no. 2 (91) (June 1, 2007): 53–79; Brad Evans, *Liberal Terror* (Cambridge: Polity, 2013), 44–46; Markus Kienscherf, "A Programme of Global Pacification: US Counterinsurgency Doctrine and the Biopolitics of Human (in)Security," *Security Dialogue* 42, no. 6 (December 1, 2011): 518–24.

40. Jasbir K. Puar, *The Right to Maim: Debility, Capacity, Disability* (Durham, NC: Duke University Press, 2017), 2; Jaclyn Pryor, *Time Slips: Queer Temporalities, Contemporary Performance, and the Hole of History* (Evanston, IL: Northwestern University Press, 2017), 18–19

41. Michael J. Hogan, *A Cross of Iron: Harry S. Truman and the Origins of the National Security State, 1945–1954* (Cambridge: Cambridge University Press, 1998); Melvyn P. Leffler, "National Security," in *Explaining the History of American Foreign Relations*, Michael J. Hogan and Thomas G. Paterson, eds. (Cambridge: Cambridge University Press, 2004), 123–36; Andrew Preston, "Monsters Everywhere: A Genealogy of National Security," *Diplomatic History* 83, no. 3 (June 2014): 477–500; Jung, *Menace to Empire*, 13–14.

42. For defensive conquest, see Deloria, *Indians in Unexpected Places* (Lawrence: University Press of Kansas, 2004), 50; Engelhardt, *The End of Victory Culture*, 5; Nick Estes, *Our History Is the Future* (New York: Verso, 2019), 247–49.

43. "Summary of the Irregular Warfare Annex to the National Defense Strategy" (Washington, DC: Department of Defense, Washington DC, 2020).

44. On the "forgetting" narrative, see Robert M. Utley, "The Contribution of the Frontier to the American Military Tradition," in James P. Tate, ed., *The American Military on the Frontier* (Washington, DC: Office of Air Force History, US Air Force, 1978), 4–9; John Gates, "Indians and Insurrectos: The U.S. Army's Experience with Insurgency," *Parameters* 13 (March 1983): 59; Russell Weigley, *History of the United States Army* (Bloomington: Indiana University Press, 1984), 161; Andrew F. Krepinevich, *The Army and Vietnam* (Baltimore: Johns Hopkins University Press, 1986), 4–7; Keith Bickel, *Mars Learning* (Boulder, CO: Westview Press, 2001), 43–47; Birtle, *Counterinsurgency*, 10–11; Davidson, *Lifting the Fog of Peace*, 28–30; Fitzgerald, *Learning to Forget*, 2–4.

45. The simultaneous absence and presence of the United States' history of colonial violence within the institutions of US militarism is an aspect of what Kevin Bruyneel calls "settler memory," in which a simultaneous absence and presence of indigeneity is a constitutive aspect of US political life. See Bruyneel,

Settler Memory, 2. See also Lisa Lowe, *The Intimacies of Four Continents* (Durham, NC: Duke University Press Books, 2015), 3.

46. Robert Cassidy, *Counterinsurgency and the Global War on Terror: Military Culture and Irregular War* (Stanford, CA: Stanford University Press, 2008); Matthew J. Flynn, *Settle and Conquer: Militarism on the American Frontier, 1607–1890* (Jefferson, NC: McFarland, 2016); Jeremy T. Siegrist, *Apache Wars: A Constabulary Perspective*, monograph (School of Advanced Military Studies, 2012); Wesley M. Pirkle, *Major General George Crook's Use of Counterinsurgency Compound Warfare during the Great Sioux War of 1876–77*, MMAS thesis (CGSC, 2015); Ike Skelton, "America's Frontier Wars: Lessons for Asymmetric Conflicts," *Military Review* July–August 2014; Kendall D. Gott, *In Search of an Elusive Enemy: The Victorio Campaign, 1879–1880* (Fort Leavenworth, KS: CSI Press, 2004); Benjamin Jensen, *Forging the Sword: Doctrinal Change in the U.S. Army* (Stanford, CA: Stanford University Press, 2016), 134. While Jensen views the Indian Wars as an early form of irregular war, he rightly cautions that there are "ethical and definitional concerns" with viewing sovereign Native nations as insurgents in their own homelands.

47. Nikhil Singh, "Racial Formation in an Age of Permanent War," in Daniel Martinez HoSang, Oneka LaBennett, and Laura Pulido, eds, *Racial Formation in the Twenty-First Century* (Oakland: University of California Press, 2012), 215–19; Man, *Soldiering through Empire*, 8–9.

48. For definitions of both militarization and militarism see M. V. Naidu, "Military Power, Militarism and Militarization: An Attempt at Clarification and Classification," *Peace Research* 17, no. 1 (1985): 2–10; Michael S. Sherry, *In the Shadow of War: The United States since the 1930s* (New Haven, CT: Yale University Press, 1995), xi; Mary A. Renda, *Taking Haiti*, 15; Kim, *Settler Garrison*, 28.

49. Amy Kaplan and Donald E. Pease, eds., *Cultures of United States Imperialism* (Durham, NC: Duke University Press, 1993); Gail Bederman, *Manliness and Civilization: A Cultural History of Gender and Race in the United States, 1880–1917* (Chicago: University of Chicago Press, 1996); Kristin L. Hoganson, *Fighting for American Manhood: How Gender Politics Provoked the Spanish-American and Philippine-American Wars* (New Haven, CT: Yale University Press, 1998); Laura Wexler, *Tender Violence: Domestic Visions in an Age of U.S. Imperialism* (Chapel Hill: University of North Carolina Press, 2000); Matthew Frye Jacobson, *Barbarian Virtues: The United States Encounters Foreign Peoples at Home and Abroad, 1876–1917* (New York: Hill And Wang, 2001); Nayan Shah, *Contagious Divides: Epidemics and Race in San Francisco's Chinatown* (Oakland: University of California Press, 2001); Amy Kaplan, *The Anarchy of Empire in the Making of U.S. Culture* (Cambridge, MA: Harvard University Press, 2002); Renda, *Taking Haiti*; Kramer, *The Blood of Government*; Penny M. Von Eschen, *Satchmo Blows Up the World: Jazz Ambassadors Play the Cold War* (Cambridge, MA: Harvard University Press, 2006).

50. Jordan T. Camp, *Incarcerating the Crisis: Freedom Struggles and the Rise of the Neoliberal State* (Oakland: University of California Press, 2016); Hannah Gurman, ed. *Hearts and Minds: A People's History of Counterinsurgency* (New York: The New Press, 2013); Singh, *Race and America's Long War*; Stuart

Schrader, *Badges without Borders: How Global Counterinsurgency Trans-formed American Policing* (Oakland: University of California Press, 2019); Estes, *Our History Is the Future*; Man, *Soldiering through Empire*; Jung, *Menace to Empire*; Lubin, *Never-Ending War on Terror.*

51. Manu Karuka's *Empire's Tracks* is emblematic of this trend, insisting on a continental imperialism that predates 1898 (and continues beyond that date). See Karuka, *Empire's Tracks*, 185.

52. Patrick Wolfe, *Traces of History: Elementary Structures of Race* (New York: Verso Books, 2016), 186; Lorenzo Veracini, *Settler Colonialism: A Theoretical Overview* (New York: Palgrave Macmillan, 2010), 33–52; Byrd, *The Transit of Empire*, 123; Bruyneel, *Settler Memory*, 8.

53. Jeffrey Ostler, "Settler Colonialism," in Kristin Hoganson and Jay Sexton, eds., *The Cambridge History of America and the World, Volume II: 1820–1900* (Cambridge: Cambridge University Press, 2022), 97.

1. COLONIAL VIOLENCE AND THE INDIAN WARS

1. Charles Devens Jr. and William T. Sherman, *Addresses to the Graduating Class of the US Military Academy, West Point, New York, June 14, 1876* (New York: D. Van Nostrand, 1876), 25–26.

2. Between 1802 and 1890 more than 50 percent of West Point graduates served on the "frontier," defined as service in Florida during the Seminole Wars or in the American West. Thomas T. Smith, "West Point and the Indian Wars 1802–1891," *Military History of the West* 24, no. 1 (1994), 26.

3. Devens and Sherman, *Address to the Graduating Class*, 25–26. Graduates of West Point often remarked on their lack of preparation once posted to the frontier. The West Point curriculum was heavy on math, science, and engineering, although some useful frontier skills, such as cavalry drills, were emphasized in the second half of the nineteenth century. Smith, "West Point and the Indian Wars," 34–41. For an analysis of the myth of the vanishing Indian as it relates to US military practices, see Stefan Aune, "Euthanasia Politics and the Indian Wars," *American Quarterly* 71, no. 3 (2019): 789–811.

4. Jeffrey Ostler, *The Plains Sioux and U.S. Colonialism from Lewis and Clark to Wounded Knee* (Cambridge: Cambridge University Press, 2004), 62–66; Jerome A. Greene, *Stricken Field: The Little Bighorn Since 1876* (Norman: University of Oklahoma Press, 2008), 11–18; Nick Estes, *Our History Is the Future* (New York: Verso, 2019), 247–48; Pekka Hämäläinen, *Lakota America: A New History of Indigenous Power* (New Haven, CT: Yale University Press, 2019), 355–70; Jeffrey Ostler, *The Lakotas and the Black Hills: The Struggle for Sacred Ground* (New York: Viking, 2010), 98.

5. C. A. Booth, "Battle of Little Bighorn Yellowstone—July 1876," July 3, 1876, Charles Austin Booth Papers, United States Military Academy.

6. Frederick Hoxie's phrase "from prison to homeland" remains a useful way of conceptualizing this period. Frederick E. Hoxie, "From Prison to Homeland: The Cheyenne River Indian Reservation before WWI," *South Dakota History* 10, no. 1 (December 1, 1979): 1–24. See also: Thomas Biolsi, *Organizing the Lakota: The Political Economy of the New Deal on the Pine Ridge and Rosebud*

Reservations (Tucson: University of Arizona Press, 1992); Vine Deloria and Clifford M. Lytle, *The Nations Within: The Past and Future of American Indian Sovereignty* (Austin: University of Texas Press, 1998); Cathleen D. Cahill, *Federal Fathers and Mothers: A Social History of the United States Indian Service, 1869–1933* (Chapel Hill: University of North Carolina Press, 2011); C. Joseph Genetin-Pilawa, *Crooked Paths to Allotment: The Fight over Federal Indian Policy after the Civil War* (Chapel Hill: University of North Carolina Press, 2012).

7. Jodi Byrd also discusses how Indians function as a ghostly presence in narratives of US history, literature, and art. See Byrd, *The Transit of Empire: Indigenous Critiques of Colonialism* (Minneapolis: University of Minnesota Press, 2011), xx.

8. Wendy Brown, *Regulating Aversion: Tolerance in the Age of Identity and Empire* (Princeton, NJ: Princeton University Press, 2008), 17–18; Holger Afflerbach and Hew Strachan, eds., *How Fighting Ends: A History of Surrender* (Oxford: Oxford University Press, 2012), 230, 444; John Fabian Witt, *Lincoln's Code: The Laws of War in American History* (New York: Free Press, 2012), 224–27.

9. My primary focus will be North America, but Spanish colonization is part of this story. In particular, Bernardo De Vargas Machuca's *The Indian Militia*, published in 1599, has been called the first counterinsurgency manual. See Geoffrey Parker, *The Military Revolution: Military Innovation and the Rise of the West, 1500–1800* (Cambridge: Cambridge University Press, 1989), 120; Laleh Khalili, *Time in the Shadows: Confinement in Counterinsurgencies* (Stanford, CA: Stanford University Press, 2012), 12. Not all early legal theorists invoked the savage exception. See Witt, *Lincoln's Code*, 92.

10. Mahmood Mamdani, *Good Muslim, Bad Muslim: America, the Cold War, and the Roots of Terror* (New York: Pantheon Books, 2004), 6–7; Paul A. Kramer, *The Blood of Government: Race, Empire, the United States, and the Philippines* (Chapel Hill: University of North Carolina Press, 2006), 83–84; Samuel Moyn, *Humane: How the United States Abandoned Peace and Reinvented War* (New York: Farrar, Straus and Giroux, 2021), 11.

11. Robert A. Williams Jr., *The American Indian in Western Legal Thought: The Discourses of Conquest* (Oxford: Oxford University Press, 1992); Stephen C. Neff, *War and the Law of Nations: A General History* (Cambridge: Cambridge University Press, 2005); Peter H. Maguire, *Law and War: International Law and American History* (New York: Columbia University Press, 2010); Stephanie Carvin, *Prisoners of America's Wars: From the Early Republic to Guantanamo* (New York: Columbia University Press, 2010); Lisa Ford, *Settler Sovereignty: Jurisdiction and Indigenous People in America and Australia, 1788–1836* (Cambridge, MA: Harvard University Press, 2010); Manu Karuka, *Empire's Tracks: Indigenous Nations, Chinese Workers, and the Transcontinental Railroad* (Oakland: University of California Press, 2019), 168. My use of *exception* draws on Giorgio Agamben's writing on the "state of exception." See Giorgio Agamben, *Homo Sacer: Sovereign Power and Bare Life*, trans. Daniel Heller-Roazen (Stanford, CA: Stanford University Press, 1998); Giorgio Agamben, *State of Exception*, trans. Kevin Attell (Chicago: University of Chicago Press, 2005). For a related use of *exception* framed around debt, see Jodi

Kim, *Settler Garrison: Debt Imperialism, Militarism, and Transpacific Imaginaries* (Durham, NC: Duke University Press, 2022), 16.

12. Mark Rifkin and Jodi Kim use the term *metapolitical authority* to describe this process whereby states except themselves from rules imposed on others. See Kim, *Settler Garrison*, 17–18. The question of colonial violence cuts across several subfields. For histories of genocide, see Benjamin Madley, *An American Genocide: The United States and the California Indian Catastrophe, 1846–1873* (New Haven, CT: Yale University Press, 2016); Jeffrey Ostler, *Surviving Genocide: Native Nations and the United States from the American Revolution to Bleeding Kansas* (New Haven, CT: Yale University Press, 2019). Native American History's attention to violence is exemplified by Ned Blackhawk, *Violence over the Land: Indians and Empires in the Early American West* (Cambridge, MA: Harvard University Press, 2006); Pekka Hämäläinen, *The Comanche Empire* (New Haven, CT: Yale University Press, 2008). For military histories of colonial violence see John Grenier, *The First Way of War: American War Making on the Frontier, 1607–1814* (Cambridge: Cambridge University Press, 2005); Robert Wooster, *The American Military Frontiers: The United States Army in the West, 1783–1900* (Albuquerque: University of New Mexico Press, 2009).

13. Emer de Vattel, *The Law of Nations; or, Principles of the Law of Nature, Applied to the Conduct and Affairs of Nations and Sovereigns* (Philadelphia: T. & J.W. Johnson, 1844), 100, 170.

14. Carole Pateman and Charles W. Mills, *Contract and Domination* (Cambridge: Polity, 2007), 35–39; Lauren A. Benton, *Law and Colonial Cultures: Legal Regimes in World History, 1400–1900* (Cambridge: Cambridge University Press, 2002), 168–70. Stuart Banner cautions that English settlers often *did* recognize some form of Native ownership of land, and thus sought to acquire it through contract rather than conquest. See Stuart Banner, *How the Indians Lost Their Land: Law and Power on the Frontier* (Cambridge, MA: Harvard University Press, 2005), 7–13.

15. Vattel, *The Law of Nations*, 347; Jeffrey Ostler, "Settler Colonialism," in Kristin Hoganson and Jay Sexton, eds., *The Cambridge History of America and the World, Volume II: 1820–1900* (Cambridge: Cambridge University Press, 2022), 82.

16. Alberico Gentili, quoted in Daragh Grant, "Francisco de Vitoria and Alberico Gentili on the Juridical Status of Native American Polities," *Renaissance Quarterly* 72, no. 3 (2019): 1–3, 910–52. See also: Mahmood Mamdani, *Neither Settler nor Native* (Cambridge, MA: Harvard University Press, 2020), 8–9.

17. Hugo Grotius, quoted in Pateman and Mills, *Contract and Domination*, 42–43.

18. Wayne E. Lee, *Barbarians and Brothers: Anglo-American Warfare, 1500–1865* (Oxford: Oxford University Press, 2011), 223–25; Maguire, *Law and War*, 6. See also Ford, *Settler Sovereignty*.

19. For defensive conquest, see Philip Joseph Deloria, *Indians in Unexpected Places* (Lawrence: University Press of Kansas, 2004); Tom Engelhardt, *The End*

of *Victory Culture: Cold War America and the Disillusioning of a Generation* (Amherst: University of Massachusetts Press, 2007), 5, 50; Estes, *Our History Is the Future*, 247–49. For retaliation, see Maguire, *Law and War*, 20; W. Fitzhugh Brundage, *Civilizing Torture: An American Tradition* (Cambridge, MA: Harvard University Press, 2018), 2.

20. Ford, *Settler Sovereignty*, 35–36, 85–86; Nikhil Singh, "Racial Formation in an Age of Permanent War," in Daniel Martinez HoSang, Oneka LaBennett, and Laura Pulido, eds., *Racial Formation in the Twenty-First Century* (Oakland: University of California Press, 2012), 293.

21. Fred Anderson and Andrew Cayton, *The Dominion of War: Empire and Liberty in North America, 1500–2000* (New York: Penguin, 2005), 45.

22. Edward Waterhouse, "A Declaration of the State of the Colony: Photographic Facsimile Edition," Dylan Ruediger, ed., *British Virginia*, January 1, 2017, 13–14; Alden T. Vaughan, "'Expulsion of the Salvages': English Policy and the Virginia Massacre of 1622," *The William and Mary Quarterly* 35, no. 1 (1978): 57–84.

23. Robert Gray, quoted in Williams, *The American Indian in Western Legal Thought*, 210; Gary Fields, *Enclosure: Palestinian Landscapes in a Historical Mirror* (Oakland: University of California Press, 2017), 126–27. On finality, temporality, and the naming of war, see Jill Lepore, *The Name of War: King Philip's War and the Origins of American Identity* (New York: Knopf, 1998), xvi–xxi; Lisa Brooks, *Our Beloved Kin: A New History of King Philip's War* (New Haven, CT: Yale University Press, 2018), 7–10. On the role played by history in masking the continuing presence of Native peoples, see Jean M. O'Brien, *Firsting and Lasting: Writing Indians out of Existence in New England* (Minneapolis: University of Minnesota Press, 2010).

24. Byrd, *The Transit of Empire*, xxi.

25. Thomas Jefferson to George Rogers Clark, Jan. 1, 1780, quoted in Ostler, *Surviving Genocide*, 64.

26. John Sullivan, *Letters and Papers of Major-General John Sullivan, Continental Army*, Vol. 15 (Concord: New Hampshire Historical Society, 1930), 48–49.

27. George Washington, *The Papers of George Washington: Revolutionary War Series, 8 April–31 May 1779*, Vol. 20, Edward G. Lengel, ed. (Charlottesville: University Press of Virginia, 1985), 716–19.

28. Lee, *Barbarians and Brothers*, 210–14.

29. James Kent, *Commentaries on American Law*, Vol. 1 (Birmingham: Gryphon, 1986), 45, 87, 193; Ellen Holmes Pearson, *Remaking Custom: Law and Identity in the Early American Republic* (Charlottesville: University of Virginia Press, 2011), 145–6; Witt, *Lincoln's Code*, 92–93; Moyn, *Humane*, 104.

30. Henry Wheaton, *Elements of International Law*, Vol. 1 (London: Stevens and Sons, 1929), 334; Witt, *Lincoln's Code*, 93.

31. Deborah A. Rosen, *Border Law: The First Seminole War and American Nationhood* (Cambridge, MA: Harvard University Press, 2015), 102.

32. Witt, *Lincoln's Code*, 95–97; Anderson and Cayton, *Dominion of War*, 234–35.

33. Samuel Putnam, *Memoirs of Andrew Jackson, Major-General in the Army of the United States, and Commander in Chief of the Division of the South*, 5th ed. (Hartford, CT: J & W Russell, 1819), 293–95. On the exterminatory aspects of the Seminole Wars, see Ostler, "Settler Colonialism," 84–85.

34. Anderson and Cayton, *Dominion of War*, 237.

35. Rosen, *Border Law*, 30–32; Andrew Jackson, quoted in Witt, *Lincoln's Code*, 96–99; Anderson and Cayton, *Dominion of War*, 237–38.

36. Rosen, *Border Law*, 111–13.

37. *The Debates and Proceedings in the Congress of the United States*, 15th Cong., 2nd Sess. (Washington, DC: GPO, 1819), 586, 638, 662–68; Rosen, *Border Law*, 187–99.

38. Francis Wharton, *A Digest of International Law of the United States*, Vol. 3 (Washington, DC: GPO, 1886), 326; Lynn Hudson Parsons, *The Birth of Modern Politics: Andrew Jackson, John Quincy Adams, and the Election of 1828* (Oxford: Oxford University Press, 2009), 50–51.

39. Tiya Miles, *Ties That Bind: The Story of an Afro-Cherokee Family in Slavery and Freedom* (Oakland: University of California Press, 2006), 81; Anderson and Cayton, *Dominion of War*, 242–44.

40. Rosen, *Border Law*, 1–10.

41. William Smith and Charles Guillaume Frédéric Dumas, *Historical Account of Bouquet's Expedition against the Ohio Indians, in 1764* (Cincinnati: R. Clarke, 1868), 94.

42. Benjamin Jensen, *Forging the Sword: Doctrinal Change in the U.S. Army* (Stanford, CA: Stanford University Press, 2016), 135. For informal doctrine, see David Fitzgerald, *Learning to Forget: US Army Counterinsurgency Doctrine and Practice from Vietnam to Iraq* (Stanford, CA: Stanford University Press, 2013), 15–16; J. P. Clark, *Preparing for War: The Emergence of the Modern U.S. Army, 1815–1917* (Cambridge, MA: Harvard University Press, 2017), 42–43.

43. Sherry L. Smith, *The View from Officers' Row: Army Perceptions of Western Indians* (Tucson: University of Arizona Press, 1990), xiii–xiv; Janne Lahti, *Cultural Construction of Empire: The U.S. Army in Arizona and New Mexico* (Lincoln: Nebraska University Press, 2012), 6; Michael L. Tate, *Frontier Army in the Settlement of the West* (Norman: University of Oklahoma Press, 1999), 27–28. Officers tended to be native born, well educated, and aristocratic, in contrast to the largely working-class enlisted soldiers. See Kevin Adams, *Class and Race in the Frontier Army: Military Life in the West, 1870–1890* (Norman: University of Oklahoma Press, 2009), 5, 31; Richard White, *The Republic for Which It Stands: The United States during Reconstruction and the Gilded Age, 1865–1896* (Oxford: Oxford University Press, 2017), 116.

44. US Army officers often held contradictory or conflicting opinions about their Native opponents. They could admire Native people even as they predicted their impending extinction; they could critique the injustice of US Indian policy even as they enforced those very policies. See Edward M. Coffman, *The Old Army: A Portrait of the American Army in Peacetime, 1784–1898* (Oxford University Press, 1986), 73–76; Brian McAllister Linn, *The Echo of Battle: The Army's Way of War* (Cambridge, MA: Harvard University Press, 2007), 74;

Smith, *The View from Officers' Row*, 113–15; Adams, *Class and Race in the Frontier Army*, 16–17.

45. On the "Indian question," see Lucy Maddox, *Removals: Nineteenth-Century American Literature and the Politics of Indian Affairs* (Oxford: Oxford University Press, 1991).

46. Henry Beebee Carrington, *The Indian Question* (Boston: De Wolfe & Fiske, 1884), 5.

47. For "euthanasia politics," see Aune, "Euthanasia Politics and the Indian Wars."

48. Linn, *The Echo of Battle*, 70–71.

49. Witt, *Lincoln's Code*, 88.

50. Dennis Hart Mahan, "Composition of Armies," 24 March 1836, Textbook Collection, Cadet George L. Weicker's Copy, unbound folio T355.6, United States Military Academy Special Collections, quoted in Smith, "West Point and the Indian Wars," 49–51.

51. Mahan, quoted in Smith, "West Point and the Indian Wars," 49–51.

52. Estes, *Our History Is the Future*, 103–4.

53. *Message from the President of the United States to the Two Houses of Congress*, 32nd Cong., 1st Sess. (Washington, DC: GPO, 1851), 225.

54. *Message from the President of the United States to the Two Houses of Congress*, 36th Cong., 2nd Sess. (Washington, D.C.: GPO, 1860), 68. For more on the rhetoric of extermination, see Karl Jacoby, "'The Broad Platform of Extermination': Nature and Violence in the Nineteenth Century North American Borderlands," *Journal of Genocide Research*, no. 2 (2008): 249–67.

55. Aune, "Euthanasia Politics and the Indian Wars."

56. Randolph Barnes Marcy, *The Prairie Traveler: A Hand-Book for Overland Expeditions* (Denver, CO: N. Mumey, 1859), xi.

57. Marcy, 200.

58. Marcy, 200.

59. Randolph Barnes Marcy, *Thirty Years of Army Life on the Border* (New York: Harper & Brothers, 1866), 67–69.

60. Marcy, 74–75.

61. Frank N. Schubert, *Other Than War: The American Military Experience and Operations in the Post–Cold War Decade* (Washington DC: GPO, 2013), endnote 31.

62. Edward Samuel Farrow, *Mountain Scouting: A Hand-Book for Officers and Soldiers on the Frontiers* (Norman: University of Oklahoma Press, 2000), 239.

63. Farrow, 239.

64. Farrow, 213–24.

65. Hämäläinen, *Comanche Empire*, 64–65.

66. Sherman to P. H. Sheridan, October 15th, 1868, Philip Henry Sheridan Papers, LOC, Container 75, Reel 80.

67. "A Buffalo Campaign," *Army Navy Journal*, June 26, 1869. John Gates acknowledges that some Indians used guerilla tactics; however, he disputes the idea that Native peoples were engaged in a guerilla war, characterizing them as "primitive people" not engaged in "true war." Diverging somewhat from Gates, I see *guerilla* as a conceptual as much as descriptive term, denoting the collapsing

of internal/external categorizations imposed on Native people by US colonialism. Gates's argument about the Indian Wars often constituting "routine though difficult police work," a complaint echoed by nineteenth-century soldiers, influenced my thinking on this point. Regardless of debates over whether, tactically speaking, Indians were "guerillas," the circulation of that term indicates uncertainties about the status of Native sovereignty (and Native violence). See John Gates, "Indians and Insurrectos: The U.S. Army's Experience with Insurgency," *Parameters* 13 (March 1983), 61–62. Recent studies in military history have characterized the Indian Wars as one of the United States' only "successful" counterinsurgencies, although not uncritically. See Matthew J. Flynn, "Settle and Conquer: The Ultimate Counterinsurgency Success," *Small Wars & Insurgencies* 32, no. 3 (April 3, 2021): 509–34.

68. Andrew C. Isenberg, *The Destruction of the Bison: An Environmental History, 1750–1920* (Cambridge: Cambridge University Press, 2000), 147; Deloria, *Indians in Unexpected Places*, 21.

69. Farrow, *Mountain Scouting*, 241.

70. Farrow, 248; White, *The Republic for Which It Stands*, 130–31.

71. William H. Leckie, *The Military Conquest of the Southern Plains* (Norman: University of Oklahoma Press, 1963), 88–89; Jerome A. Greene, *Washita: The US Army and the Southern Cheyennes, 1867–1869* (Norman: University of Oklahoma Press, 2004), 101; Hämäläinen, *Comanche Empire*, 285.

72. Sheridan to W. T. Sherman, November 1st, 1868, Philip Henry Sheridan Papers, LOC, Container 75, Reel 80.

73. Sheridan to W. T. Sherman.

74. Philip Henry Sheridan, *Personal Memoirs of P. H. Sheridan, General United States Army*, Vol. 2 (New York: C. L. Webster & Company, 1888), 297.

75. Farrow, *Mountain Scouting*, preface. On Sheridan's winter campaign that included the attack at Washita, see Paul Andrew Hutton, *Phil Sheridan and His Army* (Lincoln: University of Nebraska Press, 1985); Greene, *Washita*; Elliott West, *The Contested Plains: Indians, Goldseekers, and the Rush to Colorado* (Lawrence: University Press of Kansas, 1998); Wooster, *The American Military Frontiers*; T. J. Stiles, *Custer's Trials: A Life on the Frontier of a New America* (New York: Alfred A. Knopf, 2015), 325–36; Hämäläinen, *Lakota America*.

76. Marcos E. Kinevan, *Frontier Cavalryman: Lieutenant John Bigelow with the Buffalo Soldiers in Texas* (El Paso: Texas Western Press, 1998), 4; Russell F. Weigley, "American Strategy from Its Beginnings through the First World War," in Peter Paret, Gordon A. Craig, and Felix Gilbert, eds., *Makers of Modern Strategy from Machiavelli to the Nuclear Age* (Princeton, NJ: Princeton University Press, 2010), 439–40.

77. Russell Frank Weigley, *Towards an American Army: Military Thought from Washington to Marshall* (New York: Columbia University Press, 1962), 94.

78. John Bigelow, *The Principles of Strategy: Illustrated Mainly from American Campaigns* (Philadelphia: J.B. Lippincott Company, 1894), 104.

79. Report of Operations of the Command of Brevet Major General George A. Custer from December 7th, to December 22nd, 1868, Philip Henry Sheridan Papers, LOC, Container 72 Reel 76.

80. Theophilus Francis Rodenbough and William Lawrence Haskin, eds., *The Army of the United States: Historical Sketches of Staff and Line with Portraits of Generals-in-Chief* (New York: Maynard, Merrill & CO., 1896), 295–96.

81. Lieutenant John Bigelow, "Tenth Regiment of Cavalry," *JMSI* 13 (1892), 215–24; Coffman, *The Old Army*, 277–78; Clark, *Preparing for War*, 132.

82. White, *The Republic for Which It Stands*, 1–3.

83. Adam Jortner, "The Empty Continent: Cartography, Pedagogy, and Native American History," in Susan Sleeper-Smith et al., *Why You Can't Teach United States History without American Indians* (Chapel Hill: University of North Carolina Press, 2015), 71–86.

84. *Annual Report of the Secretary of War* (Washington DC: GPO, 1869), 24.

85. Robert M. Utley, *Frontier Regulars: The United States Army and the Indian, 1866–1891* (New York: Macmillan, 1974), 12–15; Adams, *Class and Race in the Frontier Army*, 12; Clark, *Preparing for War*, 99; Ostler, *The Lakotas and the Black Hills*, 58–59.

86. Richard White, *Railroaded: The Transcontinentals and the Making of Modern America* (New York: W. W. Norton, 2011), 455–57; White, *The Republic for Which it Stands*, 107–8; Ostler, "Indian Warfare in the West, 1861–1890," in Susan Sleeper-Smith et al., *Why You Can't Teach United States History without American Indians* (Chapel Hill: University of North Carolina Press, 2015), 152; Karuka, *Empire's Tracks*, 40.

87. Adams, *Class and Race in the Frontier Army*, 16; Lahti, *Cultural Constructions of Empire*, 127; Ostler, "Settler Colonialism," 89.

88. *Annual Report of the Secretary of War* (Washington, DC: GPO, 1866, 31–32; *Annual Report of the Secretary of War* (Washington, DC: GPO, 1867), 67–68; Utley, *Frontier Regulars*, 11.

89. White, *The Republic for Which It Stands*, 109–10; Ostler, "Settler Colonialism," 93–95; Aune, "Euthanasia Politics and the Indian Wars," 790; Mamdani, *Neither Settler nor Native*, 61–62.

90. Megan Black, *The Global Interior: Mineral Frontiers and American Power* (Cambridge, MA: Harvard University Press, 2018), 17–19.

91. Tate, *Frontier Army*, 246–47; Coffman, *The Old Army*, 254; Black, *The Global Interior*, 27–28.

92. Adams, *Class and Race in the Frontier Army*, 16–17; Tate, *Frontier Army*, 237–43; Karl Jacoby, *Shadows at Dawn: An Apache Massacre and the Violence of History* (New York: Penguin Books, 2009), 126–28; Ostler, "Indian Warfare in the West," 153–54; Black, *The Global Interior*, 26–27; Karuka, *Empire's Tracks*, 168.

93. Philip Sheridan, quoted in White, *The Republic for Which It Stands*, 129.

94. Russell Frank Weigley, *The American Way of War: A History of United States Military Strategy and Policy* (Bloomington: Indiana University Press, 1977), 171; Coffman, *The Old Army*, 278–85.

95. Utley, *Frontier Regulars*, 44; Perry D. Jamieson, *Crossing the Deadly Ground: United States Army Tactics, 1865–1899* (Tuscaloosa: University of Alabama Press, 2004), xii.

96. Report of Operations, Philip Henry Sheridan Papers.

97. Byrd, *The Transit of Empire*, 226–28; Boyd Cothran, *Remembering the Modoc War: Redemptive Violence and the Making of American Innocence* (Chapel Hill: University of North Carolina Press, 2014), 64–66, 76–78; Douglas Little, *Us versus Them: The United States, Radical Islam, and the Rise of the Green Threat* (Chapel Hill: University of North Carolina Press, 2016), 152–53; Moyn, *Humane*, 106–7, 242–46; Alex Lubin, *Never-Ending War on Terror* (Oakland: University of California Press, 2021), 76–77.

98. George Henry Williams, quoted in Moyn, *Humane*, 107.

99. Byrd, *The Transit of Empire*, 227.

100. United States Congress, *Congressional Record: Proceedings and Debates of the Forty-Fourth Congress* (Washington, DC: GPO, 1876), 3951.

101. Sen. John A. Logan, quoted in Utley, *Frontier Regulars*, 21.

102. Jacoby, *Shadows at Dawn*, 127; Lahti, *Cultural Constructions of Empire*, 25.

103. Black, *The Global Interior*, 12–13; 26–27.

104. *Annual Report of the Secretary of War* (1866), 20; Black, *The Global Interior*, 28.

105. "A Buffalo Campaign," *Army and Navy Journal* (June 26, 1869).

106. *Annual Report of the Secretary of War* (Washington, DC: GPO, 1869), 24.

107. Peter Cozzens, *Eyewitnesses to the Indian Wars, 1865–1890: The Army and the Indian* (Mechanicsburg, PA: Stackpole Books, 2001), 120–26; Linn, *The Echo of Battle*, 70–74.

108. Adams, *Class and Race in the Frontier Army*, 18–19; Tate, *The Frontier Army*, x.

109. Col. Elwell Otis, quoted in Andrew J. Birtle, *U.S. Army Counterinsurgency and Contingency Operations Doctrine, 1860–1941* (Washington, DC: Center of Military History, 1998), 92.

110. David Finkel, *The Good Soldiers* (New York: Farrar, Straus and Giroux, 2009), 29–30.

111. Utley, *Frontier Regulars*, 21.

112. Kevin Bruyneel, *The Third Space of Sovereignty: The Postcolonial Politics of U.S.–Indigenous Relations* (Minneapolis: University of Minnesota Press, 2007), xvi–xviii.

113. Parker, *The Military Revolution*, 120; Daniel E. Sutherland, *Savage Conflict: The Decisive Role of Guerrillas in the American Civil War* (Chapel Hill: University of North Carolina Press, 2009), 28–29; Peter Silver, *Our Savage Neighbors: How Indian War Transformed Early America* (New York: W. W. Norton & Company, 2009), 120; Joanne Barker, *Red Scare: The State's Indigenous Terrorist* (Oakland: University of California Press, 2021), 28–29.

114. Aaron Sheehan-Dean, *The Calculus of Violence: How Americans Fought the Civil War* (Cambridge, MA: Harvard University Press, 2018), 71–72.

115. James B. Avirett, *The Memoirs of General Turner Ashby and His Compeers* (Baltimore: Selby & Dulany, 1867), 53.

116. *Annual Report of the Secretary of War* (Washington, DC: GPO, 1863), 29.

117. Joseph M. Beilein Jr., *Bushwhackers: Guerrilla Warfare, Manhood, and the Household in Civil War Missouri* (Kent, OH: Kent State University Press, 2016), 102.

118. William Gilmore Simms, quoted in Sutherland, *Savage Conflict*, 28–29.

119. Avirett, *The Memoirs of General Turner Ashby*, 46–47, 141.

120. William McDonald, *A History of the Laurel Brigade*, Bushrod C. Washington, ed. (Baltimore: Mrs. Kate S. McDonald, 1907), 51; Paul Christopher Anderson, *Blood Image: Turner Ashby in the Civil War and the Southern Mind* (Baton Rouge: Louisiana State University Press, 2002), 105–6.

121. Kenneth W. Noe, "Exterminating Savages: The Union Army and Mountain Guerillas in Southern West Virginia, 1861–1862," in Kenneth W. Noe and Shannon H. Wilson, eds., *The Civil War in Appalachia: Collected Essays* (Knoxville: University of Tennessee Press, 1997), 114–15; George Crook, *General George Crook, His Autobiography*, Martin F. Schmitt, ed. (Norman: University of Oklahoma Press, 1986), 69–73.

122. Crook, *General George Crook*, 86–87; Michael Fellman, *In the Name of God and Country: Reconsidering Terrorism in American History* (New Haven, CT: Yale University Press, 2010), 94; Christopher J. Einolf, *America in the Philippines, 1899–1902: The First Torture Scandal* (New York: Palgrave MacMillan, 2016), 29–31.

Crook, *General George Crook*, 87. Inversely, some Confederate guerillas offered up their experience in Indian warfare as an endorsement of their ability to frustrate Union invaders. See Sutherland, *A Savage Conflict*, 28; Helen M. Kinsella, *The Image before the Weapon: A Critical History of the Distinction between Combatant and Civilian* (Ithaca, NY: Cornell University Press, 2011), 83.

123. Crook, *General George Crook*, 87; Sutherland, *A Savage Conflict*, 259.

124. Lieber's code influenced several international agreements on the rules of war in the nineteenth and twentieth centuries, including the Hague peace conferences in 1899 and 1907. See Neff, *War and the Law of Nations*, 186–87.

125. Francis Lieber, *Instructions for the Government of Armies of the United States, in the Field* (New York: D. Van Nostrand, 1863), Article 20.

126. Maguire, *Law and War*, 30; Witt, *Lincoln's Code*, 336–37; Moyn, *Humane*, 105–6.

127. Lieber, *Instructions*, Articles 20–25; 63; Linn, *The Echo of Battle*, 72.

128. *Annual Report of the Secretary of War* (1863), 29. Daniel Sutherland notes that some Union officers dismissed the code as a defense of radical abolitionism. See Sutherland, *Savage Conflict*, 128.

129. "Letter to William Tecumseh Sherman," June 14, 1867, William Tecumseh Sherman Papers, LOC, Box 21 Reel 12.

130. Lubin, *Never-Ending War on Terror*, 7–8.

131. Michael Fellman describes the history of the United States as a series of "terrorist exchanges" in which the violence of the state competes with that of nonstate actors. Fellman's study resonates with my own discussion of how Native violence was separated out from Euro-American warfare and rendered barbaric, savage, or illegitimate. See Fellman, *In the Name of God and Country*, 2–3.

132. Walter Laqueur, *The New Terrorism: Fanaticism and the Arms of Mass Destruction* (Oxford: Oxford University Press, 2000), 22–23; Linn, *The Echo of Battle*, 80.

133. Deloria, *Indians in Unexpected Places*, 20–21.

134. Bruce Hoffman, *Inside Terrorism* (New York: Columbia University Press, 2006), 4–7; Carola Dietze and Claudia Verhoeven, eds., *The Oxford Handbook of the History of Terrorism* (Oxford University Press, 2014), 4–5; Barker, *Red Scare*, 14–16.

135. There are numerous examples of "terrorism" being applied to anti-reconstruction violence in the South. An article titled "Terrorism in South Carolina" from an 1869 issue of the *Philadelphia Inquirer* describes a campaign of intimidation and murder that prevented a fair election in the Third and Fourth Congressional Districts of South Carolina. "Terrorism in South Carolina," *Philadelphia Inquirer*, April 6, 1869.

136. Mamdani, *Good Muslim, Bad Muslim*; Derek Gregory, *The Colonial Present: Afghanistan, Palestine, and Iraq* (Malden, MA: Blackwell Publishing, 2004).

137. "Our Indian Policy," *New York Times*, December 8, 1860.

138. "The Arizona Massacres," *Chicago Tribune*, December 2, 1871.

139. "Peace in Arizona," *Chicago Tribune*, May 9, 1873.

140. "Arizona Delivered," *Oakland Daily Transcript*, June 2, 1874.

141. Kevin Bruyneel, *Settler Memory: The Disavowal of Indigeneity and the Politics of Race in the United States* (Chapel Hill: University of North Carolina Press, 2021), 16; Lahti, *Cultural Construction of Empire*, 2.

142. Deloria, *Indians in Unexpected Places*, 50–51.

143. "Miles's Speech," *Los Angeles Times*, November 9, 1887.

144. Jacoby, *Shadows at Dawn*, 260–61.

145. "Kid, The Apache," *San Francisco Chronicle*, February 19, 1893.

146. See Richard Slotkin, *The Fatal Environment: The Myth of the Frontier in the Age of Industrialization, 1800–1890* (New York: Atheneum, 1985).

147. Rodenbough, *The Army of the United States*, 227; George Frederic Price, *Across the Continent with the Fifth Cavalry* (New York: D. Van Nostrand, 1883), 140–41.

148. "Indian Warfare," *Army and Navy Journal*, April 26, 1890.

149. Bvt. Major J. B. Babcock, "Field Exercises and the Necessity for an Authorized Manual of Field Duties," *JMSI* 12 (1891): 938–51, 1949.

150. "Target Practice," *Army and Navy Journal*, April 23, 1892; "Skeletonizing Is Reduction," *Army and Navy Journal*, October 30, 1897.

151. Arthur L. Wagner, "Combined Maneuvers of the Regular Army and Organized Militia," *JMSI* 36 (1905): 62–87, 65.

152. Ostler, *The Plains Sioux*, 302–4.

153. "War with Chile," *Army and Navy Journal*, January 23, 1891; João Resende-Santos, *Neorealism, States, and the Modern Mass Army* (Cambridge: Cambridge University Press, 2007), 159–60, 172–73.

154. "The Army Not Only to Watch the Indians," *JMSI* 4, (1883): 87.

155. T. R. Brereton, *Educating the U.S. Army: Arthur L. Wagner and Reform, 1875–1905* (Lincoln: University of Nebraska Press, 2000).

156. Birtle, *Counterinsurgency*, 86–87; Clark, *Preparing for War*, 136; Edward M. Coffman, *The Regulars: The American Army, 1898–1941* (Cambridge, MA: Harvard University Press, 2007), 1.

157. John Pope, quoted in Jamieson, *Crossing the Deadly Ground*, 120–21.

158. Thomas Sergeant Perry, ed., *The Life and Letters of Francis Lieber* (Boston: James R. Osgood and Company, 1882), 397.

159. Linn, *The Echo of Battle*, 71.

160. Colonel Albert G. Brackett, "Our Cavalry," *JMSI* 4 (1883): 406; Birtle, *Counterinsurgency*, 86.

161. Lt. W. P. Burnham, "Military Training of the Regular Army," *JMSI* 10 (1889): 614.

162. Hugh Lenox Scott, *Some Memories of a Soldier* (New York: The Century Co., 1928), 137.

163. Ostler, *The Plains Sioux*, 304–5.

164. August Kautz, "Military Education for the Masses," *JMSI* 17 (1895): 488.

165. "American Military Literature," *Army and Navy Journal*, April 1893, 548.

166. Captain W. H. Carter, "The Infantry and Cavalry School at Fort Leavenworth," *JMSI* 15 (1894): 752–59; Arthur L. Wagner, *The Service of Security and Information* (Kansas City, KS: Hudson-Kimberly Pub. Co., 1903), 203; Arthur L. Wagner, "From the U.S. Military Academy, April, 1903," *Journal of the United States Cavalry Association* 14 (April 1903): 150–55; Arthur L. Wagner, "The Military Necessities of the United States, and the Best Provisions for Meeting Them," *JMSI* 5 (1884): 237–68, 237–38; Arthur L. Wagner, *Organization and Tactics* (New York: B. Westermann and Co., 1895), 57.

167. Weigley, *Towards an American Army*, 69–70, 104; Stephen E. Ambrose, *Upton and the Army* (Baton Rouge: Louisiana State University Press, 1993), 106–7; Linn, *The Echo of Battle*, 69.

168. Birtle, *Counterinsurgency*, 86.

169. "British and American Armies," *Army and Navy Gazette*, May 18, 1901. The *Army and Navy Journal* made multiple references during this period to Europeans characterizing the US Army as a "militia," which was clearly an irritant. Another example can be found in the May 13, 1899, issue.

170. *Army and Navy Journal*, May 13, 1899.

171. "Filipinos Not Guerrilla Fighters," *Army and Navy Journal*, July 29, 1899.

172. "Fighting in the Philippines," *Army and Navy Journal*, March 24, 1900.

2. INDIAN/FIGHTERS IN THE PHILIPPINES

1. "Is The Philippine War Over?" *The Literary Digest*, Volume 20 (New York: Funk & Wagnalls, 1890), 503.

2. Stuart Creighton Miller, *"Benevolent Assimilation": The American Conquest of the Philippines, 1899–1903* (New Haven, CT: Yale University Press, 1982), 82–90.

3. Wayne E. Lee et al., *The Other Face of Battle: America's Forgotten Wars and the Experience of Combat* (Oxford University Press, 2021), 81.

4. Brian McAllister Linn, *The Philippine War, 1899–1902* (Lawrence: University Press of Kansas, 2000), 171–74; Christopher Capozzola, *Bound by War: How the United States and the Philippines Built America's First Pacific Century* (New York: Basic Books, 2020), 30–33.

5. "Conditions in the Philippines," *Army and Navy Journal*, April 28, 1900.

6. *The Literary Digest*, 503; Jacob Smith, quoted in Brian McAllister Linn, *The U.S. Army and Counterinsurgency in the Philippine War, 1899–1902* (Chapel Hill: University of North Carolina Press, 2000), 23.

7. "Typescripts of Ltrs 5 July 1899–Dec 1899," James C. Parker Letters, Box 8, Folder 3, United States Military Academy Special Collections; Miller, *"Benevolent Assimilation,"* 94–95.

8. One of the more extensive examinations of these connections can be found in Paul Kramer's *The Blood of Government: Race, Empire, the United States, and the Philippines* (Chapel Hill: University of North Carolina Press, 2006). However, Kramer is wary of what he calls the "export" model of imperial historiography in which historians transplant prevailing ideas about race from the metropole outward to the colonies, erasing local particularities in the process. Kramer's caution is an important one that informs this chapter; at the same time, there are numerous connections that deserve our attention. Other examples include Russell Roth, *Muddy Glory: America's "Indian Wars" in the Philippines, 1899–1935* (W. Hanover, MA: Christopher Pub. House, 1981); Peter W. Stanley, *Reappraising an Empire: New Perspectives on Philippine-American History* (Cambridge, MA: Harvard University Press, 1984); Andrew J. Birtle, *U.S. Army Counterinsurgency and Contingency Operations Doctrine, 1860–1941* (Washington, DC: Center of Military History, 1998); Matthew Frye Jacobson, *Barbarian Virtues: The United States Encounters Foreign Peoples at Home and Abroad, 1876–1917* (New York: Hill and Wang, 2000); Julian Go and Anne L. Foster, eds., *The American Colonial State in the Philippines: Global Perspectives* (Durham, NC: Duke University Press, 2003); Edward M. Coffman, *The Regulars: The American Army, 1898–1941* (Cambridge, MA: Harvard University Press, 2007); Katharine Bjork, *Prairie Imperialists: The Indian Country Origins of American Empire* (Philadelphia: University of Pennsylvania Press, 2018).

9. Coffman, *The Regulars*, 47–49; Moon-Ho Jung, *Menace to Empire: Anticolonial Solidarities and the Transpacific Origins of the US Security State* (Oakland: University of California Press, 2022), 31. "Imperial paternalism" describes a range of discourses that sought to deny Filipino's the right to self-govern based on a presumed racial inferiority. See Paul Kramer, *The Blood of Government*, 87–158; Aune, "American Empire," in David Kieran and Edwin A. Martini, eds., *At War: The Military and American Culture in the Twentieth Century and Beyond* (New Brunswick: Rutgers University Press, 2018).

10. Mary Renda calls this process "cultural conscription." See Mary Renda, *Taking Haiti: Military Occupation and the Culture of U.S. Imperialism, 1915–1940* (Chapel Hill: University of North Carolina Press, 2001), 22–27.

11. Coffman, *The Regulars*, 47–48.

12. It is important to remember that Native people also fought in the Spanish-American War and the Philippine-American War. For example, Tuscarora soldier Clinton Rickard served in the Philippines from 1901 to 1904. In one

incident he was mistaken for "a wild Indian" by his commanding officer, who called for help. See Al Carroll, *Medicine Bags and Dog Tags: American Indian Veterans from Colonial Times to the Second Iraq War* (Lincoln: University of Nebraska Press, 2008), 99–100.

13. Robert Goldthwaite Carter, Henry W. Lawton Scrapbook, Special Collections, Newberry Library.

14. "Military Papers, 1883–1900," Henry Ware Lawton Papers, Box 3, Folder 3, LOC.

15. Michael E. Shay, *Henry Ware Lawton: Union Infantryman, Frontier Soldier, Charismatic Warrior* (Columbia: University of Missouri Press, 2017), chaps. 7–8.

16. "General Lawton as Warrior, Statesman and Man," Henry W. Lawton Scrapbook.

17. "A Stronger Military Force Required," *Army and Navy Journal*, May 6, 1899; Paul C. Rosier, *Serving Their Country: American Indian Politics and Patriotism in the Twentieth Century* (Cambridge, MA: Harvard University Press, 2009), 40.

18. "The American Army Officer in Action," Henry W. Lawton Scrapbook.

19. "Lawton, Fighting Machine," Henry W. Lawton Scrapbook.

20. "Lawton, Fighting Machine," Henry W. Lawton Scrapbook.

21. John Morgan Gates, *Schoolbooks and Krags: The United States Army in the Philippines, 1898–1902* (Westport, CT: Greenwood Press, 1973), 27–29; Linn, *The Philippine War*, 42–47; Lee et al., *The Other Face of Battle*, 101; Capozzola, *Bound by War*, 19–27. Racial slurs directed at Filipinos were so pervasive in the weeks leading to the official start of the war that General Otis issued an order forbidding use of the word *nigger* by military personnel. Miller, *"Benevolent Assimilation,"* 57–58; Jung, *Menace to Empire*, 31.

22. Lee et al., *The Other Face of Battle*, 101–19.

23. Linn, *The Philippine War*, 88–95.

24. Miller, *"Benevolent Assimilation,"* 67–70, Linn, *The Philippine War*, 93–95.

25. "Will Push the Campaign," Henry W. Lawton Scrapbook.

26. *Correspondence Relating to the War with Spain and Conditions Growing Out of the Same Including the Insurrection in the Philippine Island and the China Relief Expedition*, Vol. 2 (Washington, DC: GPO, 1902), 959–61; Miller, *"Benevolent Assimilation,"* 97; Linn, *The Philippine War*, 102–3.

27. "In Pursuit of Rebels," Henry W. Lawton Scrapbook.

28. Miller, *"Benevolent Assimilation,"* 70–71; Linn, *The Philippine War*, 101–4.

29. *Correspondence Relating to the War with Spain*, 958; Linn, *The Philippines War*, 104–6.

30. *Correspondence Relating to the War with Spain*, 971.

31. "The Week at Manilla," *Army and Navy Journal*, April 29, 1899.

32. "Campaigning with General Lawton," Henry W. Lawton Scrapbook.

33. David Roberts, *Once They Moved Like the Wind: Cochise, Geronimo, and the Apache Wars* (New York: Touchstone, 1994), 260–96.

34. "Campaigning with General Lawton," Henry W. Lawton Scrapbook.

35. Miller, *"Benevolent Assimilation,"* 168–73; Linn, *The Philippine War,* 215.

36. "Tireless Lawton," Henry W. Lawton Scrapbook.

37. "Lawton, the Fighter," Henry W. Lawton Scrapbook.

38. John M. Gates, "Indians and Insurrectos: The US Army's Experience with Insurgency," *Parameters 13* (1983); Robert M. Cassidy, "Winning the War of the Flea: Lessons from Guerilla Warfare," *Military Review*, September–October (2004).

39. "Target Practice," *Army and Navy Journal*, April 23, 1892; "Skeletonizing Is Reduction," *Army and Navy Journal*, October 30, 1897.

40. "The Army and Navy Journal . . . ," *Army and Navy Journal* May 13, 1899.

41. "In Making a Comparison . . . ," *Army and Navy Journal*, April 22, 1899, 809.

42. "The Woods Must Be Full of Savages," *Santa Fe Daily*, May 31, 1899.

43. Lawton sometimes issued strict orders to protect Filipino property in an effort to "win hearts and minds," while in other cases he looked the other way (or directly encouraged) the appropriation or destruction of Filipino property. See Linn, *The Philippine War*, 103.

44. Roth, *Muddy Glory*, 17–18; Linn, *The Philippine War*, 114–16; Michael E. Shay, ed., *A Civilian in Lawton's 1899 Philippine Campaign: The Letters of Robert D. Carter* (Columbia: University of Missouri Press, 2013), 58–60.

45. George Crook, *Crook's Resumé of Operations against Apache Indians, 1882 to 1886* (London: Johnson-Taunton Military Press, 1971); Charles B. Gatewood, "The Surrender of Geronimo," *Journal of Arizona History* 27, no. 1 (1986): 53–70; Janne Lahti, *Cultural Construction of Empire: The U.S. Army in Arizona and New Mexico* (Lincoln: Nebraska University Press, 2012), 28.

46. William Thaddeus Sexton, *Soldiers in the Sun; an Adventure in Imperialism* (Freeport, NY: Books for Libraries Press, 1971), 130; Carter, *A Civilian in Lawton's Campaign*, 76.

47. Telegraph, Lawton to Adjutant General, May 14, 1899, RG 395 Entry 789 Box 1, NARA.

48. John B. Kinne Diary, Box 1, Elwyn B. Robinson Department of Special Collections, Chester Fritz Library, University of North Dakota, 40.

49. *Correspondence Relating to the War with Spain and Conditions Growing Out of the Same Including the Insurrection in the Philippine Island and the China Relief Expedition*, Vol. 1 (Washington, DC: GPO, 1902), 609.

50. Kinne Diary, 2–3.

51. Frederick Hoxie, "From Prison to Homeland: The Cheyenne River Indian Reservation Before WW 1," *South Dakota State History*, Winter 1979. For imperialist nostalgia at "vanished" Native people, see Laura Wexler, *Tender Violence: Domestic Visions in an Age of U.S. Imperialism* (Chapel Hill: University of North Carolina Press, 2000), 195.

52. Linn, *The Philippine War*, 51; Lee, *The Other Face of Battle*, 116.

53. Kinne Diary, 3, 8–15. On the frequent use of racial epithets by US soldiers in the Philippines, see Jung, *Menace to Empire*, 32; Capozzola, *Bound by War*, 30.

54. Linn, *The Philippine War*, 113.

55. Lawton to Adjutant General, June 6, 1899, Henry W. Lawton Scrapbook; Kinne Diary, 61.

56. Lawton to Adjutant General, May 14, 1899; Jerry M. Cooper and Glenn H. Smith, *Citizens as Soldiers: A History of the North Dakota National Guard* (Fargo: North Dakota Institute for Regional Studies, 1986), 97–98.

57. Telegram, Lawton to Adjutant General; Cooper and Smith, *Citizens as Soldiers*, 99.

58. Lawton to Adjutant General, June 6, 1899, Henry W. Lawton Scrapbook.

59. Kinne Diary," 63–65. Similar accounts of seek-and-destroy missions and burned supplies can be found in other American accounts of the war. See "Diary of Charles Dudley Rhodes," The Charles D. Rhodes Papers, 1940–1949, Box 1, United States Military Academy Special Collections; Journal of Harry M. Dey, Captain Harry M. Dey Papers, Box 1, Phil-Am War Day—Reports and Accounts—Soldiers' Narratives—Journal (Nov 13, 1899–July 6, 1901), University of Michigan Special Collections.

60. *Annual Report of the Secretary of War* (Washington, DC: GPO, 1899), 201–2.

61. Kinne Diary, 61.

62. Kinne Diary, 37, 44–47, 58; John Russater and William H. Lock, quoted in Cooper and Smith, *Citizens as Soldiers*, 106–7. One Navy officer even suggested that Filipinos feared Americans because General Philip Sheridan's alleged statement that "the only good Indian is a dead Indian" had been intentionally circulated in the islands. The officer claimed that "The savage and less advanced natives of Luzon are called Indians, and they were easily led to believe that Sheridan meant them, and that our soldiers meant extermination." "A Navy Officer on Aguinaldo," *Army and Navy Journal*, December 9, 1899, 354.

63. Kinne Diary, 75.

64. *Correspondence Relating to the War with Spain*, Vol. 2, 988; Operations and Casualties Lists Feb. 1899–June 1899," RG 395 Entry 764 Box 3, NARA; Cooper and Smith, *Citizens as Soldiers*, 98–99; Linn, *The Philippine War*, 115.

65. Kinne Diary, 66.

66. Lawton to Adjutant General, May 14.

67. Report of Reconnaissance of Road, RG 395 Entry 789 Box 1, NARA.

68. Roth, *Muddy Glory*, 170; Sexton, *Soldiers in the Sun*, 134–35; Linn, *The Philippine War*, 115.

69. Lawton to Adjutant General, May 14; Linn, *The Philippine War*, 185–87; Capozzola, *Bound by War*, 29.

70. "Value of Cavalry in Philippines," *Army and Navy Journal*, March 17, 1900; Linn, *The Philippine War*, 187; Jung, *Menace to Empire*, 32.

71. Linn, *The Philippine War*, 115–16.

72. Linn, 134–35.

73. "Success of the Moment against Filipino Braves," *The San Francisco Call*, June 12, 1899.

74. *Correspondence Relating to the War with Spain*, Vol. 1, 1076; Miller, *"Benevolent Assimilation,"* 81; Capozzola, *Bound by War*, 7–10, 34–41.

75. Henry W. Lawton Scrapbook.

76. "General Lawton as Warrior, Statesman and Man," Henry W. Lawton Scrapbook.

77. Senator Albert Beveridge made a similar argument in an 1898 campaign speech when he told the crowd that "we are a conquering race, and we must obey our blood and occupy new markets, and, if necessary, new lands." Beveridge would later justify the denial of self-determination to Filipino people through comparisons to Native Americans, arguing in the Senate: "You, who say the Declaration applies to all men, how dare you deny its application to the American Indian? And if you deny it to the Indian at home, how dare you grant it to the Malay abroad?" Laura E. Gómez, *Manifest Destinies: The Making of the Mexican American Race* (New York: New York University Press, 2008), 74.

78. Kramer, *The Blood of Government*, 89–90.

79. Amy Kaplan, *The Anarchy of Empire in the Making of US Culture* (Cambridge, MA: Harvard University Press, 2002), 12–14. Gail Bederman and Kristin Hoganson show how masculinity and white supremacy became powerful motivators for overseas US expansion in the late nineteenth and early twentieth centuries. Much of this masculine expression involved carefully regulated forays into a "primitive" state through organizations like the Improved Order of Red Men and the Boy Scouts. Gail Bederman, *Manliness and Civilization: A Cultural History of Gender and Race in the United States, 1880–1917* (Chicago: University of Chicago Press, 1996), 20–31; Kristin L. Hoganson, *Fighting for American Manhood: How Gender Politics Provoked the Spanish-American and Philippine-American Wars* (New Haven, CT: Yale University Press, 1998), 2–9; Robert Macdonald, *Sons of the Empire* (Toronto: University of Toronto Press, 1993), 12–13; Philip Joseph Deloria, *Playing Indian* (New Haven, CT: Yale University Press, 1998), 95–99.

80. Amy Kaplan, "Romancing the Empire: The Embodiment of American Masculinity in the Popular Historical Novel of the 1890s," *American Literary History* 2, no. 4 (1990): 659–61.

81. Deidre Johnson, *Edward Stratemeyer and the Stratemeyer Syndicate* (New York: Twayne Publishers, 1993), 64–65.

82. John M. Gates, "The Official Historian and the Well-Placed Critic: James A. LeRoy's Assessment of John R. M. Taylor's 'The Philippine Insurrection against the United States,'" *The Public Historian* 7, no. 3 (1985): 57–67; Birtle, *U.S. Army Counterinsurgency*, 10; Keith B. Bickel, *Mars Learning: The Marine Corps Development of Small Wars Doctrine, 1915–1940* (Boulder, CO: Westview Press, 2001), 42–47; Robert D. Ramsey III, *A Masterpiece of Counterguerrilla Warfare: BG J. Franklin Bell in the Philippines, 1901–1902* (Fort Leavenworth, KS: CSI, 2007).

83. Elbridge Streeter Brooks, *With Lawton and Roberts: A Boy's Adventures in the Philippines and the Transvaal* (Boston: Lothrop Publishing Company, 1900), preface.

84. Brooks, 29–36.

85. Brooks, 47–67.

86. Brooks, 315.

87. Edward Stratemeyer, *The Campaign of the Jungle; or, Under Lawton through Luzon* (Boston: Lothrop, Lee & Shepard, 1900), preface.

88. Stratemeyer, 37.

89. Kinne Diary, 61.

90. Kinne Diary, 61.

91. Jodi Kim, *Settler Garrison: Debt Imperialism, Militarism, and Trans-pacific Imaginaries* (Durham, NC: Duke University Press, 2022), 74.

92. Kinne Diary, 69–72.

93. Edgar F. Raines, "Major General J. Franklin Bell, U.S.A.: The Education of a Soldier, 1856–1899," *The Register of the Kentucky Historical Society* 83, no. 4 (1985): 340–43.

94. Ramsey III, *A Masterpiece of Counterguerrilla Warfare.*

95. Kinne Diary, 72.

96. On the "Indian sound" see Philip Joseph Deloria, *Indians in Unexpected Places* (Lawrence: University Press of Kansas, 2004).

3. THE LITERATURE OF SAVAGE WAR

1. For more on the fight at Sunset Pass, see Paul L. Hedren, "Captain Charles King At Sunset Pass," *Journal of Arizona History* 17, no. 3 (1976): 253–64; Peter Cozzens, *Eyewitnesses to the Indian Wars, 1865–1890* (Mechanicsburg, PA: Stackpole Books, 2001), 188–90; Jerome A. Greene, ed., *Indian War Veterans: Memories of Army Life and Campaigns in the West, 1864–1898* (New York: Savas Beatie, 2007), 321.

2. Charles King, "Indians and Two Young Lieutenants," *New York Herald Tribune Magazine*, August 3, 1924, Elmo Scott Watson Papers, Box 22, Folder 204, Newberry Library.

3. Richard Slotkin, *Regeneration through Violence; the Mythology of the American Frontier, 1600–1860* (Middletown, CT: Wesleyan University Press, 1973), 484–93.

4. Charles King, "Indians and Two Young Lieutenants."

5. Don Russell and Paul L. Hedren, *Campaigning with King: Charles King, Chronicler of the Old Army* (Lincoln: University of Nebraska Press, 1991), 49–51.

6. Mike Burns and Gregory McNamee, *The Only One Living to Tell: The Autobiography of a Yavapai Indian* (Tucson: University of Arizona Press, 2012), 61–63.

7. Tom Engelhardt, *The End of Victory Culture: Cold War America and the Disillusioning of a Generation* (Amherst: University of Massachusetts Press, 2007), 35.

8. C. E Dornbusch, *Charles King, American Army Novelist; a Bibliography from the Collection of the National Library of Australia, Canberra* (Cornwallville, NY: Hope Farm Press, 1963), foreword.

9. John W. Bailey, *The Life and Works of General Charles King, 1844–1933: Martial Spirit* (Lewiston, NY: Edwin Mellen Press, 1998), 96–97; Cozzens, *Eyewitnesses to the Indian Wars*, 338. King defended Buffalo Bill for the rest of his life, calling one book that questioned the showman's narrative "mendacious

and malicious reports." "Fighter, 84, Goes to Clear Name of Buffalo Bill," *Chicago Daily News*, 1929, Elmo Scott Watson Papers, Box 22, Folder 204, Newberry Library.

10. Charles King, *Campaigning with Crook: And Stories of Army Life* (New York: Harper & Brothers Publishers, 1902), 36.

11. King, 167; Louise Barnett, *Touched by Fire: The Life, Death, and Mythic Afterlife of George Armstrong Custer* (Lincoln: University of Nebraska Press, 2006), 119.

12. Bailey, *The Life and Works*, 240; Cozzens, *Eyewitnesses to the Indian Wars*, 461.

13. Edward M. Coffman, *The Old Army: A Portrait of the American Army in Peacetime, 1784–1898* (Oxford: Oxford University Press, 1986); Michael L. Tate, *The Frontier Army in the Settlement of the West* (Norman: University of Oklahoma Press, 1999), 279–80; Gretchen Murphy, "The Spanish-American War, US Expansion, and the Novel," in Priscilla Wald and Michael A. Elliott, eds., *The Oxford History of the Novel in English: The American Novel 1870–1940* (Oxford: Oxford University Press, 2014), 198–99.

14. Dornbusch, *Charles King*, iii; Kevin Adams, *Class and Race in the Frontier Army: Military Life in the West, 1870–1890* (Norman: University of Oklahoma Press, 2009), 35.

15. Tate, *Frontier Army*, 280.

16. "An Army Advocate," *Army and Navy Journal*, March 9, 1895.

17. Bailey, *The Life and Works*, 226–28; Tate, *Frontier Army*, 280.

18. Sandra K. Sagala, *Buffalo Bill on the Silver Screen: The Films of William F. Cody* (Norman: University of Oklahoma Press, 2013), 71.

19. Janne Lahti, *Cultural Construction of Empire: The US Army in Arizona and New Mexico* (Lincoln: Nebraska University Press, 2012), 4.

20. John M. Carroll, ed., *The Papers of the Order of Indian Wars* (Fort Collins, CO: Old Army Press, 1975), 113.

21. Miguel Antonio Levario, *Militarizing the Border: When Mexicans Became the Enemy* (College Station: Texas A&M University Press, 2012), 2–3; Iván Chaar-López, "Sensing Intruders: Race and the Automation of Border Control," *American Quarterly* 71, no. 2 (June 2019): 495–518.

22. Philip J. Deloria, *Indians in Unexpected Places* (Lawrence: University Press of Kansas, 2004), 4–8. For characterizations of Apache people in the late nineteenth century, see Karl Jacoby, *Shadows at Dawn: An Apache Massacre and the Violence of History* (New York: Penguin Books, 2009), 123; Katherine Benton-Cohen, *Borderline Americans: Racial Division and Labor War in the Arizona Borderland* (Cambridge, MA: Harvard University Press, 2009), 67–68; Katharine Bjork, *Prairie Imperialists: The Indian Country Origins of American Empire* (Philadelphia: University of Pennsylvania Press, 2018), 86–87.

23. Charles King, *Starlight Ranch, and Other Stories of Army Life on the Frontier* (Philadelphia: J.B. Lippincott Company, 1890), 229–33.

24. Charles King, *Sunset Pass; or, Running the Gauntlet Through Apache Land* (New York: American Publishers Corporation, 1890).

25. Lahti, *Cultural Constructions of Empire*, 116.

26. Robert K. Evans, "The Indian Question in Arizona," *The Atlantic*, August 1886.

27. George Crook, *Crook's Resumé of Operations against Apache Indians, 1882 to 1886* (London: Johnson-Taunton Military Press, 1971), 10.

28. As evidence, note the many documents produced during the War on Terror, discussed in the final chapter, that examine the Apache Wars for insight into modern counterinsurgency.

29. María Josefina Saldaña-Portillo, *Indian Given: Racial Geographies across Mexico and the United States* (Durham, NC: Duke University Press, 2016), 154–55.

30. King, *Sunset Pass*, 70.

31. King, *Sunset Pass*, 122–23.

32. King, *Sunset Pass*, 202.

33. "Gen. Charles King Here," *Chicago Daily Tribune*, June 29, 1899.

34. Charles King, "Indian Fighters in the Philippines," *Army and Navy Journal*, September 23, 1899.

35. Stefan Aune, "Indian Fighters in the Philippines: Imperial Culture and Military Violence in the Philippine-American War," *Pacific Historical Review* 90, no. 4 (January 1, 2021): 419–47.

36. "Among the Blood-Stained Trenches in the Philippines," *The Atlanta Constitution*, May 14, 1899.

37. Tom Sykes, *Imagining Manila: Literature, Empire and Orientalism* (New York: Bloomsbury, 2021), 15.

38. Charles King, *Found in the Philippines: The Story of a Woman's Letters* (New York: F.T. Neely, 1899), 52–53.

39. Charles King, *The Further Story of Lieutenant Sandy Ray* (New York: R.F. Fenno & Company, 1906), 285.

40. For American characterizations of Filipinos, see Paul A. Kramer, *The Blood of Government: Race, Empire, the United States, and the Philippines* (Chapel Hill: University of North Carolina Press, 2006), 94–95; Matthew Frye Jacobson, *Barbarian Virtues: The United States Encounters Foreign Peoples at Home and Abroad, 1876–1917* (New York: Hill And Wang, 2001), 221–23; Daniel Immerwahr, *How to Hide an Empire: A History of the Greater United States* (New York: Farrar, Straus and Giroux, 2019), 95–96.

41. Charles King, as quoted in Stuart Creighton Miller, *"Benevolent Assimilation": The American Conquest of the Philippines, 1899–1903* (New Haven, CT: Yale University Press, 1982), 41, 88.

42. King, "Among the Blood-Stained Trenches."

43. King, *Found in the Philippines*, 277.

44. Katherine E. Bishop, "The Anti-Imperialist American Literary Animal: Envisioning Empathy," *Antennae: The Journal of Nature in Visual Culture*, no. 24 (Spring 2013): 110–24, footnote 1; Philip Joseph Deloria, *Playing Indian* (New Haven, CT: Yale University Press, 1998).

45. King, *Found in the Philippines*, 284–87.

46. Occasionally, US troops in the Philippines were referred to as "Indians," most notably "Bullard's Indians," the nickname for the Thirty-Ninth Volunteer Infantry led by Colonel R. L. Bullard. See Bjork, *Prairie Imperialists*, 151–52.

47. Charles King, "Memories of a Busy Life," *The Wisconsin Magazine of History* 6, no. 1 (1922): 29–30.

48. King, 17.

49. "Captain King Fights as Well as Writes," Rufus and Charles King Collection, Carroll University.

50. Brian McAllister Linn, *The Philippine War, 1899–1902* (Lawrence: University Press of Kansas, 2000), 42–64; David J. Silbey, *A War of Frontier and Empire: The Philippine-American War, 1899–1902* (New York: Hill and Wang, 2008), 98–99.

51. Miller, *"Benevolent Assimilation,"* 67; Wayne E. Lee et al., *The Other Face of Battle: America's Forgotten Wars and the Experience of Combat* (Oxford: Oxford University Press, 2021), 117–18.

52. King, "Memories," 26–29.

53. Charles King, *A Conquering Corps Badge, and Other Stories of the Philippines* (Milwaukee: L.A. Rhodes Company, 1902), 16.

54. Sheridan to B. H. Grierson, February 23, 1869, Benjamin Grierson Papers, Box 3, Folder 117, Newberry Library.

55. King, *A Conquering Corps Badge*, 29.

56. Meg Wesling, *Empire's Proxy: American Literature and U.S. Imperialism in the Philippines* (New York: New York University Press, 2011), 34; Victor Román Mendoza, *Metroimperial Intimacies: Fantasy, Racial-Sexual Governance, and the Philippines in U. S. Imperialism, 1899–1913* (Durham, NC: Duke University Press, 2015), 102–5; Nerissa Balce, *Body Parts of Empire: Visual Abjection, Filipino Images, and the American Archive* (Ann Arbor: University of Michigan Press, 2016), 9; Lee et al., *The Other Face of Battle*, 93.

57. Charles King, *Capture: The Story of Sandy Ray* (New York: Grosset & Dunlap, 1906), 268–71.

58. Amy Kaplan, *The Anarchy of Empire in the Making of US Culture* (Cambridge, MA: Harvard University Press, 2002), 11; Kramer, *The Blood of Government*, 407–10. King's novel plays with a variety of racialized depictions of nonwhite men during this period, who were sometimes depicted as diminutive and emasculated, other times depicted as sexually threatening, particularly toward white women. See Peggy Pascoe, *What Comes Naturally: Miscegenation Law and the Making of Race in America* (Oxford: Oxford University Press, 2009), 93–104; Nayan Shah, *Stranger Intimacy: Contesting Race, Sexuality and the Law in the North American West* (Berkeley: University of California Press, 2012), 161–62; Mina Roces, "'These Guys Came Out Looking Like Movie Actors': Filipino Dress and Consumer Practices in the United States, 1920s–1930s," *Pacific Historical Review* 85, no. 4 (2016): 559–62.

59. Richard E. Welch, "American Atrocities in the Philippines: The Indictment and the Response," *Pacific Historical Review* 43, no. 2 (1974): 233–53; Linn, *The Philippine War*, 219–20; Kramer, *The Blood of Government*, 140–45; Edward M. Coffman, *The Regulars: The American Army, 1898–1941* (Cambridge, MA: Harvard University Press, 2007), 42–43; Christopher J. Einolf, *America in the Philippines: The First Torture Scandal* (New York: Palgrave Macmillan, 2014), 37–43; Samuel Moyn, *Humane: How the United States Abandoned Peace and Reinvented War* (New York: Farrar, Straus and Giroux, 2021), 110–14. Welch and Linn argue

that American atrocities in the Philippines were less widespread than sometimes depicted, with Linn also downplaying racism as an explanation for torture and other acts of violence. In contrast, Kramer and Einolf view torture as more widespread, with Kramer in particular arguing for caution with how historians treat the historical record of atrocities in the Philippines, noting that most of the concrete evidence comes from official American sources. What is incontrovertible for my argument is that Americans and their allies did use torture against Filipinos.

60. Linn, *The Philippine War*, 320–21; Kramer, *The Blood of Government*, 146.

61. Moon-Ho Jung, *Menace to Empire: Anticolonial Solidarities and the Transpacific Origins of the US Security State* (Oakland: University of California Press, 2022), 34.

62. Kramer, *The Blood of Government*, 145–46; Einolf, *America in the Philippines*, 97–109; W. Fitzhugh Brundage, *Civilizing Torture: An American Tradition* (Cambridge, MA: Harvard University Press, 2018), 175–81.

63. *Affairs in the Philippine Islands: Hearings before the Committee on the Philippines of the United States Senate,* 57th Cong., 1st Sess., 1902, Doc. No. 331, Part 2 (Washington, DC: US GPO, 1902), 950.

64. Francis Lieber, *Instructions for the Government of Armies of the United States, in the Field* (New York: D. Van Nostrand, 1863), Code 27; Brundage, *Civilizing Torture*, 178–80.

65. "One fact which . . ." *Army and Navy Journal,* September 6, 1902.

66. "Experience among Filipinos," *Army and Navy Journal,* November 29, 1902.

67. Coffman, *The Regulars*, 42–43.

68. Brian McAllister Linn, *The Echo of Battle: The Army's Way of War* (Cambridge, MA: Harvard University Press, 2007), 86.

69. Charles King, *Comrades in Arms: A Tale of Two Hemispheres* (New York: Grosset & Dunlap, 1904), 300–301.

70. King, *Comrades in Arms*, 300.

71. King, 301.

72. Jung, *Menace to Empire*, 29–30.

73. King, *Comrades in Arms*, 302–3.

74. On the Wounded Knee massacre, see Jeffrey Ostler, *The Plains Sioux and U.S. Colonialism from Lewis and Clark to Wounded Knee* (Cambridge: Cambridge University Press, 2004), 346; Nick Estes, *Our History Is the Future* (New York: Verso, 2019), 128–29.

75. Charles King to His Daughter, Jan. 31, 1899, Rufus and Charles King Collection, Carroll University.

76. King, *Comrades in Arms*, 304.

77. King, *Comrades in Arms*, 306–9; Einolf, *America in the Philippines*, 65–66; "Diary of Charles Dudley Rhodes."

78. Einolf, *American in the Philippines*, 1; Jung, *Menace to Empire*, 40.

79. King, *Comrades in Arms*, 318–19.

80. Nelson A. Miles, *The Philippines Reports by Lieutenant-General Nelson A. Miles, U.S.A. Reprinted from Army and Navy Journal, May 2, 1903* (Boston: Anti Imperialist League, 1909), 7.

81. Herbert Welsh, "Report on Herbert Yenser, Worcester's Philippine Collection," Documents and Papers, 1834–1915, Maria C. Lanzar-Carpio Papers, Welsh, Herbert, 1851–1913, Box 2, Incoming S-Z Miscellaneous, University of Michigan Special Collections.

82. King, Comrades in Arms, 316–19.

83. King, 312.

84. Moorfield Storey and Julian Codman, "Marked Severities" in Philippine Warfare. An Analysis of the Law and Facts Bearing on the Action and Utterances of President Roosevelt and Secretary Root (Boston: G.H. Ellis Co., 1902), 3.

85. In the cases that went before a court martial, American officers were hesitant to return guilty verdicts and largely sympathetic to soldiers accused of using or sanctioning torture. See Einolf, America in the Philippines, 49.

86. King, Comrades in Arms, 320–21.

87. King, 321.

88. Einolf, America in the Philippines, 37–67; Allan W. Vestal, "The First Wartime Water Torture by Americans," Maine Law Review 69 (2017): 17–21.

89. Linn, The Philippine War, 321; John Fabian Witt, Lincoln's Code: The Laws of War in American History (New York: Free Press, 2012), 359–61; Einolf, America in the Philippines, 1–2, 167–168; William L. d'Ambruoso, American Torture from the Philippines to Iraq: A Recurring Nightmare (Oxford: Oxford University Press, 2021), 58–59.

90. Miles, The Philippines Reports, 7–8.

91. "General Miles's Philippine Reports," Army and Navy Journal, May 2, 1903.

92. "General Miles Replies," Army and Navy Journal, May 16, 1903.

93. "Sensational Lying," Army and Navy Journal, April 29, 1899. Native prisoners were not always treated with "humane consideration." Apache leader Mangas Coloradas was infamously captured, tortured, and murdered by his guards, and the Cheyenne imprisoned at Fort Robinson in 1879 were starved and denied adequate shelter and warmth. See Lahti, Cultural Constructions of Empire, 23; Jerome A. Greene, January Moon: The Northern Cheyenne Breakout from Fort Robinson, 1878–1879 (Norman: University of Oklahoma Press, 2020), 185; Denise Low and Ramon Powers, Northern Cheyenne Ledger Art by Fort Robinson Breakout Survivors (Lincoln: University of Nebraska Press, 2020), 8–15.

94. Kramer, The Blood of Government, 152–55.

95. Keith B. Bickel, Mars Learning: The Marine Corps Development of Small Wars Doctrine, 1915–1940 (Boulder, CO: Westview Press, 2001), 42–47; Coffman, The Regular Army, 53–54.

96. Louis M. Hamilton, "Jungle Tactics," JMSI 37 (1905): 23–24.

97. J. P. Clark, Preparing for War: The Emergence of the Modern U.S. Army, 1815–1917 (Cambridge, MA: Harvard University Press, 2017), 217.

98. Linn, The Echo of Battle, 84–86.

99. "Insular Notes," JMSI 29 (1901): 448.

100. John M. Gates, "The Official Historian and the Well-Placed Critic: James A. LeRoy's Assessment of John R. M. Taylor's 'The Philippine Insurrection against the United States,'" The Public Historian 7, no. 3 (1985): 57–67.

101. Linn, *The Philippine War*, 213–15; Kramer, *The Blood of Government*, 152–54; Jung, *Menace to Empire*, 34–35.

102. John R. M. Taylor, *The Philippine Insurrection against the United States*, Vol. 2 (Pasay City, Philippines: Eugenio Lopez Foundation, 1971), 285–96.

103. Taylor, 299.

104. John Lawrence Tone, *The Fatal Knot: The Guerrilla War in Navarre and the Defeat of Napoleon in Spain* (Chapel Hill: University of North Carolina Press, 1994), 3–6; Richard Hart Sinnreich, "That Accursed Spanish War: The Peninsular War, 1807–1814," in Williamson Murray and Peter Mansoor, eds., *Hybrid Warfare: Fighting Complex Opponents from the Ancient World to the Present* (Cambridge: Cambridge University Press, 2012), 106.

105. Linn, *The Echo of Battle*, 86–87.

106. Robert D. Ramsey III, *A Masterpiece of Counterguerrilla Warfare: BG J. Franklin Bell in the Philippines, 1901–1902* (Fort Leavenworth, KS: CSI, 2007).

107. d'Ambruoso, *American Torture from the Philippines to Iraq*, 65.

108. J. Franklin Bell, "Telegraphic Circulars and General Orders" as quoted in Ramsey III, *A Masterpiece*, 37.

109. Andrew J. Birtle, *US Army Counterinsurgency and Contingency Operations Doctrine, 1860–1941* (Washington, DC: Center of Military History, 1998), 138–39.

110. Bell, *Telegraphic Circulars*, as quoted in Ramsey III, *A Masterpiece*, 111.

111. King, "Memories of a Busy Life," 30–33.

112. King, 30–33.

4. SAVAGE AND CIVILIZED WAR

1. Lecture, "Mountain Warfare," in Instructional Material, Infantry School, 1929–30, 1st sec., Vol. 2. Thanks to Andrew Birtle for assistance in acquiring this source.

2. Jean M. O'Brien, "'Vanishing' Indians in Nineteenth-Century New England: Local Historians' Erasure of Still-Present Indian Peoples," in Sergei A. Kan and Pauline Turner Strong, eds., *New Perspectives on Native North American: Cultures, Histories, and Representations* (Lincoln: University of Nebraska Press, 2009), 415–16.

3. On Native nations and the struggle for sovereignty, see David E. Wilkins and K. Tsianina Lomawaima, *Uneven Ground: American Indian Sovereignty and Federal Law* (Norman: University of Oklahoma Press, 2001); Kevin Bruyneel, *The Third Space of Sovereignty: The Postcolonial Politics of U.S.-Indigenous Relations* (Minneapolis: University of Minnesota Press, 2007); Audra Simpson, *Mohawk Interruptus: Political Life across the Borders of Settler States* (Durham, NC: Duke University Press, 2014).

4. Philip J. Deloria, *Indians in Unexpected Places* (Lawrence: University Press of Kansas, 2004), chap. 2.

5. John Gates, "Indians and Insurrectos: The U.S. Army's Experience with Insurgency," *Parameters* 13 (March 1983).

6. On the frontier myth, see Richard Slotkin, *Gunfighter Nation: Myth of the Frontier in Twentieth-Century America* (New York: Atheneum, 1992).

7. Lisa Lowe, *The Intimacies of Four Continents* (Durham, NC: Duke University Press Books, 2015), 3.

8. Gail Bederman, *Manliness and Civilization: A Cultural History of Gender and Race in the United States, 1880–1917* (Chicago: University of Chicago Press, 1996); Kristin L. Hoganson, *Fighting for American Manhood: How Gender Politics Provoked the Spanish-American and Philippine-American Wars* (New Haven, CT: Yale University Press, 1998); Laura Wexler, *Tender Violence: Domestic Visions in an Age of U.S. Imperialism* (Chapel Hill: University of North Carolina Press, 2000); Matthew Frye Jacobson, *Barbarian Virtues: The United States Encounters Foreign Peoples at Home and Abroad, 1876–1917* (New York: Hill And Wang, 2001); Nayan Shah, *Contagious Divides: Epidemics and Race in San Francisco's Chinatown* (Berkeley: University of California Press, 2001); Amy Kaplan, *The Anarchy of Empire in the Making of U.S. Culture* (Cambridge, MA: Harvard University Press, 2002).

9. James F. J. Archibald, *Blue Shirt and Khaki: A Comparison* (New York: Silver, Burdett and Company, 1901), 73.

10. Andrew J. Birtle, *U.S. Army Counterinsurgency and Contingency Operations Doctrine, 1860–1941* (Washington, DC: Center of Military History, 1998), 10.

11. Spencer Jones, *From Boer War to World War: Tactical Reform of the British Army, 1902–1914* (Norman: University of Oklahoma Press, 2012), 23–24.

12. Sir Alfred Milner, quoted in S. B. Spies, *Methods of Barbarism? Roberts and Kitchener and Civilians in the Boer Republics, January 1900–May 1902* (Cape Town: Human & Rousseau, 1977), 11.

13. Charles Edward Callwell, *Small Wars: Their Principles and Practice* (London: Harrison and Sons, 1899), 95; Thomas Pakenham, *Boer War* (New York: Random House, 1979), 466–67; Bill Nasson, *The South African War, 1899–1902* (London: Arnold, 1999), 211–20; Elizabeth van Heyningen, "A Tool for Modernisation? The Boer Concentration Camps of the South African War, 1900–1902," *South African Journal of Science* 106, nos. 5–6 (June 5, 2010): 1–10; Laleh Khalili, *Time in the Shadows: Confinement in Counterinsurgencies* (Stanford, CA: Stanford University Press, 2012), 28.

14. "Briton and Boer," *Army and Navy Journal*, March 31, 1900, 732.

15. Barbara Harlow and Mia Carter, *Archives of Empire: Volume 2, The Scramble for Africa* (Durham, NC: Duke University Press, 2004), 629–33; Khalili, *Time in the Shadows*, 28.

16. Brian McAllister Linn argues that many officers in the nineteenth century placed a high value on individualism, particularly in wars with Native peoples. See Brian McAllister Linn, *The Echo of Battle: The Army's Way of War* (Cambridge, MA: Harvard University Press, 2007), 75.

17. "How the Boers Trick the British," *Army and Navy Journal*, June 23, 1901; "The Turkish View of Cowardice," *Army and Navy Journal*, August 10, 1901; "A Deadly Parallel," *Army and Navy Journal*, September 29, 1900; Pakenham, *The Boer War*, 274–77; Aidan Forth, *Barbed-Wire Imperialism: Britain's Empire of Camps, 1876–1903* (Oakland: University of California Press, 2017), 134.

18. A. H. Russell, "What Is the Use of a Regular Army in This Country?," *JMSI* 24 (1899): 327–30. Marine Corps descriptions of fighting in Cuba made similar connections between Indians, individualism, and martial prowess. See Anonymous, "The Sergeant's Private Madhouse," *Marine Corps Gazette* 1, no. 3 (September 1916): 298–304.

19. Frederick Russell Burnham, quoted in Andrew Offenburger, *Frontiers in the Gilded Age: Adventure, Capitalism, and Dispossession from Southern Africa to the U.S.-Mexican Borderlands, 1880–1917* (New Haven, CT: Yale University Press, 2019), 57, 72–73.

20. Archibald, *Blue Shirt and Khaki*, 73–74.

21. Frank Geere, "Our Military Individualism," *JMSI* 39 (1906): 208; Russell Weigley, *Towards an American Army: Military Thought from Washington to Marshall* (New York: Columbia University Press, 1962), 52–53.

22. William Booth, quoted in Forth, *Barbed-Wire Imperialism*, 34. See also Paula M. Krebs, *Gender, Race, and the Writing of Empire: Public Discourse and the Boer War* (Cambridge: Cambridge University Press, 1999), 60–61; Vincent Kuitenbrouwer, *War of Words: Dutch Pro-Boer Propaganda and the South African War (1899–1902)* (Amsterdam: Amsterdam University Press, 2012), 199.

23. These were not brand-new debates. In the 1850's, Secretary of War Jefferson Davis cited French practices in Algeria for his approach to troop mobilizations on the frontier. See Robert Wooster, *The American Military Frontiers: The United States Army in the West, 1783–1900* (Albuquerque: University of New Mexico Press, 2009), 142; Khalili, *Time in the Shadows*, 13–16.

24. Regardless of how accurate Geere's claim is, the South African War did provoke a great deal of introspection in the British Army. See Jones, *From Boer War to World War*, 35–36.

25. Geere, "Our Military Individualism," 209–10.

26. Geere, 209–10.

27. See Richard Slotkin, *Regeneration through Violence: The Mythology of the American Frontier, 1600–1860* (Middletown, CT: Wesleyan University Press, 1973), 5–7; Philip Joseph Deloria, *Playing Indian* (New Haven, CT: Yale University Press, 1998), 36–37.

28. W. H. Carter, "The Infantry and Cavalry School at Fort Leavenworth," *JMSI* 15 (1894): 757.

29. John W. Shy, *A People Numerous and Armed: Reflections on the Military Struggle for American Independence* (Ann Arbor: University of Michigan Press, 1990), 160–61.

30. James Chester, "Musings of a Superannuated Soldier," *JMSI* 47 (1910): 387–97.

31. On "contamination" see Slotkin, *Regeneration through Violence*, 55.

32. "South Africa and the Philippines," *Army and Navy Journal*, December 16, 1899. This concern that "savage war" stunted military development was not confined to American observers. One German officer argued that the British, who "for years had fought none but savage people," were unprepared for modern warfare. See Lieutenant-Colonel Von Lindenau, "What Lessons Can We Draw from the Boer War for Our Infantry Attack?," *JMSI* 32 (1903): 129–36.

33. "South Africa and the Philippines," *Army and Navy Journal*, December 16, 1899.

34. For examples from the British side, see Harlow and Carter, *Archives of Empire: Volume 2, The Scramble for Africa*.

35. J. C. G., "Review of Guerilla or Partisan Warfare," *Journal of the United States Cavalry Association* 15, nos. 53–56 (July 1904): 735–36.

36. Geoffrey Demarest, "T. Miller Maguire and the Lost Essence of Strategy," Strategy Research Project (USAWC, 2007), 3; Daniel Whittingham, *Charles E. Callwell and the British Way in Warfare* (Cambridge: Cambridge University Press, 2020), 8–10.

37. Khalili, *Time in the Shadows*, 28–30.

38. Whittingham, *Charles E. Callwell*, 11, 22–23; Kim A. Wagner, "Savage Warfare: Violence and the Rule of Colonial Difference in Early British Counterinsurgency," *History Workshop Journal* 85 (Spring 2018): 217–37.

39. Callwell, *Small Wars*, 2.

40. Callwell, 40, 80, 135–36.

41. M.F.S., "Review of Tactics for Beginners," *Journal of the United States Cavalry Association* 15, nos. 53–56 (July 1904): 747.

42. Odd Arne Westad, *The Global Cold War: Third World Interventions and the Making of Our Times* (Cambridge: Cambridge University Press, 2005), 73–78.

43. Anthony Smith, *Machine Gun: The Story of the Men and the Weapon That Changed the Face of War* (New York: St. Martin's Paperbacks, 2004), vii–17.

44. Edward M. Coffman, *The Regulars: The American Army, 1898–1941* (Cambridge, MA: Harvard University Press, 2007), 161–62; Robert H. Ferrell, *Reminiscences of Conrad S. Babcock: The Old U. S. Army and the New, 1898–1918* (Columbia: University of Missouri Press, 2012), 25–32.

45. John Henry Parker, *Tactical Organization and Uses of Machine Guns in the Field* (Kansas City: Hudson-Kimberly Publishing Company, 1899), 29.

46. Smith, *Machine Gun*, 106; Jeffrey Ostler, *The Plains Sioux and U.S. Colonialism from Lewis and Clark to Wounded Knee* (Cambridge: Cambridge University Press, 2004), 343–44.

47. C.D.R., "Book Notices and Exchanges," *Journal of the United States Cavalry Association* 12, no. 41 (March 1899), 218.

48. D. R. Headrick, "The Tools of Imperialism: Technology and the Expansion of European Colonial Empires in the Nineteenth Century," *Journal of Modern History* 51, no. 2 (01 1979): 253–55; Joshua F. Berry, "Hollow Point Bullets: How History Has Hijacked Their Use in Combat and Why It Is Time to Reexamine the 1899 Hague Declaration Concerning Expanding Bullets," *Military Law Review* 206 (2010): 100–101; David J. Silverman, *Thundersticks: Firearms and the Violent Transformation of Native America* (Cambridge, MA: Harvard University Press, 2016), 245–46.

49. Berry, "Hollow Point Bullets," 100–102.

50. J. B. Hamilton, "The Evolution of the Dum-Dum Bullet," *British Medical Journal* 1, no. 1950 (May 14, 1898): 1250–51; Headrick, "The Tools of Imperialism," 256; Wagner, "Savage Warfare," 223–29.

51. Headrick, "The Tools of Imperialism," 256; Kim A. Wagner, "Expanding Bullets and Savage Warfare," *History Workshop Journal* 88 (September 2019): 282.

52. Hamilton, "The Evolution of the Dum-Dum Bullet."

53. "The Dum-Dum Bullet," *The British Medical Journal* 1, no. 1942 (March 19, 1898): 782.

54. Stephen C. Neff, *War and the Law of Nations: A General History* (Cambridge: Cambridge University Press, 2005), 186–87; Samuel Moyn, *Humane: How the United States Abandoned Peace and Reinvented War* (New York: Farrar, Straus and Giroux, 2021), 88–89.

55. James Brown Scott, *The Proceedings of the Hague Peace Conferences: Translation of the Official Texts: The Conferences of 1899 and 1907* (New York: Oxford University Press, 1920), 286; Khalili, *Time in the Shadows*, 229–30; Wagner, "Savage Warfare." A response to Wagner's article criticized the argument that Britain's use of the expanding bullet was driven by racialized logics, but I agree with Wagner that race was a key rubric in denoting "civilized" vs. "savage" warfare, and that these discourses informed the conversation around expanding bullets. For the critique, see Huw Bennett et al., "Studying Mars and Clio: Or How Not to Write about the Ethics of Military Conduct and Military History," *History Workshop Journal* 91 (Spring 2021): 274–80.

56. Scott, *The Proceedings of the Hague*, 79–81; Scott, *The Hague Peace Conferences of 1899 and 1907*, Documents (Baltimore: Johns Hopkins Press, 1909), 2:33–35. Expanding bullets remain banned for military use but are used by modern police forces. See Laleh Khalili, "The Location of Palestine in Global Counterinsurgencies," *International Journal of Middle East Studies* 42, no. 3 (August 1, 2010): 414.

57. S. D. Rockenbach, "The Service Pistol," *Journal of the United States Cavalry Association* 16, no. 57–60 (July 1905): 773–75. For more on the Philippine Scouts, see Christopher Capozzola, *Bound by War: How the United States and the Philippines Built America's First Pacific Century* (New York: Basic Books, 2020), 13–16.

58. Rockenbach, "The Service Pistol," 773–74.

59. Karl Jacoby, *Shadows at Dawn: An Apache Massacre and the Violence of History* (New York: Penguin Books, 2009), 126–28.

60. Henry Labouchère, "The Brown Man's Burden," quoted in Bonnie M. Miller, *From Liberation to Conquest: The Visual and Popular Cultures of the Spanish-American War of 1898* (Amherst: University of Massachusetts Press, 2011), 187.

61. Mira Matikkala, *Empire and Imperial Ambition: Liberty, Englishness and Anti-Imperialism in Late Victorian Britain* (London: I. B. Tauris, 2011), 17–18.

62. Senate Committee on the Philippines, *Affairs in the Philippine Islands*, 57th Cong., 1st Sess. Senate. Doc. No. 331 (Washington, DC: GPO, 1902), 2544–51; Christopher J. Einolf, *America in the Philippines, 1899–1902: The First Torture Scandal* (New York: Palgrave Macmillan, 2014), 145–47; Stuart Creighton Miller, *"Benevolent Assimilation": The American Conquest of the Philippines, 1899–1903* (New Haven, CT: Yale University Press, 1982), 241–43.

63. Senate Committee on the Philippines, *Affair in the Philippine Islands*, 2558–76; Einolf, *America in the Philippines*, 145–47.

64. Miller, *"Benevolent Assimilation,"* 241–42.

65. "Charge Perjury: Ex-Corp Richard T. O'Brien Must Face It," *Boston Daily Globe*, August 8, 1902; Senate Committee on the Philippines, *Affair in the Philippine Islands*, 2588.

66. Oliver Charbonneau, *Civilizational Imperatives: Americans, Moros, and the Colonial World* (Ithaca, NY: Cornell University Press, 2020), 6–8.

67. Brian McAllister Linn, *Guardians of Empire: The U.S. Army and the Pacific, 1902–1940* (Chapel Hill: University of North Carolina Press, 1997), 26–37; Kramer, *The Blood of Government*, 187–88.

68. Henry Hooker Van Meter, *The Truth about the Philippines, from Official Records and Authentic Sources* (Chicago: The Liberty league, 1900), 140.

69. First Lieutenant G. C. Lewis, "The Stopping Power of a Bullet," *Journal of the United States Cavalry Association* 17, no. 61 (July 1906): 121–23, 135.

70. Michael C. Hawkins, "Managing a Massacre: Savagery, Civility, and Gender in Moro Province in the Wake of Bud Dajo," *Philippine Studies* 59, no. 1 (March 2011): 84; Susan L. Carruthers, *The Good Occupation: American Soldiers and the Hazards of Peace* (Cambridge, MA: Harvard University Press, 2016), 24; Charbonneau, *Civilizational Imperatives*, 104–6; Capozzola, *Bound by War*, 67.

71. Linn, *Guardians of Empire*, 38–39; Kramer, *The Blood of Government*, 188–89; Andrew J. Bacevich, *Twilight of the American Century* (Notre Dame, IN: University of Notre Dame Press, 2018), 288–90.

72. Captain C. C. Smith, "The Mindanao Moro," *Journal of the United States Cavalry Association* 17, no. 61 (July 1906): 308.

73. Major Charles E. Woodruff, M.D., "The Normal Malay and the Criminal Responsibility of Insane Malays," *Journal of the United States Cavalry Association* 35, nos. 57–60 (July 1905): 496, 512.

74. "National Army—What It Might Be," *Army and Navy Journal*, December 21, 1889; David Woodward, *The American Army and the First World War* (Cambridge: Cambridge University Press, 2014), 3.

75. T. R. Brereton, *Educating the U.S. Army: Arthur L. Wagner and Reform, 1875–1905* (Lincoln: University of Nebraska Press, 2000); J. P. Clark, *Preparing for War: The Emergence of the Modern U.S. Army, 1815–1917* (Cambridge, MA: Harvard University Press, 2017), 270–73.

76. "Sand-30" (pseud.), "Trench, Parapet, or the Open," *JMSI* 31 (1902): 480; Linn, *The Echo of Battle*, 87.

77. Charles W. Fenton, "The Cavalry Regiment," *JMSI* 50 (1912): 387–94.

78. Fenton, 394.

79. Woodward, *The American Army*, 1.

80. *Report on the Organization of the Land Forces of the United States* (Washington, DC: GPO, 1912), 62.

81. Pershing's expedition into Mexico in 1916 took advantage of the experience his soldiers had gained in the Indian Wars and in the Philippines. See Birtle, *Counterinsurgency*, 203; Katharine Bjork, *Prairie Imperialists: The Indian*

Country Origins of American Empire (Philadelphia: University of Pennsylvania Press, 2018), chap. 10.

82. *Report on the Organization of the Land Forces*, 11–15, 62. For more on modernization in the US military, see Allan R. Millett, Peter Maslowski, and William B. Feis, *For the Common Defense* (New York: Free Press, 1984), 317–18.

83. *Annual Report of the Secretary of War* (Washington, DC: GPO, 1913), 14–15. Army historian Andrew Birtle concurs, arguing that the "constabulary" missions in the Indian War and the Philippines had impaired the Army's preparedness for modern warfare. Birtle, *Counterinsurgency*, 174.

84. *Annual Report of the Secretary of War* (Washington, DC: GPO, 1914), 151–58.

85. *Annual Report of the Secretary of War* (Washington, DC: GPO, 1915), 130–31.

86. Coffman, *The Regulars*, 200–201.

87. Greg Grandin, *The End of the Myth: From the Frontier to the Border Wall in the Mind of America* (New York: Metropolitan Books, 2019), 28–29.

88. *Annual Report of the Secretary of War* (Washington, DC: GPO, 1917), 161–62.

89. *Annual Report of the Secretary of War* (Washington, DC: GPO, 1918), 128–29.

90. "Canards Fed to Germans," *New York Times*, June 27, 1918.

91. Philip Gibbs, "War Whoops Halted a German Attack," *New York Times*, September 24, 1916.

92. Thomas A. Britten, *American Indians in World War I: At Home and at War* (Albuquerque: University of New Mexico Press, 1999), 109; Paul C. Rosier, "Native Americans, Indigeneity, and US Foreign Policy," in David C. Engerman, Max Paul Friedman, and Melani McAlister, eds., *The Cambridge History of America and the World, Volume 4: 1945 to the Present* (Cambridge: Cambridge University Press, 2022), 478.

93. Britten, *American Indians in World War I*, 151–54; Susan Applegate Krouse, *North American Indians in the Great War* (Lincoln: University of Nebraska Press, 2007), 5; Steven Sabol, "'It Was a Pretty Good War but They Stopped It Too Soon': The American Empire, Native Americans and World War I," in Richard S. Fogarty and Andrew Tait Jarboe, eds., *Empires in World War I: Shifting Frontiers and Imperial Dynamics in a Global Conflict* (London: I. B. Tauris, 2014), 193; Thomas Grillot, *First Americans: U.S. Patriotism in Indian Country after World War I* (New Haven, CT: Yale University Press, 2018), 5.

94. Britten, *American Indians in World War I*, 62–67; Grillot, *First Americans*, 37–38; Kent Blansett, *A Journey to Freedom: Richard Oakes, Alcatraz, and the Red Power Movement* (New Haven, CT: Yale University Press, 2018), 14–16.

95. Britten, *American Indians in World War I*, 7–8.

96. "American Indians Outwit the Germans," July 22, 1918, Elmo Scott Watson Papers, Box 30, Folder 448, Newberry Library.

97. Britten, *American Indians in World War I*, 111–13.

98. Sabol, "It Was a Pretty Good War," 206.

99. Britten, *American Indians in World War I*, 108–9.

100. Linn, *The Echo of Battle*, 90.

101. Maurice G. Holmes, "The Battle of the Little Big Horn," *Marine Corps Gazette* 17, no. 2 (August 1932): 15–21. The Marine Corps *Small Wars Manual*, a core text in the development of irregular war doctrine, was focused on Central and South America but at least one of its developers situated the Indian Wars as a precursor. See Harold H. Utley, "An Introduction to the Tactics and Technique of Small Wars," *Marine Corps Gazette* 15, no. 5 (May 1931): 50–53; Keith Bickel, *Mars Learning: The Marine Corps Development of Small Wars Doctrine, 1915–1940* (Boulder, CO: Westview Press, 2001), 213–14; Khalili, *Time in the Shadows*, 19.

102. E. S. Johnson, "Field Service Regulations of the Future," *Military Review* 16, no. 61 (1936), 6; Andrew F. Krepinevich, *The Army and Vietnam* (Baltimore: Johns Hopkins University Press, 1986), 39.

103. John M. Carroll, ed., *The Papers of the Order of Indian Wars* (Fort Collins, CO: Old Army Press, 1975), Article II.

104. Carroll, *The Papers of the Order*, 255.

5. FIGHTING INDIAN STYLE

1. "Indians Honor M'Arthur," *New York Times*, February 14, 1943.

2. Todd Leahy and Nathan Wilson, *Historical Dictionary of Native American Movements* (Lanham, MD: Rowman & Littlefield, 2016), 132; Tania van den Houten, "Twenty-Fifth Anniversary of the American Indian Community House," *Native Peoples Magazine* 8, no. 3 (Spring 1995): 52–55.

3. "Indian War Bonnet Awarded to Stalin," *New York Times*, February 21, 1942; "Eisenhower Is Named World Warrior of 1943," *The Christian Science Monitor*, February 18, 1944. Horn was a secretary of Local 11 of the International Association of Bridge and Structural Iron Workers. For more on the Mohawk iron workers, who played a pivotal role in constructing the skyline of New York City, see Kent Blansett, *Journey to Freedom: Richard Oakes, Alcatraz, and the Red Power Movement* (New Haven, CT: Yale University Press, 2018), 63–67.

4. "Indian Fighting," *Atlanta Constitution*, February 15, 1943.

5. Hollis Dorion Stabler, *No One Ever Asked Me: The World War II Memoirs of an Omaha Indian Soldier* (Lincoln: University of Nebraska Press, 2005), 101–4; Williamson Murray and Allan Reed Millett, *A War to Be Won: Fighting the Second World War* (Cambridge, MA: Harvard University Press, 2009), 386.

6. Homer Bigart Press, "Isles Off Riviera Taken by Stealth," *New York Times*, August 17, 1944.

7. "History of the First Special Service Force," First Special Service Force, accessed December 5, 2022, http://www.firstspecialserviceforce.net/history.html. For the history of the Indian Scouts, see Thomas W. Dunlay, *Wolves for the Blue Soldiers: Indian Scouts and Auxiliaries with the United States Army, 1860–90* (Lincoln: University of Nebraska Press, 1982); Mark van de Logt, *War Party in Blue: Pawnee Scouts in the U.S. Army* (Norman: University of Oklahoma Press, 2012).

8. David Jablonsky, *War by Land, Sea, and Air* (New Haven, CT: Yale University Press, 2010), 2; Timothy Mitchell, *Carbon Democracy: Political Power in the Age of Oil* (New York: Verso, 2011), 66.

9. David M. Kennedy, *Freedom from Fear: The American People in Depression and War, 1929–1945* (Oxford: Oxford University Press, 1999), 630–31; Murray and Millett, *A War to Be Won*, 18–19.

10. For the ways Native participation in the war effort was used to encourage a broader American patriotism, see Tom Holm, "Fighting a White Man's War: The Extent and Legacy of American Indian Participation in World War II," *Journal of Ethnic Studies* 9, no. 2 (July 1981): 69–81; Jere Bishop Franco, *Crossing the Pond: The Native American Effort in World War II* (College Station: University of North Texas Press, 1999). See also: Philip Joseph Deloria, *Playing Indian* (New Haven, CT: Yale University Press, 1998).

11. Jack Goodman, *While You Were Gone: A Report on Wartime Life in the United States* (New York: Simon and Schuster, 1946), 13; Willy Ley, "PT Boat Wins Fame," *Daily Boston Globe*, March 28, 1944.

12. Michael S. Sherry, *The Rise of American Air Power: The Creation of Armageddon* (New Haven, CT: Yale University Press, 1987), xi; John Dower, *War without Mercy: Race and Power in the Pacific War* (New York: Pantheon Books, 2012), 36–39; Ruth Lawlor, "Contested Crimes: Race, Gender, and Nation in Histories of GI Sexual Violence, World War II," *Journal of Military History* 84, no. 2 (April 2020): 563; Samuel Moyn, *Humane: How the United States Abandoned Peace and Reinvented War* (New York: Farrar, Straus and Giroux, 2021), 136–37.

13. Richard Drinnon, *Keeper of the Concentration Camps: Dillon S. Myer and American Racism* (Berkley: University of California Press, 1989), xxvii; Jodi Kim, *Settler Garrison: Debt Imperialism, Militarism, and Transpacific Imaginaries* (Durham, NC: Duke University Press, 2022), 42.

14. Juliet Nebolon, "Settler-Military Camps: Internment and Prisoner of War Camps Across the Pacific Islands during World War II," *Journal of Asian American Studies* 24, no. 2 (2021): 299–302. For "settler militarism," see also Juliet Nebolon, "'Life Given Straight from the Heart': Settler Militarism, Biopolitics, and Public Health in Hawai'i during World War II," *American Quarterly* 69, no. 1 (2017): 25.

15. Brian Masaru Hayashi, *Democratizing the Enemy: The Japanese American Internment* (Princeton, NJ: Princeton University Press, 2008), 5–6; Precious Yamaguchi, *Experiences of Japanese American Women during and after World War II: Living in Internment Camps and Rebuilding Life Afterwards* (Lanham, MD: Lexington Books, 2014), 57; Anoma Pieris and Lynne Horiuchi, *The Architecture of Confinement: Incarceration Camps of the Pacific War* (Cambridge: Cambridge University Press, 2022), 244–45.

16. Nebolon, "Settler-Military Camps," 299–302; Kim, *Settler Garrison*, 25.

17. Hayashi, *Democratizing the Enemy*, 107; Greg Robinson, *A Tragedy of Democracy: Japanese Confinement in North America* (New York: Columbia University Press, 2009), 154–55; Yasuko I. Takezawa, *Breaking the Silence: Redress and Japanese American Ethnicity* (Ithaca, NY: Cornell University Press, 2019), 127.

18. Vine Deloria Jr., *Custer Died for Your Sins: An Indian Manifesto* (Norman: University of Oklahoma Press, 1988), 54–55; Drinnon, *Keeper of the Concentration Camps*, xxvii; Hayashi, *Democratizing the Enemy*, 210–11; Paul C. Rosier, "Native Americans, Indigeneity, and U.S. Foreign Policy," in David C. Engerman, Max Paul Friedman, and Melani McAlister, eds., *The Cambridge History of America and the World, Volume 4: 1945 to the Present* (Cambridge: Cambridge University Press, 2022), 467.

19. Joanne Barker, *Red Scare: The State's Indigenous Terrorist* (Oakland: University of California Press, 2021), 37–40.

20. Howard Norton, "No Pre-Battle Tension before Hollandia 'Show,'" *Baltimore Sun*, May 9, 1944; Edward D. Ball, "Men, Mud, Machines," The AP World, October–November 1944; Gene Currivan, "Patton Now Ruler of the Rhineland," *New York Times*, March 21, 1945.

21. "French Forces of the Interior," *Yank, The Army Newspaper*, September 15, 1944.

22. Tom Engelhardt, *The End of Victory Culture: Cold War America and the Disillusioning of a Generation* (Amherst: University of Massachusetts Press, 2007), 43.

23. Hal Boyle, "Americans Hound Nazi Bands Like Indian Fighters of Old West," *Los Angeles Times*, August 13, 1944.

24. Siegfried Hutter, "Men of Air Reconnaissance," *Military Review* 23, no. 11 (1944): 89.

25. "Russian and German Tactics in World War II," *Military Review* 29, no. 6 (1949): 100–103.

26. Frank Usbeck, "Fighting Like Indians: The 'Indian Scout Syndrome' in US and German War Reports during World War II," in *Visual Representations of Native Americans: Transnational Contexts and Perspectives*, Karsten Fitz, ed. (Heidelberg: Universitätsverlag Winter, 2012), 125–44.

27. James Q. Whitman, *Hitler's American Model: The United States and the Making of Nazi Race Law* (Princeton, NJ: Princeton University Press, 2017), 9–10.

28. For more on the Code Talkers and Native service in general, see Franco, *Crossing the Pond*; Chester Nez and Judith Schiess Avila, *Code Talker: The First and Only Memoir by One of the Original Navajo Code Talkers of WWII* (New York: Berkley Caliber, 2011); Paul C. Rosier, *Serving Their Country: American Indian Politics and Patriotism in the Twentieth Century* (Cambridge, MA: Harvard University Press, 2009); Stabler, *No One Ever Asked Me*.

29. Nez, *Code Talker*, 88; Rosier, *Serving Their Country*, 87.

30. Richard Killblane and Jake McNiece, *The Filthy Thirteen: From the Dustbowl to Hitler's Eagle's Nest—The True Story of the 101st Airborne's Most Legendary Squad of Combat Paratroopers* (Philadelphia: Casemate, 2003), 23–24, 70–71.

31. Rosier, *Serving Their Country*, 260.

32. Holm, "Fighting a White Man's War," 72; Leslie Marmon Silko, *Ceremony* (New York: Penguin, 2006); N. Scott Momaday, *House Made of Dawn* (New York: Harper & Row, 1968).

33. Robert F. Berkhofer, *The White Man's Indian: Images of the American Indian from Columbus to the Present* (New York: Knopf, 1978); Richard Slotkin, *Regeneration through Violence: The Mythology of the American Frontier, 1600–1860* (Middletown, CT: Wesleyan University Press, 1973); Philip J. Deloria, *Indians in Unexpected Places* (Lawrence: University Press of Kansas, 2004).

34. Usbeck, "Fighting like Indians," 130–31.

35. Stabler, *No One Ever Asked Me*, 78; Holm, "Fighting a White Man's War," 71; "Gun's 10 Notches Make Dakotan No. 1 Commando," *Chicago Daily Tribune*, January 7, 1943.

36. Colonel Arthur Trudeau, "Tell Them Why," *Military Review* 23, no. 11 (1944): 37–39.

37. Lieutenant Colonel F. R. Waltz, "Infantry in Offensive Combat," *Military Review* 19, no. 75 (1939): 72; Orville Z. Tyler Jr., *The History of Fort Leavenworth, 1937–1951* (Fort Leavenworth, KS: CGSC, 1951), 91.

38. "Fighting Indian Style," *Chicago Daily Tribune*, November 8, 1942.

39. Lieutenant Colonel William F. Britten, "We Will Do Anything to Win the War," Military Review 22, no. 86 (1942): 20–22; Tyler Jr., *The History of Fort Leavenworth*, 97.

40. For more on the "frontier thesis" and its relation to US empire, see Greg Grandin, *The End of the Myth: From the Frontier to the Border Wall in the Mind of America* (New York: Metropolitan Books, 2019), 132–34.

41. Grandin, *The End of the Myth*, 16–17.

42. United States Army, *Ranger Handbook* (Headquarters: Department of the Army, 2016), xvii–xx; David W. Hogan, *Raiders or Elite Infantry? The Changing Role of the U.S. Army Rangers from Dieppe to Grenada* (Westport: Greenwood Press, 1992), 1–4.

43. Hogan, *Raiders or Elite Infantry*, 13–14; John Prados, *The US Special Forces: What Everyone Needs to Know* (Oxford: Oxford University Press, 2015), 17.

44. Peter Locke, "Hard-Hitting Commandos: They Are the 'Fighting-Est' Troops of the British Army," *New York Times*, April 5, 1942. See also Bernard Seeman, "Watch the Commandos!," *Los Angeles Times*, February 22, 1942.

45. Richard Slotkin, *Gunfighter Nation: Myth of the Frontier in Twentieth-Century America* (New York: Atheneum, 1992), 303–4.

46. "Stealthy British Commandos Scale Cliffs and Raid Bardia," *Washington Post*, November 15, 1941.

47. Deborah A. Carmichael, *The Landscape of Hollywood Westerns: Ecocriticism in an American Film Genre* (Salt Lake City: University of Utah Press, 2006), 111–12; Mary Lea Bandy and Kevin Stoehr, *Ride, Boldly Ride: The Evolution of the American Western* (Berkeley: University of California Press, 2012), 97–98; Engelhardt, *The End of Victory Culture*, 44–46.

48. Lucian King Truscott Jr., *Command Missions: A Personal Story* (New York: Dutton, 1954), 19–22; Hogan, *Raiders or Elite Infantry*, 14; Murray and Millett, *A War to Be Won*, 272–73.

49. Truscott, *Command Missions*, 39–40; Michael J. King, *Rangers: Selected Combat Operations in World War II* (Fort Leavenworth, KS: CSI, 1985), 5–7;

Hogan, *Raiders or Elite Infantry*, 18; Prados, *The US Special Forces*, 16–17; David Tucker and Christopher J. Lamb, *United States Special Operations Forces* (New York: Columbia University Press, 2019), 74–78.

50. Truscott, *Command Missions*, 40.

51. James J. Altieri, *The Spearheaders: A Personal History of Darby's Rangers* (Annapolis, MD: Naval Institute Press, 2014), 27–28.

52. Rice Yahner, "Taught by Commandos," *New York Times*, 1942; Hogan, *Raiders or Elite Infantry*, 19.

53. Ziebach County Historical Society, *South Dakota's Ziebach County: History of the Prairie* (Dupree, SD: Ziebach County Historical Society, 1982); "Ranger One Skunk among Invaders," *Philadelphia Inquirer*, August 20, 1942.

54. Truscott, *Command Missions*, 62–72; Hogan, *Raiders or Elite Infantry*, 20–21; Rice Yahner, "'Yanks' Rangers Named for Indian Fighters," *Washington Post*, August 20, 1942.

55. Barbara Brooks, "New England's Guerrillas: For Seven Hectic 16-Hour Days State Guard Officers Are Learning Modernized Indian Warfare among the Hills of Sturbridge," *Daily Boston Globe*, September 13, 1942.

56. "How to Be a Guerrilla," *Life* 13, no. 7 (August 17, 1942): 40–45.

57. J. Leo Loiselle, "Company 18 Vermont State Guard," *Swanton Courier*, November 12, 1942.

58. Barry M. Stentiford, *The American Home Guard: The State Militia in the Twentieth Century* (College Station: Texas A&M University Press, 2002), 163–65; John K. Howard and H. Wendell Endicott, *Summary Report: British Home Guard* (Massachusetts Committee on Public Safety, 1941); "Presentation on the 366th by James Pratt at the Fort Devens Historical Society," United States Army 366th Infantry Regiment and other Colored Divisions Collection, ca. 1940–2017, Box 1, DVD-1216, Division of Rare and Manuscript Collections Cornell University Library.

59. Brooks, "New England's Guerillas."

60. "Yank" Bert Levy, *Guerilla Warfare* (Boulder, CO: Paladin Press, 1964), 26.

61. Levy, *Guerilla Warfare*, 14–15.

62. Stentiford, *The American Home Guard*, 165; Levy, *Guerilla Warfare*, 7, 62, 100. For Native American history in New England, see Jean M. O'Brien, *Firsting and Lasting: Writing Indians Out of Existence in New England* (Minneapolis: University of Minnesota Press, 2010).

63. Brooks, "New England's Guerillas."

64. John A. Thompson, "The Exaggeration of American Vulnerability: The Anatomy of a Tradition," *Diplomatic History* 16, no. 1 (1992): 23–43.

65. Senator Edward W. Brooke, *Bridging the Divide: My Life* (New Brunswick, NJ: Rutgers University Press, 2006), 23; "Presentation on the 366th by James Pratt at the Fort Devens Historical Society."

66. Damon Runyan, "This Army Takes a Lesson from the Indians," *Atlanta Constitution*, January 10, 1943.

67. Prados, *The US Special Forces*, 16–20; Hogan, *Raiders or Elite Infantry*, 69–47; Tucker and Lamb, *United States Special Operations*, 74–78.

68. James Warner Bellah, "Long Range Penetration Groups," *Infantry Journal* 55, no. 4 (1944): 45–47; James Warner Bellah, "Encirclement by Air," *Infantry Journal* 54, no. 6 (1944): 8–13.

69. James Warner Bellah, "The Air Commando Tradition," *Air Force Magazine*, February 1, 1963.

70. James W. Bellah, "Combat Intelligence Training in New Divisions," *Military Review* 22, no. 86 (1942): 44–46.

71. David L. Preston, *Braddock's Defeat: The Battle of the Monongahela and the Road to Revolution* (Oxford: Oxford University Press, 2015), 124.

72. Fred Anderson and Andrew Cayton, *The Dominion of War: Empire and Liberty in North America, 1500–2000* (New York: Penguin, 2005), 127–28; Preston, *Braddock's Defeat*, 222–37; Colin G. Calloway, *The Indian World of George Washington: The First President, the First Americans, and the Birth of the Nation* (Oxford: Oxford University Press, 2018), 110; David L. Preston, "The Battle of the Monongahela: Braddock's Defeat, July 9, 1755," in Wayne E. Lee et al., *The Other Face of Battle: America's Forgotten Wars and the Experience of Combat* (Oxford: Oxford University Press, 2021), 20–24.

73. Major James W. Bellah, "Combat Intelligence Training in New Divisions (with 30 Training Exercises)," The James Warner Bellah Collection, Howard Gotlieb Archival Research Center, Boston University, 14.

74. Bellah, 15.

75. Bellah, 3–7.

76. Murray and Millet, *A War to Be Won*, 527.

77. For more on Bellah's influence on the western genre, see Neil McDonald, "Colonel Bellah and Admiral Ford," *Quadrant* 57, no. 12 (December 1, 2013): 98–101.

78. William Clell Howze, "The Influence of Western Painting and Genre Painting on the Films of John Ford" (PhD diss., University of Texas at Austin, 1986), 109–10; James Warner Bellah, "Massacre," *Saturday Evening Post* 219, no. 34 (February 22, 1947): 18–146.

6. INDIAN COUNTRY AND THE COLD WAR

1. Williamson Murray and Allan Reed Millett, *A War to Be Won: Fighting the Second World War* (Cambridge, MA: Harvard University Press, 2009), 525–26; "General MacArthur's Speech," Naval History and Heritage Command, accessed December 6, 2022, http://public1.nhhcaws.local/research /archives/digital-exhibits-highlights/vj-day/surrender/macarthur-speech.html.

2. Gordon Walker, "Kid-Glove Policy Still Rules Nippon; MacArthur Aides Soften Occupation," *Christian Science Monitor*, September 22, 1945.

3. US planning for postwar military governments cited Indian reservations and the Department of the Interior's management of Native peoples as a historical precedent. See Susan L. Carruthers, *The Good Occupation: American Soldiers and the Hazards of Peace* (Cambridge, MA: Harvard University Press, 2016), 24–25.

4. Odd Arne Westad, *The Global Cold War: Third World Interventions and the Making of Our Times* (Cambridge: Cambridge University Press, 2005), 86–87.

On empire and decolonization in Asia, see Simeon Man, *Soldiering through Empire: Race and the Making of the Decolonizing Pacific* (Oakland: University of California Press, 2018), 3; Moon-Ho Jung, *Menace to Empire: Anticolonial Solidarities and the Transpacific Origins of the US Security State* (Oakland: University of California Press, 2022), 17. For more on Red Power and Native activism during the Cold War, see Paul Chaat Smith and Robert Warrior, *Like a Hurricane: The Indian Movement from Alcatraz to Wounded Knee* (New York: New Press, 1996); Kent Blansett, *A Journey to Freedom: Richard Oakes, Alcatraz, and the Red Power Movement* (New Haven, CT: Yale University Press, 2018).

5. As Stuart Schrader reminds us, the domestic repression that accompanied racialized policing and the expanding carceral state was intimately related to the development of the national security state and Cold War policies intended to manage decolonization. See Stuart Schrader, *Badges without Borders: How Global Counterinsurgency Transformed American Policing* (Oakland: University of California Press, 2019), 8–9.

6. Michael H. Hunt, *Ideology and U.S. Foreign Policy* (New Haven, CT: Yale University Press, 1987), 18; Westad, *The Global Cold War*, 396–404.

7. Jordan T. Camp and Jennifer Greenburg, "Counterinsurgency Reexamined: Racism, Capitalism, and US Military Doctrine," *Antipode* 52, no. 2 (March 2020): 431–33; Greg Grandin, *The End of the Myth: From the Frontier to the Border Wall in the Mind of America* (New York: Metropolitan Books, 2019), 23.

8. Richard Slotkin, *Gunfighter Nation: Myth of the Frontier in Twentieth-Century America* (New York: Atheneum, 1992), 2–3, 446–47; Tom Engelhardt, *The End of Victory Culture: Cold War America and the Disillusioning of a Generation* (Amherst: University of Massachusetts Press, 2007), 162; Samuel Moyn, *Humane: How the United States Abandoned Peace and Reinvented War* (New York: Farrar, Straus and Giroux, 2021), 119.

9. Man, *Soldiering through Empire*, 6.

10. Melvyn P. Leffler, *A Preponderance of Power: National Security, the Truman Administration, and the Cold War* (Stanford, CA: Stanford University Press, 1992), 2–3.

11. Aaron O'Connell explains that the ballooning national security state, with its emphasis on technological solutions, expanded the US military during the second half of the twentieth century while simultaneously inhibiting its ability to wage irregular war. See O'Connell, "Moving Mountains: Cultural Friction in the Afghanistan War," in Aaron B. O'Connell, ed., *Our Latest Longest War: Losing Hearts and Minds in Afghanistan* (Chicago: University of Chicago Press, 2017), 14–15. On race, national security, and the aftermath of World War II, see Penny Von Eschen, *Satchmo Blows up the World: Jazz Ambassadors Play the Cold War* (Cambridge, MA: Harvard University Press, 2006), 4–5; Man, *Soldiering through Empire*, 2–3; Jung, *Menace to Empire*, 13–14.

12. Walter LaFeber, *The American Age: United States Foreign Policy at Home and Abroad since 1750* (New York: W. W. Norton, 1989), 457–65; Leffler, *A Preponderance of Power*, 11–13; David W. Hogan, *Raiders or Elite Infantry? The Changing Role of the U.S. Army Rangers from Dieppe to Grenada*

(Westport: Greenwood Press, 1992), 95; Murray and Millet, *A War to Be Won*, 534; Catherine Lutz, ed., *The Bases of Empire: The Global Struggle against U.S. Military Posts* (New York: New York University Press, 2009), introduction; Paul Thomas Chamberlin, *The Cold War's Killing Fields: Rethinking the Long Peace* (New York: HarperCollins, 2018), 39; Man, *Soldiering through Empire*, 8; Jodi Kim, *Settler Garrison: Debt Imperialism, Militarism, and Transpacific Imaginaries* (Durham, NC: Duke University Press, 2022), 25.

13. Melvyn P. Leffler, *For the Soul of Mankind: The United States, the Soviet Union, and the Cold War* (New York: Hill and Wang, 2007); Vladimir O. Pechatnov, "Soviet-American Relations through the Cold War," in Richard H. Immerman and Petra Goedde, eds., *The Oxford Handbook of the Cold War* (Oxford: Oxford University Press, 2013).

14. Mark Mazower, *Dark Continent: Europe's Twentieth Century* (New York: Vintage Books, 2009), 225–29; Leffler, *For the Soul of Mankind*, 57–64; Monica Kim, *The Interrogation Rooms of the Korean War: The Untold History* (Princeton, NJ: Princeton University Press, 2019), 14–15.

15. "Acceptance of Democratic Nomination for President," John F. Kennedy Presidential Library and Museum, accessed June 19, 2018, https://www.jfklibrary.org/Asset-Viewer/AS08q50YzoSFUZg9uOi4iw.aspx.

16. Schrader, *Badges without Borders*, 10–11; Camp and Greenburg, "Counterinsurgency Reexamined," 437.

17. On the frontier, see Slotkin, *Gunfighter Nation*; Grandin, *The End of the Myth*.

18. Schrader, *Badges without Borders*, 10.

19. Jeffrey Ostler, "Settler Colonialism," in Kristin Hoganson and Jay Sexton, eds., *The Cambridge History of America and the World, Volume II: 1820–1900* (Cambridge: Cambridge University Press, 2022).

20. The classic analysis of the frontier myth during the Cold War is Slotkin, *Gunfighter Nation*, particularly chapter 15. Grandin, *The End of the Myth*.

21. Brigadier General Arthur G. Trudeau, "Some Military Aspects of American Statecraft," *Military Review* 31, no. 3 (1951): 18.

22. Hogan, *Raiders or Elite Infantry*, 95–97; John Prados, *The US Special Forces: What Everyone Needs to Know* (Oxford: Oxford University Press, 2015), 20–21.

23. For a discussion of references to "Indian fighting" during the Korean War, see Moyn, *Humane*, 152–53.

24. Andrew J. Birtle, *U.S. Army Counterinsurgency and Contingency Operations Doctrine, 1942–1976* (Washington, DC: Center of Military History, 2006), 117–22, 134–50; *ST 31-20-1 1950: Operations against Guerrilla Forces* (Fort Benning, GA: The Infantry School, 1950), 4–5.

25. Schrader, *Badges without Borders*, 10–11.

26. Philip J. Deloria, *Indians in Unexpected Places* (Lawrence: University Press of Kansas, 2004), 44.

27. Megan Black, *The Global Interior: Mineral Frontiers and American Power* (Cambridge, MA: Harvard University Press, 2018), 4–5.

28. Birtle, *U.S. Army Counterinsurgency*, 159–60.

29. *President's Committee to Study the United States Military Assistance Program, Composite Report*, Vol. 2 (Washington, DC: GPO, 1959), 102–6.

30. Schrader, *Badges without Borders*, 98.

31. Michael E. Latham, *The Right Kind of Revolution: Modernization, Development, and U.S. Foreign Policy from the Cold War to the Present* (Ithaca, NY: Cornell University Press, 2011), 57–58; Westad, *The Global Cold War*, 34–35.

32. Schrader, *Badges without Borders*, 10.

33. Andrew F. Krepinevich, *The Army and Vietnam* (Baltimore: Johns Hopkins University Press, 1986), 27–30; Birtle, *U.S. Army Counterinsurgency*, 224–25; David Fitzgerald, *Learning to Forget: US Army Counterinsurgency Doctrine and Practice from Vietnam to Iraq* (Stanford, CA: Stanford University Press, 2013), 37.

34. John F. Kennedy, "Introduction," in *Special Warfare* (Office, Chief of Information, Department of the Army, 1962).

35. "Establishment of the Special Group (Counter-Insurgency)," December 19, 1961, FOIA Reading Room, Washington Headquarters Service, https://www.esd.whs.mil/Portals/54/Documents/FOID/Reading%20Room/MDR_Releases/FY12/12-M-3095%20Establishment%20of%20the%20Special%20Group%20(Counter-Insurgency).pdf; Robert D. Dean, *Imperial Brotherhood: Gender and the Making of Cold War Foreign Policy* (Amherst: University of Massachusetts Press, 2001), 186; Engelhardt, *The End of Victory Culture*, 162.

36. "The Special Group (Counterinsurgency) from January 18, 1962, to November 21, 1963," Office of the Secretary of Defense, May 13, 1964, FOIA Reading Room, Washington Headquarters Service, https://www.esd.whs.mil/Portals/54/Documents/FOID/Reading%20Room/MDR_Releases/FY12/12-M-3087%20The%20Special%20Group%20(Counterinsurgency)%20from%20January%2018,%201962,%20to%20November%2021,%201963.pdf.

37. Schrader, *Badges without Borders*, 80.

38. Walt Rostow, "Countering Guerilla Attack," in *Special Warfare*, 22; Birtle, *U.S. Army Counterinsurgency*, 163–64; Jordan T. Camp, *Incarcerating the Crisis: Freedom Struggles and the Rise of the Neoliberal State* (Oakland: University of California Press, 2016), 53; Schrader, *Badges without Borders*, 81–84. For more on Rostow's theories, see W. W. Rostow, *The Stages of Economic Growth: A Non-Communist Manifesto* (Cambridge: Cambridge University Press, 1990).

39. Mark Atwood Lawrence, *The Vietnam War: A Concise International History* (Oxford: Oxford University Press, 2008), 56. For more on Lansdale's role in the development of US counterinsurgency, see Man, *Soldiering through Empire*, 49–59.

40. Camp, *Incarcerating the Crisis*, 41–42; Schrader, *Badges without Borders*, 10–11; Joanne Barker, *Red Scare: The State's Indigenous Terrorist* (Oakland: University of California Press, 2021), 42–43.

41. "National Security Action Memoranda [NSAM]: NSAM 182, Counterinsurgency Doctrine," 962, JFKNSF-338-010-p0004, John F. Kennedy Presidential Library and Museum; Birtle, *U.S. Army Counterinsurgency*, 238–39.

42. Edward C. Banfield, quoted in Nils Gilman, *Mandarins of the Future: Modernization Theory in Cold War America* (Baltimore: Johns Hopkins University Press, 2004), 226.

43. Chamberlin, *The Cold War's Killing Fields*, 180–81, 194–95; Schrader, *Badges without Borders*, 104–5.

44. Schrader, *Badges without Borders*, 88.

45. Krepinevich, *The Army and Vietnam*, 37.

46. Andrew Krepinevich and Andrew Birtle seem to disagree somewhat on how effective (and enthusiastic) the Army's embrace of counterinsurgency was in the 1960s. Krepinevich writes that "the Army failed to create a coherent body of doctrinal literature for counterinsurgency" in the 1960s, which is at least partially correct given the necessity to keep relearning counterinsurgency after Vietnam. However, Birtle writes that in the early 1960s "the Army committed itself to the goal of indoctrinating the entire officer corps in counterinsurgency." See Krepinevich, *The Army and Vietnam*, 38–39; and Birtle, *U.S. Army Counterinsurgency*, 258–59.

47. Colonel R. W. van de Velde, "The Neglected Deterrent," *Military Review* 38, no. 5 (1958): 4–7.

48. Stahr, "Foreword," in *Special Warfare*, 5.

49. Williamson Murray and Peter R. Mansoor, *Hybrid Warfare: Fighting Complex Opponents from the Ancient World to the Present* (Cambridge: Cambridge University Press, 2012), 78; Fred Anderson and Andrew Cayton, *The Dominion of War: Empire and Liberty in North America, 1500–2000* (New York: Penguin, 2005), 132. David Preston notes that George Washington attempted to give Braddock advice (or at least recalled that he attempted to give advice) about the dangers of moving through the forested countryside, advice seemingly not taken seriously enough. David L. Preston, *Braddock's Defeat: The Battle of the Monongahela and the Road to Revolution* (Oxford: Oxford University Press, 2015), 7–9, 124.

50. Collier, "Guerillas: A Formidable Force," in *Special Warfare*, 26–27. See also Preston, *Braddock's Defeat*, 222–37; David L. Preston, "The Battle of the Monongahela: Braddock's Defeat, July 9, 1755," in Wayne E. Lee et al., *The Other Face of Battle: America's Forgotten Wars and the Experience of Combat* (Oxford: Oxford University Press, 2021), 20–24; Colin G. Calloway, *The Indian World of George Washington: The First President, the First Americans, and the Birth of the Nation* (Oxford: Oxford University Press, 2018), 110.

51. Lt. Col. Hugh H. Gardner, "The U.S. Army and Guerilla Warfare," in *Special Warfare*, 34.

52. Gardner, 34–45.

53. Gardner, 45.

54. Donald V. Rattan, "Antiguerilla Operations," *Military Review* 40, no. 2 (1960): 23–27.

55. Schrader, *Badges without Borders*, 100; Dean, *Imperial Brotherhood*, 203–4.

56. Roger Hilsman, "Internal War—The New Communist Tactic," *Military Review* 42, no. 4 (1962): 14.

266 | Notes

57. Manu Vimalassery, Juliana Hu Pegues, and Alyosha Goldstein, "Introduction: On Colonial Unknowing," *Theory & Event* 19, no. 4 (2016); Kevin Bruyneel, *Settler Memory: The Disavowal of Indigeneity and the Politics of Race in the United States* (Chapel Hill: University of North Carolina Press, 2021), 2–7.

58. Early participants were critical of the MATA course, citing the inexperience of instructors and the vague nature of the curriculum. See Krepinevich, *The Army and Vietnam*, 48.

59. Captain Richard A. Jones, "The Nationbuilder," *Military Review* 45, no. 1 (1965): 63–64.

60. Chapter 6—New Kid on the Creek, Jimmie Lambert Collection, Box 01, TTU.

61. Soldiers were trained to view Vietnamese villages as hostile before they ever arrived in Southeast Asia. Many, including the perpetrators of the My Lai massacre, trained in "mock villages" that Simeon Man calls "a simulacrum that conjured the racialized enemy through spatial enactments." See Man, *Soldiering through Empire*, 89.

62. Interview with Larry Casselman, January 31, 2009, Mr. Larry Casselman Collection, TTU, 49; Matthew Keeler, ed., "An Oral History of General Jack N. Merritt" (US Army Military History Institute, 2005), 109; Interview with David Shelly, David A. Shelly Collection, TTU, 30; Milton J. Bates, *The Wars We Took to Vietnam: Cultural Conflict and Storytelling* (Berkeley: University of California Press, 1996), 9–10; Gregory A. Daddis, *Pulp Vietnam: War and Gender in Cold War Men's Adventure Magazines* (Cambridge: Cambridge University Press, 2021), 146.

63. Grandin, *The End of the Myth*, 201–2. The mythical "Indian countries" that traveled to Vietnam could refract back to the domestic space. For example, Native efforts to exercise their fishing rights in the Pacific Northwest were sometimes described with Vietnam War–style imagery. See Paul C. Rosier, *Serving Their Country: American Indian Politics and Patriotism in the Twentieth Century* (Cambridge, MA: Harvard University Press, 2009), 225–26, 242–45.

64. Man, *Soldiering through Empire*, 89; Moyn, *Humane*, 167.

65. Andrew J. Huebner, *The Warrior Image: Soldiers in American Culture from the Second World War to the Vietnam Era* (Chapel Hill: University of North Carolina Press, 2008), 250; Bates, *The Wars We Took to Vietnam*, 9; Heather Marie Stur, *Beyond Combat: Women and Gender in the Vietnam War Era* (Cambridge: Cambridge University Press, 2011), 107; Mark Cronlund Anderson, *Holy War: Cowboys, Indians, and 9/11s* (Regina, SK: University of Regina Press, 2016), 151.

66. See Camp and Greenburg, "Counterinsurgency Reexamined," 437–41.

67. Ronald V. Dellums, *The Dellums Committee Hearings on War Crimes in Vietnam: An Inquiry into Command Responsibility in Southeast Asia* (New York: Vintage Books, 1972), 242–44.

68. *Investigation of the My Lai Incident: Report of the Armed Services Investigating Subcommittee of the Committee on Armed Services*, 99th Cong., 2nd Sess. (Washington, DC: GPO, 1970), 774.

69. Moyn, *Humane*, 166–67.

70. Heonik Kwon, *After the Massacre: Commemoration and Consolation in Ha My and My Lai* (Berkeley: University of California Press, 2006), 1–2; Man, *Soldiering through Empire*, 91–93; Daddis, *Pulp Vietnam*, 187; Moyn, *Humane*, 162–63.

71. N. Scott Momaday, "*Bury My Heart at Wounded Knee: An Indian History of the American West*," *New York Times*, March 7, 1971.

72. Dee Brown, *Bury My Heart at Wounded Knee: An Indian History of the American West* (New York, Holt, 2007), xvi.

73. Roxanne Dunbar-Ortiz, "'Indian' Wars," *Jacobin* (September 16, 2014), https://www.jacobinmag.com/2014/09/indian-wars/.https://www.jacobinmag.com/2014/09/indian-wars/.

74. Bates, *The Wars We Took to Vietnam*, 31.

75. Major David Perrine, "Review of '*Tell Baker to Strike Them Hard!*': Incident on the Marias, 23 January 1870," *Military Review* 50, no. 8 (1970): 112.

76. Bates, *The Wars We Took to Vietnam*, 32–33.

77. Frances FitzGerald, *Fire in the Lake: The Vietnamese and the Americans in Vietnam* (Boston: Little, Brown, and Co., 1972), 461; Michael Herr, *Dispatches* (New York: Vintage Books, 1991), 49.

78. Richard Drinnon, *Facing West: The Metaphysics of Indian-Hating and Empire-Building* (Minneapolis: University of Minnesota Press, 1980), 450–56.

79. Gene Roberts, "Civilian Toll 72 in Delta Mistake," *New York Times*, August 16, 1868.

80. The Army's approach to the war in Vietnam focused on concentrating massive amounts of firepower. As one general argued, the US "just sort of devastated the countryside." See Krepinevich, *The Army and Vietnam*, 199.

81. Keeler, "An Oral History of General Jack N. Merritt," 103–5.

82. Moyn, *Humane*, 168–69.

83. For more on the Ninth Infantry Division in the Mekong Delta, see Fitzgerald, *Learning to Forget*, 27–28; Chamberlin, *Cold War Killing Fields*, 236.

84. Kyle Burke, *Revolutionaries for the Right: Anticommunist Internationalism and Paramilitary Warfare in the Cold War* (Chapel Hill: University of North Carolina Press, 2018), 57–58. See also: Nick Turse, *Kill Anything That Moves: The Real American War in Vietnam* (New York: Picador, 2013).

85. Edward J. Marolda and R. Blake Dunnavent, *Combat at Close Quarters: Warfare on the Rivers and Canals of Vietnam* (Washington, DC: Department of the Navy, 2015), 37.

86. Laura M. Calkins, Interview with Clarence Jerry Wages, August 11, 2006, David A. Shelly Collection, TTU, 106–7.

87. Richard B. Verrone, Interview with Michael Sweeney, November 14, 2022, TTU, 57.

88. George W. Stocking, *Colonial Situations: Essays on the Contextualization of Knowledge* (Madison: University of Wisconsin Press, 1992), 243–44, 273; Eric T. Jennings, *Imperial Heights: Dalat and the Making and Undoing of French Indochina* (Berkeley: University of California Press, 2011), 111–13; Prados, *The US Special Forces*, 37–39.

89. Rowland Evans and Robert Novak, "Inside Report: Viet-Nam's Racial Crisis," *Washington Post*, February 19, 1965.

90. George "Sonny" Hoffman, "Mountain People," May 2, 1988, Box 03, Folder 02, Jan Churchill Collection, TTU.

91. Hoffman, "Mountain People."

92. Scott Eyman, *John Wayne: The Life and Legend* (New York: Simon and Schuster, 2015), 431.

93. Hoffman, "Mountain People."

94. Hoffman, "Mountain People."

95. Rebecca Onion, "The Snake-Eaters and the Yards," *Slate*, November 27, 2013, https://slate.com/news-and-politics/2013/11/the-green-berets-and-the -montagnards-how-an-indigenous-tribe-won-the-admiration-of-green-berets -and-lost-everything.html.

96. Engelhardt, *The End of Victory Culture*, 234–35.

97. Scott Laderman, "Camouflaging Empire: Imperial Benevolence in Ameri-can Popular Culture," in Scott Laderman and Tim Gruenewald, eds., *Imperial Benevolence: U.S. Foreign Policy and American Popular Culture since 9/11* (Oakland: University of California Press, 2018), 6.

98. Rosier, *Serving Their Country*, 249–51. For critical appraisals of the war from Native veterans, see the University of Nebraska Omaha Folklore Proj-ect interviews from the American Indian Oral History Collection, particularly: "Interview with Staff Sergeant Myan"; "Interview with Leo (Koja?)."

99. Tom Holm, *Strong Hearts, Wounded Souls: Native American Veterans of the Vietnam War* (Austin: University of Texas Press, 1995), 15, 98–106, 116.

100. Bill Paris, Interview, May 27, 2003, Mr. Bill E. Paris Collection, TTU, 80, 92.

101. Paris, 85.

102. Paris, 97, 107.

103. Paris, 122, 271.

104. Paris, 136.

105. Paris, 227. The poem in question, "Fiddlers' Green," references a field on the side of the road to hell specifically reserved for members of the cavalry. Other versions of the legend reserve Fiddlers' Green for sailors, pets, and other groups. For more, see Lieutenant Colonel Paul M. Crosby, "Legend of Fiddler's Green," *Armor* 74, no. 6 (1965): 7–11.

106. James E. Scales, Interview, June 22, 2002, Mr. James E. Scales Collec-tion, TTU, 32–33.

107. Neal Creighton, Interview, November 11, 2002, Neal Creighton Collec-tion, TTU, 106–7. For more on the body counts, see Chamberlin, *Cold War Kill-ing Fields*, 233–34; Man, *Soldiering through Empire*, 87–88; Turse, *Kill Anything That Moves*, 43; Moyn, *Humane*, 167.

108. Rosier, *Serving Their Country*, 245.

109. "U.S. Jets Meet Heavy Fire in Attacks on Hanoi Area," *New York Times*, August 6, 1967.

110. Jack Anderson, "U.S. War Intelligence Called Faulty," *Washington Post*, March 30, 1968.

111. William Eastlake, *The Bamboo Bed* (London: Michael Joseph, 1970), 23; Huebner, *The Warrior Image*, 250, Bates, *The Wars We Took to Vietnam*, 44.

112. Jerry A. Rose and Lucy Rose Fischer, "Vietnam Horrors Recounted," *USA Today*, November 2020.

113. Kathleen Belew, *Bring the War Home: The White Power Movement and Paramilitary America* (Cambridge, MA: Harvard University Press, 2018), 82.

114. See William C. Westmoreland, *A Soldier Reports* (Garden City, NY: Doubleday, 1976); Harry G. Summers, *On Strategy: A Critical Analysis of the Vietnam War* (New York: Presidio Press, 1982); H. R. McMaster, *Dereliction of Duty: Lyndon Johnson, Robert McNamara, the Joint Chiefs of Staff, and the Lies That Led to Vietnam* (New York: Harper Collins, 1997).

115. James William Gibson, *Warrior Dreams: Paramilitary Culture in Post-Vietnam America* (New York: Hill and Wang, 1994).

116. Belew, *Bring the War Home*.

117. Fitzgerald, *Learning to Forget*, chap. 2; O'Connell, "Moving Mountains," 15–16.

118. Lieutenant Colonel James R. Johnson, "People's War and Conventional Armies," *Military Review* 54, no. 1 (1974): 28.

119. For US foreign policy in Latin America, see Greg Grandin, *Empire's Workshop: Latin America, the United States, and the Rise of the New Imperialism* (New York: Metropolitan Books, 2006).

120. Paul C. Rosier, "Native Americans, Indigeneity, and US Foreign Policy," in David C. Engerman, Max Paul Friedman, and Melani McAlister, eds., *The Cambridge History of America and the World, Volume 4: 1945 to the Present* (Cambridge: Cambridge University Press, 2022), 484.

121. Robert Imrie, "Tribes Angered by General's Reference to Enemy Land as 'Indian Country,'" AP News, February 21, 1991.

7. RELEARNING THE INDIAN WARS

1. Michael G. Miller, "Red Cloud's War: An Insurgency Case Study for Modern Times," Strategy Research Project (USAWC, March 16, 2011), 49.

2. For the relationship between the Vietnam War and twenty-first-century counterinsurgency, see Fred Kaplan, *The Insurgents: David Petraeus and the Plot to Change the American Way of War* (New York: Simon and Schuster, 2013); David Fitzgerald, *Learning to Forget: US Army Counterinsurgency Doctrine and Practice from Vietnam to Iraq* (Stanford, CA: Stanford University Press, 2013).

3. Stephen W. Silliman, "The 'Old West' in the Middle East: US Military Metaphors in Real and Imagined Indian Country," *American Anthropologist* 110, no. 2 (June 2008): 237–47; Robert D. Kaplan, *Imperial Grunts: The American Military on the Ground* (New York: Random House, 2005), 4–14.

4. For a broader appraisal of how cultural differences impacted the US war in Afghanistan, see Aaron B. O'Connell, ed., *Our Latest Longest War: Losing Hearts and Minds in Afghanistan* (Chicago: University of Chicago Press, 2017).

5. John A. Kurak, "Operation Iraqi Freedom I, Al Anbar Providence" (Combined Arms Research Library Digital Library, August 17, 2006), USASMA Digital Repository.

6. David Harvey, *The New Imperialism* (Oxford: New York: Oxford University Press, 2003), 8–12; Melani McAlister, *Epic Encounters: Culture, Media, and U. S. Interests in the Middle East Since1945* (Berkeley: University of California Press, 2005), 266–69; Douglas Little, *Us versus Them: The United States, Radical Islam, and the Rise of the Green Threat* (Chapel Hill: University of North Carolina Press, 2016), 158–62; Alex Lubin, *Never-Ending War on Terror* (Oakland: University of California Press, 2021).

7. Although not the focus of this chapter, many Native soldiers deployed during the War on Terror. Hopi Lori Piestewa was the first woman to die in Iraq in 2003. See Al Carroll, *Medicine Bags and Dog Tags: American Indian Veterans from Colonial Times to the Second Iraq War* (Lincoln: University of Nebraska Press, 2008), 207–8.

8. Richard Killblane, Interview with LTC George Akin, November 2, 2005, Combined Arms Research Library, Fort Leavenworth: CSI.

9. MAJ Glen Christensen, Interview with MAJ Jerry Kung, January 30, 2006, Combined Arms Research Library, Fort Leavenworth: CSI, 11.

10. Jessica Trussoni, Interview with MAJ Shawn Carden Part I, May 11, 2009, Combined Arms Research Library, Fort Leavenworth: CSI, 5.

11. Angie Slattery, Interview with MAJ Matthew Johnson, April 20, 2010, Combined Arms Research Library, Fort Leavenworth: CSI.

12. Joseph S. Gondusky and Michael P. Reiter, "Protecting Military Convoys in Iraq: An Examination of Battle Injuries Sustained by a Mechanized Battalion during Operation Iraqi Freedom II," *Military Medicine* 170, no. 6 (June 2005): 546.

13. MAJ Doug Galuszka, Interview with MAJ Daniel Benz, February 5, 2005, Combined Arms Research Library, Fort Leavenworth: CSI, 37. For more on mental health and the US military, see David Kieran, *Signature Wounds: The Untold Story of the Military's Mental Health Crisis* (New York: New University Press, 2019).

14. Jenn Vedder, Interview with MAJ Donald Sapp, March 31, 2011, Combined Arms Research Library, Fort Leavenworth: CSI, 6.

15. Vedder, 13.

16. Major Brent Cummings, quoted in David Finkel, *The Good Soldiers* (New York: Farrar, Straus and Giroux, 2009), 30.

17. Second Lt. David Russell, quoted in Kaplan, *Imperial Grunts*, 342.

18. Kaplan, *Imperial Grunts*, 4.

19. Alan T. Mabry, "Systemic Problems within the Army during the Indian Wars (1865–1881)," MMAS thesis (CGSC, 1995), 76–77.

20. *The U.S. Army/Marine Corps Counterinsurgency Field Manual* (Chicago: University of Chicago Press, 2008), xiii–xx.

21. Gian P. Gentile, *Wrong Turn: America's Deadly Embrace of Counterinsurgency* (New York: The New Press, 2013).

22. Benjamin Jensen, *Forging the Sword: Doctrinal Change in the U.S. Army* (Stanford, CA: Stanford University Press, 2016), 132; *Counterinsurgency Field Manual*, xxxiii; Jordan T. Camp and Jennifer Greenburg, "Counterinsurgency Reexamined: Racism, Capitalism, and US Military Doctrine," *Antipode* 52, no. 2 (March 2020): 445.

23. *Counterinsurgency Field Manual*, 1-1; Moon-Ho Jung, *Menace to Empire: Anticolonial Solidarities and the Transpacific Origins of the US Security State* (Oakland: University of California Press, 2022), 13.

24. William Flavin, *Finding the Balance: U.S. Military and Future Operations* (Carlisle, PA: USAWC, 2011), 1–2, 44–45.

25. For more examples of the "Braddock analogy" from the War on Terror, see Jerry D. Morelock, "Washington as Strategist: Compound Warfare in the American Revolution, 1775–1783," in Thomas M. Huber, ed., *Compound Warfare: That Fatal Knot* (Fort Leavenworth, KS: CGSC, 2002); Douglas D. Jones, "The American Revolution: Understanding the Limiting Factors of Washington's Strategy," MMAS thesis (CGSC, 2005); Joseph A. Jackson, "March to Disaster: Major General Edward Braddock and the Monongahela Campaign," MMAS thesis (CGSC, 2008); Jared Brandon Harty, "George Washington: Spymaster and General Who Saved the American Revolution," monograph (School of Advanced Military Studies, 2012); Adam Bancroft, "Savages in a Civilized War: The Native Americans as French Allies in the Seven Years War, 1754–1763," MMAS thesis (CGSC, 2013); John M. Stevens, "Two Expeditions to Capture Fort Duquesne: A Study in Understanding the N/A Operational Environment and Attendant Failure (1755) and Success (1758)," MMS thesis (USMC Command and Staff College, 2013); Jobie S. Turner, "Victualing Victory: Logistics from Lake George to Khe Sanh, 1755–1968." PhD diss. (Maxwell Air Force Base, 2016).

26. "What Is the CAC?," United States Army Combined Arms Center, https://usacac.army.mil/.

27. Charles D. Collins Jr. and William Glenn Robertson, *Atlas of the Sioux Wars* (Fort Leavenworth, KS: CSI Press, 2006), foreword.

28. Charles D. Collins, *The Cheyenne Wars Atlas* (Fort Leavenworth, KS: CSI Press, 2012), foreword.

29. Collins, *The Atlas of the Sioux Wars*, Map 37. The atlas, while referring to Wounded Knee as a tragedy, lacks a critical perspective on the failures that led to the violence of the massacre. For more on Wounded Knee, see Jeffrey Ostler, *The Plains Sioux and U.S. Colonialism from Lewis and Clark to Wounded Knee* (Cambridge: Cambridge University Press, 2004), 346; Nick Estes, *Our History Is the Future* (New York: Verso, 2019); Pekka Hämäläinen, *Lakota America: A New History of Indigenous Power* (New Haven, CT: Yale University Press, 2019).

30. For struggles over the Dakota Access Pipeline see Estes, *Our History Is the Future*; Nick Estes and Jaskiran Dhillon, eds., *Standing with Standing Rock: Voices from the #NoDAPL Movement* (Minneapolis: University of Minnesota Press, 2019).

31. Kendall D. Gott, *In Search of an Elusive Enemy: The Victorio Campaign* (Fort Leavenworth, KS: CSI Press, 2012), iii.

32. Karl Jacoby, "Operation Geronimo Dishonors the Indian Leader," *Los Angeles Times*, May 10, 2011.

33. Gott, *In Search of an Elusive Enemy*, 43–45.

34. "Report of the Chief of Ordnance" (Washington, DC: GPO, 1878), xiii; Ari Kelman, *A Misplaced Massacre: Struggling over the Memory of Sand Creek*

(Cambridge, MA: Harvard University Press, 2013), 23; Hämäläinen, *Lakota America*, 378–79.

35. Larry Yates, *Field Artillery in Military Operations Other Than War: An Overview of the U.S. Experience* (Fort Leavenworth, KS: CSI Press, 2012), 10.

36. Yates, 42.

37. Richard E. Killblane, *Circle the Wagons: The History of US Army Convoy Security* (Fort Leavenworth, KS: CSI Press, 2005), 4.

38. Kendall D. Gott, and Michael G. Brooks, *Security Assistance: U.S. and International Historical Perspectives* (Fort Leavenworth, KS: CSI Press, 2006), 631.

39. Thomas A. Bass, "Counterinsurgency and Torture," *American Quarterly* 60, no. 2 (June 13, 2008): 234.

40. These numbers were calculated using the search engine at the Ike Skelton Combined Arms Research Library Digital Library.

41. Many of these documents can be found online at the Ike Skelton Combined Arms Research Library Digital Library, http://cgsc.contentdm.oclc.org /cdm, and the Defense Technical Information Center, https://discover.dtic.mil.

42. Amy Kaplan, *Our American Israel: The Story of an Entangled Alliance* (Cambridge, MA: Harvard University Press, 2018), 258.

43. See Stefan Aune, "Euthanasia Politics and the Indian Wars," *American Quarterly* 71, no. 3 (2019): 789–811.

44. Ronak K. Kapadia, *Insurgent Aesthetics: Security and the Queer Life of the Forever War* (Durham, NC: Duke University Press, 2019), 5–9; Lubin, *Never-Ending War on Terror*, 104.

45. Lowell S. Yarbrough, "Asymmetrical Warfare on the Great Plains: A Review of the American Indian Wars—1865–1891," Strategy Research Project (USAWC, 2002), 18.

46. See Mahmood Mamdani, *Good Muslim, Bad Muslim: America, the Cold War, and the Roots of Terror* (New York: Pantheon Books, 2004); Derek Gregory, *The Colonial Present: Afghanistan, Palestine, and Iraq* (Malden, MA: Blackwell, 2004); Jasbir K. Puar, *Terrorist Assemblages: Homonationalism in Queer Times* (Durham, NC: Duke University Press, 2007).

47. Johnny S. Williams, "A Comparison between the Insurgencies of Vietnam and the Indian Wars," 2008, USASMA Digital Library, Combined Arms Research Library Digital Library, 3.

48. Johnny S. Williams, "Comparison between the Insurgencies of Vietnam and the Indian War," 2008, USASMA Digital Library, Combined Arms Research Library Digital Library, 8.

49. Dennis Pearson, "Indian Wars and the Philippine Insurrection: A Comparison in Successful Counterinsurgency Campaigns," 2008, USASMA Digital Library, Combined Arms Research Library Digital Library, Abstract.

50. Pearson, "Indian Wars," 8.

51. For more on depictions of Muslims, Arabs, and the Middle East, see McAlister, *Epic Encounters*; Gregory, *The Colonial Present*; Puar, *Terrorist Assemblages*; Vijay Prashad, *Uncle Swami: South Asians in America Today* (New York: The New Press, 2012).

52. For a history of the 2007 "surge," see David Finkel, *The Good Soldiers*.

53. Wesley M. Pirkle, "Major General George Crook's Use of Counterinsurgency Compound Warfare during the Great Sioux War of 1876–77," master's thesis (CGSC, 2008), 2.

54. On the "doctrine of discovery" see Carole Pateman and Charles W. Mills, *Contract and Domination* (Cambridge: Polity, 2007), 36–44; Mahmood Mamdani, *Neither Settler nor Native* (Cambridge, MA: Harvard University Press, 2020), 5. For "manifest destiny," see Bruce Cumings, *Dominion from Sea to Sea: Pacific Ascendancy and American Power* (New Haven, CT: Yale University Press, 2009), 63–64; Stefan Aune, "American Empire," in David Kieran and Edwin A. Martini, eds., *At War: The Military and American Culture in the Twentieth Century and Beyond* (New Brunswick, NJ: Rutgers University Press, 2018), 32.

55. Nicholas J. Cruz, "General George Crook's Development as a Practitioner of Irregular Warfare during the Indian Wars," MMAS thesis (CGSC, 2017), 3.

56. See Amy Kaplan, *The Anarchy of Empire in the Making of U.S. Culture* (Cambridge, MA: Harvard University Press, 2002).

57. Brian McAllister Linn, *The Echo of Battle: The Army's Way of War* (Cambridge, MA: Harvard University Press, 2007), 3.

58. Collins and Robertson, *Atlas of the Sioux Wars*, foreword.

59. Laleh Khalili, *Time in the Shadows: Confinement in Counterinsurgencies* (Stanford, CA: Stanford University Press, 2012), 5.

60. O'Connell, "Moving Mountains," 6–7.

61. Cruz, "General George Crook," 2.

62. Miller, "Red Cloud's War," 44.

63. For racialized depictions of Indians see Philip J. Deloria, *Indians in Unexpected Places* (Lawrence: University Press of Kansas, 2004); Jodi A. Byrd, *The Transit of Empire: Indigenous Critiques of Colonialism* (Minneapolis: University of Minnesota Press, 2011). On depictions of Arabs, Muslims, and the Middle East, see McAlister, *Epic Encounters*; Puar, *Terrorist Assemblages*; Prashad, *Uncle Swami*. Evelyn Alsultany explores how sympathetic depictions of Arabs or Muslims served to perpetuate the idea of a "postrace" society during the War on Terror. See Evelyn Alsultany, "Arabs and Muslims in the Media after 9/11: Representational Strategies for a 'Postrace' Era," *American Quarterly* 65, no. 1 (March 1, 2013): 161–69.

64. Hannah Gurman, "Introduction," in Hannah Gurman, ed., *Hearts and Minds: A People's History of Counterinsurgency* (New York: The New Press, 2013), 7.

65. Corey A. Brunkow, "The Future of Raiding: Lessons in Raiding Tactics from the Indian Wars and Law Enforcement," MA thesis (Naval Postgraduate School, 2009), Abstract-3.

66. Master Sgt. Brian Hamilton, "Army Moves Closer to Establishing First Security Force Assistance Brigade," accessed January 10, 2018, www.army.mil/article/187991/army_moves_closer_to_establishing_first_security_force_assistance_brigade.

67. For security and the War on Terror, see Miguel De Larrinaga, and Marc G. Doucet, "Sovereign Power and the Biopolitics of Human Security,"

Security Dialogue 39, no. 5 (October 1, 2008): 517–37; Brad Evans, *Liberal Terror* (Cambridge: Polity, 2013); Lubin, *Never-Ending War on Terror*, 78–79.

68. Brunkow, "The Future of Raiding," 4.

69. See chapter 3 and the discussion of what "lessons" the US military did (and did not) preserve after the Philippine-American War.

70. Brunkow, "The Future of Raiding," 6, 38.

71. Brunkow, 74.

72. Laleh Khalili outlines this relationship in Khalili, *Time in the Shadows*, 1–6.

73. Montgomery McFate, "Anthropology and Counterinsurgency: The Strange Story of Their Curious Relationship." *Military Review* 85, no. 2 (April 2005): 24, 37.

74. "About," montgomerymcfate.com, accessed January 12, 2018, http://montgomerymcfate.com/bio/.

75. "CEAUSSIC Releases Final Report on Army HTS Program," American Anthropological Association, accessed January 12, 2018, www.americananthro.org/issues/policy-advocacy/statement-on-HTS.cfm.

76. McFate, "Anthropology and Counterinsurgency," 24.

77. *Counterinsurgency Field Manual*, 27.

78. Marshall Sahlins, "Preface," in Network of Concerned Anthropologists, *The Counter-Counterinsurgency Manual; or, Notes on Demilitarizing American Society* (Chicago: Prickly Paradigm Press, 2009), iii.

79. Anna Simons, "Anthropology, Culture, and COIN in a Hybrid Warfare World," in Robert Tomes, William Natter, and Paul Brister, eds., *Hybrid Warfare and Transnational Threats: Perspectives for an Era of Persistent Conflict* (Lexington, MA: Council for Emerging National Security Affairs, 2011), 83–91. For a military critique of the Human Terrain System, see Ben Connable, "All Our Eggs in a Broken Basket: How the Human Terrain System Is Undermining Sustainable Military Cultural Competence," *Military Review* 89, no. 2 (April 2009): 57–64.

80. O'Connell, "Moving Mountains," 3–4.

81. U.S. fixation on the tribal social structures of Afghanistan goes back at least as far as the Soviet-Afghan War. CIA documents emphasized that tribal affiliations would pose problems for Soviet efforts to legitimate the Democratic Republic of Afghanistan. See "Afghan Resistance" (Defense Intelligence Agency, Directorate for Research, November 5, 1982), The National Security Archive, https://nsarchive2.gwu.edu/NSAEBB/NSAEBB57/us.html.

82. Mamdani, *Good Muslim, Bad Muslim*, 11–21.

83. David Price, "Faking Scholarship," in *The Counter-Counterinsurgency Manual*, 72–75.

84. Price, 72–75.

85. Bancroft, "Savages in a Civilized War," 128.

86. Bancroft, abstract.

87. John D. Cross, *Decisive Battle and the Global War on Terror*, monograph (CGSC, 2005), 39.

88. Jason E. Warner, *There Shall We Be Also: Tribal Fractures and Auxiliaries in the Indian Wars of the Northern Great Plains*, monograph (CGSC, 2008), abstract.

89. Warner, 53.

90. Warner, 1.

91. For histories of pan-Indian military resistance, see Gregory Evans Dowd, *A Spirited Resistance: The North American Indian Struggle for Unity, 1745–1815* (Baltimore: Johns Hopkins University Press, 1992); Gregory Evans Dowd, *War under Heaven: Pontiac, the Indian Nations, and the British Empire* (Baltimore: Johns Hopkins University Press, 2002).

92. O'Connell, "Moving Mountains," 19–21.

93. Alan Clarke, "Tribal Identity and Conflicts with Tribes," Strategy Research Project (USAWC, 2008), abstract.

94. Clarke, 19.

95. Clarke, 6.

96. Paul Kramer, "The Water Cure" *The New Yorker*, February 18, 2008, www.newyorker.com/magazine/2008/02/25/the-water-cure.

97. Jason E. Martos, "Uncomfortable Experience: Lessons Lost in the Apache War," MMOAS thesis (Air Command and Staff College, 2015), 15.

98. George Crook and Martin F. Schmitt, ed., *General George Crook: His Autobiography* (Norman: University of Oklahoma Press, 1986), xiii; Robert Cassidy, *Counterinsurgency and the Global War on Terror: Military Culture and Irregular War* (Stanford, CA: Stanford University Press, 2008), 132.

99. William L. Greenberg, "General Crook and Counterinsurgency Warfare," MMAS thesis (CGSC, 2001), 1.

100. Greenberg, 1.

101. George Crook, *Crook's Resumé of Operations against Apache Indians, 1882 to 1886* (London: Johnson-Taunton Military Press, 1971), 1–5. On Crook vs. Miles, see David Roberts, *Once They Moved Like the Wind: Cochise, Geronimo, and the Apache Wars* (New York: Touchstone, 1994), 277–78; Janne Lahti, *Cultural Construction of Empire: The U.S. Army in Arizona and New Mexico* (Lincoln: Nebraska University Press, 2012), 235–36.

102. Greenberg, "General Crook," 112.

103. It is unclear whether the author is consciously playing on Frantz Fanon's *Black Skins White Masks* with the title, but in an author's note they address the charged language of the title, saying "The use of the term Redskin and Injun are being used in their then contemporary pejorative context to highlight the irony of different races and their interaction in the US Army, as identified by the colors red, white, and blue."

104. Michael J. Livingston, "Redskins in Bluecoats: A Strategic and Cultural Analysis of General George Crook's Use of Apache Scouts in the Second Apache Campaign, 1882–1886," MMS thesis (Marine Corps Command and Staff College, 2010) Executive Summary.

105. Livingston, vi.

106. Thomas W. Dunlay, *Wolves for the Blue Soldiers: Indian Scouts and Auxiliaries with the United States Army, 1860–90* (Lincoln: University of Nebraska Press, 1982), 165–69.

107. Crook, *Resumé of Operations*, 21.

108. Pirkle, "Major General George Crook," 4.

109. Michael L. Tate, *The Frontier Army in the Settlement of the West* (Norman: University of Oklahoma Press, 1999), 257–58; Richard White, *The*

Republic for Which It Stands: The United States during Reconstruction and the Gilded Age, 1865–1896 (Oxford: Oxford University Press, 2017), 129.

110. Crook, *Resumé of Operations*, 9.

111. Lahti, *Cultural Constructions of Empire*, 116.

112. Crook, *Resumé of Operations*, 4.

113. George Crook, "The Apache Problem," *JMSI* 7 (1886): 261–62.

114. Karl Jacoby, "'The Broad Platform of Extermination': Nature and Violence in the Nineteenth-Century North American Borderlands," *Journal of Genocide Research*, no. 2 (2008): 254–55.

115. Cruz, "General George Crook," 85.

116. Livingston, "Redskins in Bluecoats," 30.

117. Suriano, "Lessons Learned," 4.

118. Richard C. King, *Unsettling America: The Uses of Indianness in the 21st Century* (Lanham, MD: Rowman & Littlefield, 2013), 59.

119. "The Private War of Women Soldiers: Female Vet, Soldier Speak Out on Rising Sexual Assault within U.S. Military," *Democracy Now!* March 8, 2007, https://www.democracynow.org/2007/3/8/the_private_war_of_women_soldiers.

120. Daniel K. Richter, *Facing East from Indian Country: A Native History of Early America* (Cambridge, MA: Harvard University Press, 2001).

CONCLUSION

1. Max Liboiron, *Pollution Is Colonialism* (Durham, NC: Duke University Press, 2021), 11–16; Paul C. Rosier, "Native Americans, Indigeneity, and U.S. Foreign Policy," in David C. Engerman, Max Paul Friedman, and Melani McAlister, eds., *The Cambridge History of America and the World, Volume 4: 1945 to the Present* (Cambridge: Cambridge University Press, 2022), 484.

2. Sandy Tolan, "Vets Came to Protest, but They Found Mercy," *Los Angeles Times*, December 10, 2016.

3. Nick Estes and Jaskiran Dhillon, "Introduction," in Nick Estes and Jaskiran Dhillon, eds., *Standing with Standing Rock: Voices from the #NoDAPL Movement* (Minneapolis: University of Minnesota Press, 2019), 1–5; Kevin Bruyneel, *Settler Memory: The Disavowal of Indigeneity and the Politics of Race in the United States* (Chapel Hill: University of North Carolina Press, 2021), 144–45.

4. Tolan, "Vets Came to Protest."

5. Nicholas J. Cruz, "General George Crook's Development as a Practitioner of Irregular Warfare during the Indian Wars," MMAS thesis (CGSC, 2017), 3.

6. Cruz, 3.

7. Stephen W. Silliman, "The 'Old West' in the Middle East: U.S. Military Metaphors in Real and Imagined Indian Country," *American Anthropologist* 110, no. 2 (June 2008): 237–47.

8. Alleen Brown, Will Parrish, and Alice Speri, "Leaked Documents Reveal Counterterrorism Tactics Used at Standing Rock to 'Defeat Pipeline Insurgencies,'" *The Intercept*, May 27, 2017, https://theintercept.com/2017/05/27/leaked-documents-reveal-security-firms-counterterrorism-tactics-at-standing-rock-to-defeat-pipeline-insurgencies; Joanne Barker, *Red Scare: The State's Indigenous Terrorist* (Oakland: University of California Press, 2021), 50–60.

9. Nick Estes, *Our History Is the Future* (New York: Verso, 2019), 3; Brown, Parrish, and Speri, "Leaked Documents."

10. Brown, Parrish, Speri, "Leaked Documents."

11. Brown, Parrish, Speri.

12. Leslie James Pickering, *Earth Liberation Front: 1997–2002* (Minneapolis, MN: Arissa Media Group, LLC, 2007); David Naguib Pellow, *Total Liberation: The Power and Promise of Animal Rights and the Radical Earth Movement* (Minneapolis: University of Minnesota Press, 2014).

13. Barker, *Red Scare*, 57–69; Alleen Brown, Will Parrish, and Alice Speri, "TigerSwan Responded to Pipeline Vandalism by Launching Multistate Dragnet," *The Intercept*, August 26, 2017, https://theintercept.com/2017/08/26/dapl-security-firm-tigerswan-responded-to-pipeline-vandalism-by-launching-multistate-dragnet.

14. Will Parrish and Sam Levin, "'Treating Protest as Terrorism': US Plans Crackdown on Keystone XL Activists," *The Guardian*, September 20, 2018.

15. Alleen Brown, "Indigenous Water Protectors Face Off with an Oil Company and Police Over a Minnesota Pipeline," *The Intercept*, July 7, 2021.

16. James M. Suriano, "Lessons Learned from MG George Crook's Apache Campaigns with Applicability for the Current Global War on Terror," Strategy Research Project (USAWC, 2003), 1.

17. Barker, *Red Scare*, 22.

18. Steven W. Thrasher, "Talking Happiness, Security, and Counterinsurgency with Laleh Khalili," *Contexts* 15, no. 1 (February 1, 2016): 8–10.

19. Michael Hardt and Antonio Negri, *Commonwealth* (Cambridge, MA: Harvard University Press, 2009), 56–61.

20. Barker, *Red Scare*, 23.

21. For the relationship between counterinsurgency, counterterrorism, and domestic law enforcement, see Laleh Khalili, *Time in the Shadows: Confinement in Counterinsurgencies* (Stanford, CA: Stanford University Press, 2012), 245–46. See also Jordan T. Camp, *Incarcerating the Crisis: Freedom Struggles and the Rise of the Neoliberal State* (Oakland: University of California Press, 2016); Stuart Schrader, *Badges without Borders: How Global Counterinsurgency Transformed American Policing* (Oakland: University of California Press, 2019).

22. Michael Hardt and Antonio Negri, *Multitude: War and Democracy in the Age of Empire* (New York: Penguin, 2005), 22–23.

23. Khalili, *Time in the Shadows*, 247–48; Alex Lubin, *Never-Ending War on Terror* (Oakland: University of California Press, 2021), 89–108; Samuel Moyn, *Humane: How the United States Abandoned Peace and Reinvented War* (New York: Farrar, Straus and Giroux, 2021), 4–13, 268–69; Spencer Ackerman, *Reign of Terror: How the 9/11 Era Destabilized America and Produced Trump* (New York: Penguin, 2022), 122–24. Similar to Khalili's analysis, Douglas Little calls Obama's approach "contagement." See Douglas Little, *Us versus Them: The United States, Radical Islam, and the Rise of the Green Threat* (Chapel Hill: University of North Carolina Press, 2016).

24. Daniel J. Rosenthal and Loren DeJonge Schulman, "Trump's Secret War on Terror," *The Atlantic*, August 10, 2018, https://www.theatlantic.com

/international/archive/2018/08/trump-war-terror-drones/567218/; Dan De Luce and Seán D. Naylor, "The Drones Are Back," *Foreign Policy*, March 26, 2018, https://foreignpolicy.com/2018/03/26/the-drones-are-back/; Joshua A. Geltzer, "Trump's Counterterrorism Strategy Is a Relief," *The Atlantic*, October 8, 2018, https://www.theatlantic.com/international/archive/2018/10/trump-counterterrorism-strategy/572170/; Moyn, *Humane*, 114; Ackerman, *Reign of Terror*, xiv–xv.

25. Lt. Gen. Mike Lundy and Col. Rich Creed, "The Return of U.S. Army Field Manual 3-0, Operations," *Military Review* 97, no. 6 (December 2017): 14–21; Alexandre Caillot, "Forgetting Counterinsurgency, Again: Lessons from Reconstruction and Operation Iraqi Freedom," Modern War Institute at West Point, July 2, 2020, https://mwi.usma.edu/forgetting-counterinsurgency-lessons-reconstruction-operation-iraqi-freedom; Christian Tripodi and Matthew Wiger, "Worthless Coin? Why the West Should Keep Studying Counterinsurgency," Modern War Institute at West Point, July 26, 2022, https://mwi.usma.edu/worthless-coin-why-the-west-should-keep-studying-counterinsurgency.

26. "Mike Pompeo's Cairo Speech on Mideast Policy and Obama," *Haaretz*, January 11, 2019, https://www.haaretz.com/us-news/full-text-secretary-of-state-pompeo-s-speech-at-the-american-university-in-cairo-1.6829117.

27. Alex S. Vitale, *The End of Policing* (London: Verso, 2017), 221–28.

Bibliography

ARCHIVAL SOURCES

Carroll University Archives, Waukesha, WI
Rufus and Charles King Collection

Division of Rare and Manuscript Collections, Cornell University Library, Ithaca, NY
United States Army 366th Infantry Regiment and Other Colored Divisions Collection

Elwyn B. Robinson Department of Special Collections, University of North Dakota, Grand Forks, ND

Howard Gotlieb Archival Research Center, Boston University, MA
James Warner Bellah Collection

Ike Skelton Combined Arms Research Library Digital Library, Fort Leavenworth, KS
History Papers
Operational Leadership Experiences
Personal Experience Papers

John F. Kennedy Presidential Library and Museum, Columbia Point, MA
National Security Action Memoranda

Library of Congress, Washington, DC (LOC)
Henry Ware Lawton Papers
Philip Henry Sheridan Papers
William Tecumseh Sherman Papers

National Archives Building, Washington, DC (NARA)
RG 395, Records of US Army Overseas Operations and Commands

The National Security Archive, Washington, DC
Digital National Security Archive

The Newberry Library, Chicago, IL
Benjamin Grierson Papers
Elmo Scott Watson Papers
Special Collections

University of Michigan Special Collections, Ann Arbor, MI
Captain Harry M. Dey Papers
Maria C. Lanzar-Carpio Papers

US Army Infantry School, Fort Moore, GA
Infantry School Instructional Material

US Department of State, Washington, DC
Freedom of Information Act Virtual Reading Room

US Military Academy Special Collections, West Point, NY
The Charles D. Rhodes Papers
James C. Parker Letters

The Vietnam Center and Archive, Texas Tech University, Lubbock, TX (TTU)
David A. Shelly Collection
Jan Churchill Collection
Jimmie Lambert Collection

Mr. Bill E. Paris Collection
Mr. James E. Scales Collection
Mr. Larry Casselman Collection
Mr. Michael L. Sweeney Collection
Neal Creighton Collection

NEWSPAPERS AND PERIODICALS

Air Force Magazine
AP News
The AP World
Army and Navy Journal
The Atlanta Constitution
The Atlantic
The Baltimore Sun
Chicago Daily Tribune
The Christian Science Monitor
Daily Boston Globe
Democracy Now!
Foreign Policy
The Intercept
Haaretz
Jacobin
Life
The Literary Digest
Los Angeles Review of Books
The Los Angeles Times
The New York Daily News
The New Yorker
Oakland Daily Transcript
The Philadelphia Inquirer
The San Francisco Call
Santa Fe Daily
Slate
Swanton Courier
USA Today
The Washington Post
Yank, The Army Newspaper

GOVERNMENT DOCUMENTS

United States Army, *Correspondence Relating to the War with Spain and Conditions Growing Out of the Same Including the Insurrection in the Philippine
Island and the China Relief Expedition.* 2 vols. Washington, DC: GPO, 1902.
United States Congress. House. 15th Cong., 2nd sess., *The Debates and Proceedings in the Congress of the United States.* Washington, DC: GPO, 1819.

——. 32nd Cong., 1st Sess. *Message from the President of the United States to the Two Houses of Congress.* Washington, DC: GPO, 1851.

——. 36th Cong., 2nd Sess. *Message from the President of the United States to the Two Houses of Congress.* Washington, DC: George W. Bowman, 1860.

——. 38th Cong., 1st Sess. *Message from the President of the United States to the Two Houses of Congress.* "Annual Report of the Secretary of War." Washington, DC: GPO, 1863.

——. 39th Cong., 2nd Sess. *Message from the President of the United States to the Two Houses of Congress.* "Annual Report of the Secretary of War." Washington, DC: GPO, 1866.

——. 40th Cong., 2nd Sess. *Message from the President of the United States to the Two Houses of Congress.* "Annual Report of the Secretary of War." Washington, DC: GPO, 1867.

——. 41st Cong., 2nd Sess. *Message from the President of the United States to the Two Houses of Congress.* "Annual Report of the Secretary of War." Washington, DC: GPO, 1869.

——. Senate. 44th Cong., 1st sess., *Congressional Record.* Washington, DC: GPO, 1876.

——. Senate. 57th Cong., 1st Sess., *Affairs in the Philippines Islands: Hearings before the Committee on the Philippines of the United States Senate.* Washington, DC: GPO, 1902.

——. *President's Committee to Study the United States Military Assistance Program, Composite Report.* Vol. 2. Washington, DC: GPO, 1959.

——. House. 99th Cong., 2nd Sess. *Investigation of the My Lai Incident: Report of the Armed Services Investigating Subcommittee of the Committee on Armed Services.* Washington, DC: GPO, 1970.

United States War Department. *Annual Report of the Secretary of War, 1899, Volume I.* Washington, DC: GPO, 1899.

——. *Report on the Organization of the Land Forces of the United States.* Washington, DC: GPO, 1912.

——. *Annual Report of the Secretary of War, 1912, Volume I.* Washington, DC: GPO, 1913.

——. *Annual Report of the Secretary of War, 1913, Volume I.* Washington, DC: GPO, 1914.

——. *Annual Report of the Secretary of War, 1914, Volume I.* Washington, DC: GPO, 1915.

——. *Annual Report of the Secretary of War, 1915, Volume I.* Washington, DC: GPO, 1916.

——. *Annual Report of the Secretary of War, 1916, Volume I.* Washington, DC: GPO, 1917.

——. *Annual Report of the Secretary of War, 1917, Volume I.* Washington, DC: GPO, 1918.

UNPUBLISHED MANUSCRIPTS

Bancroft, Adam. "Savages in a Civilized War: The Native Americans as French Allies in the Seven Years War, 1754–1763." MMAS thesis, CGSC, 2013.

Brunkow, Corey A. "The Future of Raiding: Lessons in Raiding Tactics from the Indian Wars and Law Enforcement." MA thesis, Naval Postgraduate School, 2009.

Clarke, Alan. "Tribal Identity and Conflicts with Tribes." Strategy Research Project, USAWC, 2008.

Cross, John D. *Decisive Battle and the Global War on Terror.* Monograph, CGSC, 2005.

Cruz, Nicholas J. "General George Crook's Development as a Practitioner of Irregular Warfare During the Indian Wars." MMAS thesis, CGSC, 2017.

Greenberg, William L. "General Crook and Counterinsurgency Warfare." MMAS thesis, CGSC, 2001.

Harty, Jared Brandon. *George Washington: Spymaster and General Who Saved the American Revolution.* Monograph, School of Advanced Military Studies, 2012.

Jackson, Joseph A. "March to Disaster: Major General Edward Braddock and the Monongahela Campaign." MMAS thesis, CGSC, 2008.

Jones, Douglas D. "The American Revolution: Understanding the Limiting Factors of Washington's Strategy." MMAS thesis, CGSC, 2005.

Livingston, Michael J. "Redskins in Bluecoats: A Strategic and Cultural Analysis of General George Crook's Use of Apache Scouts in the Second Apache Campaign, 1882–1886." MMS thesis, Marine Corps Command and Staff College, 2010.

Mabry, Alan T. "Systemic Problems within the Army during the Indian Wars (1865–1881)," MMAS thesis, CGSC, 1995.

Martos, Jason E. "Uncomfortable Experience: Lessons Lost in the Apache War." MMOAS thesis, Air Command and Staff College, 2015.

Miller, Michael G. "Red Cloud's War: An Insurgency Case Study for Modern Times." Strategy Research Project, USAWC, 2011.

Pirkle, Wesley M. "Major General George Crook's Use of Counterinsurgency Compound Warfare during the Great Sioux War of 1876–77." MMAS thesis, CGSC, 2015.

Siegrist, Jeremy T. *Apache Wars: A Constabulary Perspective.* Monograph, School of Advanced Military Studies, 2012.

Stevens, John M. "Two Expeditions to Capture Fort Duquesne: A Study in Understanding the N/A Operational Environment and Attendant Failure (1755) and Success (1758)." MMS thesis, USMC Command and Staff College, 2013.

Suriano, James M. "Lessons Learned from MG George Crook's Apache Campaigns with Applicability for the Current Global War on Terror." Strategy Research Project, USAWC, 2003.

Turner, Jobie S. "Victualing Victory: Logistics from Lake George to Khe Sanh, 1755–1968." PhD diss., Maxwell Air Force Base, 2016.

Warner, Jason E. *There Shall We Be Also: Tribal Fractures and Auxiliaries in the Indian Wars of the Northern Great Plains.* Monograph, CGSC, 2008.

Yarbrough, Lowell S. "Asymmetrical Warfare on the Great Plains: A Review of the American Indian Wars—1865–1891." Strategy Research Project, USAWC, 2002.

PUBLISHED BOOKS AND ARTICLES

Ackerman, Spencer. *Reign of Terror: How the 9/11 Era Destabilized America and Produced Trump.* New York: Penguin, 2022.

Adams, Kevin. *Class and Race in the Frontier Army: Military Life in the West, 1870–1890.* Norman: University of Oklahoma Press, 2009.

Afflerbach, Holger, and Hew Strachan, eds. *How Fighting Ends: A History of Surrender.* Oxford: Oxford University Press, 2012.

Agamben, Giorgio. *Homo Sacer: Sovereign Power and Bare Life.* Translated by Daniel Heller-Roazen. Stanford, CA: Stanford University Press, 1998.

———. *State of Exception.* Translated by Kevin Attell. Chicago: University of Chicago Press, 2005.

Alsultany, Evelyn. "Arabs and Muslims in the Media after 9/11: Representational Strategies for a 'Postrace' Era." *American Quarterly* 65, no. 1 (March 1, 2013): 161–69.

Altieri, James J. *The Spearheaders: A Personal History of Darby's Rangers.* Annapolis, MD: Naval Institute Press, 2014.

Ambrose, Stephen E. *Upton and the Army.* Baton Rouge: Louisiana State University Press, 1993.

Anderson, Ben. "Population and Affective Perception: Biopolitics and Anticipatory Action in US Counterinsurgency Doctrine." *Antipode* 43, no. 2 (March 1, 2011): 205–36.

Anderson, Fred, and Andrew Cayton. *The Dominion of War: Empire and Liberty in North America, 1500–2000.* New York: Penguin, 2005.

Anderson, Mark Cronlund. *Holy War: Cowboys, Indians, and 9/11s.* Regina, SK: University of Regina Press, 2016.

Anderson, Paul Christopher. *Blood Image: Turner Ashby in the Civil War and the Southern Mind.* Baton Rouge: Louisiana State University Press, 2006.

Archibald, James F. J. *Blue Shirt and Khaki: A Comparison.* New York: Silver, Burdett and Company, 1901.

"The Army Not Only to Watch the Indians." *JMSI* 4 (1883): 87.

Aune, Stefan. "Euthanasia Politics and the Indian Wars." *American Quarterly* 71, no. 3 (2019): 789–811.

———. "Indian Fighters in the Philippines: Imperial Culture and Military Violence in the Philippine-American War." *Pacific Historical Review* 90, no. 4 (2021): 419–47.

Avirett, James B. *The Memoirs of General Turner Ashby and His Compeers.* Baltimore: Selby & Dulany, 1867.

Babcock, Bvt. Major J. B. "Field Exercises and the Necessity for an Authorized Manual of Field Duties." *JMSI* 12 (1891): 938–51.

Bacevich, Andrew J. *Twilight of the American Century.* Notre Dame, IN: University of Notre Dame Press, 2018.

———. *Washington Rules: America's Path to Permanent War.* New York: Metropolitan Books, 2010.

Bailey, John W. *The Life and Works of General Charles King, 1844–1933: Martial Spirit.* Lewiston, NY: Edwin Mellen Press, 1998.

Balce, Nerissa. *Body Parts of Empire: Visual Abjection, Filipino Images, and the American Archive*. Ann Arbor: University of Michigan Press, 2016.

Bald, Vivek, Miabi Chatterji, Vijay Prashad, Sujani Reddy, and Manu Vimalassery, eds. *The Sun Never Sets: South Asian Migrants in an Age of U.S. Power*. New York: New York University Press, 2013.

Bandy, Mary Lea, and Kevin Stoehr. *Ride, Boldly Ride: The Evolution of the American Western*. Berkeley: University of California Press, 2012.

Banner, Stuart. *How the Indians Lost Their Land: Law and Power on the Frontier*. Cambridge, MA: Harvard University Press, 2005.

Barker, Joanne. *Red Scare: The State's Indigenous Terrorist*. Oakland: University of California Press, 2021.

Barnett, Louise. *Touched by Fire: The Life, Death, and Mythic Afterlife of George Armstrong Custer*. Lincoln: University of Nebraska Press, 2006.

Bass, Thomas A. "Counterinsurgency and Torture." *American Quarterly* 60, no. 2 (June 13, 2008): 233–40.

Bates, Milton J. *The Wars We Took to Vietnam: Cultural Conflict and Storytelling*. Berkeley: University of California Press, 1996.

Bederman, Gail. *Manliness and Civilization: A Cultural History of Gender and Race in the United States, 1880–1917*. Chicago: University of Chicago Press, 1996.

Beilein, Joseph M., Jr. *Bushwhackers: Guerrilla Warfare, Manhood, and the Household in Civil War Missouri*. Kent, OH: The Kent State University Press, 2016.

Belew, Kathleen. *Bring the War Home: The White Power Movement and Paramilitary America*. Cambridge, MA: Harvard University Press, 2018.

Bellah, James Warner. "Encirclement by Air." *Infantry Journal* 54, no. 6 (1944): 8–13.

———. "Long Range Penetration Groups." *Infantry Journal* 55, no. 4 (1944): 45–47.

Bennett, Huw, et al. "Studying Mars and Clio: Or How Not to Write about the Ethics of Military Conduct and Military History," *History Workshop Journal* 91 (Spring 2021): 274–80.

Benton, Lauren A. *Law and Colonial Cultures: Legal Regimes in World History, 1400–1900*. Cambridge: Cambridge University Press, 2002.

Benton-Cohen, Katherine. *Borderline Americans: Racial Division and Labor War in the Arizona Borderland*. Cambridge, MA: Harvard University Press, 2009.

Berkhofer, Robert F. *The White Man's Indian: Images of the American Indian from Columbus to the Present*. New York: Knopf, 1978.

Berry, Joshua F. "Hollow Point Bullets: How History Has Hijacked Their Use in Combat and Why It Is Time to Reexamine the 1899 Hague Declaration Concerning Expanding Bullets." *Military Law Review* 206 (2010): 88–156.

Bickel, Keith. *Mars Learning: The Marine Corps Development of Small Wars Doctrine, 1915–1940*. Boulder, CO: Westview Press, 2001.

Bigelow, John. *The Principles of Strategy: Illustrated Mainly from American Campaigns*. Philadelphia: J.B. Lippincott Company, 1894.

———. "Tenth Regiment of Cavalry." *JMSI* 13 (1892): 215–24.

Biolsi, Thomas. *Organizing the Lakota: The Political Economy of the New Deal on the Pine Ridge and Rosebud Reservations.* Tucson: University of Arizona Press, 1992.

Birtle, Andrew J. *U.S. Army Counterinsurgency and Contingency Operations Doctrine, 1860–1941.* Washington, DC: Center of Military History, 1998.

Birtle, Andrew J. *U.S. Army Counterinsurgency and Contingency Operations Doctrine, 1942–1976.* Washington, DC: Center of Military History, 2006.

Bishop, Katherine E. "The Anti-Imperialist American Literary Animal: Envisioning Empathy." *Antennae: The Journal of Nature in Visual Culture,* no. 24 (Spring 2013): 110–24.

Bjork, Katharine. *Prairie Imperialists: The Indian Country Origins of American Empire.* Philadelphia: University of Pennsylvania Press, 2018.

Black, Megan. *The Global Interior: Mineral Frontiers and American Power.* Cambridge, MA: Harvard University Press, 2018.

Blackhawk, Ned. *Violence over the Land: Indians and Empires in the Early American West.* Cambridge, MA: Harvard University Press, 2006.

Blansett, Kent. *A Journey to Freedom: Richard Oakes, Alcatraz, and the Red Power Movement.* New Haven, CT: Yale University Press, 2018.

Boot, Max. *The Savage Wars of Peace: Small Wars and the Rise of American Power.* New York: Basic Books, 2014.

Brackett, Albert G. "Our Cavalry." *JMSI* 4 (1883): 383–407.

Brereton, T. R. *Educating the U.S. Army: Arthur L. Wagner and Reform, 1875–1905.* Lincoln: University of Nebraska Press, 2000.

Britten, Thomas A. *American Indians in World War I: At Home and at War.* Albuquerque: University of New Mexico Press, 1999.

Britten, William F. "We Will Do Anything to Win the War." *Military Review* 22, no. 86 (1942): 20–22.

Brooke, Senator Edward W. *Bridging the Divide: My Life.* New Brunswick, NJ: Rutgers University Press, 2006.

Brooks, Elbridge Streeter. *With Lawton and Roberts: A Boy's Adventures in the Philippines and the Transvaal.* Boston: Lothrop Publishing Company, 1900.

Brooks, Lisa. *Our Beloved Kin: A New History of King Philip's War.* New Haven, CT: Yale University Press, 2018.

Brown, Dee. *Bury My Heart at Wounded Knee: An Indian History of the American West.* New York: Holt, 2007.

Brown, Wendy. *Regulating Aversion: Tolerance in the Age of Identity and Empire.* Princeton, NJ: Princeton University Press, 2008.

Brundage, W. Fitzhugh. *Civilizing Torture: An American Tradition.* Cambridge, MA: Harvard University Press, 2018.

Bruyneel, Kevin. *Settler Memory: The Disavowal of Indigeneity and the Politics of Race in the United States.* Chapel Hill: University of North Carolina Press, 2021.

———. *The Third Space of Sovereignty: The Postcolonial Politics of U.S.–Indigenous Relations.* Minneapolis: University of Minnesota Press, 2007.

Burke, Kyle. *Revolutionaries for the Right: Anticommunist Internationalism and Paramilitary Warfare in the Cold War*. Chapel Hill: University of North Carolina Press, 2018.

Burnham, W. P. "Military Training of the Regular Army." *JMSI* 10 (1889): 613–40.

Burns, Mike, and Gregory McNamee. *The Only One Living to Tell: The Autobiography of a Yavapai Indian*. Tucson: University of Arizona Press, 2012.

Byrd, Jodi A. *The Transit of Empire: Indigenous Critiques of Colonialism*. Minneapolis: University of Minnesota Press, 2011.

Cahill, Cathleen D. *Federal Fathers and Mothers: A Social History of the United States Indian Service, 1869–1933*. Chapel Hill: University of North Carolina Press, 2011.

Calloway, Colin G. *The American Revolution in Indian Country: Crisis and Diversity in Native American Communities*. Cambridge: Cambridge University Press, 1995.

———. *The Indian World of George Washington: The First President, the First Americans, and the Birth of the Nation*. Oxford: Oxford University Press, 2018.

Callwell, Charles Edward. *Small Wars: Their Principles and Practice*. London: Harrison and Sons, 1899.

Camp, Jordan T. *Incarcerating the Crisis: Freedom Struggles and the Rise of the Neoliberal State*. Oakland: University of California Press, 2016.

Camp, Jordan T., and Jennifer Greenburg. "Counterinsurgency Reexamined: Racism, Capitalism, and US Military Doctrine." *Antipode* 52, no. 2 (March 2020): 430–51.

Capozzola, Christopher. *Bound by War: How the United States and the Philippines Built America's First Pacific Century*. New York: Basic Books, 2020.

Carmichael, Deborah A. *The Landscape of Hollywood Westerns: Ecocriticism in an American Film Genre*. Salt Lake City: University of Utah Press, 2006.

Carrington, Henry Beebee. *The Indian Question*. Boston: De Wolfe & Fiske, 1884.

Carroll, Al. *Medicine Bags and Dog Tags: American Indian Veterans from Colonial Times to the Second Iraq War*. Lincoln: University of Nebraska Press, 2008.

Carroll, John M., ed. *The Papers of the Order of Indian Wars*. Fort Collins, CO: Old Army Press, 1975.

Carruthers, Susan L. *The Good Occupation: American Soldiers and the Hazards of Peace*. Cambridge, MA: Harvard University Press, 2016.

Carter, W. H. "The Infantry and Cavalry School at Fort Leavenworth." *JMSI* 15 (1894): 752–59.

Carvin, Stephanie. *Prisoners of America's Wars: From the Early Republic to Guantanamo*. New York: Columbia University Press, 2010.

Cassidy, Robert. *Counterinsurgency and the Global War on Terror: Military Culture and Irregular War*. Stanford, CA: Stanford University Press, 2008.

———. "Winning the War of the Flea: Lessons from Guerilla Warfare." *Military Review* September–October (2004).

C.D.R. "Book Notices and Exchanges." *Journal of the United States Cavalry Association* 12, no. 41 (March 1899).

Chaar-López, Iván. "Sensing Intruders: Race and the Automation of Border Control." *American Quarterly* 71, no. 2 (June 2019): 495–518.

Chamberlin, Paul Thomas. *The Cold War's Killing Fields: Rethinking the Long Peace*. New York: HarperCollins, 2018.

Charbonneau, Oliver. *Civilizational Imperatives: Americans, Moros, and the Colonial World*. Ithaca, NY: Cornell University Press, 2020.

Chester, James. "Musings of a Superannuated Soldier." *JMSI* 47 (1910).

Clark, J. P. *Preparing for War: The Emergence of the Modern U.S. Army, 1815–1917*. Cambridge, MA: Harvard University Press, 2017.

Coffman, Edward M. *The Old Army: A Portrait of the American Army in Peacetime, 1784–1898*. Oxford: Oxford University Press, 1986.

———. *The Regulars: The American Army, 1898–1941*. Cambridge, MA: Harvard University Press, 2007.

Collins, Charles D., Jr. *The Cheyenne Wars Atlas*. Fort Leavenworth, KS: CSI Press, 2012.

Collins, Charles D., Jr., and William Glenn Robertson. *Atlas of the Sioux Wars*. Fort Leavenworth, KS: CSI Press, 2011.

Connable, Ben. "All Our Eggs in a Broken Basket: How the Human Terrain System Is Undermining Sustainable Military Cultural Competence." *Military Review* 89, no. 2 (April 2009): 57–64.

Cook, James W., Lawrence B. Glickman, and Michael O'Malley, eds. *The Cultural Turn in U.S. History: Past, Present, and Future*. Chicago: University of Chicago Press, 2008.

Cooper, Jerry M., and Glenn H. Smith. *Citizens as Soldiers: A History of the North Dakota National Guard*. Fargo: North Dakota Institute for Regional Studies, 1986.

Cothran, Boyd. *Remembering the Modoc War: Redemptive Violence and the Making of American Innocence*. Chapel Hill: University of North Carolina Press, 2014.

Cozzens, Peter. *Eyewitnesses to the Indian Wars, 1865–1890: The Army and the Indian*. Mechanicsburg, PA: Stackpole Books, 2001.

Crook, George. "The Apache Problem." *JMSI* 7 (1886): 257–69.

———. *Crook's Resumé of Operations against Apache Indians, 1882 to 1886*. London: Johnson-Taunton Military Press, 1971.

Crook, George, and Martin F. Schmitt, ed. *General George Crook: His Autobiography*. Norman: University of Oklahoma Press, 1986.

Crosby, Paul M. "Legend of Fiddler's Green." *Armor* 74, no. 1 (1965).

Cumings, Bruce. *Dominion from Sea to Sea: Pacific Ascendancy and American Power*. New Haven, CT: Yale University Press, 2009.

Daddis, Gregory A. *Pulp Vietnam: War and Gender in Cold War Men's Adventure Magazines*. Cambridge: Cambridge University Press, 2021.

d'Ambruoso, William L. *American Torture from the Philippines to Iraq: A Recurring Nightmare*. Oxford: Oxford University Press, 2021.

Davidson, Janine. *Lifting the Fog of Peace: How Americans Learned to Fight Modern War*. Ann Arbor: University of Michigan Press, 2011.

Dean, Robert D. *Imperial Brotherhood: Gender and the Making of Cold War Foreign Policy*. Amherst: University of Massachusetts Press, 2001.

Dellums, Ronald V. *The Dellums Committee Hearings on War Crimes in Vietnam: An Inquiry into Command Responsibility in Southeast Asia*. New York: Vintage Books, 1972.

Deloria, Philip J. *Indians in Unexpected Places*. Lawrence: University Press of Kansas, 2004.

———. *Playing Indian*. New Haven, CT: Yale University Press, 1998.

Deloria, Philip J., and Alexander I. Olson. *American Studies: A User's Guide*. Oakland: University of California Press, 2017.

Deloria, Vine, Jr. *Custer Died for Your Sins: An Indian Manifesto*. Norman: University of Oklahoma Press, 1988.

Deloria, Vine, Jr., and Clifford M. Lytle. *The Nations Within: The Past and Future of American Indian Sovereignty*. Austin: University of Texas Press, 1998.

Devens, Charles, Jr., and William T. Sherman. *Addresses to the Graduating Class of the U.S. Military Academy, West Point, New York, June 14, 1876*. New York: D. Van Nostrand, 1876.

Dhamoon, Rita. "A Feminist Approach to Decolonizing Anti-Racism: Rethinking Transnationalism, Intersectionality, and Settler Colonialism." *Feral Feminisms* no. 4 (Summer 2015).

Dietze, Carola, and Claudia Verhoeven, eds. *The Oxford Handbook of the History of Terrorism*. Oxford: Oxford University Press, 2014.

Dornbusch, C. E. *Charles King, American Army Novelist; a Bibliography from the Collection of the National Library of Australia, Canberra*. Cornwallville: Hope Farm Press, 1963.

Dowd, Gregory Evans. *A Spirited Resistance: The North American Indian Struggle for Unity, 1745–1815*. Baltimore: Johns Hopkins University Press, 1992.

———. *War under Heaven: Pontiac, the Indian Nations, and the British Empire*. Baltimore: Johns Hopkins University Press, 2002.

Dower, John. *War without Mercy: Race and Power in the Pacific War*. New York: Pantheon Books, 2012.

Drinnon, Richard. *Facing West: The Metaphysics of Indian-Hating and Empire-Building*. Minneapolis: University of Minnesota Press, 1980.

———. *Keeper of the Concentration Camps: Dillon S. Myer and American Racism*. Berkley: University of California Press, 1989.

Dunlay, Thomas W. *Wolves for the Blue Soldiers: Indian Scouts and Auxiliaries with the United States Army, 1860–90*. Lincoln: University of Nebraska Press, 1982.

Eastlake, William. *The Bamboo Bed*. London: Michael Joseph, 1970.

Einolf, Christopher J. *America in the Philippines, 1899–1902: The First Torture Scandal*. New York: Palgrave Macmillan, 2014.

Engelhardt, Tom. *The End of Victory Culture: Cold War America and the Disillusioning of a Generation*. Amherst: University of Massachusetts Press, 2007.

Engerman, David C., Max Paul Friedman, and Melani McAlister, eds. *The Cambridge History of America and the World, Volume 4: 1945 to the Present*. Cambridge: Cambridge University Press, 2022.

Enstad, Nan. "Fashioning Political Identities: Cultural Studies and the Historical Construction of Political Subjects." *American Quarterly* 50, no. 4 (December 1, 1998): 745–82.

Estes, Nick. *Our History Is the Future*. New York: Verso, 2019.

Estes, Nick, and Jaskiran Dhillon. *Standing with Standing Rock: Voices from the #NoDAPL Movement*. Minneapolis: University of Minnesota Press, 2019.

Evans, Brad. *Liberal Terror*. Cambridge: Polity, 2013.

Eyman, Scott. *John Wayne: The Life and Legend*. New York: Simon and Schuster, 2015.

Farrow, Edward Samuel. *Mountain Scouting: A Hand-Book for Officers and Soldiers on the Frontiers*. Norman: University of Oklahoma Press, 2000.

Fellman, Michael. *In the Name of God and Country: Reconsidering Terrorism in American History*. New Haven, CT: Yale University Press, 2010.

Ferrell, Robert H. *Reminiscences of Conrad S. Babcock: The Old U.S. Army and the New, 1898–1918*. Columbia: University of Missouri Press, 2012.

Fields, Gary. *Enclosure: Palestinian Landscapes in a Historical Mirror*. Oakland: University of California Press, 2017.

Finkel, David. *The Good Soldiers*. New York: Farrar, Straus and Giroux, 2009.

Fitz, Karsten, ed. *Visual Representations of Native Americans: Transnational Contexts and Perspectives*. Heidelberg: Universitätsverlag, 2012.

Fitzgerald, David. *Learning to Forget: US Army Counterinsurgency Doctrine and Practice from Vietnam to Iraq*. Stanford, CA: Stanford University Press, 2013.

———. "Warriors Who Don't Fight: The Post–Cold War United States Army and Debates over Peacekeeping Operations." *Journal of Military History* 85, no. 1 (January 2021): 163–90.

FitzGerald, Frances. *Fire in the Lake: The Vietnamese and the Americans in Vietnam*. Boston: Little, Brown, and Co., 1972.

Flavin, William. *Finding the Balance: U.S. Military and Future Operations*. Carlisle, PA: USAWC, 2011.

Flynn, Matthew J. *Settle and Conquer: Militarism on the American Frontier, 1607–1890*. Jefferson, NC: McFarland & Company, Inc., 2016.

———. "Settle and Conquer: The Ultimate Counterinsurgency Success." *Small Wars & Insurgencies* 32, no. 3 (April 3, 2021): 509–34.

Fogarty, Richard S., and Andrew Tait Jarboe. *Empires in World War I: Shifting Frontiers and Imperial Dynamics in a Global Conflict*. London: I. B. Tauris, 2014.

Ford, Lisa. *Settler Sovereignty: Jurisdiction and Indigenous People in America and Australia, 1788–1836*. Cambridge, MA: Harvard University Press, 2010.

Forth, Aidan. *Barbed-Wire Imperialism: Britain's Empire of Camps, 1876–1903*. Oakland: University of California Press, 2017.

Franco, Jere Bishop. *Crossing the Pond: The Native American Effort in World War II*. College Station: University of North Texas Press, 1999.

Gates, John M. "Indians and Insurrectos: The US Army's Experience with Insurgency." *Parameters* 13 (March 1983).

———. "The Official Historian and the Well-Placed Critic: James A. LeRoy's Assessment of John R. M. Taylor's 'The Philippine Insurrection against the United States.'" *The Public Historian* 7, no. 3 (1985): 57–67.

———. *Schoolbooks and Krags: The United States Army in the Philippines, 1898–1902.* Westport, CT: Greenwood Press, 1973.

Gatewood, Charles B. "The Surrender of Geronimo." *Journal of Arizona History* 27, no. 1 (1986): 53–70.

Geere, Frank. "Our Military Individualism." *JMSI* 39 (1906).

Genetin-Pilawa, C. Joseph. *Crooked Paths to Allotment: The Fight over Federal Indian Policy after the Civil War.* Chapel Hill: University of North Carolina Press, 2012.

Gentile, Gian P. *Wrong Turn: America's Deadly Embrace of Counterinsurgency.* New York: The New Press, 2013.

Gibson, James William. *Warrior Dreams: Paramilitary Culture in Post-Vietnam America.* New York: Hill and Wang, 1994.

Gilman, Nils. *Mandarins of the Future: Modernization Theory in Cold War America.* Baltimore: Johns Hopkins University Press, 2004.

Go, Julian, and Anne L. Foster, eds. *The American Colonial State in the Philippines: Global Perspectives.* Durham, NC: Duke University Press, 2003.

Gómez, Laura E. *Manifest Destinies: The Making of the Mexican American Race.* New York: New York University Press, 2008.

Gondusky, Joseph S., and Michael P. Reiter. "Protecting Military Convoys in Iraq: An Examination of Battle Injuries Sustained by a Mechanized Battalion during Operation Iraqi Freedom II." *Military Medicine* 170, no. 6 (June 2005): 546–49.

Goodman, Jack. *While You Were Gone: A Report on Wartime Life in the United States.* New York: Simon and Schuster, 1946.

Gott, Kendall D. *In Search of an Elusive Enemy: The Victorio Campaign, 1879–1880.* Fort Leavenworth, KS: CSI Press, 2004.

Gott, Kendall D., and Michael G. Brooks. *Security Assistance: U.S. and International Historical Perspectives.* Fort Leavenworth, KS: CSI Press, 2006.

Grandin, Greg. *Empire's Workshop: Latin America, the United States, and the Rise of the New Imperialism.* New York: Metropolitan Books, 2006.

———. *The End of the Myth: From the Frontier to the Border Wall in the Mind of America.* New York: Metropolitan Books, 2019.

Grant, Daragh. "Francisco de Vitoria and Alberico Gentili on the Juridical Status of Native American Polities." *Renaissance Quarterly* 72, no. 3 (ed. 2019): 910–52.

Greene, Jerome A., ed. *Indian War Veterans: Memories of Army Life and Campaigns in the West, 1864–1898.* New York: Savas Beatie, 2007.

———. *January Moon: The Northern Cheyenne Breakout from Fort Robinson, 1878–1879.* Norman: University of Oklahoma Press, 2020.

———. *Washita: The U.S. Army and the Southern Cheyennes, 1867–1869.* Norman: University of Oklahoma Press, 2004.

Greene, Jerome A., and Paul L. Hedren. *Stricken Field: The Little Bighorn Since 1876.* Norman: University of Oklahoma Press, 2008.

Gregory, Derek. *The Colonial Present: Afghanistan, Palestine, and Iraq.* Malden, MA: Blackwell Publishing, 2004.

———. "The Everywhere War." *Geographical Journal* 177, no. 3 (September 1, 2011): 238–50.

Grenier, John. *The First Way of War: American War Making on the Frontier, 1607–1814.* Cambridge: Cambridge University Press, 2005.

Grillot, Thomas. *First Americans: U.S. Patriotism in Indian Country after World War I.* New Haven, CT: Yale University Press, 2018.

Gurman, Hannah, ed. *Hearts and Minds: A People's History of Counterinsurgency.* New York: The New Press, 2013.

Hämäläinen, Pekka. *The Comanche Empire.* New Haven, CT: Yale University Press, 2008.

———. *Lakota America: A New History of Indigenous Power.* New Haven, CT: Yale University Press, 2019.

Hamilton, J. B. "The Evolution of the Dum-Dum Bullet." *British Medical Journal* 1, no. 1950 (May 14, 1898): 1250–51.

Hamilton, Louis M. "Jungle Tactics." *JMSI* 37 (1905): 23–28.

Hardt, Michael, and Antonio Negri. *Commonwealth.* Cambridge, MA: Harvard University Press, 2009.

———. *Multitude: War and Democracy in the Age of Empire.* New York: Penguin, 2005.

Harlow, Barbara, and Mia Carter, eds. *Archives of Empire: Volume 2, The Scramble for Africa.* Durham, NC: Duke University Press, 2004.

Harris, Alexandra N. *Why We Serve: Native Americans in the United States Armed Forces.* Washington, DC: National Museum of the American Indian, 2020.

Harvey, David. *The New Imperialism.* Oxford: New York: Oxford University Press, 2003.

Hawkins, Michael C. "Managing a Massacre: Savagery, Civility, and Gender in Moro Province in the Wake of Bud Dajo." *Philippine Studies* 59, no. 1 (March 2011): 83–105.

Hayashi, Brian Masaru. *Democratizing the Enemy: The Japanese American Internment.* Princeton, NJ: Princeton University Press, 2008.

Headrick, D. R. "The Tools of Imperialism: Technology and the Expansion of European Colonial Empires in the Nineteenth Century." *Journal of Modern History* 51, no. 2 (01 1979): 231–63.

Hedren, Paul L. "Captain Charles King at Sunset Pass." *Journal of Arizona History* 17, no. 3 (1976): 253–64.

Herr, Michael. *Dispatches.* New York: Vintage Books, 1991.

Heyningen, Elizabeth van. "A Tool for Modernisation? The Boer Concentration Camps of the South African War, 1900–1902." *South African Journal of Science* 106, nos. 5–6 (June 5, 2010): 1–10.

Hoffman, Bruce. *Inside Terrorism.* New York: Columbia University Press, 2006.

Hogan, David W. *Raiders or Elite Infantry? The Changing Role of the U.S. Army Rangers from Dieppe to Grenada.* Westport: Greenwood Press, 1992.

Hogan, Michael J. *A Cross of Iron: Harry S. Truman and the Origins of the National Security State, 1945–1954*. Cambridge: Cambridge University Press, 1998.

Hogan, Michael J., and Thomas G. Paterson, eds. *Explaining the History of American Foreign Relations*. Cambridge: Cambridge University Press, 2004.

Hoganson, Kristin L. *Fighting for American Manhood: How Gender Politics Provoked the Spanish-American and Philippine-American Wars*. New Haven, CT: Yale University Press, 1998.

Hoganson, Kristin, and Jay Sexton, eds. *The Cambridge History of America and the World, Volume II: 1820–1900*. Cambridge: Cambridge University Press, 2022.

Holm, Tom. "Fighting a White Man's War: The Extent and Legacy of American Indian Participation in World War II." *Journal of Ethnic Studies* 9, no. 2 (July 1981): 69–81.

———. *Strong Hearts, Wounded Souls: Native American Veterans of the Vietnam War*. Austin: University of Texas Press, 1995.

HoSang, Daniel Martinez, Oneka LaBennett, and Laura Pulido, eds. *Racial Formation in the Twenty-First Century*. Oakland: University of California Press, 2012.

Houten, Tania van den. "Twenty-Fifth Anniversary of the American Indian Community House." *Native Peoples Magazine* 8, no. 3 (Spring 1995): 52–55.

Howard, John K., and H. Wendell Endicott. *Summary Report: British Home Guard*. Massachusetts Committee on Public Safety, 1941.

Hoxie, Frederick E. "From Prison to Homeland: The Cheyenne River Indian Reservation before WWI." *South Dakota History* 10, no. 1 (December 1, 1979): 1–24.

Huber, Thomas M. *Compound Warfare: That Fatal Knot*. Fort Leavenworth, KS: CGSC, 2002.

Huebner, Andrew J. *The Warrior Image: Soldiers in American Culture from the Second World War to the Vietnam Era*. Chapel Hill: University of North Carolina Press, 2008.

Hunt, Michael H. *Ideology and U.S. Foreign Policy*. New Haven, CT: Yale University Press, 1987.

Hutter, Siegfried. "Men of Air Reconnaissance." *Military Review* 23, no. 10 (1944): 89.

Hutton, Paul Andrew. *Phil Sheridan and His Army*. Lincoln: University of Nebraska Press, 1985.

Infantry School. *ST 31-20-1 1950: Operations against Guerrilla Forces*. Fort Benning: The Infantry School, 1950.

Immerman, Richard H., and Petra Goedde, eds. *The Oxford Handbook of the Cold War*. Oxford: Oxford University Press, 2013.

Immerwahr, Daniel. *How to Hide an Empire: A History of the Greater United States*. New York: Farrar, Straus and Giroux, 2019.

Isenberg, Andrew C. *The Destruction of the Bison: An Environmental History, 1750–1920*. Cambridge: Cambridge University Press, 2000.

Jablonsky, David. *War by Land, Sea, and Air.* New Haven, CT: Yale University Press, 2010.

Jacobson, Matthew Frye. *Barbarian Virtues: The United States Encounters Foreign Peoples at Home and Abroad, 1876–1917.* New York: Hill and Wang, 2001.

Jacoby, Karl. "'The Broad Platform of Extermination': Nature and Violence in the Nineteenth-Century North American Borderlands." *Journal of Genocide Research,* no. 2 (2008): 249–67.

———. *Shadows at Dawn: An Apache Massacre and the Violence of History.* New York: Penguin Books, 2009.

Jamieson, Perry D. *Crossing the Deadly Ground: United States Army Tactics, 1865–1899.* Tuscaloosa: University of Alabama Press, 2004.

J.C.G. "Review of Guerilla or Partisan Warfare." *Journal of the United States Cavalry Association* 15, nos. 53–56 (July 1904): 735–36.

Jennings, Eric T. *Imperial Heights: Dalat and the Making and Undoing of French Indochina.* Berkeley: University of California Press, 2011.

Jensen, Benjamin. *Forging the Sword: Doctrinal Change in the U.S. Army.* Stanford, CA: Stanford University Press, 2016.

Johnson, Deidre. *Edward Stratemeyer and the Stratemeyer Syndicate.* New York: Twayne Publishers, 1993.

Johnson, E. S. "Field Service Regulations of the Future." *Military Review* 16, no. 61 (1936): 5–45.

Johnson, James R. "People's War and Conventional Armies." *Military Review* 54, no. 1 (1974): 24–33.

Jones, Spencer. *From Boer War to World War: Tactical Reform of the British Army, 1902–1914.* Norman: University of Oklahoma Press, 2012.

Jung, Moon-Ho. *Menace to Empire: Anticolonial Solidarities and the Transpacific Origins of the US Security State.* Oakland: University of California Press, 2022.

Kan, Sergei A., and Pauline Turner, eds. *New Perspectives on Native North America: Cultures, Histories, and Representations.* Lincoln: University of Nebraska Press, 2009.

Kapadia, Ronak K. *Insurgent Aesthetics: Security and the Queer Life of the Forever War.* Durham, NC: Duke University Press, 2019.

Kaplan, Amy. *The Anarchy of Empire in the Making of U.S. Culture.* Cambridge, MA: Harvard University Press, 2002.

———. *Our American Israel: The Story of an Entangled Alliance.* Cambridge, MA: Harvard University Press, 2018.

———. "Romancing the Empire: The Embodiment of American Masculinity in the Popular Historical Novel of the 1890s." *American Literary History* 2, no. 4 (1990): 659–90.

Kaplan, Amy, and Donald E. Pease, eds. *Cultures of United States Imperialism.* New Americanists. Durham, NC: Duke University Press, 1993.

Kaplan, Fred. *The Insurgents: David Petraeus and the Plot to Change the American Way of War.* New York: Simon and Schuster, 2013.

Kaplan, Robert D. *Imperial Grunts: The American Military on the Ground.* New York: Random House, 2005.

Karuka, Manu. *Empire's Tracks: Indigenous Nations, Chinese Workers, and the Transcontinental Railroad.* Oakland: University of California Press, 2019.

Kautz, August. "Military Education for the Masses." *JMSI* 17 (1895): 486–501.

Keeler, Matthew, ed. "An Oral History of General Jack N. Merritt." Carlisle, PA: U.S. Army Military History Institute, 2005.

Kelman, Ari. *A Misplaced Massacre: Struggling over the Memory of Sand Creek.* Cambridge, MA: Harvard University Press, 2013.

Kennedy, David M. *Freedom from Fear: The American People in Depression and War, 1929–1945.* Oxford: Oxford University Press, 1999.

Kent, James. *Commentaries on American Law.* Vol. 1. Birmingham: Gryphon, 1986.

Khalili, Laleh. "The Location of Palestine in Global Counterinsurgencies," *International Journal of Middle East Studies* 42, no. 3 (August 1, 2010): 413–33.

———. *Time in the Shadows: Confinement in Counterinsurgencies.* Stanford, CA: Stanford University Press, 2012.

Kienscherf, Markus. "A Programme of Global Pacification: US Counterinsurgency Doctrine and the Biopolitics of Human (in)Security." *Security Dialogue* 42, no. 6 (December 1, 2011): 517–35.

Kieran, David. *Signature Wounds: The Untold Story of the Military's Mental Health Crisis.* New York: University Press, 2019.

Kieran, David, and Edwin A. Martini, eds. *At War: The Military and American Culture in the Twentieth Century and Beyond.* New Brunswick, NJ: Rutgers University Press, 2018.

Killblane, Richard E. *Circle the Wagons: The History of US Army Convoy Security.* Fort Leavenworth, KS: CSI Press, 2005.

Killblane, Richard, and Jake McNiece, *The Filthy Thirteen: From the Dustbowl to Hitler's Eagle's Nest—The True Story of the 101st Airborne's Most Legendary Squad of Combat Paratroopers.* Philadelphia: Casemate, 2003.

Kim, Jodi. *Settler Garrison: Debt Imperialism, Militarism, and Transpacific Imaginaries.* Durham, NC: Duke University Press, 2022.

Kim, Monica. *The Interrogation Rooms of the Korean War: The Untold History.* Princeton, NJ: Princeton University Press, 2019.

Kinevan, Marcos E. *Frontier Cavalryman: Lieutenant John Bigelow with the Buffalo Soldiers in Texas.* El Paso: Texas Western Press, 1998.

King, C. Richard. *Unsettling America: The Uses of Indianness in the 21st Century.* Lanham, MD: Rowman & Littlefield, 2013.

King, Charles. *Campaigning with Crook: And Stories of Army Life.* New York: Harper & Brothers Publishers, 1902.

———. *Captured: The Story of Sandy Ray.* New York: Grosset & Dunlap, 1906.

———. *Comrades in Arms: A Tale of Two Hemispheres.* New York: Grosset & Dunlap, 1904.

———. *A Conquering Corps Badge, and Other Stories of the Philippines.* Milwaukee: L.A. Rhodes Company, 1902.

———. *Found in the Philippines: The Story of a Woman's Letters.* New York: F.T. Neely, 1899.

———. *The Further Story of Lieutenant Sandy Ray.* New York: R.F. Fenno & Company, 1906.

296 | Bibliography

———. "Memories of a Busy Life." *The Wisconsin Magazine of History* 6, no. 1 (1922): 3–39.

———. *Starlight Ranch, and Other Stories of Army Life on the Frontier*. Philadelphia: J.B. Lippincott Company, 1890.

———. *Sunset Pass; or, Running the Gauntlet through Apache Land*. New York: American Publishers Corporation, 1890.

King, Michael J. *Rangers: Selected Combat Operations in World War II*. Fort Leavenworth, KS: CSI, 1985.

King, Thomas. *The Inconvenient Indian: A Curious Account of Native People in North America*. Minneapolis: University of Minnesota Press, 2013.

Kinsella, Helen M. *The Image before the Weapon: A Critical History of the Distinction between Combatant and Civilian*. Ithaca, NY: Cornell University Press, 2011.

Kramer, Paul A. *The Blood of Government: Race, Empire, the United States, and the Philippines*. Chapel Hill: University of North Carolina Press, 2006.

Krebs, Paula M. *Gender, Race, and the Writing of Empire: Public Discourse and the Boer War*. Cambridge: Cambridge University Press, 1999.

Krepinevich, Andrew F. *The Army and Vietnam*. Baltimore: Johns Hopkins University Press, 1986.

Krouse, Susan Applegate. *North American Indians in the Great War*. Lincoln: University of Nebraska Press, 2007.

Kuitenbrouwer, Vincent. *War of Words: Dutch Pro-Boer Propaganda and the South African War (1899–1902)*. Amsterdam: Amsterdam University Press, 2012.

Kwon, Heonik. *After the Massacre: Commemoration and Consolation in Ha My and My Lai*. Berkeley: University of California Press, 2006.

Laderman, Scott, and Tim Gruenewald, ed. *Imperial Benevolence: U.S. Foreign Policy and American Popular Culture since 9/11*. Oakland: University of California Press, 2018.

LaDuke, Winona, and Sean Aaron Cruz. *The Militarization of Indian Country*. East Lansing: Michigan State University Press, 2013.

LaFeber, Walter. *The American Age: United States Foreign Policy at Home and Abroad since 1750*. New York: Norton, 1989.

Lahti, Janne. *Cultural Construction of Empire: The U.S. Army in Arizona and New Mexico*. Lincoln: Nebraska University Press, 2012.

Laqueur, Walter. *The New Terrorism: Fanaticism and the Arms of Mass Destruction*. Oxford: Oxford University Press, 2000.

Larrinaga, Miguel De, and Marc G. Doucet. "Sovereign Power and the Biopolitics of Human Security." *Security Dialogue* 39, no. 5 (October 1, 2008): 517–37.

Latham, Michael E. *The Right Kind of Revolution: Modernization, Development, and U.S. Foreign Policy from the Cold War to the Present*. Ithaca, NY: Cornell University Press, 2011.

Lawlor, Ruth. "Contested Crimes: Race, Gender, and Nation in Histories of GI Sexual Violence, World War II." *Journal of Military History* 84, no. 2 (April 2020): 541–69.

Lawrence, Mark Atwood. *The Vietnam War: A Concise International History*. Oxford: Oxford University Press, 2008.

Leahy, Todd, and Nathan Wilson. *Historical Dictionary of Native American Movements*. Lanham, MD: Rowman & Littlefield, 2016.

Leckie, William H. *The Military Conquest of the Southern Plains*. Norman: University of Oklahoma Press, 1963.

Lee, Wayne E. *Barbarians and Brothers: Anglo-American Warfare, 1500–1865*. Oxford: Oxford University Press, 2011.

———. "Mind and Matter-Cultural Analysis in American Military History: A Look at the State of the Field." *Journal of American History* 93, no. 4 (2007): 1116–42.

Lee, Wayne E., Anthony E. Carlson, David L. Preston, and David Silbey, eds. *The Other Face of Battle: America's Forgotten Wars and the Experience of Combat*. Oxford: Oxford University Press, 2021.

Leffler, Melvyn P. *For the Soul of Mankind: The United States, the Soviet Union, and the Cold War*. New York: Hill and Wang, 2007.

———. *A Preponderance of Power: National Security, the Truman Administration, and the Cold War*. Stanford, CA: Stanford University Press, 1992.

Lepore, Jill. *The Name of War: King Philip's War and the Origins of American Identity*. New York: Knopf, 1998.

Levario, Miguel Antonio. *Militarizing the Border: When Mexicans Became the Enemy*. College Station: Texas A&M University Press, 2012.

Levy, "Yank" Bert. *Guerilla Warfare*. Boulder, CO: Paladin Press, 1964.

Lewis, G. C. "The Stopping Power of a Bullet." *Journal of the United States Cavalry Association* 17, no. 61 (July 1906): 121–36.

Liboiron, Max. *Pollution Is Colonialism*. Durham, NC: Duke University Press, 2021.

Lieber, Francis. *Instructions for the Government of Armies of the United States, in the Field*. New York: D. Van Nostrand, 1863.

Linn, Brian McAllister. *The Echo of Battle: The Army's Way of War*. Cambridge, MA: Harvard University Press, 2007.

———. *Guardians of Empire: The U.S. Army and the Pacific, 1902–1940*. Chapel Hill: University of North Carolina Press, 1997.

———. *The Philippine War, 1899–1902*. Lawrence: University Press of Kansas, 2000.

———. *The U.S. Army and Counterinsurgency in the Philippine War, 1899–1902*. Chapel Hill: University of North Carolina Press, 2000.

Little, Douglas. *Us versus Them: The United States, Radical Islam, and the Rise of the Green Threat*. Chapel Hill: University of North Carolina Press, 2016.

Logt, Mark van de. *War Party in Blue: Pawnee Scouts in the U.S. Army*. Norman: University of Oklahoma Press, 2012.

Low, Denise, and Ramon Powers. *Northern Cheyenne Ledger Art by Fort Robinson Breakout Survivors*. Lincoln: University of Nebraska Press, 2020.

Lowe, Lisa. *The Intimacies of Four Continents*. Durham: Duke University Press Books, 2015.

Lubin, Alex. *Never-Ending War on Terror*. Oakland: University of California Press, 2021.

Lundy, Mike, and Rich Creed. "The Return of U.S. Army Field Manual 3-0, Operations." *Military Review* 97, no. 6 (December 2017): 14–21.

Lutz, Catherine, ed. *The Bases of Empire the Global Struggle against U.S. Military Posts*. New York: New York University Press, 2009.

Macdonald, Robert. *Sons of the Empire*. Toronto: University of Toronto Press, 1993.

Maddox, Lucy. *Removals: Nineteenth-Century American Literature and the Politics of Indian Affairs*. Oxford: Oxford University Press, 1991.

Madley, Benjamin. *An American Genocide: The United States and the California Indian Catastrophe, 1846–1873*. New Haven, CT: Yale University Press, 2016.

Maguire, Peter H. *Law and War: International Law and American History*. New York: Columbia University Press, 2010.

Mamdani, Mahmood. *Good Muslim, Bad Muslim: America, the Cold War, and the Roots of Terror*. New York: Pantheon Books, 2004.

———. *Neither Settler nor Native*. Cambridge, MA: Harvard University Press, 2020.

Man, Simeon. *Soldiering through Empire: Race and the Making of the Decolonizing Pacific*. Oakland: University of California Press, 2018.

Marcy, Randolph Barnes. *The Prairie Traveler: A Hand-Book for Overland Expeditions*. Denver: N. Mumey, 1859.

———. *Thirty Years of Army Life on the Border*. New York: Harper & Brothers, 1866.

Marolda, Edward J., and R. Blake Dunnavent. *Combat at Close Quarters: Warfare on the Rivers and Canals of Vietnam*. Washington, DC: Department of the Navy, 2015.

Matikkala, Mira. *Empire and Imperial Ambition: Liberty, Englishness and Anti-Imperialism in Late Victorian Britain*. London: I. B. Tauris, 2011.

Mazower, Mark. *Dark Continent: Europe's Twentieth Century*. New York: Vintage Books, 2009.

McAlister, Melani. *Epic Encounters: Culture, Media, and U.S. Interests in the Middle East Since 1945*. Oakland: University of California Press, 2005.

McDonald, Neil. "Colonel Bellah and Admiral Ford." *Quadrant* 57, no. 12 (December 1, 2013): 98–101.

McDonald, William. *A History of the Laurel Brigade*. Edited by Bushrod C. Washington. Baltimore: Mrs. Kate S. McDonald, 1907.

McFate, Montgomery. "Anthropology and Counterinsurgency: The Strange Story of Their Curious Relationship." *Military Review; Fort Leavenworth* 85, no. 2 (April 2005): 24–37.

McMaster, H. R. *Dereliction of Duty: Lyndon Johnson, Robert McNamara, the Joint Chiefs of Staff, and the Lies That Led to Vietnam*. New York: HarperCollins, 1997.

McNickle, D'Arcy. *They Came Here First: The Epic of the American Indian*. New York: Harper & Row, 1975.

Medovoi, Leerom. "Global Society Must Be Defended: Biopolitics without Boundaries." *Social Text* 25, no. 2 (91) (June 1, 2007): 53–79.

Mendoza, Victor Román. *Metroimperial Intimacies: Fantasy, Racial-Sexual Governance, and the Philippines in U.S. Imperialism, 1899–1913.* Durham, NC: Duke University Press, 2015.

M.F.S. "Review of Tactics for Beginners," *Journal of the United States Cavalry Association* 15, nos. 53–56 (July 1904): 743–48.

Miles, Nelson A. *The Philippines Reports by Lieutenant-General Nelson A. Miles, U.S.A. Reprinted from Army and Navy Journal, May 2, 1903.* Boston: Anti Imperialist League, 1909.

Miles, Tiya. *Ties That Bind: The Story of an Afro-Cherokee Family in Slavery and Freedom.* Berkeley: University of California Press, 2006.

Miller, Bonnie M. *From Liberation to Conquest: The Visual and Popular Cultures of the Spanish-American War of 1898.* Amherst: University of Massachusetts Press, 2011.

Miller, Stuart Creighton. *"Benevolent Assimilation": The American Conquest of the Philippines, 1899–1903.* New Haven, CT: Yale University Press, 1982.

Millett, Allan R., Peter Maslowski, and William B. Feis. *For the Common Defense.* New York: Free Press, 2012.

Mitchell, Timothy. *Carbon Democracy: Political Power in the Age of Oil.* New York: Verso Books, 2011.

Momaday, N. Scott. *House Made of Dawn.* New York: Harper & Row, 1968.

Moyn, Samuel. *Humane: How the United States Abandoned Peace and Reinvented War.* New York: Farrar, Straus and Giroux, 2021.

Murphy, Gretchen. *Shadowing the White Man's Burden: U.S. Imperialism and the Problem of the Color Line.* New York: New York University Press, 2016.

Murray, Williamson, and Peter R. Mansoor. *Hybrid Warfare: Fighting Complex Opponents from the Ancient World to the Present.* Cambridge: Cambridge University Press, 2012.

Murray, Williamson, and Allan Reed Millett. *A War to Be Won: Fighting the Second World War.* Cambridge, MA: Harvard University Press, 2009.

Naidu, M. V. "Military Power, Militarism and Militarization: An Attempt at Clarification and Classification." *Peace Research* 17, no. 1 (1985): 2–10.

Nasson, Bill. *The South African War, 1899–1902.* London: Arnold, 1999.

Nebolon, Juliet. "'Life Given Straight from the Heart': Settler Militarism, Biopolitics, and Public Health in Hawai'i during World War II." *American Quarterly* 69, no. 1 (2017): 23–45.

———. "Settler-Military Camps: Internment and Prisoner of War Camps across the Pacific Islands during World War II." *Journal of Asian American Studies* 24, no. 2 (2021): 229–335.

Neff, Stephen C. *War and the Law of Nations: A General History.* Cambridge: Cambridge University Press, 2005.

Network of Concerned Anthropologists. *The Counter-Counterinsurgency Manual; or, Notes on Demilitarizing American Society.* Chicago: Prickly Paradigm Press, 2009.

Nez, Chester, and Judith Schiess Avila. *Code Talker*. New York: Berkley Caliber, 2011.

Noe, Kenneth W., and Shannon H. Wilson, eds. *The Civil War in Appalachia: Collected Essays*. Knoxville: University of Tennessee Press, 2004.

O'Brien, Jean M. *Firsting and Lasting: Writing Indians out of Existence in New England*. Minneapolis: University of Minnesota Press, 2010.

O'Connell, Aaron B., ed. *Our Latest Longest War: Losing Hearts and Minds in Afghanistan*. Chicago: University of Chicago Press, 2017.

———. *Underdogs: The Making of the Modern Marine Corps*. Cambridge, MA: Harvard University Press, 2014.

Offenburger, Andrew. *Frontiers in the Gilded Age: Adventure, Capitalism, and Dispossession from Southern Africa to the U.S.-Mexican Borderlands, 1880–1917*. New Haven, CT: Yale University Press, 2019.

Ostler, Jeffrey. *The Lakotas and the Black Hills: The Struggle for Sacred Ground*. New York: Viking, 2010.

———. *The Plains Sioux and U.S. Colonialism from Lewis and Clark to Wounded Knee*. Cambridge: Cambridge University Press, 2004.

———. *Surviving Genocide: Native Nations and the United States from the American Revolution to Bleeding Kansas*. New Haven, CT: Yale University Press, 2019.

Pakenham, Thomas. *Boer War*. New York: Random House, 1979.

Paret, Peter, Gordon A. Craig, and Felix Gilbert, eds. *Makers of Modern Strategy from Machiavelli to the Nuclear Age*. Princeton, NJ: Princeton University Press, 2010.

Parker, Geoffrey. *The Military Revolution: Military Innovation and the Rise of the West, 1500–1800*. Cambridge: Cambridge University Press, 1989.

Parker, John Henry. *Tactical Organization and Uses of Machine Guns in the Field*. Kansas City: Hudson-Kimberly Publishing Company, 1899.

Parsons, Lynn Hudson. *The Birth of Modern Politics: Andrew Jackson, John Quincy Adams, and the Election of 1828*. Oxford: Oxford University Press, 2009.

Pascoe, Peggy. *What Comes Naturally: Miscegenation Law and the Making of Race in America*. Oxford: Oxford University Press, 2009.

Pateman, Carole, and Charles Mills. *Contract and Domination*. Cambridge: Polity, 2007.

Pearson, Ellen Holmes. *Remaking Custom: Law and Identity in the Early American Republic*. Charlottesville: University of Virginia Press, 2011.

Pellow, David Naguib. *Total Liberation: The Power and Promise of Animal Rights and the Radical Earth Movement*. Minneapolis: University of Minnesota Press, 2014.

Perrine, Major David. "Review of 'Tell Baker to Strike Them Hard!': Incident on the Marias, 23 January 1870." *Military Review* 50, no. 8 (1970).

Perry, Thomas Sergeant, ed. *The Life and Letters of Francis Lieber*. Boston: James R. Osgood and Company, 1882.

Pickering, Leslie James. *Earth Liberation Front: 1997–2002*. Minneapolis, MN: Arissa Media Group, 2007.

Pieris, Anoma, and Lynne Horiuchi. *The Architecture of Confinement: Incarceration Camps of the Pacific War*. Cambridge: Cambridge University Press, 2022.

Prados, John. *The US Special Forces: What Everyone Needs to Know*. Oxford: Oxford University Press, 2015.

Prashad, Vijay. *Uncle Swami: South Asians in America Today*. New York: The New Press, 2012.

Preston, Andrew. "Monsters Everywhere: A Genealogy of National Security," *Diplomatic History* 83, no. 3 (June 2014): 477–500.

Preston, David L. *Braddock's Defeat: The Battle of the Monongahela and the Road to Revolution*. Oxford: Oxford University Press, 2015.

Price, George Frederic. *Across the Continent with the Fifth Cavalry*. New York: D. Van Nostrand, 1883.

Pryor, Jaclyn. *Time Slips: Queer Temporalities, Contemporary Performance, and the Hole of History*. Evanston, IL: Northwestern University Press, 2017.

Puar, Jasbir K. *The Right to Maim: Debility, Capacity, Disability*. Durham, NC: Duke University Press, 2017.

———. *Terrorist Assemblages: Homonationalism in Queer Times*. Durham, NC: Duke University Press, 2007.

Putnam, Samuel. *Memoirs of Andrew Jackson, Major-General in the Army of the United States, and Commander in Chief of the Division of the South*. Hartford, CT: J. & W. Russell, 1819.

Raines, Edgar F. "Major General J. Franklin Bell, U.S.A.: The Education of a Soldier, 1856–1899." *The Register of the Kentucky Historical Society* 83, no. 4 (1985): 315–46.

Ramsey, Robert D., III. *A Masterpiece of Counterguerrilla Warfare: BG J. Franklin Bell in the Philippines, 1901–1902*. Fort Leavenworth, KS: CSI Press, 2007.

Renda, Mary A. *Taking Haiti: Military Occupation and the Culture of U.S. Imperialism, 1915–1940*. Chapel Hill: University of North Carolina Press, 2001.

Resende-Santos, João. *Neorealism, States, and the Modern Mass Army*. Cambridge: Cambridge University Press, 2007.

Richter, Daniel K. *Facing East from Indian Country: A Native History of Early America*. Cambridge, MA: Harvard University Press, 2001.

Rico, Monica. *Nature's Noblemen: Transatlantic Masculinities and the Nineteenth-Century American West*. New Haven, CT: Yale University Press, 2013.

Roberts, David. *Once They Moved Like the Wind: Cochise, Geronimo, and the Apache Wars*. New York: Touchstone, 1994.

Robinson, Greg. *A Tragedy of Democracy: Japanese Confinement in North America*. New York: Columbia University Press, 2009.

Roces, Mina. "'These Guys Came Out Looking Like Movie Actors': Filipino Dress and Consumer Practices in the United States, 1920s–1930s." *Pacific Historical Review* 85, no. 4 (2016): 532–76.

Rockenbach, S. D. "The Service Pistol," *Journal of the United States Cavalry Association* 16, no. 57–60 (July 1905): 773–75.

Rodenbough, Theophilus F., and William Lawrence Haskin. *The Army of the United States: Historical Sketches of Staff and Line with Portraits of Generals-in-Chief.* New York: Maynard, Merrill, & CO., 1896.

Rosen, Deborah A. *Border Law: The First Seminole War and American Nationhood.* Cambridge MA: Harvard University Press, 2015.

Rosier, Paul C. *Serving Their Country: American Indian Politics and Patriotism in the Twentieth Century.* Cambridge, MA: Harvard University Press, 2009.

Rostow, W. W. *The Stages of Economic Growth: A Non-Communist Manifesto.* Cambridge: Cambridge University Press, 1990.

Roth, Russell. *Muddy Glory: America's "Indian Wars" in the Philippines, 1899–1935.* W. Hanover: Christopher Publishing House, 1981.

Russell, A. H. "What Is the Use of a Regular Army in This Country?" *JMSI* 24 (1899): 327–30.

Russell, Don, and Paul L. Hedren. *Campaigning with King: Charles King, Chronicler of the Old Army.* Lincoln: University of Nebraska Press, 1991.

"Russian and German Tactics in World War II." *Military Review* 29, no. 6 (1949): 100–103.

Sagala, Sandra K. *Buffalo Bill on the Silver Screen: The Films of William F. Cody.* Norman: University of Oklahoma Press, 2013.

Saldaña-Portillo, María Josefina. *Indian Given: Racial Geographies across Mexico and the United States.* Durham, NC: Duke University Press, 2016.

Schrader, Stuart. *Badges without Borders: How Global Counterinsurgency Transformed American Policing.* Oakland: University of California Press, 2019.

Schubert, Frank N. *Other Than War: The American Military Experience and Operations in the Post–Cold War Decade.* Washington, DC: GPO, 2013.

Scott, Hugh Lenox. *Some Memories of a Soldier.* New York: The Century Co., 1928.

Scott, James Brown. *The Hague Peace Conferences of 1899 and 1907.* 2 vols. Baltimore: Johns Hopkins University Press, 1909.

———. *The Proceedings of the Hague Peace Conferences: Translation of the Official Texts: The Conferences of 1899 and 1907.* New York: Oxford University Press, 1920.

Sexton, William Thaddeus. *Soldiers in the Sun: An Adventure in Imperialism.* Freeport: Books for Libraries Press, 1971.

Shah, Nayan. *Contagious Divides: Epidemics and Race in San Francisco's Chinatown.* Oakland: University of California Press, 2001.

———. *Stranger Intimacy: Contesting Race, Sexuality and the Law in the North American West.* Berkeley: University of California Press, 2012.

Shay, Michael E., ed. *A Civilian in Lawton's 1899 Philippine Campaign: The Letters of Robert D. Carter.* Columbia: University of Missouri Press, 2013.

———. *Henry Ware Lawton: Union Infantryman, Frontier Soldier, Charismatic Warrior.* Columbia: University of Missouri Press, 2017.

Sheehan-Dean, Aaron. *The Calculus of Violence: How Americans Fought the Civil War.* Cambridge, MA: Harvard University Press, 2018.

Sheridan, Philip Henry. *Personal Memoirs of P. H. Sheridan, General United States Army.* Vol. 2. New York: C. L. Webster & Company, 1888.

Sherry, Michael S. *In the Shadow of War: The United States Since the 1930's.* New Haven, CT: Yale University Press, 1995.

———. *The Rise of American Air Power: The Creation of Armageddon.* New Haven, CT: Yale University Press, 1987.

Shy, John W. *A People Numerous and Armed: Reflections on the Military Struggle for American Independence.* Ann Arbor: University of Michigan Press, 1990.

Silbey, David J. *A War of Frontier and Empire: The Philippine-American War, 1899–1902.* New York: Hill and Wang, 2008.

Silko, Leslie Marmon. *Ceremony.* New York: Penguin, 2006.

Silliman, Stephen W. "The 'Old West' in the Middle East: U.S. Military Metaphors in Real and Imagined Indian Country." *American Anthropologist* 110, no. 2 (June 2008): 237–47.

Silver, Peter. *Our Savage Neighbors: How Indian War Transformed Early America.* New York: W. W. Norton & Company, 2009.

Silverman, David J. *Thundersticks: Firearms and the Violent Transformation of Native America.* Cambridge, MA: Harvard University Press, 2016.

Simpson, Audra. *Mohawk Interruptus: Political Life across the Borders of Settler States.* Durham, NC: Duke University Press, 2014.

Singh, Nikhil Pal. *Race and America's Long War.* Oakland: University of California Press, 2017.

Skelton, Ike. "America's Frontier Wars: Lessons for Asymmetric Conflicts." *Military Review* July–August 2014.

Sleeper-Smith, Susan, Juliana Barr, Jean M. O'Brien, Nancy Shoemaker, and Scott Manning Stevens, eds. *Why You Can't Teach United States History without American Indians.* Chapel Hill: University of North Carolina Press, 2015.

Slotkin, Richard. *The Fatal Environment: The Myth of the Frontier in the Age of Industrialization, 1800–1890.* New York: Atheneum, 1985.

———. *Gunfighter Nation: Myth of the Frontier in Twentieth-Century America.* New York: Atheneum, 1992.

———. *Regeneration Through Violence: The Mythology of the American Frontier, 1600–1860.* Middletown, CT: Wesleyan University Press, 1973.

Smith, Anthony. *Machine Gun: The Story of the Men and the Weapon That Changed the Face of War.* New York: St. Martin's Paperbacks, 2004.

Smith, C. C. "The Mindanao Moro," *Journal of the United States Cavalry Association* 17, no. 61 (July 1906): 287–308.

Smith, Paul Chaat, and Robert Warrior. *Like a Hurricane: The Indian Movement from Alcatraz to Wounded Knee.* New York: New Press, 1996.

Smith, Sherry L. *The View from Officers' Row: Army Perceptions of Western Indians.* Tucson: University of Arizona Press, 1990.

Smith, Thomas T. "West Point and the Indian Wars 1802–1891." *Military History of the West* 24, no. 1 (1994): 24–55.

Smith, William, and Charles Guillaume Frédéric Dumas. *Historical Account of Bouquet's Expedition against the Ohio Indians, in 1764.* Cincinnati: R. Clarke, 1868.

Special Warfare. Washington, DC: Office, Chief of Information, Department of the Army, 1962.

Spies, S. B. *Methods of Barbarism? Roberts and Kitchener and Civilians in the Boer Republics, January 1900–May 1902*. Cape Town: Human & Rousseau, 1977.

Stabler, Hollis Dorion. *No One Ever Asked Me: The World War II Memoirs of an Omaha Indian Soldier*. Lincoln: University of Nebraska Press, 2005.

Stanley, Peter W. *Reappraising an Empire: New Perspectives on Philippine-American History*. Cambridge, MA: Harvard University Press, 1984.

Stentiford, Barry M. *The American Home Guard: The State Militia in the Twentieth Century*. College Station: Texas A&M University Press, 2002.

Stiles, T. J. *Custer's Trials: A Life on the Frontier of a New America*. New York: Alfred A. Knopf, 2015.

Stocking, George W. *Colonial Situations: Essays on the Contextualization of Ethnographic Knowledge*. Madison: University of Wisconsin Press, 1992.

Storey, Moorfield, and Julian Codman, *"Marked Severities" in Philippine Warfare. An Analysis of the Law and Facts Bearing on the Action and Utterances of President Roosevelt and Secretary Root*. Boston: G.H. Ellis Co., 1902.

Stratemeyer, Edward. *The Campaign of the Jungle; or, Under Lawton through Luzon*. Boston: Lothrop, Lee & Shepard, 1900.

Stur, Heather Marie. *Beyond Combat: Women and Gender in the Vietnam War Era*. Cambridge: Cambridge University Press, 2011.

Summers, Harry G. *On Strategy: A Critical Analysis of the Vietnam War*. New York: Presidio Press, 1982.

Sutherland, Daniel E. *Savage Conflict: The Decisive Role of Guerrillas in the American Civil War*. Chapel Hill: University of North Carolina Press, 2009.

Sykes, Tom. *Imagining Manila: Literature, Empire and Orientalism*. New York: Bloomsbury, 2021.

Takezawa, Yasuko I. *Breaking the Silence: Redress and Japanese American Ethnicity*. Ithaca, NY: Cornell University Press, 2019.

Tate, James P., ed. *The American Military on the Frontier*. Washington, DC: Office of Air Force History, US Air Force, 1978.

Tate, Michael L. *The Frontier Army in the Settlement of the West*. Norman: University of Oklahoma Press, 1999.

Taylor, John R. M. *The Philippine Insurrection against the United States*. Vol. 2. Pasay City, Philippines: Eugenio Lopez Foundation, 1971.

Thompson, John A. "The Exaggeration of American Vulnerability: The Anatomy of a Tradition." *Diplomatic History* 16, no. 1 (1992): 23–43.

Thrasher, Steven W. "Talking Happiness, Security, and Counterinsurgency with Laleh Khalili." *Contexts* 15, no. 1 (February 1, 2016): 8–10.

Tomes, Robert, William Natter III, and Paul Brister, eds. *Hybrid Warfare and Transnational Threats: Perspectives for an Era of Persistent Conflict*. Lexington, MA: Council for Emerging National Security Affairs, 2011.

Tompkins, Paul J., Jr. *Irregular Warfare: Annotated Bibliography, Assessing Revolutionary and Insurgent Strategies*. Fort Bragg, NC: United States Army Special Operations Command, 2011.

Tone, John Lawrence. *The Fatal Knot: The Guerrilla War in Navarre and the Defeat of Napoleon in Spain*. Chapel Hill: University of North Carolina Press, 1994.

Trudeau, Arthur G. "Some Military Aspects of American Statecraft." *Military Review* 31, no. 3 (1951): 3–21.

———. "Tell Them Why." *Military Review* 23, no. 11 (1944): 37–39.

Truscott, Lucian King, Jr. *Command Missions: A Personal Story*. New York: Dutton, 1954.

Tucker, David, and Christopher J. Lamb. *United States Special Operations Forces*. New York: Columbia University Press, 2019.

Turse, Nick. *Kill Anything That Moves: The Real American War in Vietnam*. New York: Picador, 2013.

Tyler, Orville Z., Jr. *The History of Fort Leavenworth, 1937–1951*. Fort Leavenworth, KS: CGSC, 1951.

United States Army and Marine Corps. *The U.S. Army/Marine Corps Counterinsurgency Field Manual*. Chicago: University of Chicago Press, 2007.

Utley, Harold H. "An Introduction to the Tactics and Technique of Small Wars." *Marine Corps Gazette* 15, no. 5 (May 1931): 50–53.

Utley, Robert M. *Frontier Regulars: The United States Army and the Indian, 1866–1891*. New York: Macmillan, 1974.

Van Meter, Henry Hooker. *The Truth about the Philippines, from Official Records and Authentic Sources*. Chicago: The Liberty League, 1900.

Vattel, Emer de. *The Law of Nations; or, Principles of the Law of Nature, Applied to the Conduct and Affairs of Nations and Sovereigns*. Philadelphia: T. & J.W. Johnson, 1844.

Vaughan, Alden T. "'Expulsion of the Salvages': English Policy and the Virginia Massacre of 1622." *The William and Mary Quarterly* 35, no. 1 (1978): 57–84.

Veracini, Lorenzo. *Settler Colonialism: A Theoretical Overview*. New York: Palgrave Macmillan, 2010.

Vestal, Allan W. "The First Wartime Water Torture by Americans." *Maine Law Review* 69 (2017): 1–66.

Vimalassery, Manu, Juliana Hu Pegues, and Alyosha Goldstein. "Introduction: On Colonial Unknowing," *Theory & Event* 19, no. 4 (2016).

Vitale, Alex S. *The End of Policing*. London: Verso, 2017.

Vizenor, Gerald. *Manifest Manners: Postindian Warriors of Survivance*. Hanover, NH: Wesleyan University Press, 1994.

Von Eschen, Penny M. *Satchmo Blows Up the World: Jazz Ambassadors Play the Cold War*. Cambridge, MA: Harvard University Press, 2006.

Von Lindenau, Lieutenant-Colonel. "What Lessons Can We Draw from the Boer War for Our Infantry Attack?" *JMSI* 32 (1903): 129–36.

Wagner, Arthur L. "Combined Maneuvers of the Regular Army and Organized Militia." *JMSI* 36 (1905): 62–87.

———. "From the U.S. Military Academy, April 1903." *Journal of the United States Cavalry Association* 14 (April 1903): 150–55.

———. "The Military Necessities of the United States, and the Best Provisions for Meeting Them." *JMSI* 5 (1884): 237–68.

———. *Organization and Tactics*. New York: B. Westermann and Co., 1895.

———. *The Service of Security and Information*. Kansas City: Hudson-Kimberly Pub. Co., 1903.

Wagner, Kim A. "Expanding Bullets and Savage Warfare." *History Workshop Journal* 88 (September 2019): 281–87.

———. "Savage Warfare: Violence and the Rule of Colonial Difference in Early British Counterinsurgency." *History Workshop Journal* 85 (Spring 2018): 217–37.

Wald, Priscilla, and Michael A. Elliott, eds. *The Oxford History of the Novel in English: The American Novel 1870–1940.* Oxford: Oxford University Press, 2014.

Waltz, F. R. "Infantry in Offensive Combat." *Military Review* 19, no. 75 (1939): 65–75.

Washington, George. *The Papers of George Washington: Revolutionary War Series, Volume 20, 8 April–31 May 1779.* Edited by Philander D. Chase and William M. Ferrara. Charlottesville: University Press of Virginia, 1985.

Weigley, Russell Frank. *The American Way of War: A History of United States Military Strategy and Policy.* Bloomington: Indiana University Press, 1977.

———. *History of the United States Army.* Bloomington: Indiana University Press, 1984.

———. *Towards an American Army: Military Thought from Washington to Marshall.* New York: Columbia University Press, 1962.

Welch, Richard E. "American Atrocities in the Philippines: The Indictment and the Response." *Pacific Historical Review* 43, no. 2 (1974): 233–53.

Wesling, Meg. *Empire's Proxy: American Literature and U.S. Imperialism in the Philippines.* New York: New York University Press, 2011.

West, Elliott. *The Contested Plains: Indians, Goldseekers, and the Rush to Colorado.* Lawrence: University Press of Kansas, 1998.

Westad, Odd Arne. *The Global Cold War: Third World Interventions and the Making of Our Times.* Cambridge: Cambridge University Press, 2005.

Westmoreland, William C. *A Soldier Reports.* Garden City, NY: Doubleday, 1976.

Wexler, Laura. *Tender Violence: Domestic Visions in an Age of U.S. Imperialism.* Chapel Hill: University of North Carolina Press, 2000.

Wharton, Francis. *A Digest of International Law of the United States.* Vol. 3. Washington, DC: GPO, 1886.

Wheaton, Henry. *Elements of International Law.* Vol. 1. London: Stevens and Sons, 1929.

White, Richard. *Railroaded: The Transcontinentals and the Making of Modern America.* New York: W. W. Norton, 2011.

———. *The Republic for Which It Stands: The United States during Reconstruction and the Gilded Age, 1865–1896.* Oxford: Oxford University Press, 2017.

Whitman, James Q. *Hitler's American Model: The United States and the Making of Nazi Race Law.* Princeton, NJ: Princeton University Press, 2017.

Whittingham, Daniel. *Charles E. Callwell and the British Way in Warfare.* Cambridge: Cambridge University Press, 2020.

Wilkins, David E., and K. Tsianina Lomawaima, *Uneven Ground: American Indian Sovereignty and Federal Law.* Norman: University of Oklahoma Press, 2001.

Williams, Robert A., Jr. *The American Indian in Western Legal Thought: The Discourses of Conquest*. Oxford: Oxford University Press, 1992.

Witt, John Fabian. *Lincoln's Code: The Laws of War in American History*. New York: Free Press, 2012.

Wolfe, Patrick. *Settler Colonialism and the Transformation of Anthropology: The Politics and Poetics of an Ethnographic Event*. London: Cassell, 1999.

———. *Traces of History: Elementary Structures of Race*. London: Verso, 2016.

Woodward, David. *The American Army and the First World War*. Cambridge: Cambridge University Press, 2014.

Wooster, Robert. *The American Military Frontiers: The United States Army in the West, 1783–1900*. Albuquerque: University of New Mexico Press, 2009.

Yamaguchi, Precious. *Experiences of Japanese American Women during and after World War II: Living in Internment Camps and Rebuilding Life Afterwards*. Lanham, MD: Lexington Books, 2014.

Yates, Larry. *Field Artillery in Military Operations Other Than War: An Overview of the U.S. Experience*. Fort Leavenworth, KS: CSI Press, 2012.

Index

AMERICAN CROSSROADS

Edited by Earl Lewis, George Lipsitz, George Sánchez, Dana Takagi, Laura Briggs, and Nikhil Pal Singh

1. *Border Matters: Remapping American Cultural Studies*, by José David Saldívar
2. *The White Scourge: Mexicans, Blacks, and Poor Whites in Texas Cotton Culture*, by Neil Foley
3. *Indians in the Making: Ethnic Relations and Indian Identities around Puget Sound*, by Alexandra Harmon
4. *Aztlán and Viet Nam: Chicano and Chicana Experiences of the War*, edited by George Mariscal
5. *Immigration and the Political Economy of Home: West Indian Brooklyn and American Indian Minneapolis, 1945–1992*, by Rachel Buff
6. *Epic Encounters: Culture, Media, and U.S. Interests in the Middle East since 1945*, by Melani McAlister
7. *Contagious Divides: Epidemics and Race in San Francisco's Chinatown*, by Nayan Shah
8. *Japanese American Celebration and Conflict: A History of Ethnic Identity and Festival, 1934–1990*, by Lon Kurashige
9. *American Sensations: Class, Empire, and the Production of Popular Culture*, by Shelley Streeby
10. *Colored White: Transcending the Racial Past*, by David R. Roediger
11. *Reproducing Empire: Race, Sex, Science, and U.S. Imperialism in Puerto Rico*, by Laura Briggs
12. *meXicana Encounters: The Making of Social Identities on the Borderlands*, by Rosa Linda Fregoso
13. *Popular Culture in the Age of White Flight: Fear and Fantasy in Suburban Los Angeles*, by Eric Avila
14. *Ties That Bind: The Story of an Afro-Cherokee Family in Slavery and Freedom*, by Tiya Miles
15. *Cultural Moves: African Americans and the Politics of Representation*, by Herman S. Gray
16. *Emancipation Betrayed: The Hidden History of Black Organizing and White Violence in Florida from Reconstruction to the Bloody Election of 1920*, by Paul Ortiz
17. *Eugenic Nation: Faults and Frontiers of Better Breeding in Modern America*, by Alexandra Stern
18. *Audiotopia: Music, Race, and America*, by Josh Kun
19. *Black, Brown, Yellow, and Left: Radical Activism in Los Angeles*, by Laura Pulido
20. *Fit to Be Citizens? Public Health and Race in Los Angeles, 1879–1939*, by Natalia Molina
21. *Golden Gulag: Prisons, Surplus, Crisis, and Opposition in Globalizing California*, by Ruth Wilson Gilmore

Founded in 1893,
UNIVERSITY OF CALIFORNIA PRESS
publishes bold, progressive books and journals
on topics in the arts, humanities, social sciences,
and natural sciences—with a focus on social
justice issues—that inspire thought and action
among readers worldwide.

The UC PRESS FOUNDATION
raises funds to uphold the press's vital role
as an independent, nonprofit publisher, and
receives philanthropic support from a wide
range of individuals and institutions—and from
committed readers like you. To learn more, visit
ucpress.edu/supportus.